Party Politics in America

LONGMAN CLASSICS *in* POLITICAL SCIENCE

Party Politics in America

ELEVENTH EDITION

MARJORIE RANDON HERSHEY
Indiana University

Foreword by
JOHN H. ALDRICH
Duke University

PEARSON
Longman

New York   San Francisco   Boston
London   Toronto   Sydney   Tokyo   Singapore   Madrid
Mexico City   Munich   Paris   Cape Town   Hong Kong   Montreal

Vice President and Publisher: Priscilla McGeehon
Executive Editor: Eric Stano
Supplements Editor: Kristi Olson
Media Supplements Editor: Patrick McCarthy
Senior Marketing Manager: Megan Galvin-Fak
Production Manager: Eric Jorgensen
Project Coordination, Text Design, and Electronic Page Makeup: Electronic
    Publishing Services Inc., NYC
Cover Design Manager: John Callahan
Cover Image: J. S. Pughe/The Granger Collection, New York
Manufacturing Buyer: Roy Pickering
Printer and Binder: Phoenix Color Corp.
Cover Printer: Phoenix Color Corp.

Library of Congress Cataloging-in-Publication Data

Hershey, Marjorie Randon.
    Party politics in America / Majorie Randon Hershey. —11th ed.
        p. cm.
    Previously published: New York : Longman, 2003; in series: Longman classics in
political science.
    Includes bibliographical references.
    ISBN 0-321-20226-0
    1. Political parties—United States. I. Title.

    JK2265.H477 2005
    324.273—dc22

                                                                2004001983

 For permission to use copyrighted material, grateful acknowledgment is made to the
copyright holders on pp. 317–342, which are hereby made part of this copyright page.

 Visit us at http://www.ablongman.com

ISBN 0-321-20226-0

1 2 3 4 5 6 7 8 9 10—PBT—07 06 05 04

Brief Contents

Detailed Contents

Foreword to *Party Politics in America,* Eleventh Edition

Why should you be interested in studying political parties? The short answer is that virtually everything important in American politics is rooted in *party* politics. Political parties are at the core of American democracy and make it what it is today—just as they have virtually from the Founding.

Why should you use this book to guide you in the search for understanding democratic politics in America? The short answer is that this book is the best guide you can have, and it has been the best guide in this search for quite a long time. Now, let's turn to the longer answers.

I first encountered this text at the same stage in my life you are in now, as an undergraduate—in my case, though, that was way back in the 1960s. I read it in a form called mimeograph—think of it as a very smelly, smudgy Xerox copy—while the second edition was being prepared. At that point, the book was authored by a young, up-and-coming scholar named Frank Sorauf. Following on the heels of his important study of the impact of political parties on the Pennsylvania legislature,[1] *Party Politics in America* established him as arguably the leading scholar of political parties of his generation. In those days—less so than today—it was common for a "textbook" (that is, a book designed to be used in class) to do more than just tell you what others had written about its subject. Rather, books written for undergraduates were also designed to make a coherent argument about its subject matter—to engage you, the reader, intellectually. So it was then and so, with this book, it still is today.

In the sixth edition, published in 1988, Frank brought in Paul Allen Beck as coauthor. Paul took over the authorial duties beginning with that edition, and Marjorie Randon Hershey did so beginning with the ninth edition in 2001, leading to the book that you are about to read today. Each did so with considerable respect for the substance and the perspective that characterized the previous editions. This has brought a high degree of intellectual continuity to *Party Politics in America.* There are three important continuities (the first two of which are things you might want to keep in mind for the exams!). First, Sorauf, Beck, and Hershey very effectively use a three-part division in the discussion of political parties. More specifically, they divide the political party into its electoral, governing, and organizational roles. These three aspects of a party create a coherent system that (sometimes loosely, sometimes more tightly) provides a degree of integration to the diverse workings of any one political party. In those cases, the electoral, governing, and organizational aspects of the political party all pull together. However, as you will learn, there are often strains within

---

[1] Frank J. Sorauf, *Party and Representation, Legislative Politics in Pennsylvania* (New York: Atherton Press, 1963).

and among these three divisions. What, for example, would you do if you were an adviser to the Republican Party faced with the following choice? There is a policy stance that will help your presidential nominee win votes from undecided (typically moderate) voters and thus perhaps help your party win the presidency. That same stance, however, will hurt your party's candidates for the U.S. House of Representatives in their fund-raising campaigns and thus put at risk the narrow majority they currently hold in the House. Is it more important to hold a majority in the House or to hold the presidency? Should you risk losing potential support from moderate voters to maintain close ties with more extreme groups key to your organizational strength in fund-raising?

The second continuity is that Sorauf, Beck, and Hershey see the two major political parties in the United States as a system. The two-party system has long played a central role in the historical evolution of American politics (see especially Chapter 7). Although this two-party system has important implications for the dynamics of American politics, they also see the two-party system as a part of the intermediary groups in society. By this, the authors mean that the parties serve as points of contact between the public and its government (see their Figure 1.1, a figure that I believe has graced the beginning of this book for eleven editions now).

The third continuity is that each is a terrific scholar of political parties, and although these continuities have allowed this book to keep its unique intellectual stamp, the transition among authors has also allowed each to bring to the work his or her particular strengths. In the end, this has made the eleventh edition of the book richer and stronger than ever before. As I noted earlier, Frank Sorauf used his expertise to explain the role of the political party in government. Since then, he became one of the nation's leading experts on the role of money in politics and in later editions reflected that increasingly important but perennially controversial subject.[2] Paul Beck brings a distinguished career of scholarship, examining the role of political parties in the electorate and adding nicely to Frank's expertise about the governing role.[3] Paul is, like Frank and Marjorie Hershey, an expert on American politics. However, Paul is also, more than most of us who study American politics, genuinely knowledgeable about comparative politics. Indeed, he has not only been at the center of the study of "dealignment" from parties in the American electorate (that is, an apparent increase in the people withdrawing from partisan politics) but is also a leading scholar of dealignment in many other nations as well.[4] Marjorie, through her expertise, has made important contributions to one of the most difficult questions to study—how candidates and their campaigns shape and are shaped by electoral forces.[5] This interaction links the two most important components of the party, elections and governance, into a more coherent whole. It has allowed her to bring clarity to what has become an increasingly confused portion of the field. Mar-

[2]See, for example, Frank J. Sorauf, *Money in American Elections* (Glenview, IL.: Scott Foresman/Little, Brown College Division, 1988) or *Inside Campaign Finance: Myths and Realities* (New York: Yale University Press, 1992).

[3]He has written a great deal on this subject. One illustration that has long been one of my favorites is his "A Socialization Theory of Partisan Realignment," which was originally published in *The Politics of Future Citizens*, edited by Richard Niemi (San Francisco, CA: Jossey-Bass, 1974, pp. 199–219), and reprinted in *Classics In Voting Behavior,* edited by Richard Niemi and Herbert Weisberg (Washington, DC: CQ Press, 1992).

[4]Among his many writings, see his edited book with Russell J. Dalton and Scott Flanagan, *Electoral Change in Advanced Industrial Democracies: Realignment or Dealignment?* (Princeton, NJ: Princeton University Press, 1984).

[5]See especially her books, *Running for Office: The Political Education of Campaigners* (Chatham, NJ: Chatham House, 1984) and *The Making of Campaign Strategy* (Lexington, MA: D.C. Heath-Lexington, 1974).

jorie also has closely studied the role of gender in politics, a dimension of party politics that has not only been of long-standing importance from at least the granting of women's suffrage but has also become especially critical with the emergence and growth of the "gender gap."[6] Finally, she has made a long series of contributions to help us understand how to bring meaning to complex events.[7] One special feature of this book is the increased use of narratives from well-known and little-known party figures alike, narratives that serve to bring the subject matter to life.

One issue critical to all who study American politics is the understanding that politics matters in your life, that this is your government, and that the political parties are ways in which you can help shape what your government and elected officials do. This is one of the most important meanings of American political parties. They, and the government that they create, are the consequences of you and your political actions. So saying allows me to move more directly to the longer answer about the study of political parties themselves.

At the outset, I mentioned that you should want to study political parties because they are so important to virtually everything that happens in American politics and because political parties are so central to the workings of any democracy. Great, but you are probably asking, "So what questions should I keep in mind as I read this book; what questions will help me understand the material better?" Let me propose three questions as guidelines, ones that are neither too specific nor too general. We are looking, that is, for questions somewhere in between "Are parties good?" on the one hand, and "Why did the House Majority Leader, Tom DeLay (Republican, Texas), speak so strongly against campaign finance reform when he was House Minority Leader on February 13, 2002?" on the other hand.

You are well aware that today politicians can appear magnanimous and statesman-like if they say that they will be nonpartisan and if they call for Congress to "rise above" partisan politics to be bipartisan. Yet, essentially every elected official is a partisan, and essentially every elected official chooses to act in a partisan way much of the time. Why do politicians today, you might ask, speak as if they are of two minds about political parties? Perhaps they actually are. Even if you dismiss this rhetoric as just words, it is the case that the public is of two minds about parties, too. This book, like virtually all written about American political parties, includes quotes from the Founding Fathers warning about the dangers of party and faction, often quoting such luminaries as John Adams, Thomas Jefferson, and James Madison. Yet, these very same men not only worried about the dangers of party, they also were the founders and first leaders of our first political parties. So the first question is why are people—leaders and followers, founders and contemporary figures alike—both attracted to and repulsed by political parties?

---

[6]An especially interesting account of the ways the political parties reacted to female suffrage can be found in Anna L. Harvey, *Votes without Leverage: Women in American Electoral Politics, 1920–1970* (Cambridge: Cambridge University Press, 1998).

[7]See, for example, "Constructing Explanations for U.S. State Governors' Races: The Abortion Issue and the 1990 Gubernatorial Elections," *Political Communication* 17 (July–September, 2000), 239–262, "The Meaning of a Mandate: Interpretations of 'Mandate' in 1984 Presidential Election Coverage," *Polity* (Winter, 1995), 225–254, and "Support for Political Woman: Sex Roles," in John C. Pierce and John L. Sullivan, eds., *The Electorate Reconsidered* (Beverly Hills, CA.: Sage, 1980) 179–198.

Let me suggest two books that might give you additional ways to think about this question. One is Richard Hofstadter's *The Idea of a Party System: The Rise of Legitimate Opposition in the United States, 1780–1840* (Berkeley: University of California Press, 1969). This book is a series of public lectures that Hofstadter gave in which he roots political parties deeply in the American democratic tradition, arguing that they represent the outward manifestation of a change in philosophic understanding of the relationship between citizens and leaders in this, the world's first practicing democracy. Austin Ranney in *Curing the Mischiefs of Faction: Party Reform in America* (Berkeley: University of California Press, 1975) connects Hofstadter's view of the role of philosophic ideas and American democratic practice from our first 60 years to the contemporary era. Ranney was a leading scholar of political parties, but in this case he was also writing this book in reflection upon his time spent as a member of the so-called McGovern-Fraser Reform Commission, which revised the rules for the Democratic Party and advocated the reforms that led to the current presidential primary system. Thus, there is both a theoretical and practical dimension to this work.

This question of the purpose of parties in our democracy, both theoretical and practical, leads easily to a second major question that should be in your mind as you work through this book and your course. How does the individual connect to the political party? There are two aspects to this question. One is fairly direct—what do parties mean to the individual and how, if at all, has this changed over time? The great work that laid out this relationship in the modern era is *The American Voter* by Angus Campbell, Philip E. Converse, Warren E. Miller, and Donald E. Stokes (New York: John Wiley & Sons, 1960). Many argue that this connection has changed fundamentally. At one extreme, Martin P. Wattenberg has written about the declining relevance of political parties to the voter, such as in his *The Decline of American Political Parties, 1952–1996* (Cambridge, MA: Harvard University Press, 1998), using such striking evidence as a dramatic decline in the willingness or ability of citizens to say what they like or dislike about either of our two major political parties. Others disagree with Wattenberg. Larry Bartels, for example, has shown that partisanship remains as influential in shaping the vote as ever.[8] A second dimension of the question is whether any apparent decline, irrelevance, or dealignment of parties reflects growing distancing from the government itself. It is certainly the case that today we hear people say, "The government, they . . . ," and not, "The government, we. . . ." I suspect that few of us think that way. It is certainly common to hear politicians call for a tax cut by claiming that doing so will give the people back their money. Such a statement would not make sense if we thought of the government as being composed of us, ourselves, and thus thought of our taxes as sending our money to work in our government, doing our bidding by enacting our preferences into legislation selected by our representatives whom we chose. The question can, however, be cast even more broadly, asking whether the people feel removed from social, cultural, economic, and political institutions, generally, with political parties and the government therefore only one more symptom of a larger ill. This is certainly a part of the concerns that motivate Robert D. Putnam in his *Bowling Alone: The Collapse and Revival of American Community* (New York: Simon & Schuster, 2000).

---

[8]Larry M. Bartels, "Partisanship and Voting Behavior, 1952–1996," *American Journal of Political Science* 44 (2000): 35–50.

The change from a trusting, supportive, identified public to one apparently dramatically less so is one of the great changes that took place in American politics over the past half century. A second great change is what is often called "polarization," a growing distance between the elected officials of the two parties. That is, compared with fifty years ago, today the Democrats are more liberal and consistently more so than Republicans, who in turn are much more conservative than in the Eisenhower administration. Although this is not to say that there is anything close to an identical set of beliefs by the members of either party, there is a greater coherence of opinion and belief in, say, the congressional delegations of each party than in earlier times. Even more undeniable is a much clearer divergence between the policy interests and choices of the two parties than, say, fifty years ago. You might refer to *Polarized Politics: Congress and the President in a Partisan Era* (Washington, DC: CQ Press, 2000), edited by Jon R. Bond and Richard Fleisher, for a variety of indications of this fact. The question then is not whether there is greater polarization today; the question is whether this relative clarity of polarization matters. As usual, there are at least two ways to understand the question. One is simply to ask whether a more polarized Congress yields different policies from a less polarized one. The readings in Bond and Fleisher generally support that position. Others, for example, Keith Krehbiel in *Pivotal Politics: A Theory of U.S. Lawmaking* (Chicago, IL: University of Chicago Press, 1998) and David W. Brady and Craig Volden in *Revolving Gridlock: Politics and Policy from Carter to Clinton* (Boulder, CO: Westview Press, 1998) argue that the Founders' creation of checks and balances makes polarization relatively ineffectual in shaping legislation due to vetoes, compromises necessary between the two chambers, and so on. Even more generally, however, David R. Mayhew has argued in *Divided We Govern: Party Control, Lawmaking, and Investigations, 1946–1990* (New Haven, CT: Yale University Press, 1991) that our system generates important legislation regardless of which party is in control or whether they share power under divided partisan control of government. This carefully considered argument raises the question of whether the party really matters. As you might expect, there has been considerable interest in the challenge that Mayhew, Krehbiel, and Brady and Volden have raised. One set of responses can be seen in the Bond and Fleisher volume. Another can be found in Robert S. Erikson, Michael B. MacKuen, and James A. Stimson's book, *The Macro Polity* (Cambridge, UK: Cambridge University Press, 2002).

As you can see, we have now reached the point of very recently published work. We are, that is, asking questions that are motivating the work of scholars today. So, let's get on with it and turn to the book and the study of political parties themselves.

John H. Aldrich
DUKE UNIVERSITY

Preface

Having the opportunity to write a textbook is one of the best jobs in the world. Being able to write about politics and parties is even better. Political parties are defining features of a democratic government. They are also a continuing source of fascination, aggravation, excitement, and sometimes even complete amazement. In what other field of study do we get a chance to examine the cast of characters (130 of them, including a Sumo wrestler and a couple of porn stars) who ran for governor of California in 2003, to explain why the Republicans won control of both houses of Congress in 2002 and why it matters, and to trace the sources of political money in the early 2000s?

Three editions ago, when I became the author of *Party Politics in America*, I had the great advantage of building on the foundation provided by Frank J. Sorauf and Paul Allen Beck, two of the foremost scholars of political parties. Frank Sorauf wrote the first edition of this text and continued to revise and perfect it for almost two decades. Paul Beck brought the book into the late 1980s and 1990s with the intellectual vision and the meticulous care that has marked his research on parties and voting.

The book that they nurtured has long been known as the "gold standard" of political parties texts. Instructors and students have valued previous editions because they have provided, quite simply, the most thorough and definitive coverage of the field. These editions of *Party Politics in America* have been both an essential reference and an invitation to more than a generation of students.

My aim has been to build on the book's great strengths while making it even more readable and engaging. The current edition, for example, is notably shorter than the last one, even with the addition of a substantial amount of new research, but the text retains its comprehensive coverage, its conceptual clarity, and the comparative perspective that is so helpful for American students.

This edition continues the features that have been so well received in the last edition. The boxes titled "A Day in the Life" tell the personal stories of individuals whose experiences help to illustrate recent changes in the parties. Many of my students see political parties as remote, abstract, and a bit unseemly — something that might interest elderly people, but not teens and twentysomethings. I hope these stories will change their minds. As in the case of the challenges faced by the first person to have won a U.S. House seat as an "out" lesbian, these are compelling stories that can show readers why studying party politics is worth their time.

In other chapters, the features titled "Which Would You Choose?" present students with major debates about party politics: for instance, whether encouraging greater voter turnout would help or harm American democracy (see Chapter 8); and whether legislators ought to be listening mainly to their legislative party leaders or to their constituents (in Chapter 13). These summaries, using the point-counterpoint format with which undergraduates are familiar, could serve as the basis for class debate on these and many other fundamental concerns.

The book is constantly being updated to reflect new scholarship and examples from current politics. Chapter 3, which was extensively revised in the last edition, has been revised again to include new findings about local parties. Chapters 4 and 11 discuss the big recent changes in the national parties' approach to targeting and funding campaigns. Chapter 5 incorporates the impressive research of the early 2000s on party activists. There is a new discussion of the "invisible primary" in Chapter 10, a major revision of Chapter 11 to incorporate information about the "ground war" in 2002 and 2004, and more details in Chapter 12 about the changes in campaign finance wrought by the Bipartisan Campaign Reform Act (BCRA, often referred to as McCain-Feingold) reforms.

A new section in Chapter 1 tells students about the issue differences between the contemporary Democratic and Republican Parties. A number of instructors report that their students compare the major parties to groups of bickering children: people who complain constantly for no particular reason. Yet textbooks about political parties (including previous editions of this one) have typically said very little about the issue differences between the parties. These differences have become increasingly clear in recent years and it is time to tell students about them.

I've also tried to make the reader's job easier by putting important terms in boldface and making sure that they are clearly defined, emphasizing the central points even more, and making some of the long tables into figures or into shorter, clearer tables. And for instructors, I have worked to make sure that each chapter can stand alone, so that teachers can assign chapters in any order they choose without leaving their students puzzled because relevant concepts were explained elsewhere.

In addition, of course, colorful examples from the 2002 and 2004 elections are incorporated throughout the book. With personalities such as George W. Bush, Hillary Rodham Clinton, and Arnold Schwarzenegger among the leading characters, it is not easy to tell a dull story about current politics. The book, then, reflects the excitement of contemporary campaigns and elections as well as the important trends in party politics over time.

Like political parties and elected officials, textbooks have constituents. However, as many elected officials find, it takes a lot of effort to keep a text responsive to its users. It isn't easy for an author to get detailed information as to what readers like and don't like about a book, what could be clearer, and what could be more interesting. I have been very lucky to get reactions from some users of *Party Politics in America*, but I would like to receive many more. As you read the book, then, I'd like to ask you, whether you are a teacher, a grad or undergraduate student, or a political practitioner, to contact me with your suggestions and reactions. You can reach me at Hershey@indiana.edu. I would be most grateful for your time.

I owe thanks as well to the many people who have been so gracious with their help: to my graduate and undergraduate students, to present and former colleagues at Indiana University, particularly Bob Huckfeldt, Ted Carmines, John Williams, Leroy Rieselbach, Jerry Wright, Mike Ensley, Russ Hanson, Henry Hale, and Pat Sellers, and to departmental staff members Margaret Anderson, Fern Bennett, Kristin Brand, Scott Feickert, Steve Flinn, Marsha Franklin, Loretta Heyen, Sharon LaRoche, and James Russell.

It is an honor for me to recognize Austin Ranney, Leon Epstein, and Jack Dennis, who were most responsible for my interest in party politics and for the strength of the training I received in political science. Murray Edelman deserves special mention in that group, not only as a mentor and model for so many of us but also as a much-beloved friend. John Aldrich, one of the most insightful and systematic analysts of political parties, was kind enough to write a Foreword. Other political scientists have also been among my best and favorite teachers: Bruce Oppenheimer, Gerry Pomper, Tony Broh, Jennifer Hochschild, Burdett Loomis, Richard Fenno, Anthony King, John Kingdon, Mike Kirn, Brian Silver, Jim Stimson, and Brian Vargus. I have appreciated the comments and contributions of Nell Benton, Tom Carsey, Russ Dalton, Jim Davis, Sheldon Goldman, John Green, Rick Hardy, Paul Herrnson, Judge Michael Hoff, Bill Mayer, Jeanette Morehouse, Chuck Prysby, Brian Shoup, Ian Stirton, Robin Vuke, Brad Warren, Pat Williams, and Dick Winger.

Reviewers of the tenth edition—Shari Garber Bax, Central Missouri State University; Paul A. Djupe, Denison University; Harold F. Bass, Ouachita Baptist University; and Lisa Langenbach, Middle Tennessee State University—were generous with their constructive comments. And it continues to be a pleasure to work with the people at Longman: Editor Eric Stano, Cristine Maisano, and Jim Hill and the other members of the Electronic Publishing Services Inc. production team.

Most of all, I am very grateful to my family: my husband, Howard, and our daughters, Katie, Lissa, Lani, and Hannah. Everything I do has been made possible by their love and support.

MARJORIE RANDON HERSHEY

Party Politics in America

PART ONE

Parties and Party Systems

Who decides how old you must be to drink beer legally? Who determines how many bacteria are allowed in your hamburger meat? Who made the decision that you need a license to get married but you don't need a license to have a baby?

All three questions have the same answer. It's government that makes these decisions and thousands more that affect your life every day. In fact, you would have to look very hard to find an aspect of your life that is *not* affected by government action. The streets that you travel were built by government. Your favorite radio station is on the air because it received a license from the government. Other would-be radio stations did not. It is the political system that plays the most important role in deciding, as a famous political scientist put it, "who gets what, when, how."[1]

Because government decisions affect almost everything we do, large numbers of groups have mobilized to try to influence these decisions as well as the selection of the men and women who will make them. In a democracy, the political party is one of the oldest and most important of these groups, but it has a great deal of competition. Organized interests, such as the Gun Owners of America, Americans for Nonsmokers' Rights, and fund-raising political action committees (PACs) also work to get the government policies that they want, as do antiabortion and abortion rights groups, the Christian Coalition, and People for the Ethical Treatment of Animals. Even organizations whose main purpose is nonpolitical, such as universities, beer manufacturers, and teachers' unions, try to influence the government decisions that affect them.

All these groups serve as *intermediaries*—links or connections—between citizens and the people in government who make the decisions that affect our lives (Figure I.1). By bringing together people with shared interests, they amplify these people's voices in speaking to government. They raise issues that they want government to solve. They tell people what government is doing. In these ways, parties and organized interests, along with television and the other media, are the links between citizens and political power.

Different intermediaries specialize in different political activities. Parties focus on nominating candidates, helping to elect them, and organizing those who win. Most organized interests represent narrower groups; they are unlikely to win majorities so they try instead to influence the views of elected and appointed officials. Still others work mainly to affect public opinion and media coverage. Groups like these in other democracies may

1

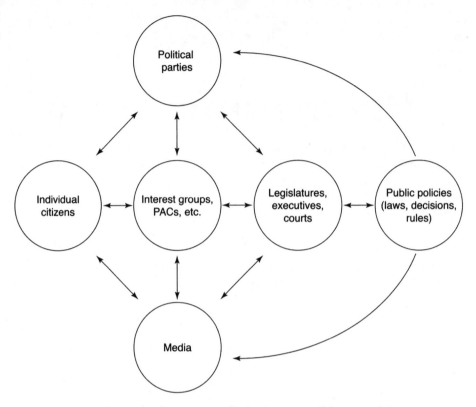

FIGURE I.1   Parties and Other Intermediaries Between Citizens and Government.

play different roles. The American parties, for example, tend to concentrate on election activities, whereas parties in Europe have been more committed to spreading ideologies and keeping their elected officials faithful to the party's program.

The competition among these intermediary groups is fierce. Parties, of course, compete with one another. They vie with powerful interest groups for the attention of legislators and for a dominant role in political campaigns; in fact, the American parties are not nearly as dominant in the business of campaigning as they were a century ago. They compete with one another for money, expertise, and volunteer help and then, with those resources in hand, for the support of individual citizens and elected officials.

As if their work was not challenging enough, political parties do this in a culture that both loves and hates them. On the one hand, many writers have celebrated the American parties as the tools with which we build and repair our democracy and as the "distinguishing marks" of a modern government.[2] In a reflection of that belief, when many nations in Eastern Europe threw off Communist rule more than a decade ago, democratic activists moved quickly to create political parties.[3]

On the other hand, political parties have been the targets of suspicion and ridicule since the United States began. James Madison and the other founders were very wary of organized factions in their new republic. About a century later, the Progressive movement—reformers intent on rooting out political corruption and returning power to middle-class people like themselves—targeted the parties' "boss rule" as the enemy to overcome. Disgust with party power in the 1960s and 1970s led to another series of party reforms that has helped to reshape current politics. Many Americans remain skeptical and even hostile to the idea of political parties.[4]

The hostile climate of public opinion has led, in turn, to a host of restrictions on how parties can organize and what they can do. Parties have tried to adapt to these rules over time by changing their organizations and the nature of their activities. The political parties of the early 2000s would not be recognizable to politicians of a century ago, and the parties that we know today may change dramatically in the coming decades.

The aim of this book is to explore the American parties: how they have developed, how they affect us, and what they are capable of contributing to a democratic politics. Given the rise of the Internet, the growth of single-issue groups, and the many other ways in which we can learn about and affect government, are political parties really as essential to the survival of a democracy as many have assumed? Are they a boon to both candidates and voters, or do they deserve the distrust with which so many Americans—and probably you yourself—view them? Let us begin by examining the parties as they evolved in and adapted to the American political environment.

CHAPTER 1

What Are Political Parties?

Try to picture American politics without political parties. Many have found it an attractive thought. George Washington, for example, stated in his Farewell Address: "Let me warn you in the most solemn manner against the baneful effects of the spirit of party," which he considered the "worst enemy" of popular government. Many contemporary Americans agree; in survey after survey, many respondents say that they think of political parties with suspicion—like the cat at the bird feeder—if they think of them at all.

Imagine, then, that we take Washington's advice in the next presidential campaign and magically make the parties disappear. There will be no party organizations to hold primary elections and no party leaders to advise or support the candidates. Would we do a better job of choosing a president?

Of course, we will have to find another way to sort through the few hundred thousand presidential wanna-bes and select a very few to run in the general election. Without party primaries and caucuses, who would make that decision? Members of Congress? Not in a system designed to separate legislative and executive powers. A convention of organized interests such as the National Rifle Association and Handgun Control, Inc.? A panel of judges selected by *People* magazine? The answer is not obvious, though it is obviously vital to our future.

Assuming that problem is solved, many other challenges remain. Strong party organizations help bring voters to the polls. Without any political parties, will voter turnout, already remarkably low in the United States, decrease even further? Most people are not very interested in politics, so how will voters decide on a candidate if they do not have the guidance that party labels provide? Will they spend hours researching each candidate's stands on issues, or will they choose the candidate who looks the best on television? When the new president takes office, how will he or she gain majority support for new programs from a Congress elected as individuals, with no party loyalties to link them?

What is this political organization that is so necessary and yet so distrusted? Does the concept of party include only the politicians who share a party label while seeking and holding public offices? Does it also include the activists who work on the campaigns and the ordinary citizens who support one party's candidates? Or is a party any grouping that chooses to call itself a party, whether Democratic or Boston Tea?

A THREE-PART DEFINITION OF PARTIES

Most scholars would agree that *a party is a group organized to nominate candidates, to try to win political power through elections, and to promote ideas about public problems.* What is that group composed of? To the scholars quoted in "What Is a Party?" on page 7, the candidates and elected officials who share a party's label are a central part of the definition (see, for example, Anthony Downs's and Edmund Burke's definitions). Many parties in democratic nations, including the United States, began as groups of political leaders who organized to advance certain programs.

Most observers, however, see the American parties as including more than just candidates and officeholders. As John Aldrich's definition (see box on page 7) reminds us, parties are organizations; they are institutions that have a life, and a set of rules, of their own. Interested individuals can join them and help set their goals and strategies, just as one would do in a softball league, a sorority, or a Teamsters Union local. These activists and organizations are central parts of the party, too.

It is tempting to close our definition at this point and to view the American parties solely as teams of political specialists—elected officials, candidates, party leaders, activists, and organizations—who compete for power and then exercise it. That leaves the rest of the population on the outside of the parties, a position that many citizens may well prefer. Yet this would ignore an important reality: Parties are rooted in the lives and feelings of citizens as well as candidates and activists. Even though the American parties have no formal, dues-paying "members," many voters develop such strong and enduring attachments to a particular party that they are willing to make their commitment public by registering to vote as a Democrat or a Republican and actively supporting their party's candidates. Further, when writers refer to a "Republican realignment" or a "Democratic area," they see parties that include voters as well as officeholders, office seekers, and activists.

The Progressive movement of the early 1900s, which promoted party registration and the practice of nominating candidates in primary elections, strengthened the case for including a citizen base in a definition of American parties. Voters in primary elections make the single most important decision for their party: who its candidates will be. In most other democracies, only a thin layer of party leaders and activists has the power to make this choice.

Because American voters have the right to nominate the parties' candidates, as well as to elect them, the line that separates party leaders from followers in some other nations becomes blurred in the United States. American voters are not only consumers who choose among the parties' "products" (candidates) in the political marketplace but also managers who decide just what products will be introduced in the first place. Making consumers into managers has transformed political parties, just as it would revolutionize the market economy. Taking this into account in our definition of parties, as do the Chambers and Key definitions in the box on page 7, makes for a messier concept of political party but a more realistic one in the American setting.

WHAT IS A POLITICAL PARTY? SOME ALTERNATIVE DEFINITIONS[1]

A party aims to promote certain policies:

[A] party is a body of men united, for promoting by their joint endeavors the national interest, upon some particular principle in which they are all agreed.

Edmund Burke (1770)

It works to gain power in government:

In the broadest sense, a political party is a coalition of men seeking to control the governing apparatus by legal means . . . [through] duly constituted elections or legitimate influence.

Anthony Downs (1957)

It inspires loyalty among voters:

[A] political party in the modern sense may be thought of as a relatively durable social formation which seeks offices or power in government, exhibits a structure or organization which links leaders at the centers of government to a significant popular following in the political arena and its local enclaves, and generates in-group perspectives or at least symbols of identification or loyalty.

William Nisbet Chambers (1967)

It is an organization with rules and durability:

Political parties can be seen as coalitions of elites to capture and use political office. . . . (But) a political party is . . . more than a coalition. A major political party is an institutionalized coalition, one that has adopted rules, norms, and procedures.

John H. Aldrich (1995)

A political party is all of the above:

Within the body of voters as a whole, groups are formed of persons who regard themselves as party members. . . . In another sense the term party may refer to the group of more or less professional political workers. . . . At times party denotes groups within the government. . . . Often it refers to an entity which rolls into one the party-in-the-electorate, the professional political group, the party-in-the-legislature, and the party-in-the-government. . . . In truth, this all-encompassing usage has its legitimate applications for all the types of groups called party interact more or less closely and at times may be as one.

V. O. Key, Jr. (1958)

In short, we can most accurately see the major American political parties as having three interacting parts. These three are the ***party organization***, which includes party leaders and the many activists who work for party causes and candidates; the ***party in government***, composed of the men and women who run for public office on the party's label and who hold public office; and the ***party in the electorate***, or those citizens who identify themselves as supporters of the party (see Figure 1.1).[2] We explore each of these

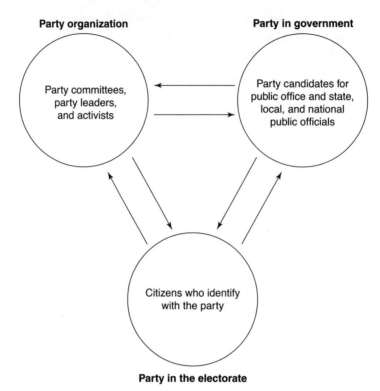

Party organization

Party in government

Party committees, party leaders, and activists

Party candidates for public office and state, local, and national public officials

Citizens who identify with the party

Party in the electorate

FIGURE 1.1   The Three Parts of American Political Parties.

parts separately, keeping in mind that the character of the American parties is defined by the ways in which they interact.[3]

The Party Organization

Party organizations are groups of people who work to promote *all* of the party's candidates and its perspectives on major issues; this contrasts with individual candidates, whose main concern must be their own chances of winning. Party organizations contain those who hold jobs with titles—the national and state party chairs and officers; the county, city, ward, and precinct leaders; and committee people—and those who don't, but who are devoted enough to give their time, money, and skills to the party. Some party leaders or activists may be waiting for the right time to run for public office (and thus cross over to the party in government); others have been pressed into service as candidates for Congress or mayor when nobody else wants the job. Many party activists prefer the tasks of answering phones in the party headquarters and plotting strategy, however, rather than the frenetic days and anxious nights that are the life of a political candidate.

The Party in Government

The party in government is made up of the candidates for public office and those who hold office, whether elected or appointed, who share a party label. The major figures here are presidents, governors, judges, mayors, Congress members, state legislators, bureaucrats, and local officials who share the same party affiliation.

The relationship between the party in government and the party organization is like that of siblings: part loyalty and part rivalry. They regularly work together to meet shared goals, but they may have different priorities in reaching those goals. A member of Congress, for example, may be trying to raise as much campaign money as possible because she wants a big victory that will boost her chances of later running for president. At the same time, the party organization's leaders may be hoping to convince the same contributors to support more vulnerable party candidates instead, in the hope of winning a party majority in Congress.

These two parts of the parties also jockey for leadership of the party as a whole. When reporters want to get a "Republican view" on an issue, they will usually interview a source in the White House, if the president is Republican, or a Republican leader in Congress; these members of the party in government are often assumed to speak for the party. Leaders of the party's organization, such as the chair of the Republican National Committee, may hold a different view on that issue. But presidents and congressional party leaders do not have to clear their pronouncements with the party organization, nor can they be controlled by it. These tensions, which lead the party organization and the party in government to compete for scarce resources, show why it is helpful to treat them as separate parts of the party.

The Party in the Electorate

The party in the electorate is the least well defined of the three parts. It consists of the men and women who *see themselves* as Democrats or Republicans: citizens who feel some degree of loyalty to the party, even if they have never set foot in the party's headquarters or met its candidates. We call them **partisans** or **party identifiers.** Many of these partisans have declared themselves to be a Democrat or Republican when they registered to vote; more than half of the states prescribe party registration. Others regard themselves as partisans even if they do not register to vote under a party label or even if they do not vote at all.

These members of the electoral party are regular consumers of the party's candidates and appeals, but they are not under the party organization's control. In general elections, they may vote for one party candidate and reject another; in primaries, they may decide to saddle the party with a candidate that the organization can't stand. However, they are vitally important as the core of the party's electoral support; without this base, the party would have to work much harder to win power.

The relationship between the party organization and party in government, on the one hand, and the electoral party, on the other, is one of the most striking characteristics of the major American parties. Other political organizations—interest groups such as labor unions and environmental groups—try to attract supporters beyond their members and workers, but these supporters remain outside the group's organization. That is not true of American parties. The party in the electorate is more than an external group to be mobilized. In addition to its power to choose the parties' candidates by voting in primaries, in many states the electoral party helps select local party officials, such as ward and precinct committee leaders. So the major American party is an open, inclusive, semipublic organization. Its combination of organization and electorate sets it apart from other political organizations and from parties in other democracies.

WHAT PARTIES DO

Political parties in every democracy engage in three sets of activities to at least some degree: They select candidates and contest elections, try to educate citizens about issues important to the party, and work to convince elected officials to support particular policies and provide other benefits, such as patronage jobs.[4] Parties and party systems differ in the degree to which they emphasize these individual activities, but no party can completely ignore any of them.

Electing Candidates

Parties often seem to be completely absorbed by their efforts to elect candidates. Electoral activity so dominates the life of the American party that its metabolism follows almost exactly the cycles of the election calendar. Party activity reaches a peak at election time; between elections, most parties go into hibernation. Parties are goal oriented, and in American politics, achieving one's goals ultimately depends on winning elections. The three parts of parties may have their differences, but they are brought together in their shared intention to elect party candidates.

Educating (or Propagandizing) Citizens

Parties also try to teach or propagandize citizens. The Democrats and Republicans do not promote all-inclusive ideologies like those of a European Marxist party. They do, however, represent the interests and issue preferences of the groups that identify with and support them. In this sense, the Republicans and Democrats can be seen as the parties of business or labor and of the wealthy or the disadvantaged. (You'll find more on this later in the chapter.) Party differences on issues have become clearer since the 1960s.

Governing

Almost all American national and state elected officials ran for office as either Democrats or Republicans, and their partisan perspectives affect every aspect of the way government works. The legislatures of 49 states[5] and the United States Congress are organized along party lines. On some issues, party cohesion may break down. Yet, in general, there is a surprising degree of party discipline in voting on legislation. In executive branches, presidents and governors usually choose cabinet officers and agency heads of their own party. Even the courts show evidence of the organizing and directing touch of the parties, though in more subtle ways.

The American parties, however, do not have a monopoly on any of these three activities. They compete regularly with interest groups, other political organizations, and even the media in all these areas. Even though the parties organize state legislatures and Congress, they must constantly battle interest groups and constituency pressures to influence legislators' votes on major bills. In nominating candidates, especially at the local level, parties face tremendous competition from interest groups and powerful local personalities who may each be pushing for pet candidates. In promoting issues, the major parties are often overshadowed by the fervor of minor (third) parties, rafts of interest groups, individual public figures, and the media.

The nature of any party's activities affects the balance of power among the party's three parts. American parties' emphasis on election activities, for example, gives the party in government an unusual degree of power, even dominance. It can often leave the party organization in the shadows when competing for the attention of the party in the electorate. In parties more strongly linked to issues and ideologies—Marxist parties, for instance—party organizations are more likely to be able to dictate to the legislative parties.

Yet individuals from all three sectors of the party often come together for specific activities. Party organization activists committed to a particular elected official may join with other members of the party in government and with loyal party voters to return that official to office. When the election is won or lost, they will probably drift apart again. These groups of individuals from different parts of a party, drawn together to achieve a particular goal, are like the nuclei of the party.[6] In American politics, alliances and coalitions are far more common within the parties than between them.

THE EFFECTS OF PARTY ACTIVITY

Parties have important effects on the functioning of American politics. As the parties work to nominate candidates, convince voters, and influence leaders, they help shape the democratic process in many other ways as well.

First, parties help people make sense of the complexities of politics. Many of us don't pay much attention to government. Parties simplify issues and elections so that citizens can make sensible choices even when they don't have a lot of information about politics. Voters can use their party attachments as guides for assessing issues and candidates. By helping citizens form political judgments, parties make it easier for people to be politically active. Further, parties preach the value of political commitment. In these ways, they take part in the political education of the American electorate by transmitting political information and values to large numbers of current and future voters.

Second, the American parties help aggregate and organize political power. They put together individuals and groups into blocs that are powerful enough to govern. So in the political world as well as in the individual, parties help to focus political loyalties on a small number of alternatives and then to build support for them. Parties also provide an organized opposition. That is not a popular role to play; the behavior of a constant adversary may seem like that of a sore loser. But an organized opposition is vital to a democracy because it has a natural incentive—its own ambition—to serve as a watchdog on a powerful government. Few of us would be willing to devote the time and effort to play this role on our own.

Third, because they devote so much effort to contesting elections, the parties dominate the recruitment of political leaders. Large numbers of legislators, political executives, and even judges entered public service through a political party or partisan candidacy for office. Because the parties work at all levels of government from local to national, they may encourage the movement of leaders from one level to another. Further, because they are constants in the election process, parties help to make changes in government leadership more routine and orderly. In nations where parties are not stable from one election to the next, leadership changes can be much more disruptive.

Finally, the parties help unify a divided American political system. The U.S. government was designed to fragment political power, to make sure that no single group could gain enough of it to become a tyrant. The division between the national government and the states, multiplied by the separation of powers at each level, does an impressive job of fragmenting power. The challenge, of course, is to enable these fragmented units to work together to solve problems. The two major parties are a unifying force in American politics. Their ability to bridge the separation of powers has limits, but the major parties can provide a basis for cooperation in a government marked by decentralization and division.

HOW DO PARTIES DIFFER FROM OTHER POLITICAL GROUPS?

We have seen that parties have a lot of competition as intermediaries in politics. *All* political organizations, not just parties, try to mobilize their supporters either to win public office or to influence those who do win. How, then, do parties differ from these other political organizations?

Parties are Paramount in Elections

Above all, a party can be distinguished from other political organizations by its role in structuring elections. In most elections, candidates are listed on the ballot as "Democrat" or "Republican"; they are not listed as "National Rifle Association" or "Planned Parenthood." It is the major parties that normally enlist the election clerks and the poll watchers, not the Chamber of Commerce. The parties are paramount among political groups in contesting elections.

They Have a Full-time Commitment to Political Activity

The major American parties are fully committed to political activity; it is the sole purpose of their existence. Interest groups and most other political organizations, in contrast, move freely and frequently from political to nonpolitical activities and back again. The Steelworkers' Union, for example, is fundamentally concerned with collective bargaining for better pay and working conditions. It may turn to political action to support sympathetic candidates or to lobby Congress for favorable legislation, but its interests are rooted in the workplace. Parties live entirely in the political world.

They Mobilize Large Numbers

An interest group, such as a political action committee representing the corporations that make diet pills, does not need millions of supporters to try to convince Congress to go easy on regulating the ingredients in diet pills; it may be able to succeed with only a few strategists and a small, well-mobilized clientele. Because winning elections is so vital to parties' goals, however, parties must recruit and mobilize an enormous range of supporters to win large numbers of races. The result is that in a system such as that of the United States, party appeals must be broad and inclusive; a major party cannot afford to represent only a narrow range of concerns.

They Endure

Political parties, at least in the United States, are also unusually stable and long-lived. Personal cliques, factions, campaign organizations, and even many interest groups are fleeting by comparison. The size and abstractness of the parties and their ability to transcend individual candidates give them a much longer life. Both major American parties can trace their histories for much more than a century, and the major parties of other Western democracies also have impressive life spans. This remarkable endurance adds to their value for voters. The parties are there as points of reference, year after year, election after election, and candidate after candidate, giving continuity to the choices Americans face and the issues they debate.

They Serve as Political Symbols

Finally, political parties differ from other political organizations in the extent to which they operate as symbols, or emotion-laden objects of loyalty. For millions of Americans, the party label is the chief cue for their decisions about candidates or issues. It helps shape their perceptions and structure their choices; it relates their political values to the real options of American politics.

Remember, however, that the differences between parties and other political organizations are differences of degree. Interest groups do become involved in elections, even extensively involved, and the larger organized interests serve as political symbols, too. They can recruit candidates, give political cues to their members and friends, and get their supporters

---

IS THIS A PARTY?

In early September 2000, the Natural Law Party formed a coalition with the Reform Party. As one reporter pointed out, with understatement, "They'll have to iron out a few differences in philosophy." The Reform Party was founded by Ross Perot, a billionaire who wanted to reduce the national debt and limit congressional terms. When Perot declined to run again as the party's presidential candidate in 2000, one faction of his party decided to nominate Pat Buchanan, a controversial conservative writer and speaker. Some Reform activists opposed that idea and looked for another candidate.

The candidate whom they found was John Hagelin, who was also the leader of the Natural Law Party. Begun by followers of the Maharishi Mahesh Yogi, a Hindu guru, Hagelin's party calls for conflict-free politics based on Transcendental Meditation (TM). Meditation, they believe, will reduce crime, violence, sickness, and accidents in the United States. An important accompaniment to TM is "yogic flying," in which meditation is said to lift the individual's body off the ground, inch by inch, beginning with "hopping" and, eventually, sailing away.

Some of the more earthbound Reform Party activists struggled mightily to mesh with their new Natural Law allies. "I don't know anything about yogic flying, but I had a sled, an American Flyer, when I was a kid," said Perot's former aide, Russ Verney, at the Natural Law convention. Another worried Reform worker asked Hagelin if he could fly and was reassured that the answer was no. Whether he was further reassured by the candidate's acceptance speech, in which Hagelin declared that "the unified field percolates infant universes at the rate of 10 to the 143rd per cubic centimeter per second," was not noted.

Source for the quotations: Dana Milbank, "The Reform Party, Feelin' Guru-vy," *Washington Post,* September 2, 2000, page C1.

to the polls on election day. Other nonparty groups may do the same. Interest groups also promote issue positions, try to influence officeholders, and (through their political action committees) give money to campaigns. They do not, however, and in most localities cannot, offer their names and symbols for candidates to use on the ballot.

In some respects, the major parties look more like some of the larger interest groups, such as the Chamber of Commerce and the AFL-CIO, than they look like minor or third parties. Most minor political parties are electoral organizations in name only. Their candidates are in no danger of needing a victory speech on election night. They may have few or no local organizations. Their membership base, often dependent on a single issue, may be just as narrow as that of most interest groups (see, for example, the box on page 13: "Is This a Party?"). However, minor parties can appear on the ballot, and their candidates can receive public funding where it is available and where they can qualify for it. In these ways (and sometimes *only* in these ways), they can be more like the major parties than the large interest groups.

HOW THE AMERICAN PARTIES DEVELOPED

The world's first political parties developed in the United States. For more than 200 years, their history has been entwined with the expansion of popular democracy. A key part of this story is the shift in the relative positions of the three parts of the party as first the party in government, then the party organizations, and then both the parties in government and in the electorate enjoyed their period of dominance.[7]

The Founding of American Parties

Although the founders of the American government were hostile to the idea of political parties, the seeds of parties were sown shortly after the new government was created. Groups within the Congress disagreed about how much power the new national government should have, relative to the states. The dominant group came to be called **Federalists**; led by the powerful Secretary of the Treasury, Alexander Hamilton, they championed some degree of centralized (federal government) control over the economy (see the box on page 15). The opposition rallied around Thomas Jefferson and James Madison, who wanted to protect the states' rights from national government interference. Each group gathered in meetings, called "caucuses," to plan strategy. During the 1790s, these alignments began to take more enduring form.

These early "parties," then, were formed "from the top" by their party in government, rather than by activists at the grassroots level. They were concerned only with the political issues that preoccupied the nation's capital, not surprisingly because most other Americans played only a marginal or indirect role in politics. In the first years of the Republic, the vote was limited in almost every state to those free men who could meet property-holding or taxpaying requirements. Even these relatively small numbers of voters had limited power, as the writers of the Constitution intended. The president was chosen not directly by the voters, but indirectly by the electoral college. Although election to the House of Representatives was entrusted to a direct popular vote, election to the Senate was not. Senators were chosen by the respective state legislatures. It was a cautious beginning for democratic self-government.

THE AMERICAN MAJOR PARTIES

The two-party drama is long, but its cast of major characters is short. In more than 200 years of history, only five political parties have achieved a competitive position in American national politics, and one of these five does not fully qualify as a party. Three lost this status; the Democrats and Republicans maintain it to this day.

1. **The Federalist Party, 1788–1816.** The champion of the new Constitution and strong national government, it was the first American political institution to resemble a political party, although it was not a full-fledged party. Its strength was rooted in the Northeast and the Atlantic Seaboard, where it attracted the support of merchants, landowners, and established families of wealth and status. Limited by its narrow electoral base, it quickly fell before the success of the Democratic-Republicans.

2. **The Democratic-Republican Party, 1800–1832.** Many of its leaders had been strong proponents of the Constitution but opposed the extreme nationalism of the Federalists. This was a party of the small farmers, workers, and less privileged citizens who preferred the authority of the states. Like its leader, Thomas Jefferson, it shared many of the ideals of the French Revolution, especially the extension of the right to vote and the notion of direct popular self-government.

3. **The Democratic Party, 1832–Present.** Growing out of the Jacksonian wing of the Democratic-Republicans, it was the first really broad-based, popular party in the United States. On behalf of a coalition of less privileged voters, it opposed such business-friendly policies as national banking and high tariffs; it also welcomed the new immigrants and opposed nativist (anti-immigrant) sentiment.

4. **The Whig Party, 1832–1854.** This party, too, had roots in the old Jeffersonian party, but in the Clay-Adams faction and in opposition to the Jacksonians. Its greatest leaders, Henry Clay and Daniel Webster, stood for legislative supremacy and protested the strong presidency of Andrew Jackson. For its short life, the Whig Party was an unstable coalition of many interests, among them nativism, property, and business and commerce.

5. **The Republican Party, 1854–Present.** Born as the Civil War approached, this was the party of Northern opposition to slavery and its spread to the new territories. Therefore, it was also the party of the Union, the North, Lincoln, the freeing of slaves, victory in the Civil War, and the imposition of Reconstruction. From the Whigs, it also inherited a concern for business and propertied interests.

The party groupings in Congress made some limited efforts to reach out to the voters at home. Party organization at the grassroots level began as "committees of correspondence" between national and local leaders, and each side established a newspaper to propagandize on behalf of its cause. And public sentiment found its way to the Capitol. Organized popular protest against some unpopular administration measures was communicated to the party in Congress.

One of these two incipient parties, the ***Democratic-Republicans*** (led by Jefferson), began organizing in the states and local communities in time for the 1800 elections. The more elitist Federalists, who had earlier dominated the Congress, failed to keep up; the result was that they began to disappear in most states soon after the defeat of their last president, John Adams, in 1800. In short, the pressures for democratization were already powerful enough by the early 1800s to scuttle an infant party whose leaders in the government could not adapt to the need to organize a mass electorate, especially in the growing states of the frontier. Yet the Federalists gave a historic gift to American democracy: They accepted Adams's defeat in 1800 and handed control of the presidency to their Democratic-Republican rivals.[8]

The Democratic-Republicans, who were the party of agrarian interests and the frontier, quickly established their electoral superiority and held a one-party monopoly for twenty years. They dominated American politics so thoroughly by the time of James Monroe's election in 1816 that the absence of party and political conflict was called the "Era of Good Feelings." Despite the decline of one party and the rise of another, however, the nature of party politics did not change much during this period. It was a time when government and politics were the business of an elite of well-known, well-established men, and the parties reflected the politics of the time. Without party competition, leaders felt no need to establish larger grassroots organizations, so the parties' further development was stalled.

American politics began to change sharply in the 1820s. By then, most states had eliminated the requirement that only landowners could vote, so the suffrage was extended to all white males, at least in state and federal elections. The growing pressure for democratization also led governments to make more and more public officials elected rather than appointed.[9]

The most obvious change in the 1820s was the emergence of the presidential election process that has lasted to this day. The framers of the Constitution had crafted an unusual arrangement for selecting the president, known as the electoral college. Each state, in a manner selected by its legislature, would choose a number of presidential voters (electors) equal to the size of its congressional delegation. These electors would meet in the state to cast their votes for president; the candidate who received a majority of the states' electoral votes was the national winner. If no candidate received a majority, the president was to be selected by the House of Representatives, with each state casting one vote.

This electoral college was an ingenious invention. By leaving the choice of electors to the state legislatures, the framers avoided having to set uniform election methods and voting requirements, issues on which they strongly disagreed (and which involved, of course, the explosive question of slavery). This also eliminated the need for federal intervention in a question on which the states had previously made their own decisions and which might have produced state opposition. Requiring electors to meet simultaneously in their respective states helped prevent a conspiracy among electors from different states to put forward their own choice for president.

At first, states used a variety of methods for selecting presidential electors, but by the 1820s, popular election was the most common method.[10] The growing enthusiasm for democratic practices—the force that propelled this movement toward popular election of presidential electors—also eroded the power of the congressional caucus to nominate a presidential candidate. Caucus nominations came to be criticized as the action of a narrow and self-perpetuating elite. The result was that the congressional party caucus was losing its role as the predominant force within the parties.

The caucus system also began to fall apart from within. The Democratic-Republicans' attempt to nominate a presidential candidate in 1824 ended in chaos. The candidate chosen by the caucus, William Crawford, ran fourth in the actual election, and because no candidate won a majority in the electoral college, the House of Representatives had to choose among John Quincy Adams, Henry Clay, and Andrew Jackson. Although Jackson was the front-runner in both the popular and electoral votes, the House chose Adams. Jackson, in turn, defeated Adams in 1828; by then, the nation was entering a new phase of party politics.

THE EMERGENCE OF A NATIONAL TWO-PARTY SYSTEM

The nonparty politics of the Era of Good Feelings gave way to a two-party system that has prevailed ever since. The Democratic-Republicans had developed wings or factions that chose divorce rather than reconciliation. Andrew Jackson led the frontier and agrarian wing of the Democratic-Republicans, the inheritors of the Jeffersonian tradition, into what is now called the ***Democratic Party***. The National Republicans, another faction of the old Democratic-Republicans who promoted Henry Clay for president in 1832, merged with the ***Whigs*** (an old English term referring to those who opposed the dominance of the King, by whom they meant Jackson). That created two-partyism in the United States.

Just as important, the parties as political institutions developed even more of a nationwide grassroots base. The Jacksonian Democrats held the first national nominating convention in 1832, which, appropriately, nominated Jackson himself for a second term. (The Whigs and the smaller Anti-Masonic Party had both held more limited conventions a year before.) Larger numbers of citizens were now eligible to vote, so the presidential campaign became more concerned with reaching out to the public and was less dominated by national political leaders; new campaign organizations and tactics brought the contest to more and more people. Jackson was then sent back to the White House for a second term as the leader of a national political party.

Party organization in the states also expanded. Candidates for state and local office were increasingly nominated by conventions of state and local leaders rather than by the narrower legislative caucuses. By 1840, the Whigs and the Democrats were established in the first truly national party system and were competitive in all the states.

During the 1840s and 1850s, the bitter issue of slavery increasingly fractured both parties. The Whigs, who were particularly divided, collapsed. Antislavery sentiment quickly moved into a new group calling itself the ***Republican Party,*** which had formed not only as a force to abolish slavery but also, like the Whigs, to promote government help for industrial development. The Republicans organized throughout the nation, with the exception of the South and the border states.

In short, modern political parties similar to those we know today—with their characteristic organizational structures, bases of loyal voters, and lasting alliances among governmental leaders—had developed by the middle of the 1800s.[11] The American parties grew hand in hand with the early expansion of the electorate in the United States. Comparable parties did not develop in Great Britain until the 1870s, after laws were passed to further expand the adult male electorate.

The Golden Age of the Parties

Just as the parties were reaching their maturity, they, and American politics, received another massive infusion of voters from a new source: European immigrants. Hundreds of thousands of Europeans, the majority from Ireland and Germany, immigrated to the United States before the Civil War. So many arrived, in fact, that their entry into American politics became a political issue. The newcomers found a ready home in the Democratic Party, and an anti-immigrant third party, the American Party (the so-called Know-Nothing Party), sprang up in response in the 1850s.

The tide of immigration was halted only temporarily by the Civil War. After the war ended, new nationalities came in a virtually uninterrupted flow from 1870 until Congress closed the door to mass immigration in the 1920s. More than five million immigrants arrived in the 1880s (equal to one-tenth of the 1880 resident population), and ten million more came between 1905 and 1914 (one-eighth of the 1900 resident population).

The political parties played an important role in assimilating these huge waves of immigrants. The newcomers gravitated toward the big cities where industrial jobs were available. It was in the cities that a new kind of party organization, the city "machine," developed in response to the immigrants' needs and vulnerabilities. The machines were impressively efficient organizations. They became social service systems that helped the new arrivals cope with the challenges of an urban industrial society. They softened the hard edge of poverty, smoothed the way with government and the police, and taught immigrants the customs of their new home.

The political machines were often indistinguishable from the government of the city; they were the classic case of "party government" in the American experience. They also were the means by which the new urban working class won control of the cities away from the largely Anglo-Saxon, Protestant elite who had prevailed for so long. As the parties again embodied the hopes of new citizens, just as they had in the 1830s, they reached their high point of power and influence in American history.

The American parties, with the party organization now their dominant part, had reached their "golden age" by the beginning of the twentieth century. Party organization now existed in all the states and localities and flourished in the industrial cities. Party discipline was at an all-time high in Congress and most state legislatures. Parties ran campaigns for public office; they held rallies, canvassed door-to-door, and brought the voters to the polls. They controlled access to many government jobs ranging from street inspectors to members of the U.S. Senate. They were an important source of information and guidance for a largely uneducated and often illiterate electorate. They rode the crest of an extraordinarily vital American politics; the highest voter turnouts in American presidential history were recorded during the latter half of the nineteenth century. The parties suited the needs and limitations of the new voters and met the need for creating majorities in the new industrial society.[12]

The Progressive Reforms and Beyond

The drive to democratize American politics continued after the turn of the century. With the adoption of the Seventeenth Amendment, U.S. senators came to be elected directly by the voters rather than by the state legislatures. Women and blacks finally gained the right to vote. As popular democracy expanded, a movement arose that would impose important changes on the parties.

The period that parties saw as their "golden age"—the height of their influence on American politics—did not seem so golden to groups of reformers. To Progressive crusaders, party control of politics had led to rampant corruption and government inefficiency.[13] The Progressives attacked party "boss rule" with the direct primary, which allowed citizens to choose the parties' candidates. Presidential nominations were made more open to the public by establishing presidential primaries in the states. Many state legislatures wrote laws to define and limit party organizations, and activists within the parties reformed their national conventions. The Progressive reforms wrested control of the parties from their professional organizations.

These reforms were shaped by the impulse to fix the problems of a democratic political system by democratizing the system even more. Because the reformers saw party power as the culprit, they tried to weaken the control that the parties, and especially the party organizations, had achieved by the late 1800s. And they succeeded; the parties would never regain the exalted position that they had enjoyed in the three decades after the Civil War. So the expectations of a democratic society, which first made the parties more public, more decentralized, and more active at the grassroots level, later turned on the party organization, leaving it less and less capable of the role that it once played in American politics.[14]

It would be too pat to conclude that these changes mark the next shift in power within the party, starting with the party in government, moving to the party organization during the "golden age" of the parties, and now to the party in the electorate. The Progressive reforms did give ordinary citizens new power in party affairs at the expense of the party organizations and their leaders. However, the reforms also tended to weaken the party's campaign capabilities, which made parties less useful to their candidates. So candidates became more independent of the party organizations and thus may have become less vulnerable to popular control.

Not all reforms in traditional party practices have undermined the party organizations. In the past 30 years, the Democratic Party, through its national committee and convention, has made its rules for selecting presidential candidates more uniform across the nation. At the same time, the Republicans enhanced the capacity of their national party organization to support candidates throughout the country, an activity the Democrats soon tried to match. The result of these two nationalizing thrusts was to strengthen the national party organizations, which has helped shift the balance of organizational power from the grassroots level toward the party's national center.

Even with all these changes, the parties remain largely what they were a hundred years ago: the leading political organizations of mass, popular democracy. They developed and grew with the expansion of the suffrage and the popularization of electoral politics. They were and are the invention by which large numbers of voters come together to select their representatives. They rose to prominence at a time when a new electorate of limited knowledge and political sophistication needed the guidance of their symbols. In that way, the American party reached its time of glory in the nineteenth century. When people talk today about a supposed decline of parties, it is the standard of that "golden age" against which the decline is measured.

WHAT DO THE PARTIES STAND FOR?

There have been many changes over time in the parties' positions on issues, even major issues. Both the Democrats and the Republicans, for example, have shifted their positions dramatically over the years on the question of civil rights for black Americans. The traditional decentralization of the American parties (discussed in the next chapter) has meant that party organizations in some states or local communities have taken stands different from organizations of the same party in other areas.

Yet there have often been times of clear party differences on big policy questions. The current period is one of those times. Although some would argue that the parties' issue stands are simply a means to attract votes, the ongoing competition between the Democrats and Republicans, and the nature of the American party system, has always been more than just a story of raw ambition. Ever since the parties began as groups of leaders in Congress, they have organized not just to gain power but to do so to achieve particular goals. Changes in the electorate and the growing strength of the national party organizations in the past three decades have encouraged the definition of clearer policy stands within both parties as well as sharper differences between them in the sources of their leadership and their core supporters.

If you explore the Republican National Committee's website, the party platform, or the votes of Republicans in Congress, you will find that the Republican Party has long believed in a strong business sector and distrusted the power of government, especially the national government, over business. These principles can be seen in the party's positions on many current issues (see Table 1.l). Tax cuts for individuals and businesses are high on the party's agenda in the early 2000s; lower taxes shrink the government's revenue and, therefore, its ability to exercise power. The tax cuts should favor those who are better off, many Republicans would argue, because that helps the economy grow. The party has traditionally argued for protecting property rights, which also limits the government's ability to interfere in the economic decisions of its citizens. In fact, the first subhead under the Republican platform's section on conservation of natural resources is "Protecting property rights."

Republican positions on other policy questions also demonstrate these commitments to private rather than governmental solutions to problems and to state and local rather than national and international authority. In education, for example, the party argues for local control over schools, and proposes that parents receive tax breaks for sending their children to private schools. In the area of defense, the Republican tradition defines a strong national defense as requiring a powerful military rather than as giving priority to international agreements on arms control and other matters.

Republicans have long been more likely than Democrats to draw their party leaders and candidates from the business sector. Consistent with that, the party's relationship with labor unions has long been somewhere between strained and nonexistent. Core groups of Republican supporters include conservatives (conservative Christians in particular), white southerners, and people with higher incomes.

The Democratic Party represents a different tradition. To Democratic activists, government is a valuable means of redressing the inequalities that the marketplace can cause. These activists believe that needed social services should be public, provided by government, rather than privatized. Tax cuts, they argue, limit the ability of government to provide these needed services. If a tax cut is needed, they say, it should be directed toward helping the needy rather than those who are more affluent.

During the past half century, the national Democratic Party has favored using government to enforce civil rights for black Americans and during the past 20 years has been the party of abortion rights and environmental action. If property rights get in the way of environmental protection, Democratic activists contend, then property rights must usu-

TABLE 1.1 Party Differences in the Early 2000s: Issues and Core Supporters

Democrats	Republicans
Core belief	
A strong government provides needed services and remedies inequalities	A strong government interferes with business and threatens freedom
Biggest exception	
Government should stay out of people's moral decisions (on abortion, homosexuality, etc.)	Government should regulate people's moral decisions (on abortion, homosexuality, etc.)
Issue agenda	
Education, health, social services Environmental protection	Strong military, tax cuts Property rights
Emphasizes	
Fairness, especially for disadvantaged groups	Individual success, not group rights
Relations with labor unions	
Close and supportive	Distant and hostile
Core supporters	
Lower-income people East and West coasts Minority groups Secular individuals Teachers, trial lawyers	Higher-income people South, Mountain West Caucasians Conservative Christians Business people

Source: Compiled by the author from materials including the 2000 Democratic and Republican platforms and the American National Election Studies 2000 *Guide to Public Opinion and Electoral Behavior* (at http://www.umich.edu/~nes).

ally give way. The party's stand on education, similarly, stresses the need for investment in public schools and equality of opportunity. That is one reason why the Democrats are more likely to draw their candidates and activists from among teachers and trial lawyers. The core of Democratic support comes from lower income people, those living on the East and West coasts, minorities, and organized labor.

Yet even today, neither party is a model of consistency on issues. In particular, as Table 1.1 shows, the parties seem to switch core beliefs on issues of individual morality. The Republican Party, which usually opposes government interference, asks for government action to limit abortions and homosexual behavior and to support conservative family values. And the Democrats, the party that sees government as an ally for the needy, wants government to stay out of individuals' lives on issues such as abortion and homosexuality. Inconsistencies such as these are the product of regional and historical forces and alliances of convenience; they show the powerful impact of their environment on the parties' development.

PARTIES ARE SHAPED BY THEIR ENVIRONMENT

Throughout their history, the nature of the parties' activities, their issue positions, and even their organizational form have been influenced by forces in their environment, and they have affected that environment in return. One of the most important of these forces has been the nature of the electorate: who has the right to vote.

Voters and Elections

As we have seen, the expansion of the right to vote has helped shape the parties' development. Each new group of voters entering the electorate challenges the parties to readjust their appeals. As they compete for the support of these new voters, the parties must rethink their strategies for building coalitions that can win elections. Parties in states where black citizens finally gained the right to vote, for example, learned to campaign differently from the days when they had to appeal to an all-white clientele.

The parties' fortunes are also bound up with the *nature* of American elections. The move from indirect to direct election of U.S. senators, for instance, transformed both the contesting of these elections and the parties that contested them. If the electoral college system is ever abolished and American presidents are chosen by direct popular vote, that change, too, would affect the parties.

A state's election rules have great impact on the parties' activities as well. If you were a party leader in a state where conventions of party activists used to nominate state and congressional candidates, imagine the changes that you would face when your state switched to the direct primary and voters gained the power to choose these candidates. Even relatively minor differences in primary law from state to state, such as differences in the form of the ballot or the timing of the primary, affect the parties. The electoral institutions of the nation and the states set the rules within which the parties compete for votes, and thus influence parties' activities and organization.

Political Institutions

The two main "rules" of American politics, federalism and the separation of powers, affect the parties profoundly. Consider, for example, the impact of the separation of powers. Nationally and in the states, American legislators and executives are elected independently of one another. That makes it possible, and in recent decades very likely, for the legislature and the governorship or the presidency to be controlled by different parties. Most other democracies, in contrast, have parliamentary systems in which the legislative majority chooses the officials of the executive branch from among its own members. When that parliamentary majority can no longer hold, a new government must be formed. An important result of the separation of powers is that American legislative parties can rarely achieve the degree of party discipline and cohesion that is common in parliamentary systems.

In addition, because the American chief executive and the cabinet secretaries are not legislative party leaders, as they would be in a parliamentary system, there is a greater opportunity for conflict between executives and legislators of their own party. This conflict is even more likely because, in a system with separated powers, legislators can vote against a president or governor of their own party on key issues without fearing that they will bring down the government and force new elections. So support for and opposition to executive programs has often cut across party lines in Congress and state legislatures to a degree rarely found in parliamentary democracies.

The federal system, in which states have a number of independent powers (rather than being "branch offices" of the national government), has also left an imprint on the American parties. It has permitted the survival of local political loyalties and traditions. It has spawned an awesome range of public offices to fill, creating a system of elections that dwarfs that of all other democracies in size and diversity. These local traditions and loyalties have nurtured a large set of semi-independent local parties within the two national parties.

Laws Governing Parties

No other parties among the world's democracies are as entangled in legal regulations as are the American parties. It was not always this way. Before the Progressive reforms a century ago, American parties were self-governing organizations, almost unrestrained by state or federal law. For most of the 1800s, for example, the parties printed, distributed, and often—with a wary eye on one another— even counted the ballots. The "Australian" (or secret) ballot changed all this, giving the responsibility for running elections to government, where it has remained ever since. During their "golden age," as noted earlier, the parties made their own rules for nominating candidates. But the arrival of the direct primary in the early 1900s and recent reforms of the presidential nominating process have severely limited the parties' autonomy. Civil service reform and court action have also largely stopped the parties from hiring workers for government jobs, a practice that was common in the late 1800s.

The existence of 50 different sets of state laws governing the parties has produced an almost bewildering 50-state variety of political parties. The forms of their organization are prescribed by the states in endless, often finicky detail. State laws define the parties themselves, often by defining the right to place candidates on the ballot. Most states try to regulate party activities; many, for example, regulate party finances, and most place some limits on their campaign practices. More recently, the federal government has added burdens of its own, including regulating parties' campaign practices and finances.[15]

Political Culture

A nation's political culture is the set of political values and expectations held by its people. It includes the public's view of how the political system works, how it ought to work, and what roles individual citizens can play in politics and government. One of the most persistent components of the American political culture is the feeling that party politics is an underhanded, dirty business. A 2000 survey, for example, demonstrated that enthusiasm for the two parties was so limited that, when given a "feeling thermometer" ranging from 0 to 100 degrees on which to indicate their level of positive feeling, respondents could muster no more than an average rating of 56 for the Democrats and the Republicans—a chilly temperature in which to live.[16]

These and other elements of the political culture help shape what the parties can be. Public distrust of parties encourages candidates to campaign as individuals rather than as members of a party team and even to avoid mentioning their party in campaign ads. The widespread view that legislators ought to vote based on their local district's interests, for example, makes it harder to achieve party discipline in Congress and state legislatures. Even the question of what we regard as fair campaigning simply reflects the values and expectations of large numbers of Americans. Whether a strongly worded campaign ad is seen as "negative" or as "hard-hitting and informative" depends on cultural values, not on some set of universal standards. These cultural values affect citizens' feelings about the parties' behavior and, as a result, they influence the behavior itself.

The Nonpolitical Environment

Parties' environment is broader than their *political* environment. Perhaps no force has been more important for party politics than the emergence of the modern mass media, especially television and the Internet. Because the media can provide so much information about politics and candidates, voters need not depend on the parties to learn about elections and issues. Just as important, candidates can contact voters directly through the media rather than having to depend on the parties to carry the message for them. That has weakened party control over candidates' campaigns. To add insult to injury, media coverage tends not to pay much attention to the parties themselves. Television attaches great importance to visual images, of course, so it is much more likely to cover individuals—candidates and public officials—than to cover institutions, such as parties, that do not have a "face."

Economic trends can also have a strong and often disruptive impact on the parties. When an economic recession occurs, for example, parties will find it harder to raise money. If the crisis is especially severe, as was the Great Depression of the 1930s, it may even fracture and reorganize the pattern of citizens' party loyalties, end the careers of prominent party leaders, and make a majority party into a weakened minority.

In this chapter, we have explored the nature of parties, what they do, and how they have developed in and been shaped by their environment. The next chapter tackles one of the biggest puzzles that students of parties face when comparing the American parties with those in other nations: why does the United States have two major parties, rather than several, or only one?

CHAPTER 2

The American Two-Party System

Many Americans think that a two-party system is normal for a democracy. Yet most democracies don't have one. In fact, most nations have either one dominant political party (Mexico is an example) or many parties competing for control of government. European democracies typically have multiparty systems with three, four, or even more parties, often without any single party being able to win a majority of the votes.[1]

One-party and multiparty systems have been part of the American experience as well. Some states and cities have had a long tradition of one-party rule; in other areas, several parties have flourished at certain times. Minor or third parties and independent candidates continue to leave their mark on American politics. Green Party candidate Ralph Nader probably took just enough votes from the Democrats in 2000 to tip the presidential election to Republican George W. Bush.[2] Ross Perot's independent presidential campaign in 1992 won the support of almost 20 million Americans—the third highest percentage of the popular vote for a minor-party candidate in U.S. history—and was transformed into a third party, the Reform Party, in 1996. At the state level, reporters were captivated by the spectacle of a former professional wrestler named Jesse "The Body" Ventura winning the governorship of Minnesota in 1998 as the Reform Party candidate.

These campaigns are colorful enough to capture a lot of media attention; not many governors have worn a pink feather boa into a public arena nor moonlighted as color commentators for the XFL (the late Extreme Football League). For better or for worse, however, they are rare. For most of American history, most elections have been contested by two parties and only two parties; the two-party system has endured for more than 160 years. Even the rapid rise of the Republican Party from its founding in 1854 to becoming one of two major parties two years later, displacing the Whig Party in the process, is the exception that proves the rule. First Democrat versus Whig and then, since 1856, Democrat versus Republican, the United States has had a two-party system in national party competition.

Why has American politics remained a two-party system for so long? Does the number of parties in a political system really matter? In this chapter, we look at the level of competition between the parties, the major theories as to how the two-party system developed, and the trends in efforts by third parties and independent candidates to break the two-party mold.

THE NATIONAL PARTY SYSTEM

Throughout this remarkably long period of two-party politics, the two major parties have been very close competitors, at least at the national level. Consider the record of presidential elections. Since 1868, the great majority of these elections (28 out of 34) have been so close that a shift of 10 percent of the vote or less would have given the White House to the other party's candidate instead. Almost half (15) were decided by a spread of less than 7 percent of the popular vote. Some of the closest presidential contests in American history have taken place in the past 40 years, including 2000, which was a virtual tie.

Elections to the House of Representatives have been even closer. Overall, during the past 70 years, the percentage of the two-party vote cast for all Democratic candidates in a given election has not differed much from the vote cast for Republicans (see Table 2.1). The two major parties are closely competitive in other contests as well. After the 2002 elections, the Senate moved from a 51–49 division in favor of the Democrats to a 51–49 split favoring the Republicans. And in 2003, 26 states had Republican governors compared with 24 led by Democrats.

As this quick survey suggests, the two major parties are extremely resilient. Media coverage may suggest otherwise because it tends to trumpet the events of the moment. However, whenever one party has taken a big advantage, in the long run the other party has been able to restore the balance. Although the Democrats seemed to be on the ropes after the Reagan victories of the 1980s and the Republican congressional sweep of 1994, they recovered quickly enough to keep the presidency in 1996 and to continue gaining

TABLE 2.1   Percentage of the Two-Party Vote Won by Republican Candidates for President and House of Representatives: 1940–2002

	Presidential Elections		House Elections	
Decade Average	% Republican of Two-party Vote	% Difference Between Republican and Democratic Vote	% Republican of Two-party Vote	% Difference Between Republican and Democratic Vote
1940s	46.3	7.3	49.8	5.9
1950s	56.6	13.1	48.1	4.2
1960s	46.3	7.8	46.7	6.7
1970s	55.4	12.6	44.5	10.7
1980s	56.1	11.9	46.1	7.6
1990s	45.9	7.1	49.5	4.3
2000s	49.7	0.5	51.6	3.2

Sources: Calculated from Harold W. Stanley and Richard G. Niemi, *Vital Statistics on American Politics 1999–2000* (Washington, DC: CQ Press, 2000), Tables 1–7 and 1–12. Data for 2000 House races were calculated from U.S. Census Bureau, *Statistical Abstract of the United States*: 2001 (Washington, DC: Government Printing Office, 2001), p. 239, and for 2002 House races from CQ *Weekly* postelection issue.

seats in Congress in 2000. By the same token, the GOP (or Grand Old Party, a nickname the Republican Party developed in the late 1800s) confounded the pessimists by springing back from the Roosevelt victories of the 1930s, landslide defeat in 1964, and the Watergate-related setbacks of the mid-1970s.

THE FIFTY STATE PARTY SYSTEMS

This pattern of close competition at the national level is an important part of the story of the American two-party system yet, interestingly enough, it coexisted for a long time with one-party dominance in many states and local communities. Georgia, for example, chose Democratic governors for 50 consecutive gubernatorial elections, starting before the end of Reconstruction, before finally electing a Republican in 2002.[3] And even now, although the House of Representatives as a whole is closely divided, many individual House districts look anything but competitive. Large numbers of House candidates are elected with a comfortable margin of victory. In 2002, almost 90 percent of the winning House candidates got at least 55 percent of the vote. In fact, more than a quarter of the winners got 75 percent of the vote or more![4]

How can we measure the level of competition in the 50 state party systems? There are many questions to answer in building a measure. Which offices should we look at: the vote for president, governor, senator, statewide officials, state legislators, or some combination of these? The competitiveness of a state's U.S. Senate seats may be strikingly different from that of its state legislative races. Should we count the candidates' vote totals, the number of offices that each party wins, or something else?

Measuring State Party Competition

The approach used most often to measure interparty competition below the national level is an index originated by Austin Ranney.[5] The Ranney index averages three indicators of party success during a particular time period: the percentage of the popular vote for the parties' gubernatorial candidates, the percentage of seats held by the parties in each house of the legislature, and the length of time plus the percentage of the time that the parties held both the governorship and a majority in the state legislature. The resulting scores range from 1.00 (complete Democratic success) through 0.50 (Democratic and Republican parity) to 0.00 (complete Republican success).

Like any other summary measure, the Ranney index picks up some trends more fully than others. One reason is that it is based wholly on state elections. This protects the measure from being distorted by landslide victories and other unusual events at the national level. Yet those national events may foreshadow what will happen in voting for state offices. In the South, for example, growing GOP strength appeared first in competition for national offices and only later worked its way down to the state and local level. In these states, the Ranney index has shown less interparty competition than really exists. A second problem is that the dividing lines between categories are purely arbitrary. There is no magic threshold that separates the category "competitive" from that of "one-party." Finally, any index score will vary, of course, depending on the years and the offices that it covers. Nevertheless, its findings provide an interesting picture of state party competition.

Figure 2.1 presents the calculations for the Ranney index through the 2002 elections. It shows much more balanced party competition at the state level than had appeared in

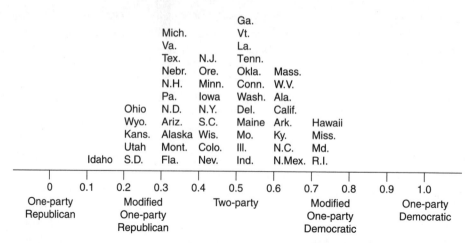

FIGURE 2.1   **Interparty Competition in the States, 1999–2003.**

Source: Data were kindly provided by John F. Bibby and Thomas M. Holbrook, "Parties and Elections," in *Virginia Gray and Russell L. Hanson, eds., Politics in the American States*, 8th ed. (Washington, DC: CQ Press, 2003), p. 88.

these calculations earlier in the years since World War II. Note especially that no states are classified as fully one-party. The driving force in this change has been the development of two-party competition in the southern states, which used to be one-party Democratic, and in formerly one-party Republican states as well. Some regional patterns can still be seen; most states of the Mountain West, for example, remain largely Republican. In fact, there has been a shift toward Republican success in the states more generally, with the tipping point coming at the time of the 1994 elections. Because the Democrats had dominated so many states in earlier years, the result has been greater competition between the two parties throughout the 50 states than had existed before.[6]

Incumbency: Limits on Competitiveness

The major restraint on competitiveness is the increased electoral value of incumbency. If you had been a candidate for elective office in the 1800s, your chance of winning would probably have depended on which party you represented. Candidates of the dominant party in one-party areas were almost sure to win. In more competitive areas, however, candidates' fates were tied to the national or statewide forces that affected their parties. Even though American candidates have been better able to insulate themselves from their party's misfortunes than have candidates in many other democracies, voters in these more competitive areas could easily turn to the other party as the political winds changed. The result was a lot of party turnover in seats and insecurity for many candidates.

Candidates for many offices since 1900, and especially since the 1950s, have had greater electoral security, mainly because incumbency has become so valuable a political resource. From 1954 through 1988, for example, the average success rates for incumbents seeking reelection were 93 percent in the U.S. House of Representatives and 81 percent in the Senate. These rates peaked in 1988 for the House when more than 98 percent of the incumbents who ran for reelection won, and in 1990 when all but one of the senators running for reelection won.[7] (A congressional incumbent in these years probably stood a greater chance of being hit by a truck in Washington, DC, traffic than of losing reelection.) Incumbents in most state legislatures were just as likely to keep their jobs.

We do not know for certain why incumbency came to be such a valuable resource in congressional elections. Incumbents certainly benefit from the "perks" of holding office—their name recognition and the attention that they receive from the media, the services they can provide to constituents, the relative ease with which they can raise campaign money, and their experience in having run previous successful campaigns. No matter what the reason, it is clear that incumbents had a great deal of job security during this time.

That job security seemed to be at risk in the early 1990s. The popular vote for House incumbents in 1990 dropped below the percentages that incumbents had come to treasure in the 1980s, even though most incumbents were still returned to office. The elections of 1992 and 1994 were even harder on incumbents. Because of redistricting, special incentives for retirement, especially strong challengers, and a well-reported scandal, fewer incumbents sought reelection to the House of Representatives in 1992 than at any time since 1954. Those who did met with a success rate of 88 percent in the primaries and general election, the lowest since the post-Watergate election in 1974. More House incumbents sought reelection in 1994, but "only" 90 percent were reelected in both the primaries and general election.[8]

The reelection rate returned to 94 percent in 1996 and 98 percent in 1998, 2000, and 2002. So, although party competition is increasing nationally and in the states, congressional incumbents still have big advantages in retaining their posts. In fact, there has been an increasing electoral advantage for incumbents of all executive and legislative offices, "from utility commissioner to governor, from state legislator to Senator."[9]

Many offices, however, do not reach the relative security of the U.S. House. Senators are not as assured of reelection as are their House colleagues; among members of the Senate who ran again, 78 percent won in 2000 and 88 percent in 2002. In addition, even the high reelection rate in the House may be misleading; many of the losing House incumbents had previously won their districts with comfortable margins, leading their colleagues to wonder whether incumbents really enjoyed the kind of long-term security that their high reelection rates would suggest.[10] Incumbency, then, is a resource with a lot of potential payoff, but it must be exploited with energy, skill, and at least some luck.

WHAT CAUSES A TWO-PARTY SYSTEM?

We have seen, then, that the American parties are durable, closely competitive with one another at the national level, and increasingly competitive in the states. Why have we had a two-party system for so long, when most other democracies do not? There are several possible explanations.

Institutional Forces

The most frequent explanation of the two-party system ties it to the nature of American electoral institutions. Called Duverger's law,[11] it argues that single-member districts with plurality elections tend to produce two-party systems. Plurality election in

PLURALITY VERSUS PROPORTIONAL REPRESENTATION: HOW IT WORKS IN PRACTICE

Does it matter whether an election uses plurality or proportional representation (PR) rules to count the votes? To find out, let us compare the results of one type of American election in which both rules are used. In presidential primaries—the elections in which party voters choose delegates to the national parties' nominating conventions—the Democrats use PR to select delegates (with at least 15 percent of the vote needed for a party to win delegates) and the Republicans generally use plurality election (also called winner-take-all).

Imagine a congressional district that can elect four delegates to the convention, in which candidates A, B, C, and D get the following percentages of the vote. The candidates would win the following numbers of delegates, depending on whether the plurality or PR rule was used:

		Delegates Won	
	% of vote	PR	Plurality
Candidate A	40%	2	4
Candidate B	30%	1	0
Candidate C	20%	1	0
Candidate D	10%	0	0

As you can see, the *plurality* rule increases the delegate strength of the leading candidate (candidate A) at the expense of the other three. The second-place candidate wins nothing but will still probably run on the chance that he or she could win more votes than candidate A. Under PR rules, in contrast, *three* candidates win delegates in rough proportion to their popular support. So in a typical Democratic primary, the less successful candidates (like candidate C) are encouraged to stay in the nomination race longer because the PR rules permit them to keep winning at least a few delegates; in a typical Republican primary, only the front-runner will win delegates, so the less successful candidates will probably drop out quickly.

The contrast is even clearer when we compare British elections with the multi-member district systems of most European legislative elections. The use of PR in the European elections promotes multiparty politics and coalition governments in which two or more different parties often share control of the executive. In the British parliamentary system, on the other hand, single-member districts operating under plurality rules typically produce a parliamentary majority for one party, giving it sole control of the executive, even if it does not win a majority of the popular vote.

a single-member district means simply that one candidate is elected to each office and that the winner is the person who receives the largest number of votes, even if not a majority. Finishing a close second, or third or fourth, brings no rewards. The American election system is, for most offices, a single-member district system with plurality election; it offers the reward of winning an office only to the one candidate who gets the most votes. So the theory suggests that minor parties will see no point in running candidates if they don't have a shot at winning.

The flip side of Duverger's law is that multimember constituencies and proportional representation result in multiparty systems. A system with multimember constituencies is one in which a particular legislative district will be represented by, say, three or four elected legislators.[12] Each party prepares a slate of candidates for these positions, and the number of party candidates who win is proportional to the overall percentage of the vote won by the party slate (see box on page 30). Because a party may be able to elect a candidate with only 15 or 20 percent of the votes, depending on the system's rules, small parties are encouraged to keep competing.

However, a puzzle remains. Single-member district systems with plurality elections exist in some other democracies that support more than two parties. Shouldn't the United States, with its great diversity, do the same? To some analysts, the nature of the American presidency is enough to sustain Duverger's law. The presidency is the most visible single-member district in the United States. It is the main prize of American politics, and only one person is elected to that office at a time. Many other democracies, using a parliamentary system, select a governing "cabinet" as the executive authority. This cabinet is made up of a number of officeholders, so it can be a coalition that includes representatives of several parties, including minority parties.

In a system with a single executive, minor parties will be weakened because they do not have a realistic chance to compete for the presidency. Even local and regional parties strong enough to elect candidates in their own localities typically find it unrealistic to run a candidate for president. That, in turn, denies a minor party a number of other important opportunities. Without a presidential candidate, a party is not likely to gain the national attention that major parties get. Add to that the uniquely American institution of the electoral college. To win, a presidential candidate must get a plurality of electoral votes—so far, at least, an impossible task for a minor-party candidate. Because the presidency is so prominent in American politics, the argument goes, it shapes the politics of the system as a whole. Because third parties have no chance of winning the presidency, they will not thrive.[13]

Of course, some minor parties try for the presidency anyway. In 1996, the Reform Party focused primarily on the presidential race. But its candidate, Ross Perot, a billionaire willing to spend tens of millions on his campaign, is clearly not typical of most minor parties, no matter how much they may dream of such an opportunity. So the importance of the single, indivisible executive office in the American system strengthens the tendency toward two-party politics.

Political scientist Leon Epstein has identified another institutional factor, the direct primary, as a force that prevented the development of third parties in areas dominated by one party.[14] Primaries, which allow voters to choose the parties' nominees, have become the main method of selecting party candidates. When disgruntled groups have the opportunity to make their voices heard within the dominant party through a primary and may even succeed in getting a candidate nominated, the resulting taste of power will probably discourage them from breaking away to pursue a third-party course. Thus, in the one-party Democratic South of an earlier era, where traditional animosities kept most people from voting Republican, factional disputes that under other conditions would have led to third-party development were contained within the Democratic Party by the existence of primary elections.

"Dualist" Theories

Some theorists believe that there is a basic duality of interests in American society that has sustained the two-party system. V. O. Key, Jr. argued that tension between the eastern financial and commercial interests and the western frontiersmen stamped itself on the parties as they were forming and fostered two-party competition. Later, the dualism shifted to North-South conflict over the issue of slavery and the Civil War and then to urban-rural and socioeconomic divisions. A related line of argument suggests that there is a natural dualism within democratic institutions: government versus opposition, those favoring and opposing the status quo, and even the ideological dualism of liberal and conservative. Therefore, social and economic interests, or the very processes of a democratic politics, tend to reduce the contestants to two great camps, and that dualism gives rise to two political parties.[15]

We can see tendencies toward dualism even in multiparty systems, in that some parties will succeed in constructing a governing coalition that pulls them together and the other parties will find themselves in opposition. In France and Italy, for example, the Socialists and other parties of the left, or the various parties of the right and center, often compete against one another in elections but then come together along largely ideological lines to contest runoff elections or to form a government. What distinguishes two-party from multiparty systems, in short, may be whether this basic tendency toward dualism is expressed in every aspect of the electoral process or only in the creation and functioning of a government.

The two major American parties play an important role in protecting a two-party system. Their openness to new groups and their adaptability to changing conditions—qualities rare among democratic parties—undermine the development of strong third parties. Just when a third party rides the crest of a new issue to the point where it can challenge the two-party monopoly, one or both of the major parties is likely to absorb the new movement. The experience of the Populists and the Progressives in the early 1900s is a good example, as is the reaction of some Perot followers in time for the 2000 campaign.

Social Consensus Theories

Another possible explanation for the American two-party system is that it reflects a broad consensus on values in American society. Despite their very diverse social and cultural heritage, early on Americans reached a consensus on the fundamentals that divide other societies. Almost all Americans have traditionally accepted the prevailing social, economic, and political institutions. They accepted the Constitution and its governmental structure, a regulated but free enterprise economy, and (perhaps to a lesser extent) American patterns of social class and status.

In traditional multiparty countries, such as France and Italy, noticeable segments of the public have favored radical changes in those and other basic institutions. They have supported fundamental constitutional change, the socialization of the economy, or the disestablishment of the national church. Perhaps American politics escaped these divisions on the essentials because Americans did not have a history of the rigid class structure of feudalism. Perhaps the early expansion of the right to vote made it unnecessary for workers and other economically disadvantaged citizens to organize in order to gain some political power. Perhaps it was the expanding economic and geographic frontiers that allowed Americans to concentrate on claiming a piece of a growing pie rather than on battling one another. Because the matters that divide Americans are secondary, the argument goes, the compromises needed to bring them into one of two major parties are easier to make.[16]

Once a two-party system has developed, the two dominant parties have a strong motivation to protect it. Naturally, the two major parties will choose and keep election systems (such as single-member districts) that make it hard for minor parties to do well. Through their control of Congress and state legislatures, the Democrats and Republicans have made it very difficult for third parties to qualify for the ballot and for third-party candidates to receive public funding. The major parties have no interest in leveling the playing field so that their minor-party competitors can take a shot at replacing them.[17] Further, after the two-party system was launched, it created deep loyalties within the American public to one party or the other and attachments to the two-party system itself.

Among all these possible reasons for a two-party system, the most important cause is the institutional arrangement of American electoral politics. Without single-member districts, plurality elections, the electoral college, and an indivisible executive, it would have been much easier for third parties to break the near-monopoly enjoyed by the two major parties. The other Anglo-American democracies, such as Britain and Canada, which share the American institutional arrangements, also tend to be dominated by two parties, although third parties are not as hobbled in these nations as in the American party system.

EXCEPTIONS TO THE TWO-PARTY PATTERN

As we have seen, the American two-party system can harbor pockets of one-party politics within some states and localities. There have been other deviations from the two-party pattern. Some areas have developed a uniquely American brand of no-party politics. Third parties or independent candidates have occasionally made their presence felt, as in recent presidential elections. Where do we find these exceptions to two-party politics?

Nonpartisan Elections

One of the crowning achievements of the Progressive movement was to restrict the role of parties in elections by removing party labels from many ballots, mostly in local elections. About three quarters of American towns and cities, including Los Angeles, Chicago, Miami, and Atlanta, conduct their local elections on a nonpartisan basis. One state, Nebraska, elects state legislators on a nonpartisan ballot, and many states elect judges in this manner.

Removing party labels from the ballot has not usually removed partisan influences where parties are already strong. The nonpartisan ballot did not prevent the development of a powerful political party machine in Chicago. A resourceful party organization can still select its candidates and persuade voters where party labels are not on the ballot. Even where local elections are nonpartisan, local voters are still affected by the partisan content of state and national elections. But nonpartisanship does add to the parties' burdens; even the strongest local parties have to try much harder to let voters know which are the party's candidates.

Typically, however, the reform tended to take root in cities and towns that already had weak parties and for offices, such as judgeships and school boards, where the traditional American dislike of party politics is most pronounced. In contrast, most northeastern cities, where strong party machines were the most visible targets of the Progressives, were able to resist the reforms and to continue to hold partisan local elections.

Beyond removing the party label from ballots and adding to the difficulties faced by party organizations, what difference does it make if an election is nonpartisan? Political scientists have found that a move to nonpartisan elections shifts the balance of power in a pro-Republican direction rather than making politics any less partisan or more high-minded. Without party labels on the ballot, the voter is more dependent on other cues. Higher status candidates tend to have more resources and visibility in the community, which can fill the void left by the absence of party. In current American politics, these higher status candidates are more likely to be Republicans.[18]

In an ingenious experiment, one group of researchers compared the behavior of state legislators in Nebraska, who are selected in nonpartisan elections, with those in partisan Kansas. They found that Nebraska legislators' votes are not as clearly structured as they are in Kansas; that makes it harder for voters to be able to predict how their representatives will behave and therefore to hold them accountable. So nonpartisan elections can weaken the policy linkage between voters and legislators.[19]

Pockets of One-Party Monopoly

In the past, the states of the Deep South were the country's best known examples of one-party domination, although the same could be said of the deeply rooted Republicanism of Maine, New Hampshire, and Vermont. Today, traces of one-party politics can still be found in thousands of cities, towns, and counties in which a mention of the other party can produce anything from raised eyebrows to raised tempers.

Where do we find these one-party areas? Since the 1930s, the major parties, especially in national elections, have divided the American voters roughly along socioeconomic lines: by income, education, and job status. (More about this can be found in Chapters 6 and 7.) A local constituency may be too small to contain the wide range of socioeconomic characteristics that leads to competitive politics. Thus, we can find "safe" Democratic congressional districts in the older, poorer, or black neighborhoods of large cities and "safe" Republican districts in the wealthier suburbs. In other words, the less diverse its people are, at least in terms of the characteristics that typically divide Republican voters from Democratic voters, the more likely the district is to foster one-party politics.

Alternatively, there may be some local basis of party loyalty so powerful that it overrides the relationship between socioeconomic status and partisanship. In the classic one-party politics of the American South, regional loyalties long overrode the factors that were dividing Americans into two parties in most of the rest of the country. Feelings about the Republicans as the party of abolition, Lincoln, the Civil War, and the hated Reconstruction were so intensely negative that, even generations after the Civil War ended, they overpowered the impact of socioeconomic differences. In other areas, the effects of a serious scandal or a bitter strike may linger, leaving only one party as a socially acceptable choice.

Once one party has established dominance in an area, it can be very hard for the weaker party to overcome its disadvantages. These disadvantages begin with stubborn party loyalties. Many voters are not easily moved from their attachments to a party, even though the reasons for the original attachment have long passed. Further, a party trying to become competitive may find itself caught in a vicious circle. Its inability to win elections limits its ability to raise money and recruit attractive candidates because, as a chronic loser, it offers so little chance of achieving political goals. The Republican Party in the South, for example, found for many years that the Democrats had recruited the region's most promising politicians and claimed its most potent appeals.

In addition, the weaker party's ability to attract voters locally is affected by media coverage of its national party's stance. If the Democratic Party is identified nationally with the hopes of the poor and minority groups, its appeal in an affluent suburb may be limited. So a nationalized politics may increasingly rob the local party organization of the chance to develop strength based on its own issues, personalities, and traditions. To the extent that party loyalties grow out of national politics, as many Democrats in the South have learned in recent years, competitiveness may be beyond the reach of some local party organizations.

As if this were not enough, the weaker party faces the hurdle of competing in electoral districts drawn up by the stronger party. The Supreme Court ruled in the 1960s that state legislatures must redraw legislative district boundaries at the beginning of each decade, following the U.S. Census, in order to keep the districts fairly equal in population. The Court halted the decades-old practice of malapportioning those districts to protect or improve the chances of majority party candidates. However, majority parties have found remarkably effective ways to draw districts that preserve their advantage. This is why parties are especially concerned with winning state legislative majorities in years when district lines must be redrawn.

Third Parties

Minor parties, often called "third" parties, have a long history in American politics, but they rarely win elections. Only seven minor parties in all of American history have carried even a single state in a presidential election, and only one (the Progressive Party) has done so twice. Theodore Roosevelt and the Progressives, in 1912, were the only minor-party candidacy ever to run ahead of one of the major-party candidates in either electoral or popular votes.

In recent years, third parties' prospects have not improved. The combined minor-party vote for president in 1992, excluding votes for independent candidates, did not even reach 1 percent of the total popular vote. In 1996, this total jumped to 9.6 million, or 10 percent, with slightly more than 8 million of those votes going to Ross Perot as the Reform Party candidate. It shrank again in 2000 (see Table 2.2). These numbers are not likely to give much hope to future third-party candidacies.

Third-party successes can be found below the presidential level, but they are as rare as they are fascinating. Of more than a thousand governors elected since 1875, fewer than 20 ran solely on a third-party ticket, and another handful ran as independents.[20] Jesse Ventura's successful candidacy in Minnesota in 1998 got enormous media attention precisely because it was so unusual, but he stepped down from the governorship in 2002, after having been largely ignored by the state legislature, and the next candidate of his party managed to attract only 16 percent of the vote.[21]

There were some third-party victories at the local level in 2000. An estimated 1,420 candidates ran on the Libertarian label alone, and almost 500 won elected or appointed

TABLE 2.2 Popular Votes Cast for Minor Parties in 2000 and 1996 Presidential Elections

2000		1996	
Parties	Vote	Parties	Vote
Green	2,882,955	Reform	8,085,402
Reform (Buchanan)	448,895	Green	685,128
Libertarian	384,431	Libertarian	485,798
Constitution	98,020	U.S. Taxpayers	184,820
Natural Law/Reform	83,714	Natural Law	113,670
Socialist Workers	7,378	Workers World	29,083
Libertarian (Arizona)	5,775	Peace and Freedom	25,332
Socialist	5,602	Socialist Workers	8,476
Others and Scattered	8,349	Others and Scattered	23,806
Total	3,925,119	Total	9,641,515

Note: Votes for independent and write-in candidates are not included.

Sources: Federal Election Commission. On the 1996 election, http://www.fec.gov/pubrec/summ.htm. On the 2000 election, http://fecweb1.fec.gov/pubrec/2000presgeresults.htm (accessed May 30, 2003).

offices in city or town councils, park and school boards, and as justices of the peace.[22] In 2002, Libertarian candidates won enough votes to throw the South Dakota Senate race and the Wisconsin governorship to the Democrats, although some Libertarians might consider that a dubious achievement. However, for every example of third-party success in local elections, there are thousands of races with no minor-party challenge. The Democratic and Republican parties have monopolized American electoral politics even more fully in the states and cities than at the national level. (For one minor-party activist's reaction, see "A Day in the Life" on page 37).

Third parties differ in their purposes, origins, and activities. Their variety is as plain as a look at their labels: Socialist Workers, Green Party, Libertarian.[23]

Differences in Scope of Ideological Commitment Most minor parties are driven by issues and ideologies, but they differ in the nature and scope of that commitment. The Right to Life and the Southern Independence Parties are very specific and targeted: the former in its antiabortion stance and the latter in favoring an independent nation of southern states. At the other extreme are socialist parties whose programs demand sweeping changes, including an end to capitalism and class privilege. The Libertarian Party advocates a complete withdrawal of government from most of its present programs and responsibilities.[24] In sharp contrast, Green Parties argue for extensive government effort on behalf of environmental, peace, and social justice issues.

Difference of Origins The minor parties differ, too, in their origin. Some were literally imported into the United States. Much of the early Socialist Party strength in the United States came from the freethinkers and radicals who fled Europe after the failed revolutions of 1848. Socialist candidates did well in cities such as Milwaukee, New York, and Cincinnati because of the concentrations of liberal German immigrants

COMPETING AGAINST THE "BIG GUYS"

The Democrats and the Republicans, Brad Warren says, have a "death grip" on the American political process. Warren, a tax attorney in Indianapolis, is a Libertarian party activist who ran for the U.S. Senate under that party's banner. "If I need a new pair of socks," he points out, "I can go to dozens of stores and pick from several different brands and dozens of colors—for something as insignificant as socks. But when it comes to politics, which has a monopoly on the lawful use of force in our society, we have only two choices. That is tremendously scary! How do you hold them accountable? If you get angry with the incumbents, you can throw them out, only to reelect the nasty incumbents you had thrown out in the previous election. Four years from now, you'll be throwing out the incumbents you elected today. There's no choice."

Third-party activists, such as Warren, find that they are competing against the "big guys"—the two major parties—on an uneven playing field. A major problem for a third party, Warren says, is simply to get its candidates' names on the ballot. In Indiana, the state legislature used to require any minor party to win just half of 1 percent of the vote for Secretary of State in order to qualify its candidates to get on the state ballot automatically in later elections. The Libertarians met that goal in 1982. The result? The legislature raised the hurdle to 2 percent. Ballot access requirements differ from state to state, making it difficult for a minor party to appear on the ballot in all 50 states.

"Even once you have ballot access," Warren argues, "you will still be excluded from any *meaningful* participation in the election. In practice, we run elections on money, not on votes, and in presidential elections, the Republicans and Democrats divide up hundreds of millions of federal dollars among themselves."

The worst problem for third parties, Warren feels, is getting noticed after the major primaries hold primary elections. "I got pretty good media coverage up to the primary election. After the primary, I was nobody. Even though the primary doesn't elect anybody to any office, it *seems to*. It legitimizes the major parties' candidates and delegitimizes everybody else. The media say we have no chance to win, so they won't cover any candidates except the [major] party-anointed ones. The debates typically don't include third-party candidates. Why? Because the commissions that decide who's going to be allowed to participate in debates are 'bipartisan' commissions, made up entirely of Republicans and Democrats, just like the legislatures that write the ballot access laws and the judges who interpret them. We understand that it would be confusing to have too many candidates in a debate. But a party that has gotten on the ballot in all 50 states, like the Libertarians, deserves to be heard."

"The two major parties won't give you any choice," Warren contends, and "if you continually vote for the lesser of two evils, what you get is evil." So what is the role of a third party? To Warren, "It's like that of a bee: You rise up, you sting, and then you die."

there. Other parties, especially the Granger and Populist Parties, were homegrown channels of social protest, born of social inequality and economic hardship in the marginal farmlands of America.

Some minor parties began as splinters or factions of one of the major parties. For example, the Progressives (the Bull Moose Party) of 1912 and the Dixiecrats of 1948 objected so strenuously to the platforms and candidates of their parent parties that they ran their own slates and presented their own programs in presidential elections. In fact, the Dixiecrats, an anti–civil-rights faction within the Democratic Party, substituted their own candidate for the one chosen by the party's national convention as the official Democratic presidential candidate in the state.

Differing Purposes   Finally, third parties differ in their intentions. The aim of some of these parties is to educate citizens about their issues; getting votes is merely a sideline. They run candidates because their presence on the ballot brings media attention that they could not otherwise hope to get. Many of these parties serenely accept their election losses because they have chosen not to compromise their principles to win office. The Prohibition Party, for example, has run candidates in presidential elections since 1872 with unflagging devotion to the cause of banning alcoholic beverages but without apparent concern for the fact that its highest proportion of the popular vote was 2 percent, and that came in 1892.

Other minor parties are serious about trying to win office. Often, their goal is local, although today they find it difficult to control an American city, as the Socialists once did, or an entire state, like the Progressives. More realistically, they may hope to hold a balance of power in a close election between the major parties, as Ralph Nader did in the 2000 presidential election and several Libertarian candidates did in 2002. Ross Perot even claimed to be looking for an outright victory in both 1992 (as an independent) and 1996.

What Difference Do They Make?   By threatening about once a generation to deadlock the electoral college, third parties have probably kept alive movements to reform it. Beyond their role as potential electoral spoiler, have third parties accomplished anything substantial?

Some argue that minor parties deserve the credit for a number of public policies— programs that were first suggested by a minor party and then adopted by a major party when they reached the threshold of political acceptability. A possible example is the Socialist Party platforms that advocated such measures as a minimum wage for 20 or 30 years before the minimum wage law was enacted in the 1930s by a Democratic administration. Did the Democrats steal the Socialist Party's idea, or would they have proposed a minimum wage for workers even if there had been no Socialist Party? There is no way to be sure. The evidence suggests, however, that the major parties make new proposals in their "time of ripeness," when large numbers of Americans have accepted the idea, so it is politically useful for the major party to do so. However, the major party might have picked up the new proposal from any of a number of groups, not only minor parties but also interest groups or the media.

If the impact of third parties is so limited, then what attracts some voters to them? Note that there aren't many such voters; the self-fulfilling prophecy that a vote for a third party is a wasted vote is very powerful in American politics.[25] Yet some voters do cast third-party ballots. To Steven Rosenstone and his colleagues, this results from the failure of major parties "to do what the electorate expects of them—reflect the issue preferences of voters, manage the economy, select attractive and acceptable candidates, and build voter loyalty to the parties and the political system."[26] So third parties tend to gain support when they promote attractive ideas that the major parties have ignored, or because of dissatisfaction with the major party candidates, rather than because a lot of voters believe in a multiparty system as a matter of principle.

Continued dissatisfaction with the major parties has certainly provided an opening for a formidable third party. When this occurs, however, the normal workings of the American electoral system make it likely that the "third" party will displace one of the major parties (as the Republicans did with the Whigs) or be absorbed by changes in one of the major parties. So alternatives to the two major parties tend to develop and gain support only when the major parties are failing.

The Rise of Independent Candidates

Recently, dissatisfaction with the two major parties has been expressed in a new way: in support for candidates running as independents rather than on third-party tickets. The independent presidential candidacy of Ross Perot in 1992 received a larger share of the popular vote than any "third" candidate in history who was not a former president. With 19.7 million popular votes, Perot also outdrew the combined total of all his third-party opponents in that race by more than 19 million ballots. Perot failed to win a single state, however, and, as has been suggested, much of his support seemed to come from voters who were more dissatisfied with the Republican and Democratic candidates than they were attracted to a long-lasting commitment to another party or candidate.[27]

Perot ran for president again in 1996 as the Reform Party candidate. The story of his two candidacies, one as an independent and the other as a third-party candidate, helps us understand some of the advantages of running an independent candidacy now. In his first presidential race, his supporters built a remarkably strong organization. Through its efforts, Perot got on the ballot in all 50 states and mounted an active campaign throughout the nation. The key ingredient in the Perot challenge, however, was money—the millions of his own dollars that Perot was willing to invest in his quest for the presidency. His money financed organizational efforts at the grassroots level and, more importantly, bought large blocks of expensive television time for the candidate's widely viewed "infomercials." No other minor party or independent candidate for president in at least a century has achieved Perot's national visibility.

By 1996, Perot had organized the Reform Party and sought to qualify it for the ballot in all 50 states. This turned out to be much harder than qualifying to run as an independent. In California, which was his toughest challenge, Perot had to get at least 890,000 signatures on a petition by October 1995 to win a place on the state's ballot thirteen months later. He failed. Using a different mechanism, Perot finally qualified in California and in all other states but found it difficult to recruit acceptable Reform candidates for other offices. On election day, Perot got less than half as many votes as a Reform Party candidate than he had four years earlier as an independent.

Why was his third-party effort less successful? Many factors were at work. One may have been simple familiarity; at times a candidate does not benefit from letting voters get to know him or her better. Another involved states' election laws, which are sometimes more restrictive for third parties than for independent candidates. In addition, it is clearly a challenge to nurture an organization to support many candidates rather than one.

Although there are some minor parties that seem to be no more than vehicles for a single candidate, third-party movements usually have to respond to the needs and demands of candidates for a variety of offices. In the 2000 presidential campaign, conflicts among Reform Party activists became so intense, especially in trying to select a candidate to take Perot's place, that the party's national convention disintegrated into a fistfight and the party split.

The Libertarians and the Greens have made real efforts since the 2000 election to establish themselves as organizations that extend beyond a relatively small number of candidates. If history is any guide, however, that is a battle which they are likely to lose. The result is that when voters consider alternatives to the major parties, independent candidates (especially if they happen to be billionaires) will continue to have real advantages over those who try to form fully elaborated third parties.

WILL THE TWO-PARTY SYSTEM CONTINUE?

This look at two-party politics and its alternatives leads us to some conflicting conclusions. In important respects, two-party dominance seems to be increasing in the United States. Both major parties are resilient. They are closely matched in strength at the national level, and with the rise of Republican strength in the South, two-party competition has spread to every region. Third parties appear and run candidates, but they show no evidence of breaking into major-party status.

Yet we have seen trends that could threaten two-party dominance and close competition. The barriers to ballot access for minor-party and independent candidates, once so substantial, have been lowered in recent years. Wealthy independent candidates such as Ross Perot can get direct access to the media without having to work through a major party. In addition, the political value of incumbency has been increasing. Fewer House districts, for example, are competitive enough to switch party control now than has been the case in decades.[28] House incumbents, in particular, have learned to nurture their many resources to protect their seats. Within a given state, these successful incumbents often come from both parties, yet their advantages can limit the scope of competition in the system. What will be the result?

The Decline of Minor Parties

The record is clear: third parties are not gaining ground. Third-party members of Congress, common in the early decades of the two-party system, were rare throughout the 1900s, and especially in recent years (Figure 2.2). Since 1952, only one member of Congress has been elected on a third-party ticket—James Buckley in 1970 as a Conservative Party senator from New York—and he aligned himself with the Republicans after taking office. (Three others have served as independent members of Congress, but two caucus with the Democrats and the other is now a Republican.) Minor-party candidates have also fared poorly in state legislative contests during this period, though there are colorful local enclaves of minor-party strength.

Minor-party and independent presidential candidates must still satisfy a patchwork of different state requirements to qualify for the ballot nationwide. Even when courts have overturned laws that discriminate against independent and third-party candidates, the decisions have been limited, requiring petitioners to mount a challenge in each state.[29]

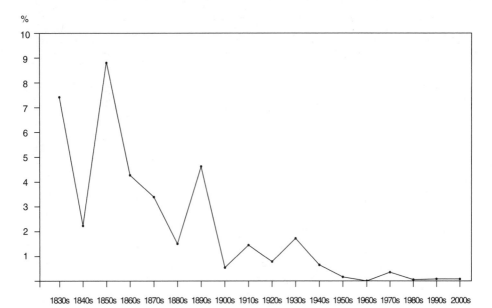

FIGURE 2.2   Third-Party and Independent Members of Congress: 1830s–2004

Note: Figures are percentages of third-party and independent senators and representatives during each decade.

Source: Updated from Norman J. Ornstein, Thomas E. Mann, and Michael J. Malbin, *Vital Statistics on Congress, 2001-2002* (Washington, DC: The AEI Press, 2002), pp. 56–58.

Quirks in local election laws continue to support a few local third parties. The classic instance is New York's minor parties, notably the Liberals and Conservatives. They survive because they can nominate candidates of a major party to run under their parties' own labels as well.[30]

The financial hurdles faced by independent and third-party candidates have come down a little. Presidential candidates outside the major-party mainstream can receive public funding for their campaign if they win at least 5 percent of the popular vote. By that time, of course, the election is over, so they can use the money only to repay campaign debts, but they then become eligible for public funding in the next election. Perot's vote in 1996 qualified the 2000 Reform Party candidate, Patrick Buchanan, for more than $12 million in federal funds.

Minor-party and independent candidates with money to spend can take advantage of the tools of high-tech campaigning, such as television and the Internet, just as major-party candidates can. So third-party and independent candidates can now reach voters throughout the United States without the need for extensive grassroots organizations, as long as they can pay for the media time or the web page design. However, the enormous cost of modern campaigns probably restricts the opportunities to only a few highly visible, or personally wealthy, third-party or independent candidates. And the rules and practices of the American two-party system are especially brutal toward third parties.

Increasing Major-Party Competitiveness

The most significant trend that we have seen in this chapter is the increasing competitiveness between the Republican and Democratic parties. No regions of the country, and very few states, can be seen as one-party areas any longer. Contests for state offices are more competitive now than they have been in decades, perhaps ever, and presidents have been winning with popular vote percentages that vary less and less from one state to another. The result is a more competitive two-party politics throughout the nation.

Increases in major-party competitiveness have the same roots as the challenges faced by local third parties: the nationalization of life and politics in the United States. It is harder and harder for one major party to maintain its dominance on the basis of regional appeals and traditions, as the Democrats did in the South from 1876 to 1950. The social and economic conditions that support one-party politics are disappearing. As Americans move more frequently, as industry comes to formerly agrarian states, as more and varied people move to the cities, each state gains the diversity of life and interests that supports national party competition. Party voters are increasingly recruited by the appeals of national candidates and issues regardless of the special appeals made by the local party. Most states have moved gubernatorial elections to non-presidential election years in order to mute the influence of these national forces, but this is only a small counterweight to the powerful pull of national politics.

This increase in two-party competition may have a downside for the major parties. The reduction in pockets of one-party strength tends to remove a source of stability in the party system. When a party has unchallenged dominance in some areas, it can survive even a catastrophic national loss because it is still winning in its own strongholds. Without those one-party strongholds to fall back on, a losing party in the future may find its loss more sweeping and devastating. Further, the increase in competition expands the scope of party activity and thus makes extra demands on party resources. When one-party areas could be written off in a presidential campaign, the area of political combat was reduced. Now the parties must mobilize more resources than ever across more of the states.

The newer challenge of independent candidates also makes elections less predictable and politics less stable. Running by themselves, without anyone else on their "tickets," they are not likely to create an enduring challenge to the Democrats and Republicans. So even though independent candidates can make headlines and the wealthiest among them can buy television time to appeal to voters, they will probably remain no more than periodic threats to the major parties' candidates. To make a sustained challenge that could fundamentally transform the American parties, these independents would need to organize to confront the major parties from the top to the bottom of the ballot. Those who try soon realize that they face a two-party system that may not be greatly beloved but is very well entrenched.

PART TWO

The Political Party as an Organization

There is much more to the American political parties than most of us see. A major party is a network of organizations that exists at all the levels at which Americans elect public officials: precincts, townships, wards, cities, counties, congressional districts, states, and the nation itself. The next three chapters examine these organizations and the activists and leaders who give them life.

We will focus in these chapters on the "private life" of the party organization, as opposed to its "public life" of recruiting and supporting candidates for office and promoting policies. In particular, we explore these questions: How do the party organizations work and how have they changed over time? What do they do well and what don't they do at all? Where does the power lie in the party organizations? What kinds of people become party activists? These internal characteristics of the party influence its ability to act effectively in the larger political system.

American party organizations vary tremendously. Parties in various parts of the nation have ranged from powerful and elaborate organizations to empty shells. Overall, however, by the standards of most Western democracies, the American party organizations would be considered to be fairly weak. Shackled by state laws, the party organizations have rarely been able to exercise much influence over the party's candidates and officeholders or over party voters.

The three parts of any party—its organization, its candidates and elected officials, and its electorate—differ in their goals, and they each seek control of the party to achieve their own ends. In the American system, the party organizations find it difficult to hold their own in this competition and to get the resources they need to influence elections and promote policies. American party organizations depend on their party in government, which writes the laws that regulate the organization. They must also work hard to court and mobilize the party electorate, who are not formally party members nor, in many cases, even especially loyal to the party in their voting.

This lack of integration among the party's three sectors is typical of *cadre parties*—one of two terms often used to describe the nature of party organizations. Imagine that party organizations are arranged along a continuum. At one end of this continuum is the cadre party, in which the organization is run by a relatively small number of leaders and activists with little or no broader public participation. These

43

officials and activists make the organization's decisions, choose its candidates, and select the strategies they believe voters will find appealing. They focus mainly on electing party candidates rather than on issues and ideology. For this reason, the party's activities gear up mainly at election time, when candidates need their party organization's help the most. The cadre party, then, is a coalition of people and interests brought together temporarily to win elections, only to wither to a smaller core once the elections are over.

At the other end of this scale is the ***mass-membership party***, a highly participatory organization in which all three parts of the party are closely intertwined. In this type of party, large numbers of voters become dues-paying members of the party organization and take part in its activities throughout the year, not just during campaigns. A mass-membership party concentrates not just on winning elections but also on promoting an ideology and educating the public. Its members vote on the party's policies as well as choose its organizational leaders. Members of the party in the electorate are so integral to the party organization that the party may even provide them with such nonpolitical benefits as insurance and leisure-time activities. Because the membership-based party organization has great power over candidate selection (it does not need to give less involved voters the right to choose party candidates, as happens in a primary election), it can also exercise much greater control over the party in government.

In important ways, the major American parties can be considered cadre parties. Most local and state party leaders and activists are not paid professionals but volunteers, whose party activities ramp up around election time. These organization leaders do not try hard to control the party's candidates and elected officials, nor are they likely to succeed. Most of the American parties' sympathizers in the public are not involved at all in the party organization.

They do not fit the cadre mold perfectly; in practice, parties have a tendency to slither out of precise definitions.[1] For example, in the days before television dominated American life, parties engaged lots of volunteers in campaign work, although these activists never gained much power in the party. And recent changes have clearly strengthened the party organizations. The parties now have the resources to employ full-time professional staffers in their national and state offices, and power in the party organizations is not as decentralized as it used to be. The parties make contact with their supporters in the electorate more frequently. Most primary elections are closed primaries in which voters have to declare a party affiliation before they are allowed to select the party's nominees.

Nevertheless, these changes have not made the major American parties into mass-membership organizations. The major parties focus on electing candidates more than on educating voters on issues. Also in contrast to mass-membership parties, the American parties do not monopolize the organization of political interests; rather, they compete in a political system in which voters are already organized by large numbers of interest groups and other organizations.

Why does it matter whether party organizations are strong or weak, cadre or mass membership? Because party organizations are at the very center of the political parties; they are the sector of the parties that can provide the continuity, even as the party's representatives in government and citizen enthusiasts come and go. A strong party organization can pursue the resources needed for long-term election success and can suggest a consolidated approach to issues. So the development of a stronger party organization can change the character of politics and elections. In fact, as American party organizations have become more robust in recent years, they have altered our politics in ways ranging from campaign fund-raising practices to the nature of political debate. Chapter 3 begins with an exploration of the party organizations closest to home: state and local parties.

CHAPTER 3

The State and Local Party Organizations

With terms such as "armies of foot soldiers," "captains," and "spoils," American party organizations were often described as military-style political "machines" in the late 1800s and early 1900s—very powerful and even fearsome in their ability to control city governments. In fact, most American party organizations were neither. Later in the 1900s, state and local party organizations were considered to be so weak that they would probably never recover. That has changed as well. Party organizations in the United States have undergone remarkable transformations in the past century.

What difference does it make if a party organization is vibrant or sickly? As the Introduction noted, in many ways the party organization is the backbone of a political party. It gives the party a way to endure, despite a changing cast of candidates and elected officeholders. More than the party in government or the party identifiers, the party organizations are the keepers of the parties' symbols—the unifying labels or ideas that give candidates a shortcut in identifying themselves to voters and that give voters a shortcut in choosing among candidates. Without this organization, a party becomes nothing more than an unstable alliance of convenience among candidates, and between candidates and groups of voters—too changeable to accomplish the important work that parties can perform in a democracy.

In this chapter, after considering what is meant by "party strength," we will explore the reality of state and local party organizations by viewing them in their environment— in particular, the environment of rules that have been enforced on the state and local parties by state law. Next, we will turn to the local party organizations, tracing their path from the fabled "political machines" that dominated a number of eastern and midwestern cities beginning in the late 1800s, to the fall and rise of local parties more recently. Finally, we will see how the state parties grew from weakness to greater strength in the closing decades of the twentieth century.

WHAT IS A "STRONG" PARTY?

Before looking at the state and local parties as organizations, we need to determine how a "strong" party could be defined. Many researchers measure a party's vigor by examining its organizational features, such as the size of its budget and staff and whether its workers are full-time professionals or occasional volunteers. Stronger parties would have larger budgets and more full-time, paid staff members. That can be termed party *organizational* strength.

There are other ways to measure party strength. A strong party would work effectively to register voters, tell them about party candidates, and get them to the polls on Election Day. It would be successful in filling its ticket with viable candidates. Its candidates would win more races than they lose. We could even measure whether the party is able to get its platform enacted into law (and we will, but not until Chapter 15).

In order for a party to do many of these things, especially to register voters, canvass, and get out the vote, it needs money, staff, and other forms of organizational strength. We will look at most of these measures of party strength in this chapter but focus mainly on party organizational strength.

THE LEGAL ENVIRONMENT OF THE PARTIES

Americans' traditional suspicion of political parties has led the 50 states to pass a blizzard of laws and rules intended to control their party organizations. These rules set the stage for the parties' activities and their organizational structure.

State Regulations

States differ markedly in their rules governing party organizations and activities.[1] State party committees are regulated "lightly" in only 17 states, most of them in the South, Plains states, and upper Midwest. At the other extreme, in 15 states—including California, New Jersey, and Ohio—lawmakers have thought it necessary to tell the state parties everything from the dates on which their central committees must meet to the types of public buildings in which they must hold their conventions.

These extensive state rules have not necessarily weakened the parties; some of the strongest party organizations in the nation are also the most tightly regulated. In fact, all these state laws help prop up the Democratic and Republican parties against competition from third parties. However, they do give state governments a set of tools for keeping an eye on their parties. They also indicate that state law does not view the parties simply as private groups. As Leon Epstein has put it, the parties are seen as public utilities, sometimes subject to a great deal of state direction.[2]

The party organizations do not face similar kinds of regulations from the federal government. The U.S. Constitution makes no mention of parties, nor has Congress tried very often to define or regulate party organizations. Only in the 1970s legislation on campaign finance (and its later amendments) is there a substantial body of national law that affects the parties in important ways.

States do not have complete freedom in regulating the parties. Over the years, the federal courts have frequently stepped in to protect citizens' voting rights (in cases to be discussed in Chapter 8) and to keep the states from unreasonably limiting third-party and independent candidates' access to the ballot (see Chapter 2). In some cases, courts have even begun to dismantle some state regulation of party organizational practices. In the 1980s, for example, the Supreme Court ruled that the state of Connecticut could not prevent the Republican Party from opening up its primary to independents if it wanted to. Soon after, the Court threw out a California law saying, among other things, that parties could not endorse candidates in primary elections.[3] As we'll see in Chapter 9, a 2000 Supreme Court decision overturned a California state initiative setting up a "blanket primary" on the ground that it violated the party organization's First Amendment right to decide who votes in its primaries.

Levels of Party Organization

Although state laws vary, the party organizations created by the states follow a common pattern. Their structure corresponds to the levels of government at which voters elect officeholders. This structure is often pictured as a pyramid based in the grassroots and stretching up to the statewide organization. A pyramid, however, gives the misleading impression that the layer at the top can give orders to the layers below. So picture these party organizations, instead, as they fit into a geographic map (Figure 3.1).

In a typical state, the smallest voting district of the state—the precinct, ward, or township—will have its own party organization composed of men and women elected to the party's local committee (and called committeemen and committeewomen). Then

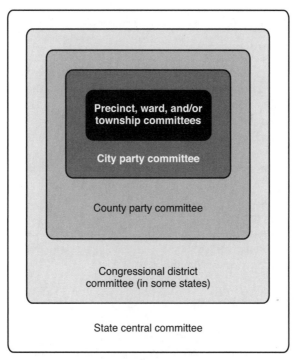

FIGURE 3.1   The Party Organizations in a Typical State.

come a series of party committees at the city, county, and sometimes even the state leg-islative, judicial, and congressional district levels. Finally, a state central committee rep-resents the state party as a whole. State laws usually determine the smallest and the largest of these levels, but the parties themselves may determine the middle levels.

Local Party Committees

The position of the local committeeman and/or committeewoman is closest to the party's grassroots. These committee leaders are typically chosen at the precinct level. Because there are more than 100,000 precincts in the United States, it would be easy to imagine a vibrant party base made up of at least 200,000 committed men and women. However, this exists only in the dreams of party leaders; in reality, many of these local committee positions are vacant because nobody wants to serve in them.

When these positions do get filled, it generally happens in one of three ways. Most committeemen and women are chosen at local party caucuses (meetings) or primary elec-tions, but in a few instances, higher party authorities appoint them. In the states that use caucuses, parties hold local caucus meetings in the wards and precincts that are open to any voters of the area who declare themselves attached to the party. These local party supporters then elect the precinct committee leaders and often elect delegates to county and/or state conventions as well. In states that choose precinct committeemen and women in the primaries, any voter may nominate him- or herself for the job by filing a petition signed by a handful of local voters. If, as often happens, there are no nominees, the com-mitteeman or woman may be elected by an even smaller handful of write-in votes. These local committee positions, in short, are not normally in great demand. So the local par-ties are far from being exclusive clubs; their "front doors" are often open to anyone who cares to walk in.

What do these precinct party leaders do? State laws often don't say. In areas where local parties are active, their leaders follow patterns that have been carved out over time. In the past, the fabled local committeemen of the American political machine knew the local voters, catered to their needs and problems, introduced the party candidates to them, and promoted the parties' issues—all with the ultimate purpose of turning out a bloc of votes for the party on Election Day. The main activities of their modern counterparts are similar: registering voters, going door-to-door (called "canvassing") to tell them about candidates, and getting voters to the polls. In the less active local parties, the commit-teemen and women may do little more than show up at an occasional meeting and cam-paign for a party candidate or two.

Several layers of party committees are built on top of the precinct level. Collectively, the precinct committeemen and women often make up the city, town, county, and con-gressional district committees, or they elect the delegates who do. The most important of these is generally the county committee.

State Central Committees

The state central committees, too, come in 50 state varieties, some highly unified and oth-ers full of conflict (see the box on page 51). State law commonly gives party central com-mittees a number of important powers: the responsibility for calling and organizing party conventions, drafting party platforms, supervising the spending of party campaign funds,

A BATTLE FOR PARTY CHAIR

Every so often, a struggle for state party leadership becomes so intense—typically because it involves a battle over the party's central principles—that it draws national attention. That was the case in 2001 when Ralph Reed, former Executive Director of the Christian Coalition, entered the race for leadership of the Georgia Republican party.

Reed campaigned on the basis of his party-building experience, not on his ideological stance. He promised that he would be a "grass-roots chairman," engaged in building a fully staffed GOP organization in every county. Others had different expectations. Backers of the opposing candidates cited a survey by a well-known Republican pollster claiming that Reed's selection would scare moderates away from statewide Republican candidates because, in the words of Emory political scientist Merle Black, "most people think he's way too far to the right." Reed supporters hired another major Republican pollster to critique these findings; he charged that the objections to Reed showed "anti-Christian bigotry."

State legislators and members of Congress from Georgia were drawn into the bitter split. A week before the vote, the contest was regarded as too close to call. Reed won the post and promised that he would be an "inclusive leader." Some feared the opposite—that the scars left by the leadership struggle would take a long time to heal.

Yet, just 18 months later, the Georgia Republicans had a lot to celebrate. In order to energize the Republican base without attracting the Democrats' attention, Reed led a well-planned, last-minute intensive canvass just before the 2002 elections. On election day, Georgia elected a Republican governor for the first time in more than 100 years, and Republican candidates beat the state's Democratic U.S. Senator and the Democratic leaders of both houses of the state legislature. Reed got much of the credit.

Sources: Charles Babington, "Ralph Reed Creates Buzz in Georgia Politics," http://www.washingtonpost.com/ac2/wp-dyn/A12942-2001Apr12 (accessed Apr. 13, 2001); Rebecca Adams, "Georgia Republicans Energized by 'Friend to Friend' Campaigns," *CQ Weekly,* November 9, 2002, pp. 2892–2893.

and selecting the party's presidential electors, representatives to the national committee, and at least some of the national convention delegates and alternates. Some other states give these powers to the party's statewide convention instead. In a few states, the party's state convention actually nominates candidates for some statewide offices, a reminder of the power that the party conventions had in the days before the direct primary.

These are the formal organizational structures that state law creates for the state and local parties. From them, we can draw three important conclusions. First, the levels of party organization have been set up to correspond to the voting districts in which citizens choose public officials in that state (for example, city, county, and congressional districts), and the main responsibility of these organizations under state law is to contest elections. State laws, then, see the party organizations as helpers in the state's task of conducting nominations and elections—tasks that before the turn of the twentieth century belonged almost entirely to the parties alone.

Second, the laws indicate that state legislators are ambivalent about what constitutes a party organization. Many of these laws treat the parties as cadre organizations (see pages 43–44) run by a small number of party officials. Yet when they specify that the party's own officials, including local committeemen and women, must be chosen in a primary election, this gives party voters—and potentially, any voters—a vital, quasi-membership role in the party organization. So state laws help to create a party that is a mix of public and private rather than a genuinely private group whose members choose its leaders and set its direction.

Finally, the relationships among these state and local party organizations are not those of a hierarchy, in which the "lower" levels take their orders from the higher levels. Instead, through much of their history, the state parties were best described as "a system of layers of organization"[4] or as a "stratarchy,"[5] in which each of the levels has some independent power. In fact, power has traditionally flowed from bottom to top in the local and state parties, as opposed to a hierarchy, where power would be centralized at the top.[6] Party organization is a system of party committees close to, and growing from, the political grassroots. The result is that the party organizations remain fairly decentralized and rooted in local politics, even in the face of recent trends toward stronger state and national committees.

THE LEGENDARY PARTY MACHINES

Perhaps the high point of local party organizational strength in the United States occurred during the heyday of the urban political "machine." Machine politics reached its peak in the late 1800s and early 1900s when, by one account, a large majority of American cities were governed by machines.[7] The party machine, accounts tell us, was a durable, disciplined organization that controlled the nominations to elective office. It had the hierarchical structure that today's local parties lack. It relied on material incentives—jobs and favors—to build support among voters. Above all, it controlled the government in a city or county.[8] Its colorful history includes the powerful Tammany Hall in New York as well as similar party organizations throughout the Northeast and big cities elsewhere.

Yet, for all their power in shaping how we think of party organizations, the great urban machines were not found in all cities, and, like the dinosaurs, they have disappeared. The last of the great party machines was Chicago's, and it declined after the death of Mayor Richard J. Daley (the father of the current mayor) in 1976. These dinosaurs were brought down by a number of forces. Some party machines, such as those in Pittsburgh and New York, never recovered from election upsets by middle-class reformers. Others, including those in Philadelphia and Gary, Indiana, lost power when racial tensions overshadowed the old ethnic politics.[9]

How the Party Machines Developed

In the late 1800s, large numbers of the immigrants arriving in major American cities had urgent economic and social needs. These newcomers were poor, often spoke no English, and faced a difficult adjustment to their new urban environment. Party leaders in many of these cities—usually Democrats, reflecting that party's history of openness to immigrants—saw the opportunity for an ingenious and mutually beneficial exchange. The populations of immigrants needed jobs, social services, and other benefits that a city government could provide. The party leaders needed large numbers of votes in order to gain control of city government. If the party could register these new arrivals to vote, their votes could put the party in power. In return, the party, which would then control the many resources that the government had available, could give the new voters the help they needed so desperately.

Jobs ranked high among the newcomers' needs. So the most visible of the benefits offered by party machines were patronage jobs in the city government—those awarded on the basis of party loyalty rather than other qualifications. During the glory days of the machine, thousands of these patronage positions were at the machine's disposal. By giving patronage jobs to party supporters, the party's leaders could be assured that city workers would remain loyal to the machine and would work to help it win elections by delivering not only their own votes but those of their friends, family, and neighbors as well.

For example, in its prime, the Chicago Democratic machine controlled an estimated 35,000 patronage jobs in government and influenced hiring for another 10,000 jobs in the private economy. Adding the families and friends of these job holders, the party machine could deliver 350,000 motivated voters at election time. Local party workers also won voter loyalties by finding social welfare agencies for the troubled or by providing Christmas baskets or deliveries of coal. Machine leaders, called "bosses," attended weddings and wakes, listened to job seekers and business executives, bailed out drunks, and helped the hungry and homeless.

The machine had favors to offer to local businesses as well. Governments purchase many goods and services from the private sector. If a bank wanted to win the city's deposits, it could expect to compete more effectively for the city's business if it were willing to contribute to the party machine. Insurance agents who hoped to write city policies, lawyers who wanted the city's business, newspapers that printed city notices, even suppliers of soap to city washrooms, all could be drawn into the web of the party machine. In addition, city governments regularly make decisions on matters that affect individuals' and businesses' economic standing, such as building permits and health inspections. If you were helped by one of these decisions, you could expect the machine to ask for your thanks in the form of contributions and votes. A political leadership intent on winning support in exchange for these so-called "preferments" can use them ruthlessly and effectively to build its political power.

How Machines Used Their Power

The classic urban machine, then, was not just a party organization but also an "informal government," a social service agency, and a ladder for upward social and economic mobility. In some ways, it looked like the local organization of a European mass-membership party, except that the American machine had little or no concern with ideology. Its world was the city; it focused on the immediate needs of its constituents, and its politics were almost completely divorced from the issues that animated national politics.

An important source of the machines' strength was their ability to appeal to ethnic loyalties. The rise and fall of the American political machine is closely linked to changes in ethnic-group migration to the big cities. The machine was a method by which ethnic groups, especially the Irish, gained a foothold in American politics.[10]

The machines were capable of creating a "designer electorate" by using force and intimidation to keep their opponents from voting. Because the party machines controlled the election process, it was possible, in a pinch, to change the election rules and even to count the votes in a creative manner. One of the indispensable tools of rival party workers in Indianapolis, for example, was a flashlight—to locate ballots that did not support the dominant party's candidates and happened to fly out of the window at vote-counting headquarters in the dark of night.

We think of machine politics as flourishing in the big cities, but American party machines took root in other areas as well. The conditions that led to the development of machines, especially a large, parochially oriented population with short-term economic needs, were also found in small southern and one-company towns. Even some well-to-do suburbs have spawned strong machine-style party organizations. In the affluent Long Island suburbs of New York City, for example, a Republican Nassau County political machine developed that controlled local government and politics "with a local party operation that in terms of patronage and party loyalty rivals the machine of the famed Democratic mayor of Chicago, Richard J. Daley."[11]

We cannot be sure how powerful the party machines really were, even at their strongest. A Chicago study found, for example, that the party machine distributed public services mainly on the basis of historical factors and bureaucratic decision rules; there was little evidence that services were provided to reward political support in either 1967 or 1977.[12] In New Haven, researchers reported that ethnic loyalties seemed more important to a party machine than even its own maintenance and expansion. The machine, led by Italian politicians, distributed summer jobs disproportionately to Italian kids from nonmachine wards, who rarely took part in later political work, and not to kids from strong machine areas.[13]

Regardless of how well they functioned, there is no doubt that the conditions that helped sustain party machines have been undercut. Economic change and political reform took away the machine's most important resources. Most city jobs are now covered by civil service protection, so the number of patronage jobs that can be used to reward the party faithful has been greatly reduced. Federal entitlement programs, such as welfare and Social Security, have reduced the need for the favors that party machines could provide. Economic growth has boosted many Americans' income levels and reduced the attractiveness of the remaining patronage jobs; the chance to work in the sewer system or on garbage pickup just doesn't have the cachet that it once may have had. Higher education levels have increased people's ability to fend for themselves in a complex bureaucratic society. And in many areas, racial divisions have overwhelmed the machine's ability to balance competing ethnic groups.

Could Political Machines Make a Comeback?

The conditions that can support machine-style parties have not completely disappeared. Major cities still have economically dependent populations. New immigrant groups have taken the places of the old. Many cities continue to deal with tremendous social service demands at the same time as they are facing a declining tax base. If party machines thrive by offering help with a confusing government bureaucracy, city governments seem more than happy to oblige by providing the confusing bureaucracy.

Where the demand for their services exists, political organizations will respond, even if they have to work within new and tighter constraints. Even past their peak, political machines were very skillful in creatively "interpreting" civil service rules in order to maintain patronage jobs (for example, Mayor Daley hired thousands of long-term "temporary" employees) and in brokering federal benefits for the poor (the summer jobs distributed by the New Haven machine were provided through a federal employment training program). Local governments continue to provide a wide array of services and play an active regulatory role, so it is still possible to sustain a patron-client form of politics in a supportive political culture.

In short, although political machines in their classic form were part of an earlier time, reports of their death may be premature. The Chicago party machine still has some strength at the ward level, although its power at the city level falls far short of the machine's glory days.[14] Party organizations often learn how to adapt to new realities, so functional equivalents to the old-time machines could emerge.[15]

HOW LOCAL PARTY ORGANIZATIONS HAVE REVITALIZED

The big city machines set the standard for effective party organizations, but it is a standard rarely achieved since the machines died away. At the other extreme—seldom written about because it offers so little to study—is virtual *dis*organization. In such cases, most of the party leadership positions remain vacant or inactive. A chairman and a handful of loyal party officials may meet occasionally to carry out the most essential affairs of the party. Their main activity occurs shortly before the primary elections, as they plead with members of the party to become candidates or step in themselves to "fill the party ticket." They are not able to raise much money for the campaigns or to attract media attention. This type of organization has probably always been common in cities and towns. Most American local party organizations lie between these two extremes.

Local Parties in the 1970s

We got the first comprehensive look at the nature of local party organizations in a 1979–1980 survey of several thousand county leaders (see Table 3.1).[16] The results showed the distinctive fingerprints of cadre parties, and fairly weak ones at that. The researchers found that most county organizations were headed by a volunteer party chair and executive committee; almost none received salaries for their efforts and only a few had a paid staff to assist them. They had few resources to work with; not many of these local party leaders enjoyed the most basic forms of organizational support, such as a regular budget, a year-round office, or even a telephone listing. They did meet regularly, had formal rules to govern their work, and, together with a few other activists, raised funds and sought out and screened candidates. However, their activity was not constant; it peaked during campaigns.

Democratic parties did not differ much from Republicans, on average, in terms of the overall strength of their local organizations. There were considerable differences among states, however, in the organizational strength of their local parties. Some states in the East and Midwest had relatively strong local organizations in both parties, while others—Louisiana, Georgia, Alabama, Kentucky, Texas, and Nebraska—had relatively weak parties at the county level. In a few states, such as Arizona and Florida, one party

TABLE 3.1 Changes in Local Parties' Organizational Strength, 1979/1980–1996

	Democrats		Republicans	
The local party organization has (in percent)	1996	1979–1980	1996	1979–1980
A complete or nearly complete set of officers	95	90	96	81
A year-round office	17	12	25	14
A telephone listing	27	11	30	16
Some paid staff members				
Full-time	4	3	4	4
Part-time	6	5	7	6
A regular annual budget	26	20	34	31
A campaign headquarters	60	55	60	60
Campaign activities				
Organized door-to-door canvassing	55	49	57	48
Organized campaign events	81	68	82	65
Arranged fund-raising events	74	71	76	68
Contributed money to candidates	75	62	78	70
Distributed posters or lawn signs	93	59	93	62
Used public opinion surveys	13	11	15	16

Note: The 1979–1980 figures are based on responses from a total of 2,021 Democratic and 1,980 Republican organizations to a mail survey; the 1996 figures are based on mail surveys of all county party chairs in nine states (Arizona, Colorado, Florida, Illinois, Missouri, Ohio, South Carolina, Washington, and Wisconsin), with responses from 340 Democrats and 335 Republicans.

Source: John Frendreis and Alan R. Gitelson, "Local Parties in the 1990s: Spokes in a Candidate-Centered Wheel," in John C. Green and Daniel M. Shea, The State of the Parties, 3rd ed. (Lanham, MD: Rowman & Littlefield, 1999), pp. 138–139.

was considerably stronger at the local level than the other party. Most often, strong organizations of one party were matched with strong organizations in the other party.[17]

There is persuasive evidence, however, that the county party organizations in 1980 were in the middle of a growth spurt. By asking 1980 county party chairs about the changes in their parties since 1964, researchers found that, on average, local parties had become much more involved in the nuts-and-bolts activities of registering voters, raising money, and publicizing candidates. When the researchers checked in again with these county organizations in 1984, they saw further development, and a national survey in 1988 indicated even higher levels of local party activity. Similar trends were reported in studies over time of local party organizations in Detroit and Los Angeles.[18]

Local Parties Today: Richer and More Active

By the late 1990s, although local parties continued to depend on volunteer effort, they were enjoying more of the benefits that money could buy. A study of the county party organizations in nine states during the 1996 presidential election found that the basic ingredients for a viable party organization (a permanent office, a budget, a telephone listing, a staff) were more widespread than they had been in 1980.[19] It seems clear that more money has been flowing to local party organizations in recent years, and the result is more energized local parties.

A majority of each party's local organizations organized campaign activities, arranged fund-raising events, gave money to candidates, sent out mailings, telephoned voters to urge them to support the party ticket, distributed yard signs, and ran get-out-the-vote efforts on election day. More local parties reported conducting these activities in 1996 than in 1980. Other types of campaign effort, using public opinion polls, buying radio or TV time for candidates, and coordinating the activities of political action committees in campaigns, were not common in either year.

The parties in Michigan are an example of this increase in local party strength. Michigan Democrats, long the minority party, were in sorry shape for the first half of the 1900s. By the end of the 1940s, more than half of the state's counties had no Democratic county committees. Then, labor unions, especially the autoworkers, stepped in and brought volunteer and financial support to the Democrats. Within two years, there was a Democratic Party organization in almost every county. After internal conflicts took their toll in both parties during the 1960s and 1970s, organized labor moved again to rebuild the Democratic organization. The county organizations are now the backbone of the state Democratic Party. Currently, the great majority of both Democratic and Republican local parties, with the help of their state organizations, raise money, donate it to candidates, buy ads and distribute literature.[20]

The impact of local parties' organizational strength on election results is hard to judge; however, local party leaders do seem to have stepped up their efforts in candidate recruitment. One study found that more than a third of people regarded as potentially strong candidates for Congress in 1998 had, in fact, been contacted by local party leaders and that those contacted were more likely to run.[21] In another study, almost half of all state legislative candidates reported that local party leaders had encouraged them to run.[22] There are some local parties, in Ohio, for example, where county party leaders can endorse candidates in primaries, fill vacancies between elections, and play an important role in registering voters and getting them to the polls.

In sum, we have good evidence that county party organizations were stronger and more active in the 1990s than they had been a generation earlier. Because there are so few reliable records prior to the 1960s, it is hard to determine whether these local organizations are as effective organizationally as they were thought to have been a century ago. Even the most active of the local parties in the early 2000s are probably no match for a powerful urban machine. Nevertheless, not many of these local parties are completely dead either. So many counties may now have more robust party organizations than they have ever had.

What accounts for the growing strength of the county parties? The short answer is money. Party organizations at all levels have developed more effective tools for raising money than they have had for some time. Local parties have benefited, in particular, from the willingness of the increasingly well-heeled state parties to share the wealth. Along with this, as we will soon see, the nature of these party organizations has changed; rather than serving as the center of election activity, they have become service providers to candidates who often have several other sources of services. So the challenge for the local parties is this: In an age of candidate-centered campaigns, does this growing county organizational presence matter as much as it would have a few decades ago?[23]

THE STATE PARTIES: NEWFOUND PROSPERITY

State parties have always been the poor relations of American party politics. Throughout the parties' history, the state committee has rarely had significant power in the party organizations. There have been exceptions, of course. Some powerful, patronage-rich state party organizations developed in the industrial heartland in the late nineteenth century.[24] But in most states, most of the time, the party's state committee has not been the site of the party's main organizational authority.

In recent years, however, state parties have grown in importance. They are richer, more professional, and more active now than they have ever been before. There has been some centralization of activity throughout the party structure. Let us start the story in the years before this change began.

Traditional Weakness

There are many reasons why the state party organizations were traditionally weak. They began as loose federations of semi-independent local party chairs. These local parties within a state differed from one another in many ways; there were rural/urban and regional differences, ethnic and religious differences, loyalties to local leaders, and, especially, conflicts between more liberal and more conservative interests. If one of these factions gained control over the state party organization, the others would be seriously threatened. So this threat was often avoided, in the past, by keeping most of the party's resources out of the hands of the state organization. Power, in other words, was decentralized, collecting in the most effective of the local organizations.

Other forces also weakened the state party organizations. Progressive reforms early in the twentieth century, most importantly the introduction of the direct primary (see Chapters 9 and 10), sapped the influence of state parties over nomination and election campaigns for state offices. Due in part to these reforms, candidates could win party nominations in primary elections without party organization support, raise money for their own campaigns and, thus, run them without party help. The Populist and Progressive influence can be seen even now, in that it is the states where the Populists had greatest strength—the western states, especially the more rural ones—where we still find relatively weak state party organizations.[25]

Beginning in the late 1960s, the national Democratic Party adopted reforms that greatly increased the number of primaries in the presidential nominating process. That weakened the state party's role in selecting a presidential candidate. It is the voters, rather than the state party organization, who choose convention delegates now; almost all the delegates come to the convention pledged to a particular candidate for the nomination rather than controlled by state party leaders. Further, extensions of civil service protections and growing unionization eroded the patronage base for many state parties. In what may have been the final indignity for patronage politics, some courts have even prevented the firing of patronage workers when the governing party changes.

The existence of one-party dominance in several states during the first half of the 1900s also kept a number of state parties weak and conflict-ridden. Southern Democratic Parties were a notable example (and southern Republican Parties were all but nonexistent). When a single party dominates a state's politics, the diverse forces within the state are likely to compete as factions within that party; the state party organization has neither the incentive nor the ability to unify, as it might if it faced a threat from a viable opposition party. For all these reasons, many state party organizations were described as "empty shells" in the 1940s and 1950s.[26]

Increasing Strength in Recent Years

Since the 1960s, however, state party organizations have become stronger and more active. The state parties began to institutionalize—to become enduring, specialized, well-bounded organizations—during the 1960s and 1970s. In the early 1960s, for example, only 50 percent of a sample of state organizations had permanent state headquarters; two decades later, in 1979–1980, that was true of 91 percent. The number of full-time, salaried, state party chairs doubled during this time, as did the number of full-time staff employed by the parties in nonelection years. These resources—full-time leaders and a stable location—are vital to the development of parties as organizations.[27]

As we found with regard to local parties, the state organizations have continued to expand since then. By 1999, more than half of the state parties surveyed in a research study had full-time party chairs, research staff, and public relations directors. Three-quarters had a field staff, and 91 percent employed a full-time executive director. The empty shells are being filled. Interestingly, southern parties, long among the weakest and most faction-ridden, have become some of the strongest state party organizations in the past two decades.[28]

Fund-raising   State parties have put special effort into developing fund-raising capabilities in recent years. By 1999, according to a study by John H. Aldrich (see Table 3.2), 98 percent of the state parties surveyed held fund-raising events, and the same percentage had direct mail fund-raising programs. The Wisconsin Republican state party is a good example; by the late 1990s, it had established a computerized marketing center with as many as 35 telemarketers in order to expand the party's small-donor base. State parties used the money to support a variety of races; party candidates for governor, state legislature, and the U.S. Senate and House received contributions from more than four-fifths of these parties. Over 90 percent of the parties surveyed by Aldrich had recruited a full slate of candidates for state races; the parties' new fund-raising skills can be very useful in convincing attractive prospects to run for an office.[29]

The parties are especially active in recruiting candidates for the state legislature, raising funds for them, and helping the candidates raise money themselves. It is the state parties, to a much greater extent than the national or local parties, that offer money and services to state legislative candidates.[30] In addition, in almost every state, these candidates get help from the legislative parties and/or leaders themselves. These state legislative campaign committees have come to play an increasingly important role in legislative campaigns.[31] Candidates for the state legislature often rely on different levels of party committees for different kinds of help. In some states, the candidates see the legislative parties as at least somewhat helpful in activities such as fund-raising and hiring consultants, whereas the local parties are thought to be more helpful in traditional grassroots activities such as get-out-the-vote drives.[32]

The increase in election-year fund-raising by the state parties between 1980 and 1999 fairly leaps off the page in Table 3.2. This was augmented by a big increase in

TABLE 3.2 Increasing Organizational Strength Among the State Parties

Party Strength and Activity	1999	1979–1980	Difference
Typical election-year budget	$2.8 mil.	$340 K	$2.46 mil.
Typical election-year full-time staff	9.2	7.7	1.5
Conducted campaign seminars	95%	89%	6%
Recruited a full slate of candidates	91%	—	—
Operated voter ID programs	94%	70%	24%
Conducted public opinion surveys	78%	32%	46%
Held fund-raising event	98%	19%	77%
Contributed to governor candidate	89%	47%	42%
Contributed to state legislator	92%	47%	45%
Contributed to state senator	85%	25%	60%
Contributed to U.S. congressional	85%	48%	37%
Contributed to local candidate	70%	—	—

Note: Data for 1999 come from a mail survey conducted by John H. Aldrich and associates of 65 state party chairs (39 Democrats, 26 Republicans). Data for 1979–1980 are from a mail survey of state parties.

Source: For the 1999 data, see Aldrich's "Southern Parties in State and Nation," Journal of Politics 62 (2000): 659. The 1979–1980 data are from James L. Gibson, Cornelius P. Cotter, and John F. Bibby, "Assessing Party Organizational Strength," American Journal of Political Science 27 (1983): 193–222.

money transferred from national party committees to the state parties and candidates. Although most of the funds moved directly into campaign advertising in competitive races, in 2000, the national party organizations transferred a whopping $430 million to parties and candidates at the state level; $230 million came from Democratic committees and $200 million from the national Republicans, many times the amounts that the national parties infused into the state organizations just a few years earlier.[33] Just as important for the development of strong party organizations, fund-raising during non-election years has been growing as well. The nonelection-year budgets of the state parties climbed from an average (in absolute dollars) of under $200,000 in 1960–1964 to $340,667 in 1979–1980, then to $424,700 by the mid-1980s, and to $900,000 by 1999. The result is that "most state parties are multimillion-dollar organizations with experienced executive directors and knowledgeable staffs."[34]

Campaign Services   Now that many state legislative and statewide candidates—even local candidates in some states—need consultants, voter lists, and computers to run a competitive campaign, they increasingly turn to the state party organizations to provide these expensive services. With their increased organizational and financial resources, the state parties have been able to comply. All the parties in Aldrich's sample operated voter identification programs to determine which voters were most likely to support their party's candidates and also took part in get-out-the-vote drives as well as joint fund-raising with county party organizations. Most provided campaign training seminars as well, and almost four-fifths conducted public opinion polls in the late 1990s.[35] Coordinated campaigns, emphasizing the sharing of campaign services among a variety of candidates, are increasingly being run through the state party organizations. Since 1996, a lot of state party money has been used to pay for issue advocacy ads promoting the party position on issues, which has at least indirect benefits for party candidates.

Republican Advantage   Unlike the situation at the county level, Republican state organizations are considerably stronger now than their Democratic counterparts. The Republican parties surveyed by Aldrich have much larger budgets and larger and more specialized staffs. Because they are larger and richer, they can provide more services to their candidates and local parties. For example, Republican state parties are more likely to conduct polls, employ a field staff and researchers, conduct joint fund-raising with county party organizations, and contribute to local parties than the Democrats are.[36] This GOP advantage reflects to a great degree the extensive subsidies the national party has been able to provide to all the state parties.

Allied Groups   State Democratic parties, however, hold an important counterweight. Labor unions, especially teachers' and government employees' unions, work closely with their state Democratic Party organizations to provide money, volunteer help, and other services to party candidates. In states such as Alabama and Indiana, the state teachers' union is so closely connected with the state party that critics might find it difficult to tell where one stops and the other begins. State Republican Parties have close ties to allied groups as well. Small business groups, manufacturing associations, prolife groups, and Christian conservative organizations often provide services to Republican candidates.

Because of the close association between parties and these allied groups, it is possible to think of the parties as networks of organizations, which include the citizen groups, issue organizations, polling and other consulting firms, and "think tanks" (research groups) that offer their resources and expertise to a party.[37] For party leaders, these allied groups can be a mixed blessing, of course; labor unions and business groups have their own agendas and they can be as likely to try to push the party into locally unpopular stands as to help in the effort to elect party candidates.

It is not easy to build a powerful state party organization. It requires having to overcome both the localism of American politics and the widespread hostility toward strong party discipline. Strong and skillful personal leadership by a governor, a senator, or a state chairman helps.[38] So does a state tradition or culture that accepts the notion of a unified and effective party. State law makes a difference as well. More centralized party organization has flourished in the states that make less use of primary elections, so the party organization has more control over who the statewide and congressional candidates will be. Good examples include both Pennsylvania parties, the Ohio Republican Party, and the North Dakota Democratic organization.

The Special Case of the South   The most striking case of party organizational development has occurred in the South. Here, several forces—notably southerners' reaction to the civil rights movement and the resulting development of two-party competition at the state level—have spurred the development of much stronger state parties. As the national Democratic Party showed greater concern for the rights of African Americans in the 1960s and 1970s, and particularly as the Voting Rights Acts greatly increased the proportion of African-American voters in southern states, conservative southern Democrats became increasingly estranged from their national party. Southern support for Republican candidates grew, first in presidential elections, later in statewide and U.S. Senate races.

In the 1980s, state legislative candidates could sense the opportunity to run and win as Republicans. By 1994, Republicans were contesting almost a third of the state legislative seats in the South and winning two-thirds of those seats. Between 1994 and 2000, Republicans won the governorship of all but two of the southern states at least once and won a majority in at least one house of the state legislature in five southern states: Florida, Texas, Virginia, and the Carolinas.[39] Republicans, in short, are now approaching parity with the Democrats in state elections—this in a region where, just a few decades before, it was often more socially acceptable to admit to having an alcoholic than a Republican in the family.

Along with these election gains, southern Republican Parties grew stronger organizationally. North Carolina's state Republican Party, for example, started in earnest to recruit state legislative candidates during the mid-1980s. By the 1990s, with a much expanded budget and staff, the party focused on attracting experienced candidates for targeted districts, producing direct mail and radio ads, and helping candidates with training and research. Even the Florida Republicans, still not very strong organizationally, have come a long way since the years when state party chairs had "portable offices" in their homes or businesses.[40]

National Party Money   The most important ingredient in strengthening the state party organizations has been the national parties' party-building efforts. The full story of these efforts is told in Chapter 4, but the central point here is that the national parties, with more energetic leadership and more lavish financial resources than ever before, have infused a great deal of money into the state parties—and local parties, too. Most of the hundreds of millions of dollars that have been channeled from the Democratic and Republican national party committees to state parties are actually bound for individual candidates' campaigns; the money is used to buy campaign ads and other services. However, at least some of the money has been directed toward helping build the organizational capacity of the state parties, which have often taken the opportunity to become major fund-raisers in their own right. State parties, so recently the poor relations of the party organizations, have come into money. Whether their new status has cost them their independence, this time from the national parties, is a question only the future can answer.[41]

SUMMING UP: HOW THE STATE AND LOCAL PARTY ORGANIZATIONS HAVE TRANSFORMED

There have been dramatic changes in party organizational strength at the state and local levels. The high point of *local* party organizations was probably reached a hundred years ago, when some parties could be described as "armies drawn up for combat" with an "elaborate, well-staffed, and strongly motivated organizational structure."[42] Although this description did not apply to party organizations throughout the nation even then, it might be impossible to find a local party organization that could be described in these terms today.

Local parties were buffeted by a variety of forces since then. Progressive reforms adopted in the early 1900s undermined party organizations by limiting their control over nominations and general elections as well as over their valued patronage resources. Since then, a number of factors—federal social service programs, the almost total demise of the patronage system, economic growth, a more educated electorate, and even racial conflict—undercut the effectiveness of the local parties.[43]

Yet local parties have come a long way toward adapting to these changes. County parties have moved to fill at least some of the void created by the decline of the urban machines. New sources of funding are enabling these county parties to expand their activities. Local party organizations, in short, are demonstrating again their ability to meet the new challenges posed by a changing environment—a resilience that has kept them alive throughout most of American history.

The state party organizations have followed a different route. Traditionally weak in all but a handful of states, the state parties were little more than vessels that could barely contain conflicting local parties. State party organizations seem to have grown remarkably robust in recent years, becoming more professional than ever before. They are providing campaign and organizational services to local parties that, in an earlier era, would not have dreamed of looking to their state headquarters for help.

In fact, the recent flow of money, resources, and leadership from the national party to the state party, and in turn from the state to the local parties, helps to modify the traditional flow of party power. Through most of their lives, the American parties have been highly decentralized, with power and influence lodged at the base of the organizational pyramid. The parties were hollow at the top, depending on the base for whatever influence and resources they had. Because of the death of urban machines and the birth of vigorous state and national party organizations, we no longer see this extreme form of decentralization. The nationalization of American society and politics has affected the party organizations as well.

Yet ironically, even though they are much stronger now, the party organizations at the state and local level probably have less impact on our politics than they once did. There are several reasons. First, they have much more competition for the attention of voters, candidates, and the media. The party organizations are often muscled aside by other groups ranging from independent campaign consultants to organized interests. The campaign communications sent out by the parties merge into a flood of direct mail fundraising and advertising by citizen groups, corporate and labor political action committees, and wealthy individuals, all of whom try to influence voters' choices. Many of these groups encourage individuals to run for office. They can offer candidates money and a means to reach voters, independent of the party organization. They have campaign expertise rivaling that of the party's experts.

Second, although most state parties have become much more able fund-raisers, the party's resources are still dwarfed by those of other actors in elections. In state legislative campaigns, for example, this new party money accounts for only about 5–10 percent of the funds received by most candidates.[44] Campaigners are happy for every dollar, of course, but these relatively small sums, even with the helpful services that accompany them, may not be enough to entice candidates to listen carefully to the party on legislative matters or any other concerns.

So the increasing organizational strength of the state and local parties has helped them adopt modern campaign skills and recapture a role in candidates' campaigns. However, it is not a *dominant* role—not in the way it could have been if party organizations, rather than voters in primaries, selected party candidates. Party organizations rarely *run* the campaigns; instead, their new resources give them more of a chance to compete for the attention of those who do—the candidates—at a time when other competitors (organized interests, consultants, and others) have become more effective as well.

Does this mean that the increases in party organizational strength are unimportant? Clearly not. In a very competitive political environment, there is little doubt that it is better to have a stronger organization than a weaker one and to have more resources rather than fewer. Further, there is evidence that where parties are stronger organizationally (and especially when both parties are strong), citizens are likely to have more supportive attitudes toward parties and partisanship.[45]

In the end, despite all the changes in party organization during the past few decades, their most basic structural features have not changed. The American state and local parties remain cadre organizations run by a small number of activists; they involve the bulk of their supporters only at election time. The parties blend easily into a surrounding network of sometimes cooperative, sometimes competitive political forces. By the standards of parties in other democratic nations, which tend to be continuously active year-round, American state and local party organizations are still weaker: more limited in their activities and authority and more easily dominated by a handful of activists and elected officials. But by the standards of American politics, the state and local organizations are more visible and active than they have been in some time.

CHAPTER 4

The Parties' National Organizations

Just a few blocks from Capitol Hill, where the House and Senate work, you'll find the national headquarters buildings of the Democratic and Republican Parties. Their quarters show a level of wealth, independence, and permanence never seen before in the history of the national parties. Their neighborhoods tell even more about the change in their status. They are now located closer to Congress than to the White House, just as the national parties have moved beyond their traditional job as aides to the president and into a new role of party building in the states and localities. The older and more imposing GOP headquarters, purchased in 1970 (the Democrats bought theirs in 1984), is testimony to the fact that the Republicans started earlier and have done more to build effective national party organizations.

The change has been remarkable. Only in the earliest years of the American parties, when presidential candidates were nominated by the congressional caucus, were the national parties as important in American politics. For much of their history, the national committees were no more than empty boxes on an organizational chart—labels at the top of a party system in which the real power collected at the bottom, as is typical in a decentralized party system. Just a few decades ago, the national committees were poor and transient renters—often moving back and forth between New York and Washington, and all but disbanding between presidential campaigns. Leading students of the national committees could accurately describe them as "politics without power."[1]

There is good reason why the parties have long been decentralized, as Chapter 3 indicated. Virtually all American public officials are chosen in state and local elections; even the voting for president is conducted mainly under state election laws. In years past, most of the incentives parties had to offer, such as preferments and patronage jobs, were available at the local and state levels, and the state governments have been the chief regulators of parties. All these forces have given the parties a powerful state and local focus that continues to restrain any shift in power within the party organizations. So state and local party organizations pick their own officers, nominate their own candidates, take their own stands on issues, and raise and spend their own funds, usually without much interference from the national party.

Yet there are powerful nationalizing forces in American society that have long since affected most other aspects of American politics. The mass media bring the same TV images into homes in all parts of the country. Government in the American federal system became more centered in Washington beginning in the 1930s. Even the other two sectors of the party have been nationalized in the past few decades. Party voters respond increasingly to national issues, national candidates, and national party symbols. And in the party in government, the president and the congressional party leaders have become more than ever the prime speakers for their parties.

The party organizations responded more slowly to these nationalizing forces, but since the 1970s, there have been striking signs of life in the national committees. Their resources and staffs have grown. They have taken on new roles, activities, and influence. They have been able to limit the independence of state and local organizations in their one collective function—the selection of delegates to the national conventions. The congressional campaign committees are vital and active. There is, in short, a greater potential for national authority within the major American parties. So although the state and local pull remains strong, the national organizations are an increasingly powerful presence in the parties.

Does this change make a real difference in the workings of American politics? Does it affect you in any way? Let us begin by exploring what the national party is and what it is capable of doing.

NATIONAL PARTY COMMITTEES

What do we mean by the "national" party? Officially, each major party's supreme national authority is the convention it holds every four years to nominate a presidential candidate. But the convention rarely does more than select the presidential and vice-presidential candidates and approve the party's platform and rules. So in practice, between conventions, the two parties' main governing bodies are their national committees.

The National Committees

Each party's national committee is a gathering of representatives from all its state parties; its leaders run the national party on a daily basis. Both national committees are venerable organizations: the Democrats created theirs in 1848 and the Republicans in 1856. For years, every state (and some territories, such as Samoa and Guam) was represented equally on both national committees, regardless of its voting population or the extent of its party support. Alaska and California, then, had equal-sized delegations to the national party committees, just as they do in the U.S. Senate. That system overrepresented the smaller states and also gave roughly equal weight in the national committees to the winning and the losing parts of the party. In practice, this strengthened the southern and western segments of each party, which tended to be more conservative.

Since 1972, when the Democrats greatly changed the makeup of their national committee, the parties have structured their committees differently. After briefly experimenting with unequal state representation in the 1950s, the Republicans have retained their traditional confederational structure by giving each of the state and territorial parties three seats on the committee. By contrast, the Democratic National Committee (DNC), now almost three times the size of its Republican counterpart (RNC), gives weight both to population and to party support in representing the states. California, for example, has twenty seats on the committee and Alaska has four.

The two national committees also differ in that the Democrats give national committee seats to representatives of groups especially likely to support Democratic candidates, such as blacks, women, and young people—a decision that shows the importance of these groups to the party—as well as to groups of elected officials. National committee members in both parties are chosen by the states and, for the Democrats, by these other groups as well.

National Party Officers

The national committees have the power to choose their own leaders. By tradition, however, the parties' presidential candidates can name their party's national chair for the duration of the presidential campaign and the committees ratify their choices without question. The national chair chosen by the winning presidential candidate usually keeps his or her job after the election. So in practice, only the "out" party's national committee actually chooses its own national chair.[2]

The chairs, together with the national committees' permanent staffs, dominate these organizations. The members of the full national committees come together only two or three times a year. Their meetings are largely for show and to call media attention to the party and its candidates. So the national chair, with a permanent staff that he or she has chosen, has, in effect, been the national party organization.

Presidents and Their National Parties

The national committees' role, and that of their chairs, depends on whether the president is from their party. When their party does not hold the presidency, the national chair and committee can provide some national leadership. They bear the responsibility for healing internal party squabbles, helping pay debts from the losing campaign, raising new money, and energizing the party organization around the country. The "out" party's national chair may speak for the party and the alternatives it proposes. So the national chair and committee play more influential roles, by default, when their party has less control over the national government.

With a party colleague in the White House, on the other hand, the national committee's role is whatever the president wants it to be. Presidents came to dominate their national committees early in the twentieth century. Their control reached a new peak in the 1960s and 1970s and has remained powerful ever since. James W. Ceaser cites the example of Robert Dole, RNC chair from 1971 to 1973, who was quickly fired by the president when Dole tried to put a little distance between the party and the president's involvement in Watergate: "I had a nice chat with the President . . . while the other fellows went out to get the rope."[3] Some presidents have turned their national committees into little more than managers of the president's campaigns and builders of the president's political support between campaigns. Other presidents, such as George W. Bush, have used their control to build up the national committees to achieve party, not just presidential, goals.

In the president's party, the national chair must be agreeable to and willing to be loyal primarily to the president. Within the opposition party, the chair needs to get along with or at least be trusted by the various segments of the party. Frequently, he or she is chosen for ideological neutrality or for lack of identification with any of the candidates for the party's next presidential nomination. Experience in the nuts and bolts of party and campaign organization is also desirable. In this respect, with the House and Senate closely divided and an expensive race expected in 2004, it is understandable that both parties have chosen national chairs with a great deal of successful fund-raising and campaigning experience (see box on page 69).

THE SUPPORTING CAST OF NATIONAL GROUPS

Clustered around the national committees are several groups that also claim to speak for the national party or for some part of it. They are often included in what many would consider the national party.

Women's and Youth Groups

The national party committees sometimes give a formal role in their organization to supportive groups that might not be otherwise well represented. For a long time, both the Democrats and Republicans have had women's divisions associated with their national committees.[4] Both have also had national federations of state and local women's groups: the National Federation of Democratic Women and the National Federation of Republican Women. The importance of these women's divisions has declined markedly in the past 30 years as women have entered regular leadership positions in the parties.

The Young Republican National Federation and the Young Democrats of America also have a long history of representation in party councils. The national committees do not control these groups, however, and at times they have taken stands and supported candidates opposed by the senior party organization. The Young Republicans, for instance, have often taken positions to the right of the regular leadership of their party, and the Young Democrats have frequently stood to the left of their national committee. In recent years, the Young Democrats have declined, while the Young Republicans have capitalized on the party's enhanced electoral strength to expand their numbers.

The Party's Officeholders in the States

State governors have long had a powerful voice in their national parties, for several reasons. They hold prestigious offices, earned by winning statewide elections. Many lead or, at least, are supported by their state party organization, and some will probably be considered potential candidates for president. As a group, they have sought influence in Washington especially since the 1960s, and by the late 1970s and early 1980s, the governors of both parties had Washington offices and staffs. Their organizational influence in the national parties, however, tends to be greatest in the power vacuum created when their party is out of power. After the 2002 elections, for example, Democratic governors, who had done better in the elections than had Democratic congressional candidates, pushed strongly for more of a role in shaping the national party's message.[5]

State legislators and local officials in both parties are organized as well and are formally represented on the Democratic National Committee, although they do not normally have much influence on either party's national operations. A more influential group is

THE NATIONAL PARTY CHAIRS: FUND-RAISING COMES FIRST

An earlier RNC chair had been forced out of the job because he was too indepen-dent; the Bush White House, like most previous administrations, wanted an offi-cial who would concentrate on raising money and leave the strategic decisions to the White House. So Bush loyalist Ed Gillespie was chosen by President Bush to become RNC chair in 2003. A corporate lobbyist as well as presidential adviser and Republican campaign consultant, Gillespie has been described as a "one-stop power broker."

Gillespie stepped into a very well-heeled RNC. By the summer of 2000, the organization had millions of dollars in the bank, an e-mail list of a million names, and a contact list containing information about 165 million voters. During the year prior to Gillespie's appointment, the RNC had overhauled its operations in preparation for the 2002 congressional elections. Out of this effort came the "72 Hour Task Force," a national program to mobilize votes for Republican candi-dates during the three days before Election Day. The program was widely cred-ited as an important reason for Republican victories in 2002.

Terry McAuliffe, newly appointed chair of the DNC in 2000, cut his fund-rais-ing teeth even earlier. McAuliffe, who started his first company when he was 14, was the top fund-raiser for the 1980 Carter presidential campaign at the ripe old age of 22. He later became the DNC's Finance Director and then National Finance Chair for the Clinton campaign in 1996.

McAuliffe claims to have raised a half-billion dollars for Democratic candi-dates, making him, in the words of *New York Times* reporter Richard L. Berke, "the party's premier fund-raiser of the last two decades" (or, in Al Gore's more expansive phrase, "the greatest fund-raiser in the history of the universe"). A home builder and mortgage financier who has also lobbied for business, McAuliffe broadened the Democrats' financial base into the business and legal communities. To Berke, who points out that "the central role of party chairman is always to raise money," the selection of McAuliffe as DNC chair represents the triumph of the political preoccupation with money.

Source: Thomas B. Edsall, "A Broker of Power, Able to Wear Many Professional Hats," *Washington Post,* June 24, 2002, p. A17; and Richard L. Berke, "The Man Who Would Be Democratic Chairman Leaves Little to Chance," *New York Times,* February 1, 2001, p. A15.

the Democratic Leadership Council. Founded in 1985, it brings together Democratic elected officials, led by influential members of Congress and governors and some prospective candidates for president. The Democratic Leadership Council represents the moderate-to-conservative wing of the party and works to make the party more appeal-ing to southern and western voters. On the Republican side, groups such as the Repub-lican Liberty Caucus and the Heritage Foundation also try to affect party policy.

Congressional Campaign Committees

The most important of all the supporting cast are each party's House and Senate campaign committees (called the "Hill committees" because they used to be housed on

Capitol Hill). The House committees were founded in the immediate aftermath of the Civil War; the Senate committees came into being when senators began to be popularly elected in 1913. The Democratic Congressional Campaign Committee (DCCC), the National Republican Congressional Committee (NRCC), the Democratic Senatorial Campaign Committee (DSCC), and the National Republican Senatorial Committee (NRSC) are organized to promote the reelection of their members and the success of other congressional candidates of their party. They are the campaign organizations of the congressional party in government, much as the national committee serves as the campaign organization of the presidential party.

Although incumbent House and Senate members control these committees, they have resisted the pressures to work only on behalf of incumbents' campaigns; they also support their party's candidates for open seats and challengers who have a good chance of winning. In short, they concentrate their money where they think they are likely to get the biggest payoff in increasing the size of their party's representation in Congress. During the past two decades, the congressional campaign committees have developed their own fund-raising and service functions. They provide party candidates with an impressive range of campaign help, from production facilities for television ads to hard cash (see box on page 71). They also help to channel money from political action committees to the party's candidates. In resources and campaigning skills, they are often as influential as their parties' national committees.

TWO PATHS TO POWER

The two national parties have traveled two different roads to reach these new levels of effectiveness. The Republicans have followed a service path by building a muscular fund-raising operation in order to provide needed services to their candidates and state parties. The Democrats, in contrast, first followed a procedural path, strengthening their national party's authority over the state parties in the selection of a presidential nominee.

The central element in both national parties' development, however, was their ability to attract thousands of small contributions through mass mailings to likely party supporters; this gave the national parties, which formerly depended on assessments provided by the state parties, an independent financial base. Ironically, then, at a time when some were warning that the parties were in decline, the national party organizations were reaching levels of strength that had never been seen before in American politics.

The Service Party Path

The service party was born during the 1960s, when a quiet revolution began in the Republican National Committee. The committee's chairman at the time, Ray Bliss, involved the committee more and more in helping state and local parties with the nuts and bolts of party organizational work. Chairman William Brock continued this effort in the mid- to late 1970s, as a means of reviving the party's election prospects after the Republican losses of the post-Watergate years. Under Brock, the RNC helped to pay the salaries of the executive directors of all 50 state Republican Parties, provided expert help to the state parties in organizing, strategizing, and fund-raising and also gave financial help to more than 4,000 state legislative candidates. Bliss and Brock fashioned a new role for the RNC by making it into an exceptionally effective service organization for the state and local parties.[6]

RUNNING FOR CONGRESS? HERE'S WHAT THE PARTIES' NATIONAL COMMITTEES CAN DO FOR YOU

The national party organizations now offer these services to candidates:

- Training for candidates, campaign managers, and other workers in up-to-date campaign techniques, management, fund-raising, and field work
- "Issue packages" for selected candidates: information about issues relevant to their campaigns and talking points to use in discussing these issues
- State-of-the-art television and radio production facilities and consultants to help candidates make effective ads at low cost
- Satellite capabilities to let candidates broadcast live interactive programs with constituents
- Contributor lists given to selected candidates on the condition that these candidates give their own contributor lists to the party after the election
- Party fund-raising events in Washington
- Party leaders' visits to candidate events, live and via satellite uplink, to help candidates raise money and attract votes
- "Hard-money" direct contributions to campaigns*
- "Coordinated spending" to buy polls, media ads, or research for a candidate*
- "Issue advocacy" ads in support of candidates* and generic ads promoting the party as a whole
- Help in raising money from political action committees (PACs) and individuals

---

*Explained in chapter 12.
Sources: Paul S. Herrnson, *Congressional Elections*, 3rd ed. (Washington, DC: CQ Press, 2000), pp. 100–115, and Victoria A. Farrar-Myers and Diana Dwyre, "Parties and Campaign Finance," in Jeffrey E. Cohen, Richard Fleisher, and Paul Kantor, eds., *American Political Parties: Decline or Resurgence?* (Washington, DC: CQ Press, 2001), pp. 143–146.

There were two keys to success in performing the new service role: money and mastery of the new campaign technologies. Using the new ability to generate computer-based mailing lists, the Republicans began a program of direct-mail solicitations that brought in ever-higher levels of income, as you can see in Table 4.1. By the 1983–1984 election cycle, the RNC had raised $105.9 million in "hard money" (contributions regulated by federal law; these terms are explained in Chapter 12)—a record for national committee fund-raising that has been broken only recently. The national Republican committees used the money, as Bliss and Brock had, to provide a broad array of services to candidates and to state and local party organizations—candidate recruitment and training, research, public opinion polling, data processing, computer networking and software development, production of radio and television commercials, direct mailing, expert consultants, and legal services. State party leaders were glad to accept the help; as the party more closely identified with the business community, Republicans felt comfortable with these innovations.

TABLE 4.1 Party "Hard Money" Receipts: 1975–76 to 2001–02 (in millions)

	National	Senate	House	State/Local	Total
Democratic committees					
1975–1976	$13.1	1.0	0.9	0.0	15.0
1977–1978	$11.3	0.3	2.8	8.7	26.4
1979–1980	$15.1	1.7	2.1	11.7	37.2
1981–1982	$16.4	5.6	6.5	10.6	39.3
1983–1984	$46.6	8.9	10.4	18.5	98.5
1985–1986	$17.2	13.4	12.3	14.1	64.8
1987–1988	$52.3	16.3	12.5	44.7	113.8
1989–1990	$14.5	17.5	9.1	44.7	78.5
1991–1992	$65.8	25.5	12.8	73.7	163.3
1993–1994	$41.8	26.4	19.4	55.6	132.8
1995–1996	$108.4	30.8	26.6	93.2	221.6
1997–1998	$64.8	35.6	25.2	63.4	$160.0
1999–2000	$124.0	40.5	48.4	149.3	275.2
2001–2002	$67.5	48.4	46.4	114.2	217.3
Republican Committees					
1975–1976	$29.1	12.2	1.8	0.0	43.1
1977–1978	$34.2	10.9	14.1	20.9	84.5
1979–1980	$ 76.2	23.3	28.6	33.8	169.5
1981–1982	$ 83.5	48.9	58.0	24.0	215.0
1983–1984	$105.9	81.7	58.3	43.1	297.9
1985–1986	$ 83.8	84.4	39.8	47.2	255.2
1987–1988	$ 91.0	65.9	34.7	66.0	251.3
1989–1990	$ 68.7	65.1	33.2	39.3	202.0
1991–1992	$ 85.4	73.8	35.3	72.8	264.9
1993–1994	$ 87.4	65.3	26.7	75.0	244.1
1995–1996	$193.0	64.5	74.2	128.4	416.5
1997–1998	$104.0	53.4	72.7	89.4	285.0
1999–2000	$212.8	51.5	97.3	176.6	465.8
2001–2002	$170.1	59.2	141.1	132.5	441.6

Note: Beginning with 1987–1988, total receipts do not include monies transferred among the listed committees.

Source: Federal Election Commission at http://www.fec.gov/press/20030320party/demfederalye02.xls and http://www.fec.gov/press/20030320party/repfederalye02.xls (accessed June 10, 2003).

The Democrats' Procedural-Reform Path

At about the same time, the national Democrats had begun to expand the power of the national party organization for other reasons. Reformers supporting the civil rights movement and opposing American involvement in the Vietnam War pressed for change in the Democratic Party's positions on these issues. The reformers focused on changing the rules for selecting presidential candidates. Their aim was to make the nominating process more open and democratic and, in particular, more representative of the concerns of people like themselves: blacks, women, and young people.

In the mid-1960s, these reforms began with efforts to keep southern states from sending all-white delegations to the national convention. After the 1968 election, the first of a series of reform commissions worked to dramatically overhaul the party's rules for nominating presidential candidates. (This story is told in more detail in Chapter 10.) In doing so, the Democrats limited the autonomy of the state parties and the authority of state law in determining how convention delegates were to be selected, thus giving the national party the authority over the presidential nominating process.[7] Key court decisions upheld these actions, further solidifying the newfound authority of the national party.

Why would the state party leaders have been willing to go along with this erosion of their independence? Some may still be asking themselves that question. The reformers' success indicates that state Democratic leaders were not sufficiently aware of the threat posed by the reforms; it also reflects the unusual politics of that time and the existence of a power vacuum at the top of the Democratic Party in the 1960s. This change, however, was limited to the Democrats. Republican leaders, consistent with their party's long-standing states' rights orientation, had no real desire to centralize power in their own party organization.[8] Yet the GOP was still affected by the tide of Democratic Party reform because the bills passed by state legislatures to implement the reforms applied to both parties.

In the early 1980s, the Democrats took stock of the reforms and did not like what they saw. The newly centralized authority in nominating a presidential candidate and the increased grassroots participation in the nominating process had done little to win elections. Further, it had divided the party and alienated much of the Democratic Party in government, many of whom stayed home from party conventions in the 1970s. So the national Democrats decided to soft-pedal organizational reforms and move toward the Republican service model. The party rushed to broaden the base of its fund-raising and to provide the means and know-how to recruit candidates and revitalize local parties. When the dust from all this effort settled, authority over party rules had been nationalized, and what had been two models for strengthening the national party were rapidly converging into one.[9]

Both Parties Take the Service Path

The good news for the Democrats in the 1980s was that they were dramatically improving their fund-raising capacities, reducing their long-standing debt, and increasing their activities in the states and localities. The bad news was that the Republicans were far ahead of them to begin with and were continuing to break new ground. The national Democrats made no secret of their effort to imitate the Republican success in raising money and using it to buy services. Slowly, they began to catch up; what began as a three-to-one and even five-to-one financial advantage for the Republicans was later cut by about half (see Figure 4.1).

Both national parties' committees took advantage of the development of unrestricted "soft money" in the early 1990s (see Chapter 12) to expand their fund-raising even more. In 2000, for example, the national Republicans established the "Republican Regents" program for individuals and corporations who gave at least $250,000 in soft money to the party during a two-year period, which helped produce record soft-money donations, and the Democratic "Jefferson Trust" honored givers of at least $100,000.[10] When court decisions put the legality of soft money in doubt in 2002, both parties encouraged big donors to ask friends and colleagues for smaller contributions and "bundle" the checks to give to the party. The NRCC, in particular, has moved heavily into telemarketing to attract small donors, tailoring the phone appeal to the individual being called—asking for donations from a business executive, for instance, in exchange for a position on the NRCC's Business Advisory Council.[11]

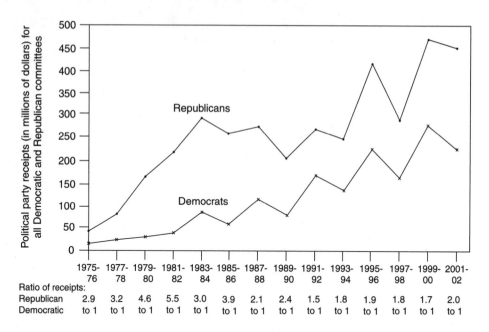

FIGURE 4.1   Republicans Lead in Fund-raising: 1975–76 to 2001–02.

Note: Soft money is not included.

Source: Same as Table 4.1.

How has the money been used? Some of it has gone into building up the state and even the local parties (see "Who Got the Most National Party Money in 2001–2002?" on page 75). In the 2002 election cycle, for example, the RNC and the Republican Hill committees transferred $145.6 million to their state and local organizations and the three Democratic committees transferred $158.6 million.[12] Most of this was soft money, which could be used for campaign advertising as long as it did not use words such as "elect" or "defeat" in connection with a candidate. But at least some of this money went into voter mobilization drives that could help the state party more generally.

In fact, the NRCC had so much soft money left at the end of the 2002 campaign— money that would no longer be usable after the election because of change in campaign finance laws—that it donated large amounts to candidates and party organizations right before the election. So the Fairfax County, Virginia, Republican Party, the home county of the NRCC chair, got $250,000 for a new headquarters. And as they had in 1984, Republican national committees funneled major investments into state legislative races during the spring of 2000. Their aim was to improve the chances that these legislatures, which would be drawing new legislative districts after the 2000 U.S. Census, would have Republican majorities.

A much larger portion of the national parties' money has gone into races for the U.S. House and Senate. Ever since the mid-1980s, both parties have provided increasing levels of aid to selected candidates. Here as well, the Republican committees have taken the lead. The stunning success of GOP candidates in the 1994 congressional elections, for

WHO GOT THE MOST NATIONAL PARTY MONEY IN 2001–2002?

State parties

Texas Democratic Party	$15,341,003
Minnesota Republican Party	12,191,930
Florida Republican Party	12,168,808
Minnesota Democratic Party	11,645,519

Senate candidates (including party direct contributions, coordinated spending, and party independent spending)

John Cornyn, Texas Republican (won)	$ 2,217,863
Suzanne Haik Terrell, Louisiana Republican (lost)	1,469,314
Doug Forrester, New Jersey Republican (lost)	961,500
Saxby Chambliss, Georgia Republican (won)	901,864

House candidates

John Swallow, Utah Republican (lost)	472,877
Steve Pearce, New Mexico Republican (won)	220,945

Note: National party money includes money transferred by all six national party committees (DNC, RNC, NRSC, DSCC, NRCC, DCCC).
Source: Federal Election Commission data, indexed at http://www.fec.gov/press/20030320party/20030103party.html

example, was due in part to aggressive fund-raising and candidate recruitment by their Hill committees.

In the 2002 congressional campaigns, the Republican Hill committees acted strategically to maximize the value of their fund-raising by trading funds with state parties and candidates' committees in order to put the money where it was most needed and could be used legally. Overall, the two Republican Hill committees amassed an impressive $200 million in federally regulated "hard" money for use in the 2002 elections; note especially in Table 4.1 the big jump in the House campaign committee's fund-raising from 2000 to 2002, plus about $136 million in "soft money." Their fund-raising success made a big difference in the Republicans' successful fight to hold the House and regain control of the Senate. The national Republican committees, closely directed by the White House, set out a plan to give even more party money in 2004, but only to candidates who met certain criteria, including a commitment to using Spanish-language media to attract Latino voters.[13]

The Democrats' Hill committees have expanded their fund-raising much more gradually, as the slow rise in Table 4.1 shows. Their "bottom line" improved in 2000, when they greatly increased their courtship of business and, taking advantage of the closeness of the congressional races, brought in soft money at levels well beyond those they had reached in previous years. With the end of soft money fast approaching in 2002 (see Chapter 12), the two Democratic Hill committees surpassed their Republican counterparts with soft-money collections of $151 million, to add to $95 million in hard money. For both parties, the greatest advances in fund-raising and organizational development have come when their party is not holding the presidency. Adversity breeds innovation.

All together, the national parties broke all fund-raising records in the period leading up to the 2002 elections. The six national party committees collectively raised almost $1.2 *billion*—substantially more than in any previous midterm race and almost as much as the two parties had raised in the 2000 general election, when they had a presidential candidate to support. Over time, these fund-raising advances have permitted both national parties to hire increasing numbers of professional staff members, who in turn have been able to put new campaign technologies into practice (see Table 4.2). Since the mid-1980s, then, both national parties have become institutionalized as active, well-staffed "service parties" working to support party candidates and state and local organizations throughout the nation.[14]

WHAT IS THE IMPACT OF THESE STRONGER NATIONAL PARTIES?

The dramatic changes in the national parties have helped to beef up the parties' roles in nominating and electing candidates, roles that had been seriously undercut a century ago with the advent of the direct primary. To an important degree, the national and state parties (especially the Republicans) have begun to "muscle in" on the campaign support functions that political action committees (PACs) and private campaign consultants had monopolized just a few years ago. It is not likely that party organizations can displace PACs and consultants, but the money and services provided by the national parties have helped to raise their profiles in the eyes of candidates. The increasing strength of the national parties also has the potential to alter the relationships within the parties.

TABLE 4.2 The Growth of National Party Committee Staff: 1972–2000

	1972	1976	1980	1984	1988	1992	1996	2000
Democratic Party committees								
National committee	30	30	40	130	160	270	264	150
House campaign committee	5	6	26	45	80	64	64	75
Senate campaign committee	4	5	20	22	50	35	38	40
Republican Party committees								
National committee	30	200	350	600	425	300	271	250
House campaign committee	6	8	40	130	80	89	64	63
Senate campaign committee	4	6	30	90	88	135	150	75

Note: These numbers fluctuate a lot from month to month and year to year. Generally, the size of the national committees peaks in the presidential election year and is smaller in the interelection period.

Source: 1972–1984: Paul S. Herrnson, Party Campaigning in the 1980s (Cambridge, MA: Harvard University Press, 1988), p. 39; 1988: Herrnson, "Reemergent National Party Organizations," in L. Sandy Maisel, ed., The Parties Respond (Boulder, CO: Westview Press, 1990), p. 51; 1992: Herrnson, "The Revitalization of National Party Organizations," in Maisel, ed., The Parties Respond (Boulder, CO: Westview Press, 1994), p. 54; 1996: Herrnson, "National Party Organizations at the Century's End," in Maisel, ed. The Parties Respond (Boulder, CO: Westview Press, 1998), pp. 60–61; 2000: Data were graciously provided by Paul S. Herrnson.

Effects on Candidates' Campaigns

The impact of the new national party strength on the campaigns of congressional candidates is increasingly concentrated in a few states and districts. In the 1980s and 1990s, the national party committees supported a wide range of viable candidates; the committees tended to protect their incumbents when they expected a lean election year and invested in challengers and open seats when a big victory looked likely. By the early 2000s, though, the two parties were so evenly matched in the House and Senate and the number of truly competitive races had shrunk so dramatically that both parties' congressional committees were pouring the great majority of their money and help into those few competitive races.[15]

The volume of party funds and field staff coming into the small number of competitive campaigns in 2002 was unprecedented. In one of the most visible cases, a runoff for a Louisiana Senate seat offered the GOP the chance to expand the razor-thin edge that it had won in the Senate on Election Day. National Republican committees, free from their responsibilities in all the other races, ran the runoff campaign of the Republican challenger from Washington, DC, and the state party headquarters. The challenger, Suzanne Haik Terrell, had been recruited to run by the White House. The national party designed her message and spent $500,000 on get-out-the-vote efforts. The NRSC made and funded ads on her behalf. "The result," according to a reporter, "is that Terrell's tiny headquarters in Baton Rouge is oddly quiet."[16]

When the candidate's headquarters is quiet and the national party committees in Washington are humming, we have an indicator that at least in these few targeted races, the national party committees' money and other resources have given them real power over the campaign. For instance, in 2002, the national parties spent more in a closely fought Colorado congressional race than the candidates' own campaigns did, and the national party committees specified exactly what the campaigns were to do with the party money. The race, the candidates acknowledged, was in large part under the parties' control, not their own. The Democratic candidate's campaign manager probably spoke for both candidates in his exasperation at the national party's micromanaging: "They crawl up our . . . on a daily basis."[17] The national parties' heavy investment in campaigns, then, can lead to conflicts as well as to cooperation with party candidates (see the box on page 78).

This level of party influence on campaigns is unusual, however. In most other congressional campaigns, the national party committees have not put in enough money or other resources to attract even much attention, much less power, relative to the candidates and their staffs. National party involvement in the targeted House and Senate races in 2002 shows the potential for greater party impact on campaigns, but the potential is far from being realized.

Effects on State and Local Parties

More generally, have the increasing visibility and resources of the national parties led to a shift in power from the state and local to the national party organizations—to centralization rather than decentralization of the parties? Probably not. The Democrats are somewhat more comfortable with centralization; they have had more experience than the Republicans in enforcing national rules and a stronger inclination to accept centralized authority. However, the forces that encourage a state and local party focus remain strong.

WHO KNOWS BETTER? CONFLICT BETWEEN NATIONAL PARTY COMMITTEES AND CAMPAIGNS

As if being a moderate in an increasingly conservative party were not challenging enough, Jim Leach's life got a lot tougher in 2002. In the redrawing of congressional district lines that followed the 2000 Census, Leach, a Republican member of the U.S. House from Iowa, found himself in a new district where most of the voters were Democrats.

Leach had won 13 elections to Congress by campaigning with a local focus, accepting no out-of-state money. However, in 2002, Leach and his Democratic opponent, Dr. Julie Thomas, felt like puppets in a contest where the real power lay at the national level. There were very few truly competitive House races in 2002, and Leach's race was one of them. If Leach lost, Republicans risked losing control of the closely divided House.

National Republican Congressional Committee (NRCC) strategists disapproved of Leach's style of campaigning; they pronounced it "perhaps the worst incumbent campaign in the country." So the NRCC stepped in. Chair Thomas M. Davis III promised, "I'm not going to let them [the Democrats] buy it from him. I'm not going to let them take the House on that." The NRCC poured campaign advertising into the district, some of it negative.

Leach objected to the volume of ads and also to their tone; "I think he [Davis] looks at me as if I'm naïve [for trying to run a local, positive campaign]," said Rep. Leach. Dr. Thomas felt the same frustration. The Democratic Congressional Campaign Committee ran sharp-edged campaign ads and the AFL-CIO, the League of Conservation Voters, and other national groups also funneled money and volunteers into the race.

Leach's and Thomas's predicament was echoed in highly competitive races all over the nation: with the infusion of national party and interest group money, neither candidate had control over what messages would be broadcast in their campaign.

Source: Quotations are from Robin Toner, "Where Candidates May Fear to Tread, National Parties Stampede In," *New York Times,* September 30, 2002, p. A18.

Although the parties are far from centralized, the national aid to state and local parties and campaigns and the national intervention in their nomination processes have caused some shift in party power toward the national organizations. When the national parties have a lot of money and services to give, their suggestions are likely to be taken more seriously by candidates and state and local parties. The result may be more of a national imprint on the issues discussed in state and local campaigns, the kinds of candidates recruited, and the ways in which the parties are organized. State and local organizations that resist the national party's suggestions could find themselves on the short end of the national party's money and help. Is this a good thing for American politics? "Which Would You Choose?" on the next page, gives you arguments on both sides of this question.

This increased national influence can produce some interesting strains among party organizations at different levels of government, just as it has produced strains between

COULD A STRONGER NATIONAL PARTY HELP YOU?

YES! Political parties offer you a valuable shortcut. Government decisions affect almost everything you do, but you may not have time to research dozens of complicated issues (health care, energy prices) and candidates in order to vote for those who will act in your interest. A party can do the research for you. If you generally agree with, say, the Republican Party, it can offer you a set of recommended candidates with no effort on your part. But if each state and local Republican organization can act independently, and if some of these organizations are moderate and others are conservative, then how can you be sure that your state and local Republican candidates will support the positions that drew you to the party? A strong national party could help recruit candidates whose views are consistent with the party's philosophy and help them get elected. Besides, who would you rather have raising campaign money: the national party, or the individual candidates who will soon be voting on bills affecting the donors' interests?

NO! The United States is very diverse; the concerns of Democrats in Omaha may well be different from those in San Francisco, New Hampshire, and the Florida Panhandle. If a national party is strong enough to promote a clear set of ideas on what government should be doing, then whose ideas should it promote: those of the Omaha Democrats or those of the San Francisco Democrats? If a national party is strong enough to elect its candidates, wouldn't it be capable of telling them how to vote in Congress, whether or not their constituents agreed? Even if a national party organization confines itself to raising money and giving it to candidates, doesn't that give the national organization a great deal of influence over state and even local candidates? In a nation with a tradition of hostility to "boss rule," couldn't a strong national party raise those fears again?

the parties and their candidates. One of the areas of greatest conflict between the national parties and their state and local brethren centers on national party involvement in primaries. It is always a temptation for national party officials to try to select and groom the candidate they think will have the best chance of winning in a district. The House and Senate campaign committees, whose chance for a majority in Congress depends on the effectiveness of candidates in competitive races, find it very frustrating to watch a less capable candidate win their party's primary and go on to run a less-than-professional campaign for the seat.

There are big risks involved when a national party organization tries to endorse a candidate in a primary. If the party organization backs a candidate who then loses the primary, the party alienates the winning candidate, perhaps splits the state party in the process, and makes itself look weak to boot. The DCCC provided a textbook example of these hazards when it decided to endorse four congressional candidates in the 2000 primaries. Two of the four lost, and the effort caused intraparty fighting that became a public embarrassment to the national Democrats.

National Democratic committees stayed out of party primaries in the next election, but the national Republicans chose to wade boldly into this thicket and came out relatively unscathed. Anxious to regain control of the Senate in 2002, the NRSC focused early on 10 states that it considered winnable for a strong Republican candidate. Using public opinion polls to measure the favorability ratings of various possible candidates, NRSC strategists identified the strongest prospective contenders and, with President Bush, worked to persuade these people to run. The NRCC did the same in some key House races. All three national Republican committees then raised record amounts of money to pour into the closest races.[18]

The Republican Hill committees were able to recruit many of those on their wish list and to win enough races to capture the Senate. Yet this national intervention, according to one reporter, "infuriated" several state Republican Party leaders when the NRCC chair campaigned in their states for the national party's preferred candidates.[19] When the national party committees use their money to affect the choice of candidates or the direction of a campaign, it is likely that there will be ruffled feathers within the state party and the campaign, who feel that they are better judges of what works in the district. In addition, state party leaders may worry that the national intervention will make it that much harder to unite the party after the primary.

Effects on the Presidency

Is a stronger national party likely to compete with the president's power or to add to it? Clearly, the increasing resources of the national committees give them the opportunity for a more independent political role. This independence has been developing since the 1980s, when the Republican National Committee came into its own as an important actor in party politics. Federal funding of presidential campaigns, with its strict limits on party spending for presidential races, freed the national committees from their traditional concentration on presidential elections and allowed them to dedicate their now considerable resources to party-building at the state and local level. At the same time, the party committees carved out new roles in raising soft money for the presidential campaign and channeling this money to the state and local parties for grassroots voter mobilization.

On the other hand, these new capabilities make the national committee an even more attractive resource for presidents. Naturally, presidents want the new party power to be at their service, and every president in recent memory has kept his party's national committee on a short leash. RNC Chair Jim Gilmore was edged out in late 2001, for example, because he clashed with the White House over control of the committee. Presidents will certainly want the party committees to mobilize all those members of Congress whom they recruited, trained, financed, and helped elect to support the president's program. Also, presidents in their first term will want to draw on the assets of the national party for their reelection campaigns, as much as the Federal Election Campaign Act permits. So there is considerable pressure on these stronger national parties to put their capabilities at the service of presidential goals.[20]

The situation is different in the "out" party. During the four years after its presidential candidate has been defeated, a national party suffers constant jockeying for the right to lead. The defeated presidential candidate may or may not remain an important voice within the party, depending on his or her popularity and the credibility of his or her losing campaign.

Al Gore, for instance, fell out of the speed-dial lists of many national Democratic leaders after he lost the electoral college vote in 2000. Most often, the leadership of the "out" party falls to its leaders in Congress, supported by the resources of their congressional campaign committees. The reason is that the congressional party, simply because its legislative responsibilities force it to take policy stands, is a logical source of the party's positions and of challenges to the program of the opposition's president. An invigorated national party committee can also help fill the void in national leadership, as can its chair.

Effects on Congress

As we have seen, the Hill committees have become much more active in recruiting and supporting party candidates. At about the same time as this expansion in the Hill committees' resources, there has also been an increase in the extent to which Congress members cast legislative votes with the majority of their party (as Chapter 13 shows). Did these new campaign resources help convince congressional incumbents to support their party's positions on bills? To this point, the campaign committees have not given out campaign money and services on the basis of a candidate's support for the party's program. Their support goes to competitive races rather than to candidates who are ideologically "pure."[21] However, the committees have not been bashful in reminding members, especially newly elected members, that the party played some role in their election success.

The remarkable cohesion of the post-1994 Republican majority in the House surely stems, in part, from the party leadership's financial and other support for Republicans in the 1994 elections. Constituency pressures will always come first in Congress, but the more senators and representatives can count on campaign support from the congressional party, the more open they will be to party-based appeals.

Relationships Within the National Party

The three national committees of each party—the DNC or RNC and the party's Hill committees—have a number of reasons to cooperate with one another. All three committees benefit from voter registration and get-out-the-vote drives, and it is often cost-effective for them to work together on candidate recruitment and campaigns. A good example was the coordinated campaign conducted by DNC, the DSCC, and the Iowa Democratic Party in 2002, where Senator Tom Harkin and Governor Tom Vilsack were both facing close races for reelection. With money provided by the campaigns and the national Democratic organizations, the state party and labor unions assembled large numbers of volunteers and paid staff. These staffers then contacted 250,000 homes in Iowa to identify likely Democratic supporters, create a database of their concerns, and deliver absentee ballot requests. The result was a substantial harvest of absentee ballots in races that Harkin and Vilsack narrowly won.[22]

On the other hand, the three national party committees compete with one another in several ways, and especially in raising money. They seek financial support from the same contributors (and jealously guard their contributor lists), recruit political talent from the same limited pool and sometimes seek conflicting goals. Resources are scarce in party organizing, so it is not surprising that different organizations from the same party will struggle over them.

THE LIMITS OF PARTY ORGANIZATION

Even the new strength in the national party organizations, however, may not be enough to revive the parties in the minds of many Americans. More professional, service-oriented parties may be better at helping candidates run for office than in stimulating voter attachments to parties or involving people at the grassroots. The strengthening of parties at the center is a fascinating change, but it may not have contributed much to expanding their role in American politics.[23]

Remember that even with these changes, American party organizations remain weak by international standards. In this era of large-scale business, government, universities, and voluntary organizations, the parties cut an unimpressive figure. They lack the top-down control and efficiency, the unified setting of priorities, and the central responsibility that we often find in parties in other nations. Where the party organizations of other Western democracies have had permanent, highly professional leadership and large party bureaucracies, most American party organizations have generally done without a professional bureaucracy or leadership. Especially at the local level, the business of American party organization is still often in the hands of part-time activists and inexperienced professionals, which may indicate that its activities do not normally require much specialization or professionalism.[24]

It is not surprising that the American party organization's development remains stunted, even in these times of unprecedented strength at its national level. There is little in American political values that would welcome an efficient or "businesslike" operation of the parties. Americans' traditional fears of party strength combine with legal limits on the parties, the effects of the separation of powers, and the federal structure of our political system to produce a hostile climate for party organizational development. Even the campaign finance reforms since the 1970s have contributed to the weakness of the party organizations by treating them as just another source of campaign money, along with PACs and individuals, rather than as the central organizations in campaign funding, essential to the electoral process.

Besides, a strong organization implies routine and continuity—an arrangement that may be more compatible with a party of unchanging principle rather than with a party committed to making the adjustments necessary to do well in a pragmatic political system. The American parties are fundamentally flexible and election oriented, concerned mainly with supporting candidates for office and active mainly during campaigns. For that reason, they have long been led by candidates and officeholders, not by career bureaucrats. So even though they now have active and vibrant national committees, the electoral focus of the American parties may have tipped the scales against the development of any centralized, elaborate party organization. As they have for some time, the American parties remain candidate-centered organizations in a candidate-centered political world.

CHAPTER 5

Party Activists

Fighting the bitter cold on a snowy evening in Iowa, thousands of Democrats and Republicans headed for schools, firehouses, and other locations to begin the process of choosing their party's candidate for president in January 2004. These were not state party leaders. Many of them were—or would become—party activists, contributing their time and energy to their party on a purely voluntary basis. Even the professional party workers who staff the national and state offices share many of the attributes of these volunteers. Their activity and motivations are at the heart of party politics.

Why would people spend their precious free time on volunteer work for a political party? Most likely because they feel that they get something in return. People who become active in a party organization have some reasons—seek some payoffs—for devoting their time to the party's activities rather than to their television programs, their church, or their tennis game. The party organization, of course, has goals of its own. So the party has to be able to work toward its aims—winning elections, educating the public, and governing—while at the same time allowing its volunteers and leaders to achieve theirs. If it fails to do so, its future as a viable party may be short. How it accomplishes this tricky challenge (and whether it does) is determined by the ways it recruits party activists, organizes them, and mobilizes them for action.

WHAT DRAWS PEOPLE INTO PARTY ACTIVITY?

The American political parties have never operated primarily in a cash economy. They have rarely bought or hired more than a small proportion of the millions of labor hours they need. Today, in spite of the increasing professionalism of the national and state party headquarters, most Americans who volunteer in their local parties get no cash in return for their considerable time and skills. Even the old customs of paying precinct workers on Election Day or using government employees as the party's workers at election time are vanishing. What, then, induces all these people to donate their time and effort to try to meet their party's goals?

In their seminal theory, Peter B. Clark and James Q. Wilson identified three types of reasons why individuals become active in organizations of all kinds. ***Material incentives*** are tangible rewards for activity—direct cash payments or other concrete rewards for one's work. ***Solidary incentives*** are the intangible, social benefits that people can gain from associating with others, from networking and being part of a group. ***Purposive incentives*** are intangible rewards of a different kind—based on the sense of satisfaction that comes when people are promoting an issue or principle that matters to them or feel that they are involved in a worthwhile cause. By exploring these three types of incentives, we can learn a lot about people's motives for becoming and staying involved in party work and about the functioning of party organizations as well.[1]

Material Incentives

Over time, the main material, or tangible, reasons why people became involved in party activity were the opportunity to share in the "spoils" gained when a party controlled the government. These "spoils" came in the form of patronage and preferments. ***Patronage*** refers to the appointment of an individual to a government job as a reward for party work. Although patronage is very limited today, the party can still provide loyal workers with a base of support if they seek elected office. ***Preferments*** involve, more generally, granting the favors of government to party supporters. Patronage, access to elected office, and preferments have all played important roles in building and sustaining the American party organizations.

Patronage   Early in the life of the Republic and for many decades afterward, Americans were attracted to party work by the prospect of being rewarded with government jobs. Patronage has been used in other nations as well, but no other party system has relied on patronage as fully and for as long as the American system. In the heyday of the political machine, for example, city governments were staffed almost entirely by loyalists of the party in power.[2] As the price to be paid for their jobs, patronage appointees traditionally "volunteered" their time, energy, and often even a part of their salary to the party organization.

Campaign help was especially expected; American party politics is rich with tales of the entire staff of certain government departments being put to work in support of their boss's reelection. Money, too, has always been an important resource in campaigns, and patronage workers have been called upon to "invest" in the party that gave them their jobs. Even now, when such practices are increasingly frowned on and sometimes illegal, government employees can still face a lot of pressure to contribute time or money to their party.

But at the same time as the various levels of government were growing to include more than 18 million public employees, the number of patronage jobs available to the parties was declining dramatically. Most government employees are now hired under civil service and merit systems, in which applicants get jobs based on their scores on competitive exams. The number of full-time federal positions filled by political appointees has dwindled over the years to fewer than 10,000 today, many of them high-level policy-making positions. States and cities have followed the same path, though more slowly.

The Supreme Court has helped to dismantle patronage at the state and local levels. In 1976 and 1980, the Court ruled that some county political employees could not be fired simply because of a change of the party in power. The Court went further in a 1990 Illinois case, determining that politically based hiring and promotion violated the First

Amendment freedoms of speech and association. In each case, the Court agreed that party affiliation might be a relevant qualification in filling policy-making positions, but not in lower level offices.[3]

Even where patronage positions remain, it has gotten harder for parties to use them as incentives for party activity. The politics of patronage worked best among the disadvantaged, who were willing to accept whatever city or county jobs were offered. However, most of the available patronage positions do not tempt the educated, respected, middle-class leadership that the parties would like to attract. And in an age of candidate-centered politics, elected executives are more interested in using patronage to build their own political followings than to strengthen the party organization.

Yet some patronage is likely to survive as long as it is attractive to both political leaders and their followers. Mayors, governors, and presidents will continue to reserve top policy-making positions for their loyal supporters. Legislatures at all levels of government will remain reluctant to bring their staff members under the protection of civil service systems. Civil service rules for governmental employees can be bypassed by hiring politically loyal, "temporary" workers outside of the civil service system, or by channeling party loyalists into jobs in private firms that depend on government business. A few big campaign contributors will continue to be named ambassadors to small and peaceful countries. Wherever political leaders retain discretion over personnel appointments, in short, they will find a way to award them to their trusted political supporters. The promise of such awards, in turn, will keep attracting people to political activity, although not the large numbers who once served as the "foot soldiers" of the traditional political machines.

Keep in mind that some thoughtful observers are sorry to lose the practice of patronage (as unsavory as it now seems). The use of patronage was promoted by the presidency of Andrew Jackson as a means of encouraging a more democratic and less elitist government.[4] When government jobs are filled (and then protected) only by civil service procedures, it becomes almost impossible for reform-minded leaders to replace a sluggish or ineffective bureaucrat with a more efficient worker. Besides, replacing political (patronage) appointees by neutral professionals may actually make government bureaucracies less responsive to elected political leaders and maybe even less sympathetic to the public they serve.

Patronage was also thought to be a means of keeping party organizations strong as instruments of democracy. Material incentives can often be very effective lures in attracting workers; without the opportunity to award patronage jobs, parties can find it harder to recruit the labor that they need. Those who participate for reasons other than material rewards may make other demands, for example, for the party to take an ideological stance that might alienate moderate voters. That could undermine the ability of a party organization to act pragmatically and inclusively.

Patronage jobs in government are not the only employment opportunities a party can offer. In recent years, party organizations at the state and national levels have become important employers of professional campaign workers. To provide services to their candidates, party organizations need computer specialists, pollsters, media production experts, field directors, researchers, fund-raisers, strategists, webmasters, direct mail specialists, and other experts in current campaign techniques. Some activists are attracted to party work by the chance of landing these jobs, but in general, patronage, so important in attracting party workers in years past, is now a less important force in motivating activists.

Elected Office   Some women and men become party activists because they see party work as a first step toward running for office. This has been the case for a long time; about 40 percent of the county chairs interviewed in a 1979–1980 national survey hoped to hold public office, and an earlier study found that one-third of all state party chairs became candidates for elective office after serving the party.[5] Few party organizations, of course, can simply "give" nominations to public office to loyal party activists. That level of party organizational control over primary elections is rare. It is far more common for candidates to see the party as one of the bases of support for election or reelection and, in some areas, as the most important one. Candidates need advice, know-how, people (staff and volunteers), and money, and the party remains a likely source of all of these. So the lure of party support in a later campaign for elected office may bring some people into party work.

Preferments   Party activity can bring tangible rewards for some people, other than elective or appointive office. Because public officials can use at least some discretion in distributing government services and in granting government contracts, there is the potential for political favoritism. Many people become involved in party activity and in making contributions to their party in the hope of attracting these favors. A big giver might, for example, be hoping to win a government contract to build a new school or library. It is no accident that leaders of the construction industry are so active politically in states and localities that spend millions every year on roads and public buildings.

Preference may take other forms as well. Potential activists may hope for special treatment such as tolerant inspection of their restaurant by the health department, faster than usual snow removal in front of their place of business, or admission to a crowded state university. It may also involve the granting of scarce opportunities, such as liquor licenses, cable television franchises, or the calculated "overlooking" of drug trafficking, in return for some form of political support.

Reformers have promoted a number of safeguards over the years to limit the discretion available to governments in giving out benefits and buying goods and services from private firms. Examples are competitive and sealed bidding, conflict of interest statutes, and even affirmative action. Yet, because the potential benefits are so great for both sides, there always seem to be ways of evading even the tightest controls. There is understandable resistance, in the name of both democracy and efficiency, to sacrificing *all* discretion in order to eliminate *political* discretion. The result is that preferments may have taken the place of patronage as the main material incentive for political activity. Unfortunately for party leaders, however, it is elected officials who grant the preferments, not the party leaders themselves.

Solidary (Social) Incentives

Other motivations for party activity are not as easy to measure as a government job or the awarding of a contract. Many people are drawn to party work by the social contact that it provides. In an age when some people's closest relationship is with their computer or their television, the face-to-face contact found at a party headquarters or caucus provides a chance to meet like-minded people and feel a part of an active group. Family traditions may lead some young adults to go to party activities looking for social life, just as others may look to a softball league or a church group. The chance to meet local officials whose photos appear in the newspaper may be a draw. For whatever reason, researchers find that a large number of party activists cite the social life of party politics as a valuable reward.[6] This is especially true for those who involve themselves in campaign activities; those who confine their party activism to writing checks, of course, are not likely to get much social benefit.

These social contacts may produce other rewards as well. Networking has become a standard means of looking for a job and searching for new business. Young lawyers may find potential clients among the activists and elected officials they meet in the party organization. Real estate agents can learn about prospective home sellers and buyers in party activities. More generally, involvement in a party can help people feel a part of something larger than themselves—a charismatic leader, an important movement, a moment in history. The party can be a small island of excitement in a sea of routine.

Purposive (Issue-Based) Incentives

To an increasing extent, people are led to party activism by their commitment to particular issues or attitudes about the proper role of government. Someone dedicated to abortion rights, for example, might begin by working for a prochoice Democratic candidate and then come to see the candidate's party as a vehicle for protecting abortion rights in Congress. A property rights activist may be attracted to the Republican Party by its statements about the value of limited government.

Other groups compete for the attention of these activists; the abortion rights supporter, for instance, could also work effectively through organized interests, such as NARAL Pro-Choice America and Planned Parenthood. But the parties hold enough attraction for issue-oriented activists that in recent years, most of those who volunteer for party work seem to be motivated by a desire to use the party as a means to achieve policy goals.[7] Although we do not have comparable data on earlier periods, there is reason to believe that this was far less true of party workers a generation or two ago.[8] The energy and passion in party organizations come increasingly from issue-driven activists—those on the right in the Republican Party and those on the left for the Democrats.

A large proportion of these issue-based activists are convinced that their activity has made a difference; in a massive survey conducted in 1990, three-quarters of those who reported that they had volunteered in a campaign believed that their involvement had affected at least some votes.[9] So even though it might seem irrational to spend a lot of time on party activity in support of an issue that could be termed a "collective good"—one that, if achieved, will benefit the whole society rather than just the activists who worked hard to achieve it—large numbers of people become active in a party to do just that. Others become party activists out of a more general sense of civic obligation or a belief that citizen participation is essential in a democracy.

Issue-based party activism has played a vital role in shaping politics at the national level. The victories of Ronald Reagan in the 1980s owed a lot to the efforts of Christian fundamentalists in the Republican Party, who backed Reagan in order to legalize school prayer, end legal abortion and pornography, and overturn gay rights laws. Many conservative Christian groups have worked for George W. Bush's reelection for the same reasons. As these examples show, it is often the force of an attractive leader that brings ideologically motivated activists into a party. Even without a charismatic leader, some issues and ideological movements have had sufficient power to motivate activists, even to the extent of causing them to switch parties. The abortion and race issues, for example, induced many formerly Democratic prolifers and southern conservatives to join the Republican Party beginning in the 1970s, and they soon cemented a set of favored issue positions into the platform of their new party.[10]

Mixed Incentives

Most party organizations rely on a variety of incentives. Activists who hope for a political job or some other preferment work together with those motivated by a particular issue and with those who come to party activities for social contact. That can produce conflict among party volunteers who are motivated by different incentives. Someone who became a Democratic activist to work for abortion rights, for instance, is not likely to be satisfied with a party that supports a prolifer running on the Democratic label. Others who have become active in the party for social reasons may feel that the party ought to be a "big tent," including people who differ in their attitudes toward abortion.

The incentive that recruits people to party work, of course, may not be the incentive that keeps them there. Several studies suggest that activists who come to the party to fulfill purposive goals—to fight for certain issues—are more likely to remain in the party if they come to value the social contact they get from party activism. The motive that sustains their party work, in short, tends to shift to solidary incentives: friendships, identification with the party itself, and other social rewards[11] (see "A Day in the Life," page 89). It may be that committed issue activists simply burn out or that the pragmatic American parties, in their effort to remain flexible enough to win elections, cannot provide the level of ideological dedication needed to sustain party workers whose political lives revolve around a set of uncompromising ideals.

Professionals and Amateurs

Drawing on research on these incentives for party work, scholars have classified party activists into two types, based on the role that they play in the organization and the expectations that they have for it. One type of party activist is the ***professional***—the party worker whose first loyalty is to the party itself and whose operating style is pragmatic. These are the party "regulars" who support their party in good times and bad, when it nominates candidates whom they approve of and even when it doesn't. A very different type is the ***amateur***—the issue-oriented purist, motivated by purposive incentives who sees party activity as only one means of achieving important political goals.[12] (On the differences between these two types, see Table 5.1).

A party organization populated by amateurs will probably behave very differently from a party dominated by professionals. Above all, amateur activists are drawn into the party in order to further some issues or principles; for them, the issue is the goal and the party is the means of achieving it. If the party, or its candidates, pulls back on its commitment to their issue, they may pull back on their commitment to the party. So they tend to be less willing to make compromises in their positions in order to win elections. (An example of this is the real-life amateur activism of Martin Sheen, star of television's "The West Wing"; see the box on page 91.) Further, amateur activists are likely to insist on an active, participatory role within the party organization in order to put their issue concerns at the top of the party's agenda. When they come to lead party organizations, they often

A DAY IN THE LIFE

A NONTRADITIONAL REPUBLICAN ACTIVIST

"I always abhorred party politics," says Robin Vuke. "I thought it was a nasty business. It's unfortunate that we have to be involved in it." Yet Vuke, an African-American woman who graduated from college in 1990, became a Republican activist. How did it happen?

David Duke, a former Ku Klux Klan leader and friend of the American Nazi Party, had campaigned successfully for a Louisiana state legislative seat in 1989. The following year, he filed as a Republican to run for the U.S. Senate seat of Democrat J. Bennett Johnston. To the embarrassment of Republican leaders, Duke became the leading Republican candidate in the race, and until very close to the election, it appeared that he would force Johnston into a runoff in Louisiana's unusual "blanket primary" (see Chapter 9). "David Duke really scared me," Vuke states. "It was frightening that someone like that could get that far. Everyone has the right to run, but winning state office gives someone a lot of power, and to come that close to a U.S. Senate seat. . . . "

"My parents weren't involved in party politics. But my interest in politics was triggered in elementary school. We had a mock presidential election; they brought in a voting machine, we waited till the end of the day to get the results and that experience stuck with me! Then my government teacher in high school really opened my eyes to politics and the analysis of governments. I always saw myself as a behind-the-scenes person. But after Duke's campaign, I felt it was time for me to get involved. I felt there has to be a point where I can affect someone and show that there are good, rational people in the Republican Party who are willing to listen."

Vuke began, in short, as an activist who would be called an "amateur"; her concerns revolved around issues and principles, rather than the promotion of the party itself. She is prochoice, very concerned about environmental issues—"values that sometimes run counter to traditional Republican beliefs."

Why, then, is she a Republican? "I believe in fiscal responsibility," she says. "I think it's our responsibility as African-Americans to take control of our futures. But that has to be balanced with other commitments I have: to a clean environment, to make sure no one goes without." Vuke's local Republican organization is located in a college town. Do you think she would have felt less comfortable in a Republican local party in Dallas or in rural Wyoming?

As often happens with issue-oriented activists, Vuke has remained in the party for social reasons. "Specific issues come and go," she says. "But now it's really the people who help with the party who keep me here. I don't always agree with everybody in the party. In fact, I found it embarrassing to see the beliefs of the Religious Right gain so much power in the party; I'd like to see us move away from that. I'm in the 'liberal leg' of the party. That can make for a lot of pressure. You can't do anything without criticism. But I wouldn't want to walk away from the party; there are a lot of good people involved, and I want to support them."

bring a strong push for reform in both the party's internal business and in the larger political system.

For professionals or pragmatists, on the other hand, the goal is the success of the party in elections; issue positions and candidates are the means of achieving that goal. If

TABLE 5.1 Comparing Professionals and Amateurs

	Professionals	Amateurs
Political style	Pragmatic	Purist
What do they want?	Material rewards (patronage, preferments)	Purposive rewards (issues, ideology)
Their loyalty is to:	Party organization	Officeholders, other political groups
They want the party to focus on:	Candidates, elections	Issues, ideology
The party should choose candidates on the basis of:	Their electability	Their principles
The style of party governance should be:	Hierarchical	Democratic
Their support of party candidates is:	Automatic	Conditional on candidates' principles
They were recruited into politics through:	Party work	Issue or candidate organizations
Their SES level is:	Average to above average	Well above average

they believe that their party is most likely to win by downplaying an issue, moderating a position, or nominating a candidate who is popular, but not in lockstep with their views on major issues, then that is the course they are likely to favor. Party leaders, then, must find a balance between the demands of the growing numbers of issue-oriented, purist activists and those of their more pragmatic colleagues. It is a common problem in modern society: whether to remain loyal to the group (or the nation) in order to keep it strong and vibrant or to give priority to the principles for which the group was formed.

There is some evidence, however, that these differences in attitudes between amateurs and professionals do not always show up clearly in their behavior. In a study of delegates to state nominating conventions, amateurs were just as likely as professionals to support candidates who seemed electable rather than those whose ideology they shared.[13] Among county party chairs in 1972, a time when amateurs were thought to hold the upper hand, at least in the Democratic Party, the amateurs did not differ from professionals in their effort to communicate within the party, maintain party morale, or run effective campaigns.[14] In current politics, the lines between the two groups have been blurred in that the national parties are hiring more strategists and consultants who are dedicated not just to winning races but to a set of principles as well.

HOW DO PARTIES RECRUIT ACTIVISTS?

Like almost all other volunteer groups, party organizations have had an increasingly difficult time attracting willing volunteers. Except at the national level and in some states where there has been an increase in paid positions and exciting professional opportunities, parties often have few effective means of enlisting new activists. To add to the challenge, state laws often take at least part of the recruitment process out of the party's hands. Rules requiring open party caucuses and the election of party officials in primaries limit the party's control over its personnel. This can lead to the takeover of a local (or even a state) party organization by an intense group of issue activists. At the least, it

MARTIN SHEEN: "AMATEUR" DEMOCRATIC ACTIVIST

Martin Sheen is a liberal Democrat who plays one on television. The actor, who stars as President Josiah Bartlet on NBC's award-winning series "The West Wing," first became involved in political activism in the early 1980s when he rejoined the Catholic Church and became committed to the work of peace activists and priests Philip and Daniel Berrigan. Since that time he has taken part in numerous demonstrations for social justice, including a prayer vigil to protest the war in Iraq in 2003.

His support for environmental protection and gun control, among other issues, has led him to endorse and work for some Democratic candidates. Sheen campaigned for Democratic presidential candidate Al Gore in 2000 and filmed a television ad criticizing candidate George W. Bush's gun control record in Texas; in a media appearance he termed Bush a "moron."

Sheen's political activities are driven primarily by his commitment to particular issues, not to individual candidates or to the Democratic Party as a whole. "I don't have a personal interest in politics per se," he says. "I have a great interest in the issues that are publicly debated, but I have a far greater interest in social justice and peace."

His commitment is intense enough that Sheen has been arrested for civil disobedience 64 times at peace and social justice demonstrations. In fact, the future of "The West Wing" depends in part on Sheen's political activity; on probation for a previous arrest, he would risk a prison sentence if he were to be arrested again.

Just as Sheen fits the definition of a political "amateur," Robert Strauss is the consummate party "professional." A former Democratic National Committee chair, Strauss has supported both conservative southerners and liberal Democrats. In the 2000 Democratic presidential primaries, he supported Al Gore for the nomination, but he also donated money to the primary campaign of Gore's rival, Bill Bradley. Why? For Strauss, the important point is the success of the party rather than any specific candidate or issue.

Sources: Jacqueline Cutler, "Martin Sheen—Acting President and Tireless Activist," *Television,* December 14, 2002, p. 2; "That's Entertainment," Feb. 3, 2001; Susan Feeney, "Texans Making Dual Donations in Presidential Race," *Dallas Morning News,* Aug. 22, 1999, p. 1.

leaves a party vulnerable to shifts in its direction as some leaders and activists move on and new, self-recruited leaders take their places.

Finding Volunteers: Is Anybody Home?

In a much discussed set of writings, political scientist Robert Putnam has shown that there has been a drop in participation in community activities in recent years. Party organizations are not alone in having to search for volunteers; groups ranging from churches to bowling leagues have been starved for participants. Fewer people are involving themselves in the face-to-face activities of politics—attending a political speech or a community meeting—but the lonely activities of check writing and Internet surfing are on the increase. Many culprits have been identified, from the numbers of hours Americans spend watching television to the increasing numbers of dual-career families. The consequences, Putnam argues, are profound: a reduction in the "social capital"—the social connections, values, and trust that enable communities to solve their problems more easily.[15]

The lack of participation in party organizations has been carefully documented. One well-designed survey found in the 1990s that only 8 percent of its national sample reported working on a campaign and just 5 percent said they were involved in a party organization, among the smallest percentages reporting activity in any type of civic organization. Much larger percentages of people say that they take part in charitable groups, sports, and business and professional groups.[16] Similarly grim conclusions come from the American National Election Studies, in which, in each year since 1994, only 5 percent reported going to any political meetings and only 3 percent said they worked for a party or a candidate in 2000.[17] Granted, that is still a lot of people; 3 percent of the adult population would be about 6 million party and campaign activists. But although some of these activists spend a considerable amount of time on political work, mainly at the local level, many others are "checkbook participants" who mail in their contributions but do not volunteer their time and energy.

Party organizations have a constant need for activists of any kind, so at a time when volunteers are in short supply, the parties are very likely to accept whatever help is available. The nature of that help often varies from one political period to another, depending on the events in the larger political world at that time. The nature and direction of the Democratic Party were heavily influenced by the influx of liberals activated by the Vietnam War and the civil rights movement in the 1960s and 1970s. Tax revolts in the 1980s and efforts to limit the number of terms that incumbents could serve brought new blood into state and local Republican Parties. Because this recruitment process often depends on the presence of magnetic personalities and powerful issues, it tends to take place in spurts rather than continuously. It produces generational differences among party activists in which political outlooks may differ considerably, depending on the time at which individuals became active.[18]

The nature of the parties' recruitment system, then, is pretty informal and haphazard, yet it has major impact on the parties' ability to achieve their goals. A local Democratic Party whose activists come largely from labor unions will have different concerns and styles from a local Democratic Party dominated by environmental activists, and a Republican organization run by local business leaders can differ from one dominated by the Religious Right. Depending on the nature of the community that these parties are trying to persuade, these local parties may have different levels of success in elections as well.

Means, Motive, and Opportunity

We have seen that there are several incentives for people to become active in a party, but relatively few people do. What influences an individual's decision to try to meet his or her needs through involvement in party politics? Three sets of factors are most important. They include whether the individual has the resources to take part, the attitudes that support involvement, and whether anybody has asked him or her to do so.[19]

The resources—the means—needed to become a party activist include time, money, and civic skills. It takes free time to help plan a party's activities, canvass or call people, or attend other party events. People need money if they plan to make contributions to the party organization or its candidates, and they may need funds as well to get to party conventions and other events. Their educational levels help to determine how much money and time they have available.

Their attitudes toward politics are also important. People are more likely to take part if they are interested in what happens in campaigns and concerned about the workings of government, if they have a feeling of attachment to a party, and if they believe that their involvement could make a difference. Most of these attitudes are related to one's income and education levels and thus add to their impact.

The third important characteristic is quite simple: has anybody asked them? The parties now have a whole arsenal of tools to contact potential activists: e-mail, regular mail, telemarketing, and in-person canvassing. However, most appeals to take part in campaign work—and especially most *successful* appeals—come from friends or other people known to the potential activist. Over the years, most activists have reported that they first became involved with the party as a result of these informal, personal requests for help.[20] Being asked to participate is a powerful motivator; in the 1990 study, almost half of those who were asked to do campaign work said yes. Most people are never asked; only about 12 percent of the respondents in that study reported that anyone had asked them to work on a campaign.[21] That helps to explain why the proportion of party activists is relatively small.

WHAT KINDS OF PEOPLE BECOME PARTY ACTIVISTS?

These various incentives and recruitment processes come together to produce the party activists—the men and women who do the work of the parties. These activists play a wide range of roles in party affairs, from campaigning on behalf of party candidates and serving as delegates to party nominating conventions to answering phones and e-mail at party offices. Who are they? How representative are they of the rest of the American population? How do they affect the parties that they serve?

People from "Political Families"

Although they differ in motivations, American party activists have several characteristics in common that set them apart from the general population. First, they often come from families with a history of party activity. Study after study indicates that many party activists had an adult party activist in their immediate family as they were growing up. Think of the case of George W. Bush. His grandfather was a long-time Republican state and national party official and U.S. senator from Connecticut. His dad, a former Republican National Committee chair, had served his party in many other posts as well before becoming president. Some of his siblings have been involved in Republican politics, including his brother Jeb, who served in the cabinet of a Republican governor and then won the governorship of Florida himself. His nephew, George P. Bush, was youth chair of the Republican National Convention in 2000. With such a background, politics becomes the family business.

Better Educated and Wealthier than Average

A second distinctive characteristic of party activists is that they tend to have higher incomes, more years of formal education, and higher status occupations than does the average American.[22] People with incomes over $75,000 are four times more likely to do campaign work as are people whose income is at or below the poverty line. Some types of higher income occupations are especially well represented among party activists: lawyers, for example. As would be expected, this gap between wealthy and poor is even greater among those who contribute money to the parties.[23]

This tendency for party activists to be better educated and wealthier than the average citizen may seem perfectly natural; people with more money and higher education are more likely have the means to participate in politics, the interest in political affairs, and the expectation that they would be successful at it. So we might expect this pattern to hold in other democratic nations as well. But that is not the case. Most other democracies have a viable socialist party that recruits many of its activists from the ranks of organized labor. That tends to dampen the relationship between party activism and higher education and wealth.

In fact, it was not always true of American politics either. The urban political machines tended to recruit party workers and leaders who were more representative of the populations with which they worked. For many lower status Americans, the jobs and favors the machines could provide were probably the crucial reasons for their activism. When patronage and other material incentives dwindled, the social character of these parties changed. A comparison of county committee members from both Pittsburgh parties in 1971, 1976, and 1983 shows that, as machine control declined, the education levels of party workers increased.[24] So as issue-based incentives become more common in the American parties, the educational and income differences between party activists and the average citizen tend to grow.

The social characteristics of Democratic activists differ from those of Republicans, just as the social bases of the parties' voters do. Democratic activists are more likely than their Republican counterparts to be black, union members, or Catholic. But differences in education, income, and occupation between the parties' activists have declined in recent years. Although they may come from different backgrounds and certainly hold different political views, the leaders of both parties are drawn especially from the higher status groups in American society—even more now than in decades past.[25] As a result, it is even more true in the United States than in many other nations that party activism and other forms of active political participation amplify the voices of privileged groups.

Different Agendas

In addition to these differences in income, education, and family background, party activists also tend to differ from other Americans in the types of issues that concern them the most. When one group of researchers asked campaign workers what issues had led to their activism, at the top of their lists were questions of education, abortion, human needs (including Social Security and Medicare, jobs, health care, and housing), and the economy. Almost one in five mentioned abortion, a larger proportion than is usually found in polls of citizens as a whole, and one in four mentioned education. International issues were close to the bottom of the list, as were such social issues as pornography, school prayer, gay rights, and environmental protection.[26]

The activists' issue agendas varied according to their income and education. Higher income activists expressed greater concern about abortion and the environment, whereas lower income activists' involvement is more likely to have been motivated by a concern about basic human needs.[27] To the extent that higher income activists are better represented in the parties, issues such as abortion may get more attention in party activities than such issues as welfare and health care, at least in recent years.

The types of issues that most clearly divide Democratic from Republican activists have changed over time. In the early 1970s, one of the primary distinctions between the two major parties' activists was the question of social welfare—how much of a role government should have in issues such as welfare and other social services. At that time, there was much greater overlap between the two parties' activists on the abortion issue. Today, in contrast, there are few issues that more clearly divide Democratic from Republican activists than their views on abortion.[28]

More Extreme Views

Most significantly, party activists (and people who take active roles in other areas of politics as well) tend to hold more extreme views on issues than does the average American. In recent decades, there has been a tendency for liberals to become more active as Democrats and for conservatives to dominate activity within the Republican Party.[29] This has been true of Democrats and Republicans in Congress, too, as we will see in Chapter 13.

Fitting all these findings together creates a complicated picture of party activists. The major parties attract men and women with the time and financial resources to afford political activity, the attitudes that make politics a priority to them, and the connections with others who are similarly engaged. These activists also tend to be brought into party activity by controversial issues, and are more polarized by party than was the case in the mid-1900s. These findings raise an important question. If the parties' volunteers differ from the average American in their income levels, their concern about the issues of current politics, and the intensity and extremism of their views, then how well can they connect their interests and their issue stands with those of the public whom they hope to persuade?

PARTY ACTIVISTS AND DEMOCRACY

By learning what kinds of people become active in party organizations, and why they decide to spend their time in party work rather than in other types of activities, we can learn more about the nature of the party organizations and about American politics more generally. This chapter concludes with three major questions about these findings. Does it matter if party activists are not very representative of adult Americans as a whole? What effects will the increase in issue-oriented, "amateur" activists have on the party organizations? How do the characteristics of Republican and Democratic activists affect party organizational strength?

The Problem of Representation

We have seen that relative to many other democratic nations, there is a greater difference between American party activists and other citizens in their income and education levels. Other qualities seem to widen the gulf between party activists and the people whom they aim to represent. Activists are more concerned with some types of issues—abortion is a good example—than are most nonactivists, and they are often more extreme in their issue positions than are other people who identify with their party. The Democratic Party is led by office holders, party officials, and volunteers who are typically more liberal than the average Democrat, and the leaders and activists of the Republican Party tend to be more conservative than other Republican identifiers.

If party activists do not seem to share the concerns of other citizens, then it is not surprising that many Americans think of the party organizations as alien places. When those most involved in party activities give the appearance of being "true believers" on contentious issues, that might further drive away average citizens. There is a delicate balance to be achieved in party politics. When the two parties sound too much alike on issues, citizens may not feel that they have clear choices in politics. Democracy can be well served when the major parties take clear and distinctive stands on major policy questions. However, when the debates between Republican and Democratic activists focus on questions that are not central to most Americans' daily lives, then the parties expose themselves to public distrust, an old problem in American politics.

Amateurs and Pressure for Internal Party Democracy

Another important influence on the party organizations is the increase in the proportion of amateur activists. These activists tend to be not just issue oriented but also concerned with internal party democracy; in the past four decades, they have come to demand a much louder voice in the party's organization and activity, and their demands have been heeded. Party leaders depend on activists for many things. So party leaders at various levels work hard to mobilize support within their own organizations and to tolerate at least some degree of internal party democracy in order to retain their volunteers' loyalty.

It could be argued that their success in making the parties—and especially the Democratic Party—more participatory has weakened the discipline of the party organization. Much of the discipline in the classic party machine resulted from the willingness and ability of party leaders to give or withhold material rewards. A disobedient or inefficient party worker sacrificed a patronage job or the hope of one. The newer incentives cannot be given or taken away so easily. A local Republican organization is not likely to punish an errant, ideologically motivated activist by ending the party's support of school prayer. Even if it did, the activist could find many other organizations that may be more effective at pursuing that goal, such as religious lobbies or other organized interests.

On the other hand, a party organization dominated by amateur activists could be strengthened by its commitment to internal democracy. Rank-and-file activists who are contributing their time and effort in the service of a strongly held principle and who feel sure that their views are taken seriously by party leaders may be even more likely to work hard on the party's behalf. Granted, it is easier to imagine a strong and disciplined party organization when it is composed of party professionals who are dedicated to the party's success above all else. But the growing importance of issue-based motives for party activism does not necessarily mean a threat to strong party organizations.

Activists and Party Strength

Strong party organizations, however, have often been considered a threat to American politics. Since the beginning, American political culture has been dominated by a fear that a few people, responsible to no one but themselves, will control the selection of public officials and set the agendas of policy making in "smoke-filled rooms." The result has been a series of efforts to keep the parties from playing too powerful a role in the lives of candidates, elected officials, and voters.

Several characteristics of party activists help to keep the parties decentralized and limited in power. The shortage of volunteers means that party organizations have to pay attention to their activists' concerns; that prevents a centralization of party power (unless, of course, the party activists push for such a centralization, as they sometimes have). The concern of many activists for internally democratic parties also restrains the authority of party leaders at the top. And, in turn, because power in the American parties is diffused through the various levels of party organization, precinct committee members, city leaders, county officials, and activists at all levels are free to define their own political roles and nourish their separate bases of party power.

The traditional worry about the excesses of party power, then, is probably misplaced. There have been few occasions in American history when the parties have been able to corral the kinds of incentives and resources that they would need in order to flesh out the party organization that they would like or that the state laws detail. The thousands of inactive precinct workers and unfilled precinct positions testify to that. The parties have had no alternative but to try to recruit activists who vary in their backgrounds, styles, and motives, with all the challenges and limits that involves. The parties are, after all, the products of their people.

PART THREE

The Political Party in the Electorate

If there were a Pollsters' Hall of Fame, surely the first question in it would be: Generally speaking, do you usually think of yourself as a Republican, a Democrat, an independent, or what? The question is meant to classify *party identifiers*—people who feel a sense of psychological attachment to a particular party. If you respond that you do usually think of yourself as a Democrat or a Republican, then you are categorized as belonging to the *party in the electorate*—the second major sector of the American parties. These party identifiers make up the core of the party's support: the people who normally vote for a party's candidates and who are inclined to see politics through a partisan's eyes. They are more apt to vote in their party's primary elections and to volunteer for party candidates than are other citizens. They are, in short, the party organization's, and its candidates', closest friends in the public.

Survey researchers have measured Americans' party loyalty since the 1940s. The dominant measure, cited above, has been used in polls conducted by the University of Michigan, now under the auspices of the American National Election Studies (ANES). After asking whether you consider yourself a Republican or a Democrat, the question continues:

[If Republican or Democrat] Would you call yourself a strong [Republican or Democrat] or a not very strong [Republican or Democrat]? [If independent, no preference, or other party] Do you think of yourself as closer to the Republican Party or to the Democratic Party?

Using these answers, researchers classify people into seven different categories of party identification: strong party identifiers (Democrats or Republicans), weak identifiers (Democrats or Republicans), independent "leaners" (toward the Democrats or Republicans), and pure independents.[1]

Note that this definition is not based on people's actual voting behavior. Strong party identifiers usually vote for their party's candidates, but the essence of a party identification is an attachment to the idea of the party itself, distinct from feelings about any particular candidates. Someone can remain a committed Republican, for example, even while choosing to vote for the Democratic candidate in a specific race. Given the large number of elective offices in the United States and the value American culture places on

99

independence, we can often find party identifiers who vote for a candidate or two, or more, of the other party. In the same sense, we do not define the party electorate in terms of the official act of registering with a party. Almost half of the states do not have party registration, and in states that do, some voters change their party attachments without bothering to change their official registration.[2]

The party electorate's relationship with the other two party sectors, the party organization and the party in government, can be both slippery and frustrating. Clearly, the party cannot survive without the party identifiers' support. Party organizations and candidates, however, see their identifiers as a group of customers to be courted at each election but largely ignored between elections. Party identifiers, in turn, seldom feel any obligation to the party organization other than to vote for its candidates, if they choose. Party identifiers are not party "members" in any real sense. In these ways, the American parties resemble cadre parties: top-heavy in leaders and activists without any real membership, in contrast to the mass-membership parties that have been such an important part of the European democratic experience.

Despite their independence, party identifiers give the party organization and its candidates a continuing core of voter support. The parties do not, in other words, have to start from scratch in every campaign. The party in the electorate also largely determines who the party's nominees for office will be by voting in primaries. It is a reservoir of potential activists for the organization. Its members may donate money to the party or they may work in a specific campaign. They help keep the party alive by transmitting party loyalties to their children. The loyalty that links these groups and individuals to their party can be strong enough to act as a filter through which people see and evaluate candidates and issues. It can structure an individual's mental map of the political world.

A party in the electorate is not just a group of individuals; it is a coalition of social groups. Our images of the two parties often spring from the types of people the parties have attracted as identifiers. When people speak of the Democrats as the party of the disadvantaged, or of the Republicans as the party of business, they are probably referring, at least in part, to the party in the electorate. The interplay between a party's supporters and its appeals (its candidates, issues, and traditions)—each one shaping and reinforcing the other—comes very close to determining what the parties are.

The three chapters in Part 3 explore the nature and importance of these parties in the electorate. Chapter 6 looks at the development of party identification and its impact on individuals' political behavior. Chapter 7 examines the parties as coalitions of social groups and traces the changes in those coalitions over time and the meaning of the changes. Chapter 8 focuses on the differences between the people who vote and those who do not. These differences have an important effect on the parties' choices in mobilizing their faithful and recruiting new supporters.

CHAPTER 6

Party Identification

Think back to your years in elementary school. If you are like millions of other Americans, by the time you completed sixth grade, you had begun to identify yourself as a Democrat, a Republican, or an independent. What led you to develop at least a minimal sense of attachment to a party (or to reject party labels)? Do you still identify with the same party? What difference does it make? How does the existence of party identification affect the lives of the political parties and the nature of American politics?

A party identification is a useful shortcut for voters. Politics is complicated, even for political junkies who pay close attention to the news. Americans cope with more elections, and therefore more occasions on which they need to make large numbers of political choices, than do citizens of any other democracy. On any given day, three levels of legislatures—national, state, and local—may be passing laws that affect our lives. It is hard enough for reporters and political activists to keep track of all the action. The challenge is so much greater for other citizens who spend less time thinking about politics (even though their lives are just as greatly affected by political decisions).

To help them cope with all this complexity, most Americans develop an *identification*, or sense of psychological attachment, to a political party.[1] More than 30 percent of Americans call themselves "strong" partisans, and another 25 percent express some party attachment, though not a strong one. Even among those who at first claim to be independents, more than two-thirds confess to some partisan feeling. This party identification, or party ID, serves as a framework through which individuals can see political events. It gives the individual a predisposition to support Democratic candidates or Republican candidates without having to do all the research necessary to make a separate decision on each candidate for office or to develop an opinion on each bill the legislature considers.

Partisanship can be measured in various ways.[2] However we measure it, people's party ID tells us more about their political perceptions and behavior than does any other single piece of information. A party ID will probably be the individual's most enduring political attachment. For that reason, it often acts as a kind of stabilizer, protecting political outlooks against the buffeting of short-term influences. Where do these party identifications come from?

HOW PEOPLE DEVELOP PARTY IDENTIFICATIONS

Families are the most common source of our first party ID, as they are of so much else in our early lives. People often say that they are Democrats or Republicans because they were brought up that way, just as they may have been raised as a Methodist or a Jew. As children become aware of politics, they absorb their family's judgments about political parties and typically come to think of themselves as sharing their family's partisanship.

Childhood Influences

Party loyalty often develops as early as the elementary grades. Although they do not usually consciously indoctrinate their children into party loyalty, parents are the primary teachers of political orientations in the American culture (see the cartoon on page 103). Their casual conversations and references to political events are enough to convey their party loyalties to their children. These influences can be powerful enough to last into adulthood, even at times when young adults are pulled toward independence.

This early party ID usually takes hold before children have much information as to what the parties stand for. It is not until the middle-school and high-school years that students begin to associate the parties with general economic interests—with business or labor, the rich or the poor—and thus to have some reasoning to support the party ID that they have already developed. Note the importance of the sequence here. Party loyalty comes first, so it tends to have a long-lasting impact on attitudes toward politics. Only later do people learn about political issues and events, which will then be filtered, at least in part, through a partisan lens.[3]

Once developed, people's party loyalties are often sustained because their friends, relatives, and co-workers typically share the same partisanship.[4] Some people do leave the party of their parents. Those whose early party loyalty is weak are more likely to change. So are people whose mother and father identified with different parties or who live in a community or work in a setting where the prevailing party influences differ from their own. But when parents share the same party ID, they are more likely to produce strong party identifiers among their children.

Other sources of political learning tend to support a person's inherited party loyalty or at least do not challenge the family's influence. Schools typically avoid partisan politics; they are probably more inclined to teach political independence than partisanship. During most of the 1900s, American churches usually steered clear of partisan conflict even at a time when church-connected political parties existed in Europe. Churches and other religious groups have clearly entered the political fray in recent years, but they are not likely to lead young people away from their parents' partisan influence. The American parties themselves do very little direct socialization; they do not maintain the youth clubs, the social or recreational activities, or the occupational groups that some European parties do.

Influences in Adulthood

These influences on children's and teenagers' political learning are more likely to be challenged beginning in young adulthood, when an individual moves into any of several new environments: college, work, marriage, a new community, and the unexpected honor of paying taxes. At this point in the life cycle, adults can test their childhood party loyalties against their own personal experience with politics. They can see how their favored party

THE FAITHFUL REPUBLICANS

performs in matters that concern them, and they can watch the behavior of the other party as well. Their adult experiences may reassure them that their early-learned loyalties are the right ones for them or may undermine those loyalties.[5]

The longer that people hold a particular party ID, the more intense it tends to become. Older adults are most likely to hold strong party attachments and least likely to change them. Perhaps party ID is more likely to become a habit after decades of political observations and activity. Partisanship may grow stronger across the life cycle because it is so useful a shortcut for simplifying the political decision making of older voters.[6]

There are times, however, when even committed Democrats and Republicans are driven to change their partisanship. During realigning periods, when the issue bases of partisanship and the party coalitions themselves are being transformed, some voters desert the partisan tradition of their parents. (We look more fully at the idea of realignment in the next chapter.) This happened during the New Deal realignment of the 1930s, and we can find more recent examples of the power of major issues to change some people's partisanship. The Bush tax cuts, debate on an abortion bill, and even a local struggle over development can make someone aware that she no longer feels close to the party of her parents. Older adults may be caught up in the excitement of the moment as well, but their partisanship, typically reinforced by years of consistent partisan behavior, resists change much more effectively. So when partisan turmoil begins, young adults are more likely than older adults to embrace the change.[7]

PATTERNS OF PARTISANSHIP OVER TIME

Large-scale change in party identifications is the exception, however, and not the rule. Most Americans, once they have developed party loyalties, tend to keep them; partisanship becomes a fairly stable anchor in an ever-changing political world. People who do change their party ID normally change only its intensity (for example, from strong to weak identification) rather than convert to the other party.

At the national level, we can see this stability in Americans' responses to the poll question measuring party ID that has been asked since 1952 by researchers for the American National Election Studies (see Table 6.1).[8] The percentage of respondents in each category of partisanship has not changed much from one election year to the next; the biggest change is 7 percent, and the usual difference is just 2 percent. Look, for example, at the percentage in Table 6.1 who call themselves strong Republicans. Over almost 50 years of history, from years when the Republican Party was triumphant to years when it seemed almost dead, the proportion of strong Republicans has stayed within a 7 percentage–point range, never less than 9 nor more than 16 percent of those surveyed.

There is one possible exception to this story of stable partisanship, and it appears at both the national and individual levels. During an especially turbulent period in recent history—in 1972, 1974, and 1976, a time that included Richard Nixon's landslide reelection as president, the Watergate scandals that caused Nixon's resignation, Nixon's subsequent pardon by President Ford, and Ford's own 1976 defeat—researchers interviewed the same set of individuals in three successive surveys. Almost two-thirds of the respondents remained in the same broad category of party identification (44 percent were stable strong/weak Democrats or Republicans, 20 percent stable independents) throughout all three surveys. Only 3 percent actually changed parties.[9] People were more likely to alter their evaluations of prominent politicians and issues than their party ID. Many researchers felt that it would be hard to find better evidence of the stability of party identification than its consistency during these agitated times.[10]

Yet a third of the respondents did change from party identification to independence during these three waves of surveys. In particular (as you can see in Figure 6.1), at the national level, there was a big drop in the proportion of respondents calling themselves *strong* partisans (Democrats or Republicans) at this time, and an increase in the percentage of independent "leaners." The three categories of independents grew from 28 percent of the respondents in 1964 to almost 40 percent in 1976. Combined with other events of that time—the political turmoil of the civil rights movement, the protests against American involvement in the Vietnam War, the women's movement, environmental activism—this suggested to a lot of observers that partisanship was fading in the United States.

Has There Been a Decline in Partisanship?

Research in other democracies bolstered the argument that such a decline in partisanship was occurring. Across the western industrialized world, analysts found a rise in

TABLE 6.1 Party Identification: 1952–2000

	1952	1956	1960	1964	1968	1972	1976	1980	1984	1988	1992	1996	2000
Strong Democrats	22%	21%	20%	27%	20%	15%	15%	18%	17%	17%	18%	18%	19%
Weak Democrats	25	23	25	25	25	26	25	23	20	18	18	19	15
Independents, closer to Democrats	10	6	6	9	10	11	12	11	11	12	14	14	15
Independents	6	9	10	8	11	13	15	13	11	11	12	9	12
Independents, closer to Republicans	7	8	7	6	9	10	10	10	12	13	12	12	13
Weak Republicans	14	14	14	14	15	13	14	14	15	14	14	15	12
Strong Republicans	14	15	16	11	10	10	9	9	12	14	11	12	12
Others	3	4	2	1	1	1	1	2	2	2	1	1	1
	101%	100%	100%	101%	101%	99%	101%	100%	100%	101%	100%	100%	99%
Cases	1,793	1,762	1,928	1,571	1,556	2,707	2,864	1,614	2,236	2,033	2,478	1,714	1,785

Note: Based on surveys of the national electorate conducted immediately before each presidential election in recent years as part of the American National Election Studies program at the University of Michigan. Due to rounding, percentages do not always add up to 100 percent.

Source: Data made available through the Inter-University Consortium for Political and Social Research at http://www.umich.edu/~nes/nesguide/toptable/tab2a_1.htm (accessed June 19, 2003).

the proportion of independents, a decline in confidence expressed in political parties, and an increase in ***split-ticket voting*** (supporting candidates of more than one party).[11] The consequences of this "party decline" would have been profound.[12] What caused it? Education levels were steadily increasing in democratic nations; perhaps the better educated voters had so much other information available that they didn't need parties as a decision shortcut any more. Maybe candidates were becoming more independent of party ties and influencing other citizens. Perhaps media coverage of politics stressed nonpartisanship or ignored parties.

These explanations produced even more questions, however. If Americans have more information available than ever before, wouldn't they need a device, like a party ID, to help them sift through it? Even though education levels are rising, one of the things we know with greatest certainty about public opinion is that most of us are not very interested in politics, do not know very much about it, and therefore depend on shortcuts with which to make sense of the voting decisions that face us. We may have a wealth of information, but most of us are not motivated to make use of it. Party ID, then, would probably remain a helpful tool.[13]

In fact, indicators of partisanship *have* rebounded since the 1970s. In particular, there has been a resurgence of strong partisanship (see Figure 6.1). The level of strong partisanship among voters in 2000 was not much different from what it had been in the 1950s, which was considered a very partisan time. At least among those who vote, the decline in

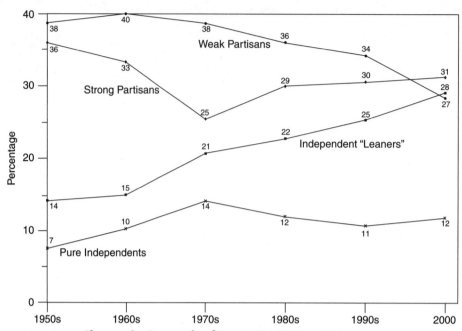

FIGURE 6.1   **Change in Strength of Party ID: 1950s–2000.**

Note: This is a "folded" party ID scale in which Democrats and Republicans in each category are combined (i.e., the category "Strong Partisans" includes strong Democrats and strong Republicans).

Source: Calculated from the full time-series of American National Election Studies data at http://www.umich.edu/~nes/nesguide/toptable/tab2a_1.htm (accessed June 22, 2003).

party ID has been largely reversed.[14] The main difference is a decrease in the proportion of weak partisans combined with a large increase in the numbers of independent "leaners," those who initially call themselves independents but then admit, when probed by poll takers, that they lean toward one party.

The relative strength of the two parties in the electorate has remained fairly constant in recent years. If we count independent leaners as independents, then about four in ten adults call themselves independent of party ties, and Democrats outnumber Republicans among the partisans. If we include the leaners among the party identified—and there is good reason to do so—then Democrats have hovered around 50 percent of the electorate and Republicans at a little less than 40 percent for most of this time, with occasional ups and downs in landslide election years. The Democratic edge has narrowed since the 1950s.

Perhaps the revival of party attachment in the 1990s was prompted by greater partisanship in Congress and by more partisan political leaders such as Ronald Reagan and former House Speaker Newt Gingrich. Perhaps partisanship is the normal state of affairs for most Americans, disrupted only temporarily by the ferment of the 1970s. Whatever the reason, party remains an influential political attachment. The evidence of party decline is no longer as convincing.

PARTY IDENTIFICATION AS A FILTER FOR POLITICAL VIEWS

Because of their early development and stability, party loyalties can affect the ways that individuals view politics. People often develop evaluations of candidates that are heavily colored by their attachment to a party. Whether these images are accurate or not, people tend to *project* favorable characteristics and acceptable issue positions onto the candidates of the party they favor and are *persuaded* to support particular candidates or issues because they are associated with the individual's party.[15]

Projection and Persuasion

When a new political candidate begins to get public notice and before most voters know much about him or her, many partisans in the electorate will react to the candidate positively or negatively based solely on party affiliation. Many people will project their favorable image of the party onto its new candidate and will be persuaded to support him or her. "The stronger the voter's party bias, the more likely he is to see the candidate of his own party as hero, the candidate of the other party as villain."[16]

Even when a popular nonpolitician such as Arnold Schwarzenegger is first mentioned as a possible candidate, evaluations of that person quickly diverge along partisan lines once the name is associated with a party. When a current politician does something controversial, public reactions have a partisan tinge. When former Senate Majority Leader Trent Lott, a Republican, made a racially insensitive remark in late 2002, for instance, almost two-thirds of Democratic identifiers said he should step down, but 56 percent of Republicans said Lott should keep his post.[17]

Party loyalty can have a big impact on people's attitudes even when it has to compete with other valued loyalties. Democrat John F. Kennedy was only the second Catholic presidential candidate in American history. Catholics tended to view Kennedy more favorably in that election than Protestants did. Catholic Republicans, however, were not as positive toward Kennedy as were Catholic Democrats. Party ID still made a difference, even among those with the same religious loyalty. So party ID helps to condition the way people feel about candidates and public officials.[18]

PARTY IDENTIFICATION AND VOTING

The most important effect of party attachments is their influence on people's voting behavior. Party identifiers' support for candidates of their party can't be taken for granted. The American electoral system discourages faithful party voting; partisans have to fight their way through long ballots, the culture's traditional emphasis on the individual rather than the party, and its distrust of strong parties. Nevertheless, party identifiers have tended to support their party with a lot of fidelity.

Party Voting

During the past half century, party identifiers have voted for their party's candidates most of the time. As you can see in Table 6.2, a majority in each category of partisanship has voted for their party's presidential candidate in every year, except for weak Democrats

TABLE 6.2 Voting for Their Party's Presidential Candidates Among Party Identifiers: 1952–2000

	1952	1956	1960	1964	1968	1972	1976	1980	1984	1988	1992	1996	2000
Strong Democrats	84%	85%	90%	95%	85%	73%	91%	86%	87%	93%	93%	96%	97%
Weak Democrats	62	62	72	82	58	48	74	60	67	70	69	82	89
Independents closer to Democrats	60	68	88	90	52	60	72	45	79	88	71	76	72
Independents	—	—	—	—	—	—	—	—	—	—	—	—	—
Independents closer to Republicans	93	94	87	75	82	86	83	76	92	84	62	68	79
Weak Republicans	94	93	87	56	82	90	77	86	93	83	60	70	85
Strong Republicans	98	100	98	90	96	97	96	92	96	98	87	94	97

Note: The table entries are the percentages of each category of partisans who reported a vote for their party's candidate for president. To find the percentage voting for the opposing party's candidate or some other candidate, subtract the entry from 100 percent. Individuals who did not vote for president are excluded from the table.

Source: American National Election Studies, Center for Political Studies, University of Michigan; data made available by the Inter-University Consortium for Political and Social Research.

in 1972 and independent Democrats in 1980 (both GOP landslide years). The most faithful are the strong partisans. Even in the Reagan landslide victory of 1984, when voting Democratic clearly ran against the tide, almost nine out of ten strong Democrats voted for Reagan's Democratic opponent, Walter Mondale. However, the prize for party loyalty goes to strong Republicans; only once in 50 years has their support for the GOP presidential candidate dipped below 90 percent.

Party voting among several groups of party identifiers decreased during the late 1960s and early 1970s, just as the proportion of strong and weak partisans did. As had happened with party ID, the decline was temporary. Recent studies show that the impact of party ID on voting behavior increased in each of the presidential elections from 1976 through 1996, reaching a level in the late 1990s higher than in any presidential election since the 1950s.[19] The polarization of the Republican and Democratic parties in recent decades has probably helped some people to clarify their stands on major issues and relate those stands more easily to a party ID, which could encourage more party voting.

These patterns appear in congressional elections as well (Table 6.3). A majority within each group of partisans has voted for their party's congressional candidates in each election, and strong partisans have been the most regular party voters. One key to the Democrats' ability to continue winning congressional majorities in the 1970s and 1980s, even at a time when their electoral base was eroding, might have been that they were more faithful than their GOP counterparts in voting for their party's congressional candidates.

Similar results appear in voting at the state and local level. ***Straight-ticket voting***— voting for one party's candidates only—declined among all the partisan groups during

TABLE 6.3 Voting for Their Party's Congressional Candidates Among Party Identifiers: 1952–2000

	1952	1956	1960	1964	1968	1972	1976	1980	1984	1988	1992	1996	2000
Strong Democrats	89%	94%	93%	94%	88%	91%	89%	85%	89%	88%	86%	88%	87%
Weak Democrats	77	86	86	84	73	80	78	69	70	82	82	71	73
Independents closer to Democrats	64	83	84	79	63	80	76	70	78	87	74	69	70
Independents	—	—	—	—	—	—	—	—	—	—	—	—	—
Independents closer to Republicans	81	83	74	72	81	73	65	68	61	64	65	79	67
Weak Republicans	90	88	84	64	78	75	66	74	66	70	63	79	79
Strong Republicans	95	95	90	92	91	85	83	77	85	77	82	97	86

Note: The table entries are the percentages of each category of partisans who reported a vote for their party's candidate for Congress. To find the percentage voting for the opposing party's candidate or some other candidate, subtract the entry from 100 percent. Individuals who did not vote or did not vote for Congress are excluded from the table.

Source: American National Election Studies, Center for Political Studies, University of Michigan; data made available by the Inter-University Consortium for Political and Social Research.

the 1960s and 1970s. But most strong Democrats and strong Republicans remained straight-ticket voters. The stronger an individual's party identification was, the more likely he or she was to vote a straight ticket.[20] And as with other indicators of party influence, the decline seems to have stopped and reversed. In fact, the proportion of respondents voting a straight ticket for president and the House of Representatives in 2000 increased to 76 percent, more than 10 percent higher than in 1980.

Although party voting is common in American elections, we still see some fascinating hints of weakened partisanship. For example, even though the majority of party identifiers have been Democrats during the past 50 years, Democrats have won the presidency only three times during this period. At no other time in American history has the majority party had so little success at the presidential level. As Tables 6.2 and 6.3 indicate, party voting has not been constant; it has decreased sharply in some election years, especially among the weak partisans and independent leaners (see, for example, the Democrats in the 1980 Reagan election), and then bounced back in other years (e.g., among Republicans when Reagan was reelected in 1984).

The most recent congressional midterm elections provide more evidence of this bumpy ride. Republican partisanship was especially strong in 1994 and 1998. Unlike their typical behavior since the 1960s, more Republicans than Democrats supported their party's candidates for the House of Representatives. In both years, Republicans also won a clear majority of the support of independents, but it was probably the extra boost in loyalty from their own partisans that gave them control of Congress for the first time in forty years. In mirror image, Democratic voting fidelity decreased in the 1990s.

Party Versus Candidates and Issues

What causes these ups and downs in the level of party voting? Individuals' voting decisions are affected by the give-and-take of two sets of forces: the strength of their enduring party loyalty (if they have one) and the power of the *short-term forces* operating in a given election. These short-term forces include the attractiveness of particular candidates running that year and the pull of various issues in the campaign. Usually these two sets of forces incline the voter in the same direction; as we have seen, a party ID leads an individual to see the party's candidates and issue stands in a favorable light.

However, there are times when an especially attractive candidate or a particularly appealing issue stance—a tax cut proposal or a promise to keep the nation safe from terrorism—may lead a voter to desert one or more of his or her party's candidates. At least by some measures, split-ticket voting has been fairly frequent for decades.[21] Voters do not usually split their tickets out of a conscious desire to create a divided government. Rather, voters are more likely to defect from their party ID because they are attracted to a very visible candidate running a well-funded campaign, most often an incumbent of the other party.[22] In the 2000 elections, for example, Democratic presidential candidate Al Gore lost West Virginia with 46 percent of the vote, but popular incumbent Democratic Senator Robert C. Byrd was reelected with 78 percent. Similarly, although Gore won Vermont with 51 percent of the vote, incumbent Republican Senator James Jeffords got 66 percent. Typically, those with the weakest party ID are the most likely to defect.

Partisanship as a Two-Way Street

A big challenge in determining the relative importance of party ID, candidate characteristics, and issues in affecting individuals' voting decisions is that these three forces are strongly interrelated. The early studies of party ID in the 1950s assumed that party "came first" in the causal ordering—that it influenced people's feelings about candidates and issues but was not in turn influenced by them. These early studies did not have good measures of how close the voter felt to the candidates on the issues.

Since then, with the use of better measures, researchers have shown that there are reciprocal relationships among these three influences. Just as an individual's party loyalty influences the way he or she views politics, feelings about candidates and issues can affect the individual's party ID as well. In particular, there is powerful evidence that negative reactions to a president's management of the economy (so-called *retrospective evaluations*, in that they refer to past actions rather than hopes for the future) can feed back on party loyalties and weaken or change them. In this way, partisanship can be seen as a kind of "running tally" of party-related evaluations.[23] Even if party ID is usually stable enough to withstand an individual's disappointment in a particular party candidate or in the party's position on an issue or two, an accumulation of these negative experiences can shake or change an individual's partisanship—as happened over several decades to the long-standing Democratic loyalties of many conservative white southerners.

In the short run, then, issues and the candidates in a particular election can have a major impact on the outcome, especially now, when the two major parties are so closely matched in numbers of adherents.[24] But party ID has continuing power to influence voters' choices and to affect their feelings about issues and candidates as well. So whether we want to explain the general trends of American voting behavior or the choices of voters in a particular election, party ID plays a prominent role.[25]

PARTY IDENTIFICATION AND POLITICAL ACTIVITY

Another important effect of party ID is that individuals who consider themselves Democrats and Republicans are more involved in political life than are those who call themselves independents. It is the strongest partisans who are the most likely to vote, to pay attention to politics, and to take part in political activities. As in previous years, the 2000 American National Election Studies survey shows that strong Democrats and strong Republicans were more likely than weak identifiers or independents to be interested in politics and to follow reports about public affairs and the campaign on television and in newspapers (Table 6.4).

The strongest partisans are also the most active in other ways. A total of 84 and 92 percent, respectively, of the strong Democrats and Republicans reported having voted in 2000—higher than the turnout levels among weaker partisans or independents.[26] They were also more likely than other citizens to try to persuade other people to vote a certain way, to wear campaign buttons, to display bumper stickers or yard signs, to attend political meetings, and to contribute money to a party. The combatants of American electoral politics, in short, come disproportionately from the ranks of the strong Democrats and strong Republicans.

TABLE 6.4 Political Involvement of Partisans and Independents: 2000

	Democrats		Independents			Republicans	
				Closer to			
	Strong	Weak	Dem.	Neither	Rep.	Weak	Strong
Very much interested in politics	54%	30	38	24	42	31	65
Follow public affairs most of time	28%	14	23	14	28	11	32
Great deal of attention to campaign via TV	35%	22	31	18	34	21	43
Read about campaign in newspapers	65%	53	56	40	62	61	74
Voted	84%	76	71	54	78	76	92
Tried to persuade people to vote certain way	44%	26	35	22	38	34	44
Displayed button, bumper sticker, sign	14%	5	7	2	12	10	18
Attended rally or meeting	10%	3	5	2	6	1	8
Contributed money to							
Candidate	6%	3	8	3	9	4	14
Party	7%	4	5	2	6	4	15

Source: 2000 American National Election Study, Center for Political Studies, University of Michigan; data made available by the Inter-University Consortium for Political and Social Research.

PARTY IDENTIFICATION AND ATTITUDES TOWARD THE PARTIES

Strong party identifiers tend to see a greater contrast between the Republican and Democratic parties than do weak identifiers and independents, both in general and on specific policy issues (see Figure 6.2). They are more polarized in their evaluations of the two parties' candidates as well as of the parties' abilities to govern for the benefit of the nation. Strong partisans are more inclined than weaker partisans and independents to say that their party's president has done his job well and that a president of the opposing party has performed poorly.[27] In the mind of the strong partisan, in short, the political parties are clearly defined and highly polarized along the important dimensions of politics.

These data do not necessarily prove that party ID alone results in greater activity or sharper party images. Other factors also affect people's willingness to become involved in politics. In particular, higher socioeconomic status and the greater political sophistication and easier entry into politics that it often brings can lead people into

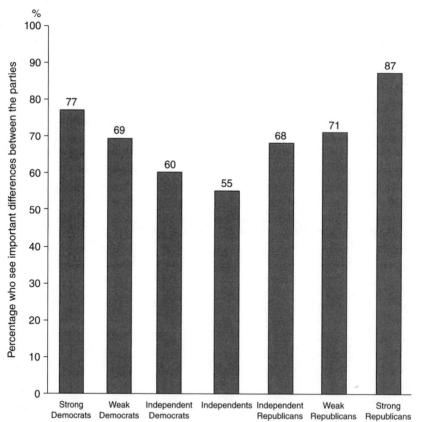

FIGURE 6.2   Differences Between the Parties as Seen by Partisans and Independents: 2000.

Source: 2000 American National Election Study, Center for Political Studies, University of Michigan; data made available by the Inter-University Consortium for Political and Social Research.

political activity. The relatively greater involvement of partisans (and, in most years, of Republicans) comes in part from their generally higher socioeconomic status levels as well as from their more ideological commitment to politics.[28] Even so, party ID has a major impact on people's political activity.

THE MYTH OF THE INDEPENDENT

It is intriguing that party loyalties govern so much political behavior in a culture that so warmly celebrates the independent voter. There is clearly a disconnect between the American myth of the high-minded independent—the well-informed citizen who is moved by issues and candidates, not parties—and the reality of widespread partisanship. The problem is with the myth.

Attitudinal Independents

The definition of "independent" that we have used so far in this chapter is someone who tells a poll taker that he or she does not identify with a political party. Studies show that these independents split their tickets more often than other voters do and that they wait longer in the campaign to make their voting decisions. In those ways, they would seem to fit the myth of the thoughtful, deliberative citizen. But they fall short of the mythical picture of the independent in most other ways. They are less well informed than party identifiers are, less concerned about specific elections, and less active politically. They are also less likely to vote. In 2000, as you saw in Table 6.4, independents stayed home from the polls at a higher rate than did party identifiers.

Within this group, it is important to distinguish between independents who say they feel closer to one of the two parties (independent leaners) and those who do not ("pure" independents). The independent leaners usually turn out to be more politically involved (see Table 6.4) and sometimes even more partisan in voting (especially for president) than weak partisans are (see Tables 6.2 and 6.3). It is only in comparison with strong partisans that these leaners fall short. By contrast, the pure independents typically have the most dismal record, with relatively low levels of political interest and information, turnout, and education. It is the pure independents who are the least involved and least informed of all American citizens.[29]

Behavioral Independents

We can also define independents in terms of their behavior. In his final work, the unparalleled researcher, V. O. Key, Jr., explored the idea of political independence. The picture of the American voter that was emerging from the electoral studies of the 1950s and 1960s was not a pretty one; it showed an electorate whose voting decisions were determined by deeply ingrained party loyalties—an electorate that had not grasped the major political issues and didn't care that it had not.[30]

Key looked for evidence of rational behavior among voters and focused his attention on "party switchers"—those who supported different parties in two consecutive presidential elections—rather than on the self-described independents. In practice, Key's switchers came much closer to the flattering myth of the independent than did the self-styled independents. These party switchers, Key found, expressed at least as much political interest as did the "stand-patters" (those who voted for the same party in both elections). Above all, the switchers showed an issue-related rationality that well fitted the mythical picture of the independent. They agreed on policy issues with the stand-patters toward whose party they had shifted, and they disagreed with the policies of the party from which they had defected.

It is the attitudinal independents, however—those who call themselves independents and express no party preference—who are the subject of the most research. Researchers conclude that they have always been a diverse group containing some who resemble the image of the sophisticated independent but also many of the least involved and informed voters in American politics. The myth that they are a carefully informed and active group of voters who operate above the party fray has withered under the glare of survey research.

Are Independents a Likely Source of Support for Third-Party Candidates?

Even if the attitudinal independents don't know much about politics and don't get involved in much political activity, they still could play an important role in elections. Because they have the weakest ties to the two major parties, they could be more open to the charms of third-party and independent candidates than other citizens are. We can see some evidence of this in presidential elections during the 1990s. One of the biggest stories of the 1992 presidential election was the unprecedented showing of independent candidate Ross Perot. A very rich man, Perot spent millions on a campaign criticizing the two major parties as irresponsible and corrupt. Unlike most independents, Perot flourished rather than faded as the campaign came to an end. He finished with almost 20 million votes, 19 percent of those cast.

On Election Day, Perot did draw most of his votes from self-identified independents and to a lesser extent from independent leaners, as had third-party candidates John Anderson (in 1980) and George Wallace (in 1968) before him.[31] Fully 37 percent of the pure independents said they voted for Perot, compared with only 4 percent of the strong Democrats and 11 percent of the strong Republicans. The same was true of Perot's third-party candidacy in 1996, although the percentages decreased by more than half. [32] In the end, however, there were not enough independents and disgruntled partisans to make a majority for Perot. Even if there were, it would be very hard for any single candidate to construct a winning coalition from a group as diverse as independent voters, who have little in common other than their lack of interest in politics and parties.

This doesn't mean, of course, that independents have no impact. Ralph Nader's well-publicized presidential run in 2000 as a candidate of the Green Parties got enough votes, most of them from independents, to have given the election to Republican George W. Bush. In the very close party competition that has characterized the early 2000s, even a small percentage of independent voters has the power to determine the winner. It is a sobering thought that when an election is close, the voters with the least interest and information about the candidates may be the ones who tip the balance.

CHANGE IN THE IMPACT OF PARTY ID

Party ID, then, is a psychological commitment that is often strong enough to guide other political beliefs and behavior. Democratic and Republican partisans often see issues and candidates through "party-tinted" glasses. They are more likely to vote for their party's candidates and to be active on behalf of the party or its candidates than other citizens are. For those reasons, party ID is a significant force in American politics. Yet partisanship functions in a very different context now than it did a century ago.

A More Candidate-Centered Politics

As we have seen in earlier chapters, American politics has changed in some marked ways in the past century. The great majority of Americans still hold a party ID, at least in the sense that they "lean toward" one of the two major parties. But, their party loyalties face more competition for their votes. Almost a century ago, states began adopting the direct primary, in which voters had to choose candidates without the useful guidance of a party label. Partisanship remains a helpful shortcut in general elections but does not distinguish one candidate from another in a party's primary. New campaign and fund-raising technologies developed that were harder for the party organizations to monopolize. Candidates with enough money could find ways, using television, direct mail, and other media, to reach voters directly, over the parties' heads.

During the turbulent years of the 1960s and 1970s, as we have seen, the number of self-identified independents grew and the impact of party ID on people's voting choices declined. Candidates found it helpful to downplay their party label, running instead as individual entrepreneurs. Now, even though party loyalties have regained much of their frequency and influence, candidates still tend to downplay their partisanship or even to emphasize their independence from their own party's leadership as a means of attracting voter support. The consequence is that elections have become less party centered and more candidate centered.[33]

In addition, other elements of American politics—organized interests, independent campaign consultants—have diversified and strengthened and so can compete more effectively with party loyalties for the attention and allegiance of citizens. It is not that party ID is weaker now but that it has more competition from other potential influences on voters. These short-run forces—candidates' characteristics, issues, and the particular events of the current campaign—have important effects on the campaign strategies that party organizations develop (see box on page 116) as well as on the role of the parties in government.

What have we lost as a result and what have we gained? A strongly party-identified electorate has a stabilizing influence on politics. When people vote straight-party tickets in election after election, vote outcomes are predictable. Patterns of party support are stable geographically. To the extent that it can be time-consuming and stressful to adapt to political change, predictable elections can be a benefit. When split-ticket voting is more common, we get the patterns of divided party government and more frequent switches in party control of Congress and the presidency that we have seen in the past two decades.

The Continuing Significance of Party

Yet we should not underestimate the persistence of party ID. Most Americans—a clear majority if we count only strong and weak identifiers, and almost all Americans if leaners are included as well—still report some degree of attachment to either the Democratic or the Republican Party. Large numbers of Americans are faithful to these loyalties

PARTY CAMPAIGN STRATEGIES IN THE 2000 AND 2004 PRESIDENTIAL RACES

The first rule of campaigning is to mobilize your own party identifiers while using issues and attractive candidates to appeal to independents and supporters of the other party. How you implement this rule depends on whether you are in the majority or the minority party. The job of the majority party is to rally its loyalists by appealing to the party's core issues. Democrats since the 1930s, for example, have stressed the economic issues that gave them their majority status: keeping employment high and protecting people's incomes with strong Social Security and Medicare programs.

The minority party has a different task: to divert attention from these issues by choosing candidates who seem to be "above" politics (Ronald Reagan, for instance, whose attractive personality had wide appeal) or by raising issues that cross party lines (such as the GOP emphasis on patriotism and family values) or that threaten to split the other party's coalition.

George W. Bush came into the 2000 presidential race with his party's identifiers in the minority. He stressed that he was a "compassionate conservative" in order to appeal to independents and Democrats who valued such issues as education and health care and who feared that Republicans were not committed to these issues. Bush also emphasized bipartisanship and an end to "partisan bickering," just as a minority-party candidate would logically do.

As a majority-party candidate would do, Democratic Vice President Al Gore emphasized the traditional Democratic core issues of Social Security and Medicare and his concern for "the people, not the powerful." He failed to stress his role in the nation's economic expansion because that would tie him to President Clinton, who had presided over that expansion but whose personal reputation had sunk very low with many groups of voters. Even so, Gore almost pulled it off. He won a majority of the popular vote but lost in the electoral college.

As the incumbent, Bush began his 2004 campaign for reelection with one of those issues that cross party lines: an emphasis on the threat of terrorism and the need for Americans to unite. That posed an interesting challenge for his potential Democratic rivals. There is no point debating an opponent on a bipartisan issue; none of the Democrats was in favor of terrorism. So the Democrats would need to change the subject and focus public attention on the economic and social welfare issues that are the Democrats' trademark. But how could Bush's Democratic challenger change the subject when American troops were still fighting in Iraq and the terrorist threats were regularly in the headlines?

As it turned out, he couldn't. Disagreements among Democratic candidates on the war in Iraq ensured that war and terrorism would remain high on the campaign agenda, to the Republicans' delight. Even worse for the Democrats, their ability to stress economic issues was undercut by President Bush's tax cuts. The Democratic candidates argued that the Bush tax cuts favored the wealthy and should be rolled back. That put the Democrats in the position of arguing for a tax increase, not a position that normally wins votes in American elections!

in voting for candidates for office. Voters may stray from the party fold; the abundance of elected offices encourages such defections. But voters continue to perceive candidates, issues, and elections in partisan terms and often vote accordingly.

Probably the most recent dramatic sign of this party influence could be seen in the 1994 congressional elections, which were the most party-oriented contests in years. The Republicans were able to overcome the localism that protected (mainly Democratic) incumbents by appealing to national issues, especially dissatisfaction with the Democratic president. Republican House candidates rallied around a "Contract with America," presented as a set of party pledges. When the Republicans won control of the House in that election (for the first time since 1954), they behaved like a cohesive party. Four years later, party voting remained high among Republicans, although it declined among Democrats. The 2002 congressional races were almost as partisan.

These congressional elections show that party-dominated contests are still possible, even when so many other forces are competing with parties for voters' attention. It would be hard to find clearer evidence of party influence than in the unprecedented recount of the 2000 presidential election vote, when activists, commentators, and even judges saw and interpreted the events of the recount with a partisan mindset. Will this continue or will the instability of modern politics eat away at the parties' base of support? The story continues in the next chapter, where we look more closely at the two major parties' supporting coalitions and their changes over time.

CHAPTER 7

Party Support and Party Realignments

A "Terminator" with political aspirations, Arnold Schwarzenegger has a mixed marriage, politically speaking. Schwarzenegger, a wealthy, middle-aged white man whose father was a military officer, owns several businesses. His wife, Maria Shriver, is Catholic and a journalist and comes from a family of lawyers and activists for nonprofit groups. On the basis of this description, would you have been able to tell which member of this couple is a Democrat and which is a Republican?

Party identifications are not distributed randomly among Americans. Some social groups lean heavily toward a Republican identification—business executives and "born-again" white Protestants, for example—and other groups, such as women, African Americans, and Jews, are more likely to consider themselves Democrats. Without any knowledge of their voting record, then, and purely on the basis of their links with certain social groupings, we could predict (accurately, in fact) that Schwarzenegger is the Republican and Shriver is the Democrat.

The groups that support a party make up what is called the party's *coalition*—the types of people most inclined to favor that party's candidates through good times and bad. These groups' interests, in turn, are likely to affect the party's platform and its strategic choices in campaigns. So the differences between the two parties' coalitions at a particular time are a helpful clue as to which issues dominate the nation's politics at that time. The facts that African Americans have identified so overwhelmingly as Democrats in recent decades, for example, and that southern whites' loyalty to the Democratic Party has seriously eroded, remind us that racial issues continue to be powerful in American elections.[1] At various times in U.S. history, regional conflicts, ethnic and religious divisions, disputes between agriculture and industry, and differences in social class have also helped form the basis for differences between the two parties' coalitions, as they have in other Western democracies.

Because the alignment of social groups with parties is so significant in shaping a nation's politics, great and enduring changes in those coalitions, often called *realignments,* are well worth exploring.[2] In this chapter, then, we will look at the nature of realignment and other types of party change and tell the story of these changes over time. Then we'll examine the development and nature of the coalitions that currently support the Democrats and the Republicans: from what educational backgrounds, occupations, regions, religions, and other social groups do these supporters come and what interests attract them to one party rather than the other? Finally, we will consider whether the parties' coalitions have shifted markedly enough in the past 30 years to constitute another realignment or whether the current relationship between social groups and parties is something entirely new.

REALIGNMENTS: THE FIVE AMERICAN PARTY SYSTEMS

In the last chapter, we saw that although party identification has a major impact on people's voting, the extent of that impact can vary from one election to the next. Elections can be classified into three types, depending on the degree to which party identifiers vote for their party's presidential candidate:

> In *maintaining elections*, the party attachments of the recent past continue without any great change. In these elections, the candidate from the largest party in the electorate wins.

> In *deviating elections*, short-term forces (candidates' characteristics or issues) are powerful enough to cause the defeat of the majority party's candidate, but the basic distribution of party loyalties is not changed.

> In periods of *realigning elections*, the coalition of groups supporting the parties changes in significant ways, as does its issue base. The new coalition then endures. These elections often (but not always) produce a new majority party.

In recent years, deviating elections have been very common; since 1952, the Democratic Party has consistently had more party identifiers than the Republicans but has won the presidency in only five of thirteen elections. Prior to that time, if we had survey data with which to measure party identifications since about 1800, many scholars believe that we would find long periods of relative stability in the components of each party's coalition—in other words, maintaining elections—punctuated fairly regularly by realigning periods. Unfortunately, survey data were not available until the late 1930s. For earlier years, we can only estimate the composition of the parties in the electorate from aggregated voting returns. These voting patterns suggest a division of American politics into a series of electoral eras.[3]

Many analysts agree that the United States has experienced at least five different electoral eras or party systems. Each of these party systems has had a distinctive pattern of group support for the parties. Each party system can also be distinguished by the kinds of issue concerns that dominated it and the types of public policies that the government put into effect. (See Table 7.1 for a summary of each party system.) In Chapter 1, we looked at party history to learn about the interrelationships among the three parts of the party. Now let us get a different take on these events, from the perspective of changes in the social group support for the parties.

The First Party System

The initial American party system (1801–1828)[4] emerged out of a serious conflict between opposing groups within the Washington administration: How much power should the national government exercise relative to that of the states? As noted in Chapter 1, the Federalists, led by Alexander Hamilton, wanted to build the new economy through the efforts of a strong national government that would collaborate closely with business and

TABLE 7.1 Years of Partisan Control of Congress and the Presidency: 1801–2004

	House		Senate		President	
	D-R	*Opp.*	*D-R*	*Opp.*	*D-R*	*Opp.*
First party system						
(1801–1828)	26	2	26	2	28	0
	Dem.	*Opp.*	*Dem.*	*Opp.*	*Dem.*	*Opp.*
Second party system						
(1829–1860)	24	8	28	4	24	8
	Dem.	*Rep.*	*Dem.*	*Rep.*	*Dem.*	*Rep.*
Third party system						
(1861–1876)	2	14	0	16	0	16
(1877–1896)	14	6	4	16	8	12
Fourth party system						
(1897–1932)	10	26	6	30	8	28
Fifth party system						
(1933–1968)	32	4	32	4	28	8
(1969–1980)	12	0	12	0	4	8
(1981–2004)	14	10	10	14	8	16
(1969–2004)	26	12	22	14	12	24

Note: Entries for the first party system are Democratic-Republicans and their opposition, first Federalists and then Jacksonians; for the second party system, Democrats and their opposition, first Whigs and then Republicans; for subsequent party systems, Democrats and Republicans. In 2001, Republicans were in the majority in the Senate for the first five months and Democrats for the last seven, so the Senate is counted as being under Democratic control.

industry. A national bank would centralize the state banking systems. This plan would benefit business owners and wealthier citizens, who were concentrated in New England; these groups were the core support for Hamilton's Federalists.

Small farmers and the less well-off, living in the southern and mid-Atlantic states, could see that the Federalists' proposals would harm them financially; it was the small farmers who would pay the taxes while businesses and speculators would gain. They supported Thomas Jefferson and James Madison's demand for a limited national government, for states' rights, and a more egalitarian vision of the new democracy. The Jeffersonians won the debate; in the hotly contested 1800 election, these Democratic-Republicans, as they came to be called, gained the presidency. The Federalists slowly slipped into a fatal decline, and the party of Jefferson and Madison then enjoyed more than two decades of almost unchallenged dominance.

The Second Party System

The next party system (1829–1860) developed when the one-party rule of the Democratic-Republicans could not contain all the conflicts generated by a rapidly changing nation. The party split into two factions on the major issues of the period: how the Union should expand, what the national government's economic powers should be, and, increasingly, how to handle the explosive question of slavery. One faction continued the Jeffersonian tradition of opposition to a strong national government; it included the small farmers of the South and the western frontier as well as urban workers and their political bosses. Led by Andrew Jackson, it would later call itself the Democratic Party or, at times, "the Democracy." The other, a more elitist and eastern faction represented by John Quincy Adams, referred to itself as the National Republicans and was eventually absorbed into the Whig Party.[5]

This second party system was just as class based as the first; wealthier voters supported the Whigs and the less privileged identified as Democrats. The Democrats dominated, growing as the franchise was extended to more and more Americans. Their rule was interrupted only twice, both times by the election of Whig war heroes to the presidency. As the issues of this period grew more disruptive, however, several minor parties developed and the Whigs began to fracture, especially over the issue of slavery.

The Third Party System

One of these new parties, an antislavery party called the Republicans, was quickly propelled into major party status; it was founded in 1854 and had already replaced the seriously divided Whigs by 1856. Its rapid rise signaled the end of the second party system. The intense conflict of the Civil War ensured that the new third party system (1861–1896) would have the most clearly defined coalitions of any party system before or since. War and Reconstruction divided the nation roughly along geographic lines: the South became a Democratic bastion after white southerners were permitted to return to the polls in the 1870s, and the Northeast and Midwest remained a reliable base for Republicans.

So sharp was the sectional division that the Democratic Party's only strongholds in the North were in the cities controlled by Democratic machines (for example, New York City's Tammany Hall) and areas settled by southerners (such as Kentucky, Missouri, and the southern portions of Ohio, Indiana, and Illinois). In the South, GOP support came only from blacks (in response to Republican President Abraham Lincoln's freeing of the slaves) and people from mountain areas originally opposed to the southern states' secession. By 1876, when southern whites were finally reintegrated into national politics, there was close party competition in presidential voting and in the House of Representatives as these sectional monopolies offset one another.[6] Competition was so intense that this period contained two of the four elections in American history in which the winner of the popular vote for President lost the vote in the electoral college.

As industrial expansion proceeded, economic issues, particularly the growth of huge industrial monopolies, became a major focus of the party cleavage. Along with the white South, which was universally Democratic, the Democrats gained support in other parts of the country from farmers and the working class—groups that had been passed over by economic expansion and who were deeply suspicious of capitalism. On the other hand, the Republicans "were from the beginning the party more identified with moral Puritanism and emerging industrial capitalism."[7]

The Fourth Party System

The imprint of the Civil War continued to shape southern politics for the next century. However, the Civil War party system soon began to fade elsewhere, under the weight of farm and rural protest and the economic panic of 1893. Tensions within the Democratic Party between poor whites and the more conservative party leaders erupted into a fight over the party's leadership in the 1890s. The less wealthy, egalitarian wing won with the nomination of populist William Jennings Bryan in 1896. Bryan went down to crashing defeat, and Republicans began a long domination of American national politics, disrupted only by their own internal split in 1912.

This fourth party system (1897–1932) reflected both regional and economic conflicts. It pitted the eastern business community, which was heavily Republican, against the western and southern "periphery," with the South even more Democratic than before. Southern Democrats, out from under the heavy hand of Reconstruction, were able to reinstitute racially discriminatory laws and to prevent blacks from voting in the South. The waves of immigrants into the large cities swelled the ranks of both parties, although Catholic immigrants, especially from Europe, tended to be drawn into Democratic Party organizing.

Just as earlier party systems began to weaken a decade or two after they began, the fourth party system showed signs of deterioration in the 1920s. The Progressive Party made inroads into major party strength early in the decade, and in 1928, Democratic candidate Al Smith, the first Catholic ever nominated for the presidency, brought even more Catholic voters into Democratic ranks in the North and drove Protestant southerners temporarily into voting Republican.

The Fifth Party System

It took the Great Depression of 1929 and the subsequent election of Franklin D. Roosevelt to produce the fifth, or New Deal, party system. During the 1930s, as a means of pulling the nation out of economic ruin, Roosevelt pushed Congress to enact several large-scale welfare state programs. These Roosevelt New Deal programs—Social Security, wages and hours laws, protection for labor unions—strengthened the Democratic Party's image as the party of the have-nots and as the party of social and economic reform. Even groups such as blacks, long allied with the Republicans as the party of Lincoln, were lured to the Democratic banner; socioeconomic issues were powerful enough to keep both blacks and southern whites as wary allies in the Roosevelt coalition.

By 1936, the new Democratic majority party had become a grand coalition: a *New Deal coalition* of the less privileged minorities—lower income people, industrial workers (especially union members), poor farmers, Catholics, Jews, blacks—plus the South, where the Democratic loyalty imprinted by the Civil War had become all but genetic. The Republican Party, committed to capitalism free of government restraints, was reluctant to accept the Roosevelt programs. The costs of the New Deal and the impact of its programs heightened the stakes of the conflict between higher income and lower income groups, so the socioeconomic stamp on the party system again became pronounced.

It is clear from this brief tour of party history that the effects of socioeconomic, racial, and regional divisions have waxed and waned, but all have had a continuing and powerful role in shaping the parties' coalitions over time. What is the nature of the two parties' coalitions today? As we explore the fate of the New Deal coalition, we'll ask whether there is convincing evidence that another realignment has taken place, introducing a sixth party system, in the closing years of the twentieth century.

THE SOCIAL BASES OF PARTY COALITIONS

Socioeconomic Status Divisions

Most democratic party systems reflect divisions along social class lines, even if those divisions may have softened over the years.[8] James Madison, one of the most perceptive observers of human nature among the nation's founders, wrote in the *Federalist Papers* that economic differences are the most common source of factions.[9] The footprints of socioeconomic status (SES) conflict are scattered throughout American history. Social and economic status differences underlay the battle between the wealthy, aristocratic Federalists and the less privileged Democratic-Republicans. These differences were even sharper between the Jacksonian Democrats and the Whigs a few decades later, and again at the time of the fourth party system beginning in the 1890s.

The relationship between party and SES established in the New Deal party system can still be seen in American politics today (see Table 7.2, sections A–C). Read across the top row of section A, for instance. You will find that among survey respondents in the lower third of incomes, 24 percent call themselves strong Democrats and, toward the right side of the row, only 10 percent are strong Republicans. The next column, titled "Dem. minus Rep.," shows that there are 19 percent more Democrats (counting strong plus weak identifiers) than Republicans among these lower income people.

The same story can be seen among those with lower educational levels (section C). Like people with lower incomes, those with less education are more likely to call themselves Democrats than Republicans. Here, 26 percent of those who didn't finish high school identify as strong Democrats, and only 5 percent call themselves strong Republicans, for an overall Democratic edge (counting both strong and weak partisans) of 28 percent. Why do we see these trends if the impact of social class is diminishing in politics? The overall decline in class voting among whites since the time of the New Deal has been counterbalanced by the very high Democratic identification among blacks, who are predominantly lower income.[10]

Socioeconomic forces, then, continue to leave their mark on American party politics. In fact, some observers argue that, outside the South, less affluent voters have become even more supportive of Democrats in recent decades. The substantial gulf between rich and poor in the United States and the differences between the parties' stands on issues of special concern to lower income people (such as government-provided health care and social services) may help sustain the impact of SES on party identification. The result is that, especially in congressional elections, Republicans are even more likely to win races in higher income districts now, and Democrats are more likely to win in lower income districts than they were 20 years ago.[11]

The current relationship between SES and party differs in some interesting ways from that of the New Deal coalition, however. As Table 7.2 shows, although less educated respondents are much more Democratic than Republican, those with a college education now divide themselves fairly evenly between the parties. The same is true with regard to income and occupation. Those with service jobs (which tend to be lower paying) and blue-collar jobs remain more likely to be Democrats. Upper income people, on the other hand, are no longer distinctively Republican—perhaps because this group now contains fewer business people and more professionals, many of whom are concerned with quality-of-life issues such as the environment and women's rights. The identification of many

TABLE 7.2 Social Characteristics and Party Identification: 2000

	Democrats		Independents			Republicans			
			Closer	Closer to	Closer			Dem.	
	Strong	Weak	to Dem.	Neither	to Rep.	Weak	Strong	Minus Rep.	Cases
A. Income									
Lower third	24%	16	16	13	10	11	10	19	495
Middle third	18%	16	16	13	14	13	9	12	521
Upper third	17%	14	14	8	15	13	18	0	562
B. Occupation									
Service	16%	20	18	10	12	12	12	12	139
Blue collar	20%	15	16	14	14	9	11	15	221
White collar	15%	17	16	11	13	14	13	5	367
Professional	16%	14	16	10	13	15	15	0	466
Farm	13%	0	7	7	20	27	27	–41	15
C. Education									
No high school	26%	20	14	13	8	13	5	28	174
High school grad	21%	15	17	16	12	9	10	17	511
College	17%	15	14	9	14	13	16	3	1,095
D. Region									
South	21%	15	12	13	13	11	14	11	646
Nonsouth	19%	15	17	11	13	12	13	9	1,139
E. Religion									
Jews	44%	14	21	7	5	5	2	51	43
Catholics	20%	15	15	10	15	11	13	11	457
Protestants	24%	19	13	11	9	13	11	19	618
White "Born-again" Protestants	12%	12	10	10	16	16	23	–15	367
F. Race									
Blacks	46%	22	16	10	3	3	1	64	206
Whites	16%	14	14	12	14	14	15	1	1,377
G. Gender									
Female	20%	18	15	12	12	11	12	15	1,006
Male	18%	11	15	11	14	14	15	0	779

Note: Totals add up to approximately 100 percent reading across (with slight variations due to rounding). Dem. minus Rep. is the party difference calculated by subtracting the percentage of strong and weak Republicans from the percentage of strong and weak Democrats. Negative numbers indicate a Republican advantage in the group.

Source: 2000 American National Election Study, Center for Political Studies, University of Michigan; data made available by the Inter-University Consortium for Political and Social Research.

professionals with the Democratic Party is reflected in the support Democratic candidates often receive from teachers' unions and trial lawyers' associations.

The impact of SES should not be overstated. Socioeconomic status has been less important as a basis for party loyalty in the United States than in many other Western democracies,[12] and even at the height of the New Deal, the SES differences between the parties were less clear than the parties' rhetoric would suggest. The electorates of both American parties in the early 2000s contain a significant number of people from all status groups. Some groups locate themselves in the "wrong" party from an SES point of view; for example, white fundamentalist Protestants have trended Republican in recent years even though their average income is closer to that of the average Democrat than to the average Republican.[13] The SES divisions between the Republicans and Democrats, then, can be muddy, and as a result, the parties do not usually promote blatantly class-based appeals; they try to attract votes from a variety of social groups.

Sectional (Regional) Divisions

Historically, the greatest rival to SES as an explanation for American party differences has been sectionalism. Different sections of the country have often had differing political interests. When a political party has championed these distinct interests, it has sometimes united large numbers of otherwise different voters.

The most enduring sectionalism in American party history was the one-party Democratic control of the South. Well before the Civil War, white southerners shared an interest in slavery and an agriculture geared to export markets. The searing experience of that war and the Reconstruction that followed made the South into the "Solid South" and delivered it to the Democrats for most of the next century. The 11 states of the former Confederacy cast all their electoral votes for Democratic presidential candidates in every election from 1880 through 1924, except for Tennessee's defection in 1920. Al Smith's Catholicism frightened five of these states into the Republican column in 1928, but the Roosevelt economic programs brought the South back to the Democratic Party for the four Roosevelt elections.

Only the beginnings of the civil rights movement had the power to peel away the South from its Democratic loyalties. When Democratic administrations began to use federal power to end the racial segregation of schools and public accommodations such as restaurants and hotels, some conservative white southerners looked for an alternative. They found it in the Republican Party when its 1964 presidential candidate Barry Goldwater defended states' rights against these federal civil rights initiatives. Democratic strength eroded in the South, even when the Democrats nominated southern candidates for president and vice president. By 2000, southerners were no more likely to claim a Democratic identification than were people in other regions (Table 7.2, section D). In fact, white southerners have become fairly reliable Republican voters in national elections, though traces of the Democratic habit have survived in state and local races.[14]

At times as well, the party system has reflected the competition between the economically dominant East and the economically dependent South and West. In the first years of the Republic, the Federalists held to an ever-narrowing base of eastern seaport and financial interests, while the Democratic-Republicans expanded westward with the new settlers. Jackson aimed his party appeals at the men of the frontier, and the protest movements that thrust William Jennings Bryan into the 1896 campaign sprang from the agrarian discontent of the western prairies and the South. Many of the Populists' loudest complaints were directed at eastern bankers and eastern capitalism. The geographic distribution of the 1896 presidential vote, with the Democrats winning all but three states in the South and West, but losing all northern and border states east of the Mississippi River, is a striking example of sectional voting.

Sectional divisions are no longer as obvious. As society has nationalized, the isolation that maintained sectional interests has broken down. Sectional loyalties have not completely disappeared, of course; Democrat Al Gore, who lost every southern state in 2000, could attest to that. The mountain West has sometimes acted as a unified bloc in national politics on concerns that these states share, such as protecting the coal deposits and the ranchers in the western states against federal environmental laws. So in recent presidential elections, commentators have referred to the "Republican L," the substantial support for Republican candidates in the Rocky Mountain and Plains states and then across the South.

In the fourth and fifth party systems, regional divisions tended to dampen two-party competition in the nation as a whole. That has not happened recently; two-party competition has increased throughout the nation, as we saw in Chapter 2. And although minor party presidential candidates used to draw on a regional base of support, that was not the case with Ross Perot in 1992 or 1996 or Ralph Nader in 2000. Sectionalism, it seems, has less influence on the parties now.

Religious Divisions

There have always been religious differences between the American party coalitions, just as there are in many other democracies. In the early days of the New Deal, Catholics and Jews were among the most loyal supporters of the Democratic Party, although Catholic support for Democrats has declined somewhat in recent years (Table 7.2, section E). Some of the relationship between religion and party loyalty is due to the SES differences among religious groupings. Yet religious conviction and group identification also seem to be involved.

Internationalism and concern for social justice, rooted in the religious and ethnic traditions of Judaism, have disposed many Jews toward the Democratic Party as the party of international concern, support for Israel, and social and economic justice.[15] The long-standing ties of Catholics to the Democratic Party reflected the party's greater openness to Catholic participation and political advancement. Most of the national chairmen of the Democratic Party during the past century have been Catholics and the only Catholic presidential nominees of a major party have been Democrats.

Northern white Protestants have trended Republican ever since the party began, but the relationship is complex. In recent years, we have seen an interesting difference between mainline Protestant denominations and white evangelicals. Greater support for the Republicans among white "born-again" Protestants, especially in the South, in part reflects the parties' stands on issues such as abortion and school prayer as well as Republican leaders' social conservatism and emphasis on traditional values.[16] More generally, voters who consider themselves very religious, who pray and attend church often, and especially those who believe the Bible to be literally true and to be the word of God, are substantially more Republican than Democratic. So in current politics, the greatest religious difference in voting preferences may not be the difference between Catholics and Protestants but between frequent church attenders and those who are "unchurched."

Racial Divisions

Decades ago, the Republican Party, the party founded to abolish slavery and the party of Lincoln, the Civil War, and Reconstruction, was associated with racial equality in the minds of both black and white Americans. Between 1930 and 1960, however, the partisan direction of racial politics turned 180 degrees. It is now the Democratic Party that is viewed as standing for racial equality.

As a result, blacks identify as Democrats in overwhelming numbers today, as they have since at least the 1960s, regardless of their SES, region, or other social characteristics (Table 7.2, section F). In a recent poll, two-thirds of blacks interviewed agreed that the Democratic Party is committed to equal opportunity; only three in ten blacks said that about the Republican Party.[17] In 2000, 90 percent of blacks reported voting for Gore, compared with only 44 percent of whites.[18] There is no closer tie between a social group and a party than that between blacks and the Democrats.[19]

Ethnic Divisions

Hispanics and Latinos are the fastest growing segment of the U.S. population. The 2000 U.S. Census showed that the Hispanic population grew by nearly 60 percent in the previous decade to more than 35 million. By 2002, Hispanics had surpassed non-Hispanic blacks as the nation's largest minority group. Hispanics have long exercised a great deal of voting strength in states such as California, Texas, and Florida. But as their numbers shoot up nationwide, both parties work harder to attract Hispanic voter support, just as Hispanics seek to gain political influence to the same degree achieved by blacks. In fact, a White House pollster warned in 2002 that unless Republicans steadily increased their share of the Hispanic vote in 2004 and beyond, Republican candidates would lose those elections.[20]

Yet winning the Hispanic vote is easier said than done, mainly because Hispanics and Latinos include many different nationalities with differing interests. The Cuban émigrés who settled in Miami after Fidel Castro took power in the 1950s tend to be conservative, intensely anti-Communist, and inclined to vote Republican, whereas the larger Mexican-American population in California leans Democratic. Surveys show that most Hispanic voters identify themselves as Democrats, but Republican strategists see Hispanics as potentially responsive to a socially conservative message.[21]

Gender Divisions

For more than two decades, the votes and stands of women have diverged from those of men. In 1980, about 6 percent more women voted for Jimmy Carter than men did. The so-called gender gap grew after that. Men rated President Reagan much more positively than women did, and by the mid-1980s, the gender difference had extended to partisanship; men were less likely than women to identify as Democrats. This partisan gender gap increased in the 1996 election and remained large in 2000 (Table 7.2, section G). There is evidence that it stems to a greater extent from men becoming more Republican rather than from women becoming more Democratic.[22]

Why should gender be related to partisanship? Studies of the gender gap suggest that there are differences between men's and women's attitudes on some major issues; on average, women express greater support for social programs and less support for defense spending. These differences correspond with the two parties' issue agendas; the Democratic Party tends to emphasize education, health care, and other social programs, while the Republicans put a priority on military strength and tax cuts. Surveys show that people's attitudes toward gender equality and abortion, in particular, have become more closely correlated with their party identification during the past three decades.[23] The national parties also project some lifestyle differences that may affect men's and women's party identification. Among members of the U.S. House and Senate first elected in 2002, for instance, 80 percent of those who list their spouse as sharing their last name were Republicans, and almost 70 percent of those whose spouse had a different last name were Democrats.[24]

ISSUES ARE CENTRAL TO THE PARTIES' COALITIONS

As this discussion of the gender gap suggests, the links between groups and political parties are typically closely related to issues. A group's presence in a party coalition suggests that the members of the group, white fundamentalists, for instance, have some shared reactions to major issues and candidates. These shared reactions can lead them to support one party rather than the other. Over time, that party will probably come to speak for at least some of the group's hopes and interests, further strengthening the tie between them. Most social groups are not monolithic; although white fundamentalists may agree on some religious doctrines, they don't necessarily agree on all political issues, from energy policy to estate taxes. The relationships between parties and social groupings can tell us a lot about the views and the interests to which each party must respond.

Fortunately, we have a huge arsenal of public opinion polls to examine the attitudes on issues within each party's supporting coalition. Table 7.3 shows the preferences of Democratic identifiers, independents, and Republican identifiers on a range of issues that left their mark on recent presidential campaigns. There are big differences between Democrats and Republicans (seen in the "Dem. minus Rep." column) in attitudes toward programs of the welfare state. Democrats are much more favorable than are Republicans to greater government spending on services and a government role in providing jobs for the unemployed (sections A and B). The recipients of these services and jobs tend to be lower SES people, whose Democratic leanings can be seen in Table 7.2. Note, however, that factors other than an individual's own SES can affect his or her views on these issues. Even more important are people's perceptions of how the economy is doing as a whole.[25]

Party differences are also apparent on non-SES issues, such as civil rights, defense spending, and the question of abortion (see Table 7.3, sections C–E). Since the 1960s, for example, party identifiers have been sharply divided in their attitudes toward racial policy, with Democrats much more likely to favor a government role in helping minorities than Republicans are. (Recall from Table 7.2 the strong tendency for blacks to identify as Democrats.) In 2000, defense and foreign policy issues and concerns about abortion separated Democrats from Republicans to a significant degree. In their voting choices, those who supported abortion rights were much more likely to vote for Gore than for Bush in 2000, provided that they were aware of the two candidates' positions on the issue.[26]

Interestingly, the abortion issue had not been related to party identification as recently as 1988. Then, attitudes toward abortion cut across party lines, dividing Democrats from Democrats and Republicans from Republicans.[27] An issue with the power to affect party identification can threaten to rearrange the two parties' coalitions and possibly even create major change in the party system. It did happen to at least some extent; prochoice sentiment is now much stronger in the Democratic than the Republican Party, suggesting that some people changed their partisanship to correspond with the prochoice position of Democratic Party leaders or the prolife stance of Republican leaders.

TABLE 7.3 Issues, Ideology, and Party Identification: 2000

	Democrats		Independents			Republicans			
	Strong	Weak	Closer to Dem.	Closer to Neither	Closer to Rep.	Weak	Strong	Dem. Minus Rep.	Cases
A. Government spending on services									
More	28%	18	18	12	8	8	8	30	575
Same	17%	16	16	11	15	13	13	7	626
Less	4%	8	6	7	22	21	33	−42	281
B. Government role in providing jobs and a good standard of living									
Gov. help	33%	17	18	15	7	7	4	39	307
In between	23%	16	19	10	14	11	8	20	501
Help self	11%	13	11	10	16	16	22	−10	763
C. Government role in improving position of minorities									
Gov. help	35%	16	18	10	7	8	5	38	281
In between	20%	16	18	11	12	13	10	13	678
Help self	12%	15	11	11	17	15	19	−7	589
D. Government spending on defense									
Decrease	22%	20	28	10	8	8	5	29	173
Same	21%	17	16	10	14	11	11	16	677
Increase	14%	12	10	10	14	14	24	−12	552
E. Abortion									
Own choice	22%	18	19	11	12	10	8	22	742
In between	17%	13	13	11	15	14	17	−1	778
Illegal	16%	8	8	16	11	13	17	−6	211
F. Ideological self-identification									
Liberal	34%	20	24	7	8	4	3	47	414
Moderate	19%	20	20	15	14	10	2	27	417
Conservative	9%	8	5	8	18	21	31	−35	618

Note: Totals add up to approximately 100 percent reading across (with slight variations due to rounding). Dem. minus Rep. is party difference calculated by subtracting the percentage of strong and weak Republicans from the percentage of strong and weak Democrats. Negative numbers indicate a Republican advantage in the group. Individuals who were unable to describe themselves in ideological terms were not included in the data in section F.

Source: 2000 American National Election Study, Center for Political Studies, University of Michigan; data made available by the Inter-University Consortium for Political and Social Research.

There is additional evidence that the two parties' coalitions are more sharply divided on issues than they were a few decades ago. Look, for example, at the striking party difference between those who call themselves liberals and those who identify themselves as conservatives (Table 7.3, section F). As one pollster puts it, "We have two massive, colliding force. . . . One [i.e., the Republican coalition] is rural, Christian, religiously conservative, with guns at home, terribly unhappy with (then-President Bill) Clinton's behavior. . . . And we have a second America [the Democratic coalition] that is socially tolerant, pro-choice, secular, living in New England and the Pacific coast, and in affluent suburbs."[28] Party divisions, then, increasingly reflect differences that have been termed "the culture wars."[29]

These findings show that there is a close and reciprocal relationship between the stands that a party takes and the groups that form the party's core support. Parties take positions on issues to maintain the support of the groups in their existing coalition. Sometimes party leaders use issue positions to draw members of other social groups to the party, as both parties are now doing to win the support of Latino voters. At times, it is the group that tries to put its issue on the party's agenda; prolifers did so in the Republican Party as abortion rights activists did with the Democrats. As these newer groups become a larger force within the party, the party's leadership will probably try to firm up their support with additional commitments on their issues. So there is a dynamic and fascinating interaction between the social groups in a party's coalition and the party's stands on issues.

IS THERE A SIXTH PARTY SYSTEM?

There is no doubt that the party system of the early 2000s is different from that of the 1930s. But how can we characterize that difference? Are we now in a sixth American party system or even a seventh? On the one hand, the patterns of group support that launched the fifth party system can still be seen in polls. On the other hand, almost all these relationships have weakened in recent decades; only the tendency of black voters to identify as Democrats has increased.

In Figure 7.1, the size of each bar represents the extent to which each group was distinctively either Democratic or Republican in 1960 and again in 2000. All these social groups were predominantly Democratic in 1960 (the black columns), other than college-educated and upper income respondents. With the important exception of black Americans, almost all the distinctively Democratic groups in 1960 are less Democratic in 2000 (the white columns), and the two pro-Republican groups in 1960 are less Republican in 2000. In other words, almost all these groups—educational, income, regional, religious, and gender—are less distinctively associated with one party or the other in 2000 than they were four decades earlier.

The SES and sectional differences in party ID that were so important to the New Deal party system must now compete with other forces. As the box on page 132 shows, the current Republican and Democratic coalitions also differ in terms of marital status and sexual orientation (with single people and gays more likely to identify as Democrats) and attitudes toward "hot button" social issues. To some researchers, these changes are substantial enough to justify a conclusion that the New Deal coalition is dead.[30]

Alternatively, we could argue that the nature of the party system itself has changed fundamentally since the New Deal. The party organizations do not expect to anoint candidates now, run their campaigns, or hand out patronage jobs. Rather, the party organizations work primarily to help fund and serve campaigns that are run by candidates and their paid consultants. This major change in party functioning could be considered just as significant as a realignment of group support.

Evidence of a Realignment

One way to characterize these changes is to argue that another realignment has taken place, superseding the New Deal party system. Recall that a realignment is defined as a significant and enduring change in the patterns of group support for the parties, usually (but not always) leading to a new majority party. Has there been a significant and

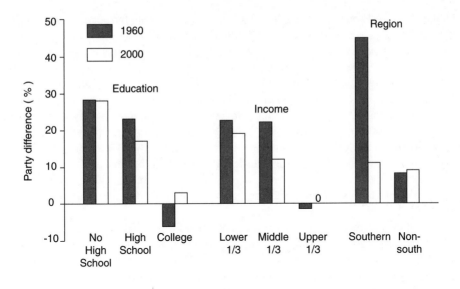

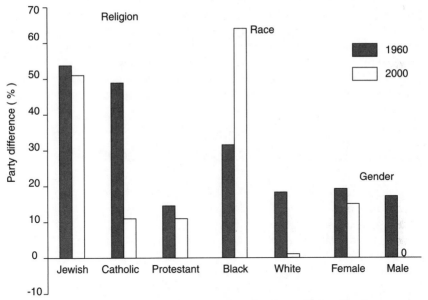

FIGURE 7.1 Changes in Group Support for the Two Major Parties.

Note: Entries are the proportion of Democrats (strong + weak) minus the proportion of Republicans (strong + weak) within each group in each year. So the size of the bar represents the extent to which the group is distinctively Democratic in its party identification.

Source: 1960: Warren E. Miller and Santa A. Traugott, *American National Election Studies Sourcebook, 1952–1986* (Cambridge, MA: Harvard University Press, 1989). 2000: American National Election Studies; data made available through the Inter-University Consortium for Political and Social Research.

enduring change in the pattern of group support for the parties? A few differences do seem evident in Figure 7.1. In 1960, Catholics and Jews were much more likely to be

Democrats than Protestants were, as can be seen by comparing the black columns; now, among religious groups (see the white columns), only Jews are distinctively Democratic. And although there was little party difference between men and women in 1960 (black columns), there is a big difference now.

The most significant changes, however, involve southerners and blacks. There has been a massive transfer of party power in the South. Southerners were strikingly Democratic in 1960; now, they barely differ from nonsoutherners in their party idenfication. In presidential races, southern whites have become a bedrock of Republican support. African Americans were predominantly Democratic in 1960. Today they are almost exclusively Democratic. The Republican coalition, then, has become more southern, and a Democratic Party that used to draw much of its strength from the white South has lost the loyalty of many southern white conservatives and now depends to a much greater extent on the votes of African Americans.

Do these changes matter? Clearly, they do. There is good evidence that the national Democratic Party's shift in the 1960s to policies favoring racial integration and affirmative action has been a primary factor in these changes and thus in the weakening of the New Deal coalition.[31] These changes in group support, in turn, affect other stands taken by the two parties. A Democratic Party that draws a large minority of its followers from African Americans is likely to take different stands from a Democratic Party that depended heavily on conservative white southerners, not only on civil rights, affirmative action, and racial profiling, but also on welfare reform, aid for inner cities, and support for public schools. These demographic changes in the Democratic coalition correspond with changes in the Democratic platform, as we will see in Chapter 15. If we take seriously the definition of realignment as a change in the party coalitions, then these changes are too dramatic to dismiss.

THE DEMOCRATIC COALITION IN 2000

Percentage Reporting a Vote for Al Gore for President

Income under $15,000	57%
No high school degree	59
Postgraduate degree	52
African American	90
Hispanic	62
Jewish	79
Catholic	50
Union member	62
Live in a large city	61
Gay or lesbian	70
Unmarried woman	63
Liberal	80
Abortion should always be legal	70
Government should do more	74
Support stricter gun control laws	62

Source: Voter News Service exit polls, at
http://cnn.com/ELECTION/2000/results/index.epolls.html (accessed Feb. 22, 2002).

Or Maybe Not

The second element of the definition—a new majority party or even a clear change in the two parties' share of the electorate—is more elusive. According to the University of Michigan's American National Election Studies polling (see Figure 7.2), more Americans called themselves Democrats than either Republicans or Independents throughout the 1952–1964 period. The Democratic edge began to erode after 1964, but Republicans did not immediately benefit. In 1969, analyst Kevin Phillips published a book that he believed would be prophetic titled *The Emerging Republican Majority*,[32] but, in fact, the proportion of Republican identifiers decreased from 1964 through 1980. Even Richard Nixon's landslide victory in the 1972 presidential contest failed to add party loyalists to GOP ranks. Instead, since the mid-1960s, more Americans have characterized themselves as independents. In this sense, then, there was no sign of a traditional realignment in the late 1960s and 1970s; both parties lost supporters, and neither won an obvious advantage.

The 1980s were a different story. Republican identification was on the rise during the decade. President Ronald Reagan's popularity, unlike Nixon's, seemed to have translated into growth for his party. Democratic strength showed a corresponding decline. Another piece of evidence suggesting a realignment was the Republican surge among young voters who, in the 1980s, became more Republican than Democratic for the first time in the 50 year annals of public opinion polling.[33]

The argument that there was a Republican realignment at this time focuses on the successes of Republican presidential candidates, the growth of the GOP in the once one-party Democratic South and the Republican gains in Congress.[34] The drop in Democratic Party ID in the South led to many more election victories for Republican candidates.

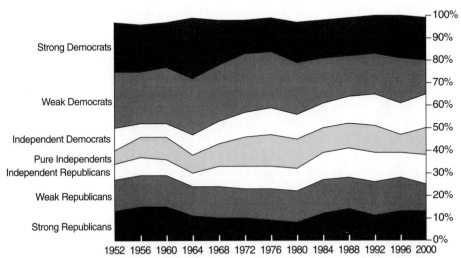

FIGURE 7.2 Democrats, Republicans, and Independents: 1952–2000.

Note: The data for this figure can be found in Table 6.1 on page 105. The small percentage of "others" (apoliticals and third-party identifiers) is not included.

Source: American National Election Studies, University of Michigan; data made available through the Inter-University Consortium for Political and Social Research.

In the 1980s, the party was able to compete effectively with the Democrats in statewide races and in 1994, there was a GOP majority among the region's U.S. representatives, U.S. senators, and governors for the first time since Reconstruction. (In fact, in recent years, most Republican leaders in the U.S. House and Senate have been from southern states.) In addition to its southern successes, the size of the Republican *partisan* victory in the 1994 congressional races was unexpectedly large across the nation, not only among southern whites but also among white men generally, especially those with less education.[35]

But if the Republican resurgence was really a realignment, why had Republican identifiers (combining "strong" and "weak" Republicans) leveled out at about one-quarter of the electorate in 2000? Even by 2004, with Republican majorities in both houses of Congress and a Republican in the White House, most polls showed only about one-third of Americans calling themselves Republicans, about on par with the percentages of self-identified Democrats and those claiming to be independent of party ties. The evidence of a realignment, then, is not strong enough for a conviction.

Evidence of a Dealignment

These changes in party loyalties strike many scholars as resembling a different pattern: a ***dealignment*** or decline in party loyalties, as opposed to a realignment, in which people develop new party loyalties. To these scholars, it seems clear that the New Deal party system has eroded and Democratic dominance has faded, but the Republican Party has not been able to capitalize fully on the Democrats' losses. In spite of the decline in the percentage of Democratic loyalists since the 1950s, the GOP has not yet won the hearts of a plurality of party identifiers. Republicans have won the presidency most of the time in recent decades, but these GOP presidents have usually had to deal with a Congress in which at least one house was under Democratic control. Divided government is alive and well in most states. Split-ticket voting is fairly common, and there has been a steady stream of independent and third-party candidates.[36]

If a dealignment is the best way to characterize the current party system, what will come next? Some scholars see dealignment as the final phase of a party system, occurring just before a realignment. As the electoral conflicts that established the party system begin to age, they argue, voters start to shake themselves loose from their party identifications, election results become less predictable, and new party coalitions can then emerge. It is the newest voters who tend to be the leading edge of such a dealignment; because they do not have the experiences that shaped the partisanship of earlier generations, when the party coalitions were being formed, they are more likely to find the major parties irrelevant to their present needs.[37]

If this argument is correct, then the dealignment will be followed by the emergence of a new party system. Yet the signs of dealignment—ticket splitting, the shifts in party control at the national level, the increase in self-identified independents—have been present for decades. Why should this particular realignment, if one is in fact coming, be taking so long?

Other observers argue that the long-awaited realignment will never come. Conditions have changed so much, they feel, that a return to a stable party system through realignment may not happen. Walter Dean Burnham has written that the American parties were so fractured by the loss of party control over nominations and the insulation of many state and local elections from national forces, through the scheduling of these elections in off years, that they may no longer be capable of realignment.[38] Candidates are so independent of their party organizations that a party realignment would have little meaning.

It may be that the New Deal succeeded so well that it eliminated the desperation that could cause another realignment. Programs such as Social Security and food stamps provide a "social safety net" for many of the most vulnerable. The absence of truly large-scale poverty, some argue, has given citizens the freedom to pursue a wide variety of other issues through a wide variety of interest groups. When a big, enduring, and contentious issue such as a Depression dominates politics, parties are the only institutions capable of creating a majority to deal with the issue. When the agenda is dominated by a large set of conflicting issues, then parties' capabilities are weakened.[39] If so, then economic change and the resulting dealignment have undermined the foundations of the New Deal party system without building a new party system in its place. Yet this argument, however, does not help us to explain why the impact of party identification on voting seems to have been recovering in recent years.

So Which Is It?

What we are witnessing, in short, is a genuine puzzle about the fate of American party politics. Analysts have mustered arguments for three different scenarios: that the party system is in a long-term dealignment, that this dealignment is about to give way to a realignment of the major parties, or that the realignment has already occurred. A fourth alternative, perhaps the argument that best fits the evidence, is that the very idea of a realignment is an exception to the more usual pattern in which some issues (race and abortion, for example) have a greater capacity than others to stimulate people's interest, cut across the existing party lines, and lure some party identifiers to reevaluate and change their party loyalty.[40] Does it matter which scenario is most accurate? It matters a lot. It will affect the amount of political conflict that we will have, the kinds of issues that we will be debating, and the volatility or predictability of our elections.

What we *do* know is that in the mid-2000s, the American electorate is composed of three groups of roughly similar size. There are two groups of partisans whose composition has changed in significant ways: an expanding group of Republicans dominated by conservatives, southerners, and churchgoers, and a group of Democrats, including liberals, lower-income people, and minorities, whose size has shrunk a bit in recent years. And there is a third group that could truly be termed dealigned, in that it feels no lasting party loyalties and usually stays out of political activity.[41]

But because the Democratic and Republican camps are so close in size and because so many Americans consider themselves independent of party, it is also an electorate capable of producing mercurial election results, within and across elections. This highly competitive party system could soon produce the Republican majority that Phillips envisioned decades ago. It could also sustain the divided control of government that has been so characteristic of American politics for the past three decades. The trajectory of American politics, then, has the potential for rapid change.

CHAPTER 8

Who Votes—and Why It Matters

In the end, the 2000 presidential election came down to 537 votes in Florida. That was the margin by which George W. Bush beat his Democratic opponent, Al Gore, in the state. Under Florida's winner-take-all rules, Bush thus won all of its electoral votes— enough to give him a bare majority in the electoral college and, as a result, the presidency. At the same time, about 2.6 *million* Floridians who were registered to vote did not go to the polls—almost 5,000 times the size of Bush's tiny margin of victory.

Does it matter who votes and who doesn't? Ask Al Gore. If just a few more African Americans or fewer conservatives had come out to vote in each Florida county, the nation might have had a different president. The question of who votes, then, is a central concern of candidates, especially the thousands of candidates in close races each year, and party organizations. The question of how well these voters reflect the opinions, social characteristics, and partisanship of the larger adult population is a major issue for those interested in preserving democracy.

In a more basic sense, the American parties have grown and changed in response to expansions of the *right* to vote. As the electorate was enlarged to include lower status people and then women, minorities, and younger people, the parties were forced to change their organizations and appeals. Parties that failed to adjust to the new electorates, the early Federalists, for example, became extinct. Others, such as European socialist and labor parties, have gained strength by fighting to secure the vote for lower status citizens and then using these voters' support to win power.

In short, the nature of the parties, as well as the success of individual candidates, depends on the kinds of people who have the right to vote and on the types of people who take advantage of that right. In turn, parties try to expand the right to vote (or limit its expansion), and to bring some groups to the polls and not others, in order to improve their odds of winning elections. Because groups have different profiles of support for the parties, as Chapter 7 showed, the composition of the active electorate affects the balance of party power. The remarkably low voter turnout in American elections heightens the impact of these group differences in party support.

THE LOW TURNOUT IN AMERICAN ELECTIONS

Only 51 percent of the eligible electorate cast a ballot for president in 2000. Four years earlier, the turnout rate was 49 percent. These voting rates are low even by American standards. Prior to 1996, voter turnout had dropped below 50 percent in just two presidential elections since 1824: the first two elections of the 1920s, before many women had become accustomed to their new right to vote (see Figure 8.1).[1]

The overall figures hide even lower turnout rates in many states. In the 2000 presidential contest, for example, the U.S. Census reported that 44 percent of the voting-age citizen population cast a ballot in Hawaii in comparison with around 70 percent in North Dakota, Wisconsin, Maine, and Minnesota. Even fewer people vote in off-year elections; in 2002, a mere 39 percent of those eligible cast a vote for the top office on the ballot. Turnout rates drop further in local elections and party primaries.

These low turnouts have long generated serious debate. Some observers ask: how healthy can our democracy be when fewer than half of its citizens bother to vote? Others have the opposite concern: that the nation might be harmed by encouraging less interested, and presumably less informed, citizens to participate. Nevertheless, at other times and in other places, democracies have enjoyed much broader participation. Voting turnout in the United States reached an all-time high toward the end of the nineteenth century.[2] In more recent times, presidential turnout reached 63 percent in 1960 and turnout in off-year elections peaked at 48 percent in 1966. However, even these percentages are low compared

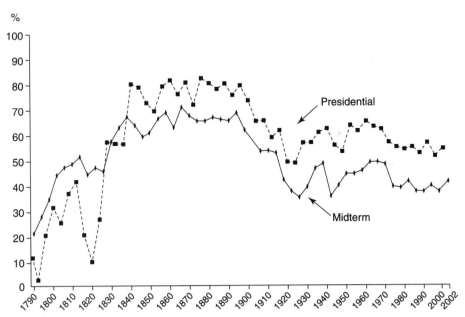

FIGURE 8.1   Turnout in American Elections: 1790–2002.

Note: These are the percentages voting for president and for the office with the highest vote in midterm elections, calculated as described in note 1 to this chapter.

with other countries. In almost no other democratic nation in the world does such a small share of the voters take part in choosing the most important government officials.[3]

How did American voter participation sink to this level? There are two stories to tell here. On the one hand, the *right* to vote has greatly expanded; on the other, Americans are increasing reluctant to exercise that right. The major parties have played an important role in both these stories. Let us start with the expansion of voting rights.

THE EXPANDING RIGHT TO VOTE

The Constitution leaves it to the states to decide who is eligible to vote. Since the Civil War, however, the national government has acted occasionally, most often through constitutional amendments, to keep states from imposing especially offensive restrictions on voting.

White males were given the right to vote earlier in the United States than in any other democracy. In the early 1800s, the states gradually repealed the property, income, and tax-paying qualifications for voting by which they had so severely limited male suffrage.[4] By 1860, no states required property holding and only four required substantial taxpaying as a condition for voting. About a century later, the Supreme Court, and then the Twenty-fourth Amendment, finally ended even the small poll tax as a requirement for voting.[5]

Women did not win the right to vote in all states until much later. By the mid-1870s, activists had begun to press state governments to let women vote; in 1890, when it was admitted to the Union, Wyoming became the first state to grant full voting rights to women. The push for women's suffrage then bogged down, especially in the eastern states, and women suffragists shifted their hopes to the U.S. Constitution. The Nineteenth Amendment, forbidding states to deny the vote on grounds of gender, was finally ratified in 1920.

Black Americans' right to vote has a more checkered history. Some New England states granted blacks the suffrage before the Civil War. The Fifteenth Amendment, adopted after that war, declared that no state could abridge the right to vote on account of race. However, the federal government soon turned its attention to other matters, and southern states worked effectively to undermine the amendment's purpose by using devices such as poll taxes, outrageous "literacy tests," and outright intimidation to keep blacks from voting. By the early 1900s, black turnout in the South had dropped to negligible levels. It remained that way in most southern states until the 1960s, when the federal government began to enforce the Fifteenth Amendment and new voting rights laws on the reluctant states.

The most recent change in the legal definition of the electorate has been to lower the voting age to 18. In the 1960s, only a handful of states allowed people under the age of 21 to vote. In 1970, Congress lowered the minimum voting age to 18 in both state and federal elections. When the Supreme Court decided that the act was unconstitutional for state and local elections,[6] Congress passed a constitutional amendment lowering the age to 18 for all elections; this was quickly ratified by the states in 1971.

The national government has taken other steps to expand the electorate. Congress banned literacy, understanding, and "character" tests for registration and waived residence requirements for voting in presidential elections. The so-called "motor voter" law, passed in 1993, required the states to let citizens register to vote at driver's license bureaus, by mail, and through agencies that give out federal benefits. Voter registration has surged in many areas as a result, although these increases have not been matched by greater voter turnout in most elections.[7]

LEGAL BARRIERS TO VOTING

In sum, the right to vote has been expanded enormously since the early 1800s; political pressures for universal adult suffrage have resulted in constitutional amendments, congressional legislation, and supervision by the Supreme Court. But states continue to impose some major restrictions and burdens on those who would vote, including citizenship requirements, residence requirements, and the need to register before going to the polls.

Citizenship

Since the 1920s, all states have required that voters be citizens of the United States. As surprising as it may now seem, prior to 1894, at least twelve states permitted noncitizens to vote,[8] although some required that the individual had to have applied for American citizenship. The requirement of citizenship remains the biggest legal barrier to voting. There are millions of adults living in the United States, most of them concentrated in California, Florida, Texas, and New York, who cannot vote until they are "naturalized" as citizens, a process that can take two or three years to complete.

Residence

For most of American history, states could require citizens to live in a state and locality for a certain period of time before being allowed to vote there. Most states had three-layer residence requirements: a minimum period of time in the state, a shorter time in the county, and an even shorter period in the local voting district. Southern states had the longest residence requirements (which kept migrant farm workers from voting), but other states also had long waits for eligibility.

A few states had begun to lower their residence requirements in the 1950s and 1960s as society became more mobile; many states set up even lower requirements for newcomers wishing to vote in presidential elections. In 1970, Congress established a national requirement of thirty days' residence within a state for voting in presidential elections. Since then, almost half of the states have dropped residence requirements altogether and most of the rest have fixed them at one month.

Despite these changes, residency requirements are still a barrier to voting. The United States is a nation of movers. Almost one in every six Americans moved between March 1999 and March 2000, including about 6 percent who moved to a different county and 3 percent to a different state.[9] Those who have moved recently are much less likely to vote, in part because they must take the time and initiative to find out where and when they need to register (see below). Researchers estimate that with the impact of mobility removed, turnout would be about 9 percent higher.[10]

Registration

One of the greatest obstacles to voting is the registration requirement—the rule in most states that citizens must register in advance in order to vote in an election. During most of the 1800s, voters needed only to show up on Election Day to cast a ballot or to be listed on the government's voting roll—the same rules that most European democracies use today. Progressive reformers near the end of the nineteenth century urged states to require advance registration in order to limit illegal voting in the big cities. That increased the motivation needed to vote because it required a trip to the registration office well before the excitement of the campaign had reached its peak. These registration requirements reduced the high turnout levels of that time.[11]

These requirements have since been relaxed. States differ in what they require and thus in the burden they place on citizens. The relevant provisions involve the closing date for registration (which ranges from none to 30 days before the election), the frequency with which registration rolls are purged (a few states remove voters from the rolls after missing one election, but most do it only after four years of nonvoting), and the accessibility of registrars.[12] North Dakota does not require its citizens to register at all, and six other states permit registering on Election Day, which tends to increase turnout.

The requirements that remain, however, still make it more inconvenient to vote. The higher these "costs" of voting are, the more citizens will choose not to participate in elections. Studies estimate that turnout in presidential elections would be much higher if all states allowed Election Day registration, set regular as well as evening and Saturday hours for registering, and did not purge for nonvoting. The greatest gains would be realized by eliminating the closing date, which would let citizens cast a ballot even if they did not get interested enough to take part until the last, most engaging days of the campaign.[13]

THE SPECIAL CASE OF VOTING RIGHTS FOR AFRICAN AMERICANS

Legal barriers to voting were especially effective in denying the vote to southern blacks, at least until fairly recent times. The disenfranchisement of southern black voters was a case of blatant manipulation of the electoral system in order to control election results. It was accomplished by a variety of laws, capricious election administration, and intimidation and violence when these subtler methods were not effective. By these means, blacks were kept away from the polls in the former Confederacy and some neighboring states for almost a century.

Southern states employed an arsenal of weapons to restrict the black vote. Residence requirements were most strict in the South. Most states in that region required payment of a poll tax in order to vote—just one or two dollars, but often demanded well before an election, with the stipulation that the taxpayer keep a receipt and present it weeks later at the voting booth. Many states also required some prospective voters to pass a literacy test measuring reading ability and understanding. Local voting officials, who were usually hostile to blacks voting, had the power to decide who was "literate" enough to pass the test. These laws were intentionally directed at the poor and uneducated black population. They created huge barriers to voting.

If the law was not enough to discourage blacks from voting, other devices were available. Blacks hoping to register found themselves blocked by endless delays, unavailable or antagonistic registrars, and technicalities (see box on page 141). Those who kept trying were often faced with economic reprisal (the loss of a job or a home) and physical violence. It is not surprising, in this relentlessly hostile environment, that only 5 percent of voting-age blacks were registered in the 11 southern states as late as 1940.[14]

BARRIERS TO BLACK REGISTRATION IN THE SOUTH

In their account of the civil rights movement in the South, Pat Watters and Reese Cleghorn describe how blacks were prevented from registering by simple but effective administrative practices:

> Slowdowns were common. Separate tables would be assigned to whites and Negroes [the customary term for African-Americans before the mid-1960s]. If a line of Negroes were waiting for the Negro table, a white might go ahead of them, use the empty white table, and leave. In Anniston, Alabama, a report said the white table was larger, and Negroes were not allowed in the room when a white was using it. Another variation was to seat four Negroes at a table, and make three wait until the slowest had finished, while others waited outside in line. These methods were particularly effective when coupled with the one or two day a month registration periods. . . . In one north Florida county, the registrar didn't bother with any of these refinements, and didn't close his office when Negro applicants appeared. He simply sat with his legs stretched out across the doorway. Negroes didn't break through them.

Source: Pat Watters and Reese Cleghorn, *Climbing Jacob's Ladder* (New York: Harcourt Brace Jovanovich, 1967), pp. 122–123.

The Long Struggle for Voting Rights

For years after the end of Reconstruction, southern states and the Supreme Court played a game of constitutional "hide and seek." States would devise a way to disenfranchise blacks, the Court would strike it down as unconstitutional, and the states would find another. One example was the "white primary." Faced with the threat of blacks voting in the Democratic primary, some states simply declared the party a private club open only to whites; blacks, therefore, could not vote in the primary. This was done at a time when the Republican Party was weak to nonexistent in the South, so the candidate who won the Democratic primary was assured of winning the general election. It took 21 years of lawsuits and five Supreme Court cases to end this practice.[15]

Court action was not nearly as effective against the more informal hurdles faced by blacks trying to vote, so reformers tried legislative and administrative remedies. The federal Voting Rights Act of 1965, extended in 1982, made a frontal assault on these forms of discrimination by involving the national government directly in local registration practices. It authorized the U.S. Justice Department to seek injunctions against anyone who prevented blacks from voting. When the Justice Department could convince a federal court that a "pattern or practice" of discrimination existed in a district, the court could send federal registrars there to register voters. It could also supervise voting procedures in states and counties where less than 50 percent of potential voters had gone to the polls in the most recent presidential election. It put local registrars under greater regulation and control.[16]

The Growth of Black Registration in the South

This unprecedented federal intervention in state elections, combined with the civil rights movement's efforts to mobilize black voters, enabled the black electorate to grow enormously in the South. Black registration increased from 5 percent of the black voting-age population in 1940 to 29 percent in 1960 and then surged dramatically by the 1990s to a level close to that of white southerners. White registration also increased slightly during this period. Yet black registration levels vary among the southern states even now, depending on the size and socioeconomic characteristics of states' black populations, their political traditions, and the barriers that they continue to raise to black participation (Figure 8.2).

From Voting Rights to Representation

Even though they are no longer systematically prevented from voting, African Americans still find it hard to gain an effective political voice in many areas of the South. In the debate over extending the Voting Rights Act in 1981 and 1982, the major issue was the effort by some states and localities to dilute the impact of black votes or to limit the opportunities for blacks to choose black officeholders. This was most commonly done by redrawing legislative district lines in order to divide black voters among several districts and by annexing white suburbs to offset black majorities in the cities or towns.

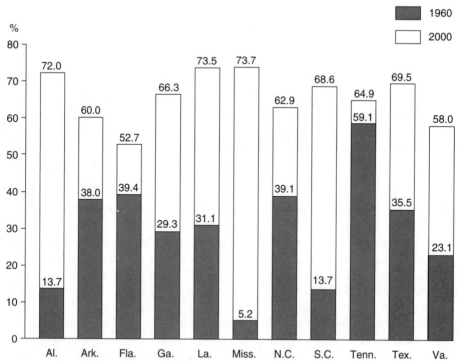

FIGURE 8.2   **Black Voter Registration in the South: 1960 and 2000.**

Note: Bars show the percentage of blacks in the two years who were registered to vote.

Source: U.S. Census Bureau.

After the 1990 census, the first Bush administration pressed southern states to redraw congressional district lines so as to create some districts with a majority of black voters, called *"majority-minority" districts*. It was assumed that these districts would be very likely to elect black legislators to Congress and thus improve the representation of African Americans. A number of these districts were created by an interesting alliance of black and Hispanic Democrats with white Republicans. The result was to increase the number of congressional seats held by black Americans.

Another effect of these majority-minority districts, however, was to elect more Republicans to Congress from the South—one reason why Republicans supported their creation. Because the districts are fashioned by packing as many (heavily Democratic) black voters into a district as possible, the neighboring districts are left with a higher proportion of whites and Republicans. So, according to one estimate, "for every overwhelmingly black Democratic district created, there is a good chance of creating two or more districts that are overwhelmingly white and Republican."[17] In turn, Democratic state legislatures try to pack the GOP vote into as few districts as possible and to draw other districts that are 25 to 40 percent black which, coupled with the third or so of white voters who still support Democrats, are very likely to send Democratic representatives to Congress.

In a series of close decisions since the early 1990s, the Supreme Court rejected the most flagrantly engineered of these majority-minority districts. The Court ruled that race cannot be the "predominant" factor in drawing district lines, overriding such considerations as county boundaries, compactness, and protecting incumbents. However, a closely divided Court continues to rule that race can be an element in redrawing district lines, as long as it is not the controlling factor.[18]

Getting Blacks' Votes Counted

Americans learned from the 2000 presidential election that even when people get to the polls, their votes are not always counted. Poorer and minority-dominated districts tend to have older and less reliable voting machines that are more likely to make errors in counting votes. The U.S. Commission on Civil Rights reported in 2001 that although it found no evidence of a systematic effort to disenfranchise blacks, they were ten times more likely than whites to have their ballots undercounted or rejected in the 2000 Florida balloting because they lived in districts with less reliable voting systems.[19]

These frustrations are compounded by the fact that as many as 12.5 percent of black males have lost the right to vote because they have felony convictions. The recent spate of mandatory sentences for drug use appear to target drugs used more often by blacks, and most states deny felons the right to vote, at least while they are serving their sentences.[20] So although black turnout rates are much higher now than they were in the mid-1900s, more subtle challenges to blacks' voting rights remain.

POLITICAL INFLUENCES ON TURNOUT

The *right* to vote, we have seen, is now almost universal in the United States. But people differ in their willingness to exercise that right. Among the forces that can draw voters to the polls or drive them away are various political factors, including the importance of the contest, the level of public interest it generates, the amount of competition between the parties, and the efforts of parties and other political groups to stimulate voter turnout.

The Excitement of the Election

American voters face more frequent elections than almost any other population in the democratic world. Within four years, they will be called to the polls to select scores of legislators, executives, and even judges at the national, state, and local levels. Most of these elections are preceded by primaries. In some areas, voters will have to deal with initiatives, referenda, and even an occasional recall election. Just 11 months after they had elected a governor, for instance, Californians were asked to vote in 2003 on whether he should be recalled. Campaigns are lengthy and often disappointingly negative. Americans pay dearly, in the currency of many and frequent voting decisions, for the right to keep government on a short electoral leash.

Voter participation varies a great deal depending on the type of election.[21] It is usually highest in presidential elections and lowest in local races. General elections normally attract far more voters than primaries. It is understandable why the more intense general election campaigns for the presidency and governorships entice more voters to participate. The personalities and issues involved are more highly publicized. Because party fortunes are involved, people's party loyalties are aroused, in contrast with the situation of many nonpartisan local elections.

Initiatives and referenda, the Progressives' devices for allowing voters to decide issues directly, bring out fewer voters than candidate elections. At times, an emotionally charged referendum can attract public interest, but the issues are often complicated enough to confuse many would-be voters. Yet under some conditions, even these Progressive reforms can provoke a large voter turnout, as in the 2003 California recall election, whose colorful list of candidates included movie star Arnold Schwarzenegger, a porn actress, the publisher of *Hustler* magazine, a bounty hunter, and a sumo wrestler. They, and the 130 other candidates on the recall ballot, were apparently enough to shake California voters out of their election-induced lethargy.

Close Competition

Political competition brings voters to the polls. Turnout is higher in areas where the parties and candidates regularly compete on a fairly even basis, for example, in the states in Table 2.2 (in Chapter 2) that fall into the two-party range. Voting participation increases in races that are hotly contested, regardless of the type of office, the nature of the electorate, and the district's historical voting trends.[22] Closely fought races generate excitement and give voters more assurance that their vote will make a difference.

Changes in party competition, historically brought about by realignment, have affected turnout levels. National politics was fiercely competitive in the two decades before 1900; control of government turned on razor-thin margins of victory. The realignment of 1896 brought an abrupt end to this close competition: in the South, the Populist movement was absorbed into the Democratic Party, and outside the South, the Democrats' appeal declined. After the realignment, participation in presidential elections dropped markedly—from almost 80 percent of the voting-age population in prior elections to about 65 percent in the early 1900s. Some scholars argue that the realignment was the culprit; because of the decline in party competition, the parties did not have as great an incentive to work at mobilizing voters, which resulted in a decrease in turnout. Even the realignment of the 1930s failed to restore the competition and high voter turnouts of that earlier era.[23]

There are other possible explanations for this decrease in turnout. At around the time of the 1896 realignment, such devices as poll taxes and literacy tests began to increase the "cost" of voting, as did the introduction of the secret ballot and tightened registration requirements.[24] More evidence would be needed to resolve this controversy, but the decline in party competition produced by that realignment probably had at least some role in reducing turnout.

The Representativeness of the Party System

Turnout tends to be much higher in European multiparty systems, where each sizable group in the society is often represented by its own party. The broad, coalitional nature of the two major American parties may make it more difficult for citizens to feel that a party gives voice to their individual needs. One price that the United States may pay for its two-party system, then, is lower turnout. The particular types of conflicts that shape the party system, whether social, economic, religious, or racial, can also affect voter involvement. Citizens who feel that they have a big stake in the prevailing political conflicts are more likely to see a reason to vote: for example, elderly Americans at a time when their Social Security and Medicare benefits, which depend so heavily on government decisions, are consistently an issue in national campaigns.

Organized Efforts to Mobilize Voters

One of the most important findings about voter turnout is that people go to the polls when somebody encourages them to do so. Researchers show that personal canvassing, at least when it uses nonpartisan appeals, does a better job of getting voters to the polls than do mail or phone appeals. Thus, the decline in face-to-face voter mobilization, at least until recent years, can probably explain some of the decrease in voter turnout.[25] Yet turnout increased only slightly in 2000, even though parties and other groups seemed to have hit a recent high in their voter contacting efforts; 44 percent of a national sample said they had been contacted by someone with regard to registration or voting.[26]

In a nation with low voter turnouts, bringing more voters to the polls has long been an appealing strategy, not only for the parties but for other groups as well. American history is filled with examples of group efforts to increase turnout. Civil rights groups, as we have seen, helped to achieve dramatic gains in voter registration and turnout since the 1960s and worked closely with the Democratic Party in the 2000 and 2002 elections to encourage African Americans to go to the polls.[27] Organized labor mounted a major, and apparently effective, get-out-the-vote drive in 2000, built on union members' contacts with other members and their friends and neighbors.[28] Christian conservatives expanded their influence in the Republican Party by developing a base of loyal followers that could be mobilized in elections.

Not all such efforts have been as effective. Mobilizing groups of people is hard to do. MTV's "Rock the Vote" campaign, aimed at teens and young adults, for example, has not made much of a dent in the low voting turnout of that age group. Because new campaign techniques allow campaigns to target the people most likely to vote, the existing racial and socioeconomic status (SES) differences between voters and nonvoters can be further entrenched. Once the mobilization has brought an individual to the polls, however, he or she is likely to return. Voting becomes a habit, which can help to explain the increasing tendency to vote as people age.[29]

TURNOUT: INDIVIDUAL DIFFERENCES

Differences among individuals also affect their likelihood of voting. Voter turnout is related to a variety of economic and social forces, from citizens' levels of education to their social connections. We can think about the decision to vote in terms of its costs and benefits to the individual. Each of us pays some costs for the privilege of voting, not in cash but in time, energy, and attention. What we get in return may seem minimal; the influence of a single vote in most elections is likely to be small. From that perspective, it may be remarkable that anyone votes at all.[30] Many factors affect the costs and benefits that individuals weigh in choosing whether to go to the polls.

Socioeconomic Status

The greatest difference between voters and nonvoters is their SES; lower status Americans are much less likely to vote.[31] A careful study of voting argues that education level is the most powerful influence on turnout (see Figure 8.3, section A); the impact of income and occupational differences is minimal once education is taken into account. More education helps people understand the complexities of politics and gives them the tools to get the information they need to make political choices. People with more education are more likely to feel that they ought to vote, to gain satisfaction from voting, and to have the experience with meeting deadlines and filling out forms that will be necessary to register and vote.[32]

This relationship between SES and voting sounds so obvious that we would expect to see it in other democracies too. Interestingly, however, the relationship is less strong in many other democratic nations. In these nations, labor parties and other groups work hard enough to bring less educated and lower income people to the polls that they seem to compensate for the disadvantages of low SES that are so marked in American politics.[33]

Youth

After socioeconomic explanations, the next most powerful personal factor in accounting for differences between voters and nonvoters is youth. For a long time, younger Americans have been less likely to go to the polls than are older people, especially those over the age of 65, and the gap is growing, not shrinking (see Figure 8.4). Much of the difference reflects the high "start-up" costs younger people must pay when voting: the difficulties of settling into a community, registering for the first time, and establishing the habit of voting, all at a time when other, more personal interests dominate their lives. The lowering of the national voting age to 18 and the entry of the unusually large "baby boom" generation into the electorate helped to depress voting rates more generally.

As a result, campaign agendas became even more attuned to the concerns of older voters—Social Security, Medicare, prescription drugs—because they are much more likely to vote. Studies show that young adults hold attitudes different from those of their parents and grandparents. Younger people, on average, are more likely to accept the idea of privatizing public services (for instance, letting people invest some of their Social Security taxes in the stock market) than older people are and also more tolerant of diversity, including women's rights, affirmative action, and gay marriage.[34] But the low turnout rates of young adults make it less likely that these views will be heard.

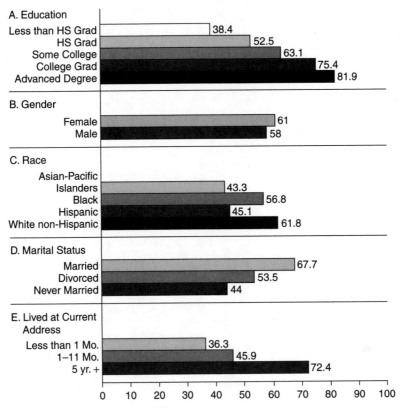

FIGURE 8.3   Voter Turnout in 2000.

Note: Bars show the percentage of each group who reported having voted in the 2000 presidential election, based on the voting-age citizen population.

Source: U.S. Census, *Voting and Registration in the Election of November 2000* (Feb. 27, 2002), p. 6; at http://www.census.gov/prod/2002pubs/p20-542.pdf (accessed August 13, 2003).

Gender and Race

For many decades after getting the right to vote in 1920, women voted less often than men, but women's increasing education levels and changes in women's roles in society have largely eliminated this gender difference (see Figure 8.3, section B). The gap in voting rates between blacks and whites still persists, although it has gotten smaller (see Figure 8.3, section C). The remaining racial differences in voting are due almost entirely to the differences in education and occupational status, on average, between whites and blacks.[35] Hispanics and Asian Americans have the lowest rates of voter turnout.

Social Connectedness

People who have a lot of social ties—those who belong to a variety of organizations and are closely connected with friends and family—are much more likely to participate in elections than others are. Social interaction itself increases the likelihood of involvement

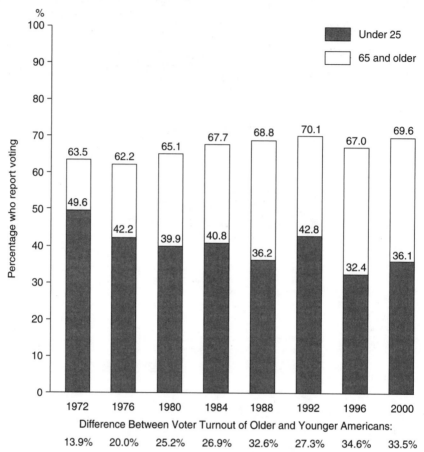

FIGURE 8.4   Voter Turnout of Younger and Older Americans: 1972–2000.
Source: U.S. Census, *Voting and Registration in the Election of November 2000* (Feb. 27, 2002), p. 6; at
http://www.census.gov/prod/2002pubs/p20-542.pdf (accessed August 13, 2003).

in politics. Members of organizations have much higher voting rates than nonmembers; this adds weight to the conclusion that organizations play an important role in mobilizing voters. Voting is also more common among people who are well integrated into the community through home ownership, long-time residence, church attendance, or a job outside the home. Even marriage or the loss of a spouse affects the likelihood that an individual will vote (see Figure 8.3, sections D and E).[36]

Personal Costs of Voting

There are several reasons why the occasion to vote may seem like a threat. For some adults whose political cues are mixed, for example, those who have Democratic relatives and a Republican spouse, voting can be stressful.[37] Less educated citizens may find the length and complexity of the ballot intimidating. Some people refuse to register because the registration rolls are used to choose citizens for jury duty, which they may want to avoid, or there may be less pressing reasons to avoid voting (see box on page 149).

WHY DIDN'T YOU VOTE?

Here's why people said they didn't go to the polls in the 2000 election:

I was too busy	21%
Illness or emergency	15
Just not interested	12
Out of town	10
Didn't like the candidates	8
I don't know why	8
Problems with registration	7[1]
I forgot	4
It was inconvenient	3
Transportation problems	2
The weather was bad	1
Other	10

[1]Only the answers of registered voters are reported here.

Source: U.S. Census Bureau, *Voting and Registration in the Election of November 2000* (issued Feb. 27, 2002), p. 10, at http://www.census.gov/prod/2002pubs/p20-542.pdf (accessed July 17, 2003).

Political Attitudes

Attitudes toward politics affect individuals' motivation to vote. Those who find the current campaign more interesting and who have stronger party loyalties are more involved in elections. In addition, study after study has shown that a cluster of "civic attitudes" predisposes individuals to vote. The most important of these are perceptions that government is responsive to citizens (termed ***external political efficacy***) and can be trusted to do what is right (***trust in government***) and a sense of responsibility to take part in elections (***citizen duty***).[38] Individuals' attitudes probably interact with the reality of the political system: divided government and separated powers may depress turnout by making it harder for individuals to know who is responsible for what the government does.[39]

THE PUZZLE OF DECLINING VOTER TURNOUT

Turnout in American elections has declined substantially since the 1960s. Voting in presidential elections decreased by almost 15 percentage points from its postwar peak in 1960 (63 percent) to the 1996 low of 49 percent. Turnout in midterm elections also dropped, from a postwar high of 48 percent in 1966 to 33 percent in the 1998 House elections. There was an upswing in 2000 and 2002, but it was not dramatic. Interestingly, there has been a marked recent decrease in British voter turnout as well.[40]

Explaining the Decline

This decline in voter turnout is puzzling because it has occurred at a time when powerful forces should have propelled turnout upward instead. Educational levels have increased substantially and higher SES is associated with higher voter turnout. The costs of voting have been reduced by liberalized residence and registration rules. New voting methods make it easier to cast a ballot; Oregon, for example, now votes entirely by mail. Earlier generations of women who were not accustomed to voting have been succeeded by generations accustomed to an active political role. Since 1960, groups have worked hard to bring southern blacks to the polls. Yet turnout has declined, at least outside the South.[41]

One main reason is that the political attitudes that support participation, especially the belief that government is responsive to its citizens (external political efficacy), have declined since 1960. Alienation and cynicism have increased. When people don't feel connected to the political process, they don't vote. Variations over time in the strength of partisanship have also played a role. These two attitudes contributed separately to the turnout declines from 1960 through 2000, with partisanship accounting for more of the change than efficacy. Their combined effects were even stronger.[42]

Other forces have also taken their toll on voting turnout. Since 1960, the American electorate has become more mobile, less inclined to attend religious services on a regular basis, and less likely to be married. These indicate a decrease in social "connectedness"—a weakening of the ties binding Americans to the social networks that stimulate participation. At least in the 1970s and 1980s, parties' and groups' efforts to turn out the vote through labor-intensive campaigning seemed to decline, as did social movement activism. With this slackening of effort to arouse the electorate, voters had less motivation to go to the polls.

Could Voter Participation Revive?

The decline in turnout seemed to halt in the 1992 and 1994 elections. Although participation was still low by most standards, it reached its highest levels in a decade for midterm contests and in two decades for presidential contests. These two elections proved to be a "blip"; low turnouts returned in 1996 and have remained since then. Yet the reasons for these brief improvements in voter turnout suggest that the long-term turnout decline could be interrupted again.

The excitement of the 1992 election probably explains the surge in presidential turnout in that year. It was the closest election since 1976; public opinion polls showed a tight race through the fall campaign. Most states were won by only a small plurality. It was also a genuine three-candidate contest packed with dramatic events in which independent candidate Ross Perot posed a serious challenge to the major-party standard-bearers. As a result, interest in the election was considerably higher than the 1964 to 1988 average and that buoyed turnout. Perot was able to rally many disaffected Americans who were looking for an alternative to the two major parties.

Similarly, the political situation leading up to the 1994 congressional elections probably led more people to the polls. The Republicans seemed to have their best chance in decades to capture the Congress and to gain more governorships and state legislative seats. Media attention focused on the "Contract with America," a statement of conservative principles signed by most Republican congressional candidates in an effort to nationalize the campaign. It was an effective strategy; otherwise, the localism typical of midterm elections would probably have advantaged incumbent Democrats. The result was an unprecedented surge of Republican support. GOP House candidates drew almost 9 million more votes than they had in 1990 and Democrats lost nearly a million votes.

Such one-sided mobilization is rare; it last appeared in the 1934 election during the realignment that created the New Deal party system.

The 1992 and 1994 campaigns were a hard act to follow. In fact, 1996 and 1998 were business as usual—low turnouts, low political interest. The 2000 presidential election turned out to be the closest in history, but the campaign and the candidates did not generate much public excitement. The lesson of the early 1990s, then, is that when an important race is up for grabs, when the candidates are entertaining, and when elections turn on an identifiable set of divisive themes, political interest should increase and carry voter turnout along with it. Without the stimulation of an interesting contest, or the active mobilization of partisans, turnout levels are not likely to recover.

WHY DO THESE CHANGES IN TURNOUT MATTER?

We have been following two related stories in this chapter: the expansion of voting rights to new groups and the decline in Americans' willingness to take advantage of these rights. Both of these trends have important effects on the parties and on representation more broadly.

Long-Range Effects

The addition of new groups to the electorate has reshaped the parties. When blacks began to vote in large numbers in the 1960s and 1970s, they voted overwhelmingly for Democratic candidates; more than 80 percent of blacks have voted Democratic in each presidential election since 1964. At the same time, there was a countermovement of whites away from the Democrats, particularly in the South.[43] These trends have been responsive to, and have helped to reinforce, major changes in the two parties' stands on issues ranging from civil rights to welfare reform, as we will see in Chapter 15.

The enfranchisement of young adults between the ages of 18 and 21 has had more mixed effects on the parties. The new young voters were more likely to be Democrats than Republicans in the 1970s. That trend reversed in 1984 and 1988 and re-reversed in the early 1990s. On balance, the youngest voters have tended to pay more attention to the short-term forces of a particular election than to the parties' more fundamental appeals.

The voting population has changed in other ways. An increasing proportion of the voting-age population lives in the South and West, areas where Republicans do well in elections. The aging of the population has enlarged the group of elderly voters in each successive presidential election. As these groups expand, their distinctive interests carry greater weight in the electorate. If the parties hope to thrive, they must adapt to these changes when choosing candidates and taking positions on issues.

In the same sense, groups that shrink as a proportion of the electorate, either because they are becoming a smaller part of the population as a whole or because they are going to the polls in smaller numbers, may lose political influence. Elected officials and parties, understandably, are more likely to pay attention to the needs of those who affect election results than to those who don't. A recent study shows that members of Congress direct more federal spending to counties in their district with higher voter turnout than to those with lower voter turnout.[44]

The implications of this potential loss of influence are all the more serious because nonvoters are more likely than voters to come from disadvantaged groups. On average, the 70 million adults who are not registered to vote tend to have a lower SES than those who are registered, to be African American, Asian, or Latino, and to be younger. Some careful studies report that nonvoters do not differ much from voters in their views on issues.[45] Yet we cannot be sure that this would continue to be true if these nonvoters were to become politically involved.

Effects on Particular Elections

Changes in turnout from election to election can affect the parties as well. The conventional wisdom is that large turnouts favor Democratic candidates. Most nonvoters come from groups, in particular, those of lower SES, usually inclined to vote Democratic. That is why proposals to make it easier to register (as did the "motor voter" law), to allow voters to register at the polls, and to make illegal aliens eligible for citizenship are often assumed to benefit the Democrats. It explains why organized labor spends so much money and effort on registration and get-out-the-vote campaigns. It is one reason why Republicans have lobbied to schedule gubernatorial elections in non-presidential election years, because the smaller voter turnout would advantage Republican candidates. It even explains politicians' belief that rainy weather is Republican weather, in that Republicans will come to the polls anyway.

This conventional wisdom is not always correct, however. We have seen that people who are more interested and involved in politics are more likely to vote. So an increase in voter turnout in a particular election is likely to come from the segment of the electorate that is less politically interested. Those who are less concerned with politics tend to vote only if they are motivated by a dramatic issue or a popular candidate, whether Democratic or Republican; in fact, Republican presidential candidates have won most of the large-turnout elections in the past five decades.[46] In addition, people seem to register mainly in response to group efforts to mobilize them, and especially in the Sunbelt, it has been the Republicans who have made large-scale efforts at voter registration.[47]

THE CHALLENGE TO THE PARTIES

This chapter began by citing one of the most striking facts about current American politics: that even in the most high-profile elections, almost half of the potential voters stay home. The case for democracy often rests on the argument that the best decisions are made when the responsibility for decision making is most widely shared. Full participation in democratic self-governance, then, would seem to be a valuable ideal (see "Which Would You Choose?" on page 153). Yet American politics falls far short of that ideal, a finding that is all the more bitter when we see that voting turnouts are higher in most other democracies.

If widespread nonvoting is an insult to the democratic spirit, it also raises questions as to whether the major parties—the groups most directly concerned with contesting elections—are doing an effective job of involving the whole electorate. The parties are the organizations that developed to mobilize citizens for political action. They have the great strength, compared with other kinds of organized interests, of being able to recruit large and diverse groups of people into politics. As instruments of mass democracy, it would seem that the parties ought to strive for the greatest possible citizen participation in elections.

If that is so, then the parties have failed. Although they have, at times, actively competed for the support of new voters, the parties do not always seem to relish the challenge of attracting new voting groups, especially those of low SES. They have adjusted their strategies to the electorate as it now exists. The party in government, which helps

WHICH WOULD YOU CHOOSE?

WE NEED EVERY VOTE . . .

Democracy is most vibrant when there is full debate among all viewpoints. When as many people as possible take part in elections, government is more likely to come up with the creative solutions needed to solve public problems.

Politicians pay more attention to the needs of those who vote than to those who do not. So the views and interests of the nonvoters, although real, may well go unrepresented.

The most committed voters tend to be more educated, have higher incomes, and are often more extreme in their viewpoints than other citizens are. These people will thus get more than their share of government benefits and attention from elected officials anxious to get their votes.

It is the more alienated and dissatisfied people who stay away from the polls. They can become ripe for extremist appeals. It is better to bring them into the political system where they can voice their concerns in more productive ways.

LET SLEEPING DOGS LIE . . .

Those who are least likely to vote are also the least interested in government and the least well informed. Why, then, should we encourage them to have a voice in elections? If they don't care enough to vote or don't know enough, shouldn't we be grateful that they don't show up at the polls?

If people have the right to vote and choose not to, maybe that means they are satisfied with things the way they are. If they really wanted change, they could use their votes to obtain it.

If we relax registration and residence requirements to encourage more people to vote, we are opening the floodgates to vote fraud: people voting more than once or voting under other people's direction.

American democracy has been vibrant enough to survive impeachments, financial scandals, and candidates who lose the presidency even though they won the popular vote. If it "ain't broke," why try to fix it?

to make the rules as to who can vote, has won office with the support of the current voters; understandably, they do not welcome the uncertainties that a large expansion of the electorate would bring.

The fact that the active electorate in the United States is not as diverse as the nation's population probably reduces the amount of conflict in American politics and the range of political interests to which the parties must respond. That, in turn, makes it easier for the parties to be relatively moderate and pragmatic, compared with many parties in European democracies. In turn, these fairly pragmatic parties, accustomed to low-turnout elections, probably do not jump at the chance to appeal to the more alienated, less well-educated individuals who do not customarily show up at the polls.

Many Americans may consider that to be a worthwhile tradeoff. They may fear that a sudden influx of new and uninformed voters could threaten our democracy. Elections might become more vulnerable to manipulation or unthinking reaction. That seemed to happen in Germany in the 1920s and 1930s, when the Nazi Party, which killed off the democracy Germany had developed, gained power with the support of less informed and less involved citizens. Most other Western democracies seem to have avoided these problems even though their electorates are more inclusive; yet the fears remain. We are left, then, with a troubling challenge. Do we have to choose between greater participation and greater political stability? Are there ways to reconcile our concerns about the quality of democracy with the democratic value of engaging as many of the people as possible in American politics?

PART FOUR

Parties, Nominations, and Elections

Elections are great political spectacles, full of crisis and resolution, comedy and tragedy.[1] They are also the main bridge that links the party organizations and identifiers, the first two parts of the American parties that we explored in Parts 2 and 3, with the party in government. During campaigns, party activists try to energize party identifiers and get them to the polls to support candidates who share the party label. The need to unite around the party's nominees and to work together in the general election are powerful reasons for the three parts of the parties to reconcile their differences—at least until the votes are counted. Elections also link the parties at different levels of government. The process of nominating and electing a presidential candidate binds the state and local parties into at least a brief coalition with the national party. Similarly, a statewide election focuses the energies of local party organizations and leaders within the state.

There is good reason why elections ought to encourage cooperation within the party. When candidates run more capable campaigns, they improve not only their own ability to attract money and other resources but also that of their party organization. When candidates win, their party's activists stand a better chance of getting action on their issue agenda. When a party's candidate wins the governorship or the local executive office in some areas, then party leaders may gain access to patronage jobs, which in turn can bring more activists into the party organization. In the effort to win, candidates and party activists have to mobilize as many of the party's identifiers as possible. Because victory holds so many attractions for all three parts of the party, it is a powerful lure for them to work together.

All this cooperative activity does not come easily. Almost every aspect of the electoral process, and especially the nominating process, can also pit the needs of one part of the party against those of another. Whenever primaries are used to select a party's candidates, there will be times when party voters choose a nominee regarded as a disaster by party leaders. Efforts by the party organization to raise money will compete with candidates' own fund-raising. Candidates get to choose which issues they will emphasize, which advisers they will hire and which strategies they will adopt, and these choices will affect the image of the party as a whole, even when the party's leaders,

155

activists, and voters do not share these preferences. Once in office, the party's candidates may have reason to ignore or downplay some questions that are "hot button" issues to party activists.

In addition to the competition within each party, the parties also compete on the larger electoral stage with other political organizations. Groups such as single-issue organizations, labor unions, religious lobbies, reform groups, and corporations all get involved in campaigns in order to achieve their political goals. Some of these groups work very aggressively to help candidates get nominated, raise money, influence public opinion, and win the election. Democratic state party leaders, for example, will probably have to compete with environmental groups, women's rights groups, civil rights organizations, prochoice activists, and unions representing teachers, trial lawyers, government employees, and a variety of other occupations to get the attention of a Democratic candidate for statewide office.

This competition and cooperation is guided by a set of rules, just as the cooperation and competition in a basketball game are. These rules range from laws to standard practices, and, as in basketball, they have a tremendous impact on the results. One of these "rules" is the widespread use of primary elections, which poses a major challenge to the party organizations in their effort to control the nomination of candidates. Another "rule" is the set of voting systems used in communities across the nation, whose limitations became so painfully obvious in the 2000 and 2002 elections and which can affect Democratic and Republican efforts differently. Yet another is the set of rules that govern campaign fund-raising.

The first two chapters in this section focus on parties' involvement in nominating candidates. Chapter 9 explores the nomination process in general, and Chapter 10 considers the fascinating and peculiar practices through which the parties select their presidential candidates. In Chapter 11, we turn to the role of parties in general elections, and finally, Chapter 12 discusses money in politics. The constant search for dollars to run campaigns gave rise to extensive reform efforts in the 1970s and has prompted more recent debate about the effects of these reforms, leading to the passage of a new campaign finance reform law in 2002. This chapter traces the flow of money into campaigns and considers how it can both expand and contract the influence of parties on their candidates.

CHAPTER 9

How Parties Choose Candidates

In addition to public opinion polls, drive-through restaurants, and other means of democratizing life, Americans invented primary elections. In a primary (more formally known as a *direct primary*), the party electorate chooses which candidates will run for office under the party's label. Then, in a later *general election*, all voters can make the final choice between the two parties' nominees for each office. To American voters neck-deep in primaries during an election season, this may seem like the "normal" way for parties to nominate candidates. It is not; although the idea of a primary election is spreading, candidates in much of the rest of the democratic world are still selected by party leaders, activists, or elected officials, not by voters.[1]

These differences in nomination procedures explain a great deal about the contrasts between American party politics and those of other democracies. The shift to primaries has forced the American parties to develop a different set of strategies in making nominations, contesting elections, and trying to hold their candidates accountable after winning public office than we would find in nations that do not hold primaries.

The direct primary permeates every level of American politics. The great majority of states use it in all nominations, and the rest use it for most elective offices. It dominates the presidential nominating process (see Chapter 10). Even though it is just the first of two steps in electing public officials, it does the major screening of candidates, at least for the major parties, by reducing the choices to two in most races. The choice of nominees in the primary can affect the party's chance for winning the general election. In areas where one party dominates, the voters' only real choice is made in the primary. What led to the use of this two-step election process? How does it work and how well does it serve the needs of voters, candidates, and parties?

HOW THE NOMINATION PROCESS EVOLVED

For the first 110 years of the American republic, candidates for office were nominated by party caucuses and, later, by party conventions. In both cases, it was the leaders and activists of the party organizations who chose the party's nominees, not the rest of the voting public.

Nominations by Caucus

In the early years, as the parties expanded from being coalitions in the Congress to establishing local and state organizations, they held local caucuses (meetings) to choose candidates for county offices. Caucuses of like-minded partisans in Congress continued to nominate presidential and vice-presidential candidates. Similar caucuses in state legislatures nominated candidates for governor and other statewide offices. These caucuses were informal; the participants were self-selected. There weren't even any procedures for ensuring that all the major figures of the party would take part.[2]

Nominations by Convention

As the push for popular democracy spread, these caucuses came to be seen as an aristocratic elite—"King Caucus"—that ignored public opinion. In 1831, opponents of Andrew Jackson decided to hold a national convention to nominate their own presidential candidate, on the assumption that a convention would bring press and public attention to their efforts. Jackson's followers held their own convention the next year. From then on, through the rest of the nineteenth century, conventions were the main means of nominating presidential candidates. These nominating conventions were composed of delegates chosen by state and especially local party leaders, often at their own lower level nominating conventions.

These large and chaotic conventions looked more broadly representative than the caucuses but often were not. Delegates were chosen and the conventions managed by the heavy hands of the party leaders. So reformers began to denounce the convention system as yet another form of boss rule. By the end of the nineteenth century, the Progressive movement led the drive against conventions. Sympathetic journalists, called "muckrakers," wrote stories about party leaders crushing any outbursts of democracy at national conventions.[3]

Nominations by Direct Primaries

The Progressives proposed a new way to nominate candidates. Instead of giving party leaders the power to choose, they suggested, let the voters select their party's candidates for each office. This direct primary election reflected the core belief of the Progressives: that the best way to cure the ills of a democracy was to prescribe larger doses of democracy. Robert M. La Follette, a Progressive leader, argued that the caucus and convention serve only to "give respectable form to political robbery." In a primary, in contrast, "the citizen may cast his vote directly to nominate the candidate of the party with which he affiliates. . . . The nomination of the party will not be the result of 'compromise' or impulse, or evil design . . . but the candidates of the majority, honestly and fairly nominated."[4]

Some southern states had adopted primaries at the local level in the years after the Civil War, often to legitimize the nominees and settle internal disputes in their one-party Democratic systems. In the first two decades of the twentieth century, all but four other states turned to primaries for at least some of their statewide nominations. This was a time when one party or the other dominated the politics of many states—the most pervasive one-party rule in American history. It might be possible to tolerate the poor choices made by conventions when voters have a real choice in the general election, but when the nominees of the dominant party have no serious competition, those shortcomings were harder to accept. So the Progressives, who fought economic monopoly with antitrust legislation, used the direct primary as their major weapon in battling political monopoly.

Although the primary was designed to democratize the nominating process, many of its supporters hoped that it would go further and cripple the political party itself. They felt that the best way to weaken the parties was to divest the party organization of its most important power—the nomination of candidates—and give it instead to party voters. In fact, some states, such as Wisconsin, adopted a definition of the party electorate so broad that it included any voters who chose to vote in the party's primary on Election Day.

Primaries were not the first cause of party weakness in the United States; if party leaders had been strong enough throughout the country when primaries were first proposed, then they would have been able to keep these primary laws from passing. But primaries did undermine the party organizations' power even further. Elected officials who were nominated by the voters in primaries were unlikely to feel as much loyalty to the party organization as were officials who owed their nominations to party leaders. Largely because of the existence of primaries, party leaders in the United States have less control over who will receive the party nomination than in most other democratic political systems. In some states, the reforms required that the party organization's own leaders be chosen in primaries; the result was that the parties risked losing control even over their own internal affairs.

THE CURRENT MIX OF PRIMARIES AND CONVENTIONS

Although conventions are no longer common, they are still used to nominate candidates in a few states and, most conspicuously, in the contest for the presidency. Because states have the legal right to design their own nominating systems, the result is a mixture of primaries and conventions for choosing candidates for state offices.

All 50 states now use primaries to nominate at least some statewide officials, and 38 of them (plus the District of Columbia) use this method exclusively.[5] In Alabama and Virginia, the party may choose to hold a convention instead of a primary, but only in Virginia has the convention option been used in recent years as a means of unifying the party behind a particular candidate.

The remaining states use some combination of convention and primary. Iowa requires a convention when no candidate wins at least 35 percent of the primary vote. Three states (Indiana, Michigan, and South Dakota) use primaries for the top statewide offices but choose other nominees in conventions. Five (Colorado, New Mexico, New York, North Dakota, and Utah) hold conventions to screen candidates for the primary ballot. Connecticut used to hold nominating conventions, although any candidate who received at least 15 percent of the convention vote could challenge the endorsed candidate in a primary. The state legislature changed that rule in 2003 to grant a line on the primary ballot to any candidate who filed a petition signed by 2 percent of party members in the district.[6] This variety of choices reminds us that, in spite of the national parties' growing strength, party power is still largely decentralized.

TYPES OF PRIMARIES

States also differ in the criteria that they use to determine who can vote in their primaries. There are three basic forms, although each has many variations.[7] In the states with so-called closed primaries, only voters who have formally declared their affiliation with a party can participate. Voters in states with "open" primaries have more freedom to choose which party's primary they want to vote in. And there is still one state where Democratic and Republican candidates all run on the same primary ballot, so a voter can select some candidates of each party.

Closed Primaries

A slim majority of states hold *closed primaries*, in which there must be a permanent record of the voter's party affiliation before he or she can vote in that party's primary. In the 14 states with *fully closed* primaries, voters have to register as a Democrat or a Republican prior to the election.[8] Then they receive the primary ballot of only their own party when they enter the polling place on Election Day. If they want to vote in the other party's primary, they must formally change their party affiliation on the registration rolls well in advance of the primary. States with traditionally strong party organizations, such as New York and Pennsylvania, are among those that have been able to keep their primaries closed.

In the other 14 closed-primary states, often called *"semiclosed,"* voters can change their party registration at the polls or they can simply declare their party preference at the polling place; they are then given their declared party's ballot and, in about half of these states, are considered to be enrolled in that party. The lack of preregistration makes it possible for independents and even the other party's identifiers to become "partisans for a day" and vote in a party's primary. From the point of view of the voter, these semiclosed primaries are not very different from an open primary. The difference is important from the party's perspective, however, because in many semiclosed primaries there is a written record of party registration that can then be used by party organizations to target campaigning to the people who claim to support them.

Open Primaries

Citizens of 20 states can vote in the primary of their choice without ever having to make a public declaration as to which party they favor.[9] There are different types of *open primaries*. In *"semiopen"* primaries, used by 11 states (most of them in the South), voters can pick whichever party's ballot they choose but will need to ask for a particular party's ballot at the polls. (They often do not need to say that they favor that party but simply that they want to vote in its primary.) The other nine states hold *fully open* primaries, in which voters receive either a consolidated ballot or ballots for every party and they select the party of their choice in the privacy of the voting booth. They cannot, however, vote in more than one party's primary in a given election. Many of these states have histories of Progressive strength.

Blanket Primaries

The state of Washington adopted the *blanket primary* in 1935. It gives voters even greater freedom. The names of candidates from all parties appear on a single ballot in the primary, just as they do in the general election, so that a voter can choose a Democrat for one office and a Republican for another. In short, just as with an open primary, voters who are not affiliated with a party are permitted to help choose that party's candidates. Alaska later adopted the blanket primary system as well.

California voters approved an initiative in 1996 to hold a blanket primary. Proponents said it would boost voter participation in the primary, which it did, and encourage the choice of more moderate candidates. Party leaders saw it differently; they claimed that the plan prevented the party's loyal supporters from choosing the candidates who best represented their views. That, they said, would keep the party from offering a clear and consistent message to the voters. The result, they argued, was to violate the First Amendment's guarantee of freedom of association. In 2000, the U.S. Supreme Court sided with the parties and gave the right to decide who votes in a primary, at least in California, back to the party organization.[10] California then moved to a semiclosed primary. An appeals court ruled in 2003 that Alaska could no longer use the blanket primary system, and the Washington state legislature decided to abolish its 2004 primary altogether.

Louisiana still uses a type of blanket primary, sometimes called a "unitary" or "non-partisan" primary, in which any candidate who wins more than 50 percent of the votes in the primary is elected to the office immediately. If no candidate wins an outright majority, then the general election serves as a runoff between the top two vote getters, even if they are of the same party.

WHY DOES THE TYPE OF PRIMARY MATTER?

These varieties of primaries represent different answers to a long-standing debate: Is democracy better served by competition between strong and disciplined parties or by a system in which the parties have relatively little power? The closed primary reflects the belief that citizens benefit from having clear choices in elections, which can best be provided by unified, strong parties; therefore, it makes sense for a party's candidates to be selected by that party's loyal followers. In contrast, open and blanket primaries are consistent with the view that rigid party loyalties are harmful to a democracy, so candidates should be chosen by all voters, regardless of party.

Party organizations clearly prefer the closed primary in which voters must register by party before the primary. It pays greater respect to the party's right to select its candidates. Prior party registration also gives the parties a bonus—published lists of their partisans. Further, the closed primary limits the greatest dangers of open and blanket primaries, at least from the perspective of party leaders: crossing over and raiding. Both terms refer to people who vote in the primary of a party that they do not generally support. They differ in the voter's intent. Voters *cross over* in order to take part in a more exciting race or to vote for a more appealing candidate in the other party. *Raiding* is a conscious effort to weaken the other party by voting for its least attractive candidates.

Studies of primary contests in Wisconsin and other states show that crossing over is common in open primaries. Partisans rarely cross over in gubernatorial primaries because that would keep them from having a voice in other party contests. But because only one office is at stake in a presidential primary, both independents and partisans often cross over; in the 2000 presidential race, for example, more Democrats and independents voted in some Republican primaries than Republicans did. Candidates running in open primaries often encourage cross overs by discussing issues that appeal to the other party's voters.[11]

Organized raiding would be a bigger problem. It is a party leader's nightmare that opponents will make mischief by voting in the party's primary for the least appealing candidate. Studies of open primaries have found little evidence of raiding, however.

Voters usually cross over to vote their real preferences rather than to weaken the party in whose primary they are participating.[12]

HOW CANDIDATES QUALIFY

States also vary in the ease with which candidates can get their names on the primary ballot and in the support required to win the nomination.

How Do Candidates Get on the Ballot?

In most states, a candidate can get on the primary ballot by filing a petition. State election laws specify how many signatures the petition has to contain—either a specific number or a percentage of the vote for the office in the past election. States vary a lot in the difficulty of this step. New York, with its complicated law that favored party insiders, long had the strictest requirements for filing (see box on page 163) but liberalized them in 2003. In some other states, a candidate needs only to appear before the clerk of elections and pay a small fee. A few states, including California, even put candidates on the ballot if they are "generally recognized" to be running.

These simple rules have consequences for the parties. The easier it is for candidates to get on the ballot, the more likely it becomes that dissident, or even crackpot, candidates will enter a race and engage the party's preferred candidates in costly primary battles. Sometimes such candidates even win. In states with easy ballot access, citizens can be treated to grudge campaigns, in which people file to oppose the sheriff who arrested them, for instance, or who simply enjoy the thought of wreaking havoc in a primary.[13]

Runoffs: When Too Many Candidates Get on the Ballot

What if the leading candidate in a primary gets less than a majority of the votes? In most states' primaries, a plurality is enough. Almost all the southern and border states, however, hold a runoff between the top two candidates if one candidate does not win at least 50 percent. This southern institution was developed in the long period of one-party Democratic rule of the South. Democratic factionalism often produced three, four, or five serious candidates for a single office in a primary. The runoff was used to ensure a majority winner in order to present a unified face to the electorate and ward off any challenges from blacks and other Republicans.

In recent years, the southern runoff primary has become very controversial. Citing instances in which black candidates who received a plurality in the first primary in the South have lost to whites in the runoff, some have charged that runoffs discriminate against minority groups and are in violation of the Constitution and the federal Voting Rights Acts. Others have countered that it is the voters, not the runoff, who produce this result and that, in fact, the runoff helps to force southern parties to build biracial coalitions. This debate is far from being resolved.[14]

WHAT PARTIES DON'T LIKE ABOUT PRIMARIES

The Progressives designed the direct primary to break the party organization's monopoly control of nominations, and, in important respects, it did. In the process, it compromised parties' effectiveness in elections more generally, in several ways.

JUMP HOW HIGH? GETTING ON THE BALLOT IN NEW YORK

Five weeks before the New York primary in the 2000 presidential race, a state judge threw Senator John McCain off the primary ballot in much of the state. McCain was one of the two leading contenders for the Republican nomination. The state's Republican establishment, which supported Texas Governor George W. Bush for the nomination, had initiated the action, reportedly in order to help the governor of New York, who hoped to become Bush's running mate.

Under New York's ballot access rules, passed by the state legislature at the request of the state party, candidates had to circulate petitions in each of the state's congressional districts under very restrictive rules. This system, described as "tortuous," was the toughest in the nation. It was especially hostile to candidates who did not have the state party's support; those who did could rely on party volunteers to conduct the separate petition drives in each district. A McCain lawyer commented, "It demonstrates the absurdity of the election law when a candidate such as John McCain, who is a leading candidate in the race, can't get on the ballot in more than a third of the election districts."

McCain's campaign made good use of the controversy in portraying himself as an outsider running against a corrupt political system. He was later added to the ballot after a successful appeal to a federal judge. Imagine battling to get on the primary ballot in New York despite these hurdles and then dealing with the varying ballot access rules of 49 other states as well!

As a result of the controversy, the state legislature modified its rules for 2004. Now a presidential candidate gets on the ballot if he or she is discussed in the media, qualifies for federal matching funds, or submits 5,000 signatures.

Sources: New York Times stories by Clifford J. Levy: "McCain Off Ballot in Much of Upstate New York," Jan. 28, 2000, p. A1; "McCain on Ballot Across New York as Pataki Gives In," Feb. 4, 2000, p. A1; and "Judge Adds McCain to New York Ballot and Rejects Rules," Feb. 5, 2000, p. A1.

Difficulties in Recruiting Candidates

Candidate recruitment has never been an easy job, especially for the minority party. The direct primary makes the challenge even more difficult. If an ambitious candidate has the opportunity to challenge the party favorite in the dominant party's primary, he or she is less likely to consider running for office under the minority party's label. So, some argue, the minority party will find it even harder to recruit good candidates for races that it is not likely to win, and the office goes to the other party's nominee by default. Little by little, the majority party becomes the only viable means of exerting political influence and the minority party atrophies.[15]

This argument should not be taken too far. One-party politics has declined in recent years as primaries have become common. (There are still a number of uncontested races in state legislative and other, less visible elections in many states, however.[16]) Even in areas still dominated by one party, the internal competition promoted by primaries can keep officeholders responsive to their constituents.[17] But researchers do find greater competition in the primary of the dominant party than in that of the weaker party.[18] Further, because parties cannot control access to their own primaries or guarantee the outcome, they have less to offer candidates whom they are trying to recruit.

The damage primaries can do to the minority party is an unintended result of this Progressive reform. The Progressives were intent on destroying the party monopoly in nominations, but they certainly did not aim to make general elections less competitive. A modern-day version of a Progressive reform—the movement to limit the number of terms public officials can serve—could have a similar unintended effect. By preventing an official from staying in office decade after decade, term limits may produce more competition, but probably only in the year when the term limit has been reached and then only in the majority party's primary in a one-party area. In the other years, competition may be reduced as attractive candidates sit back and wait until the officeholder's term limit has been reached.

The Risk of Unattractive Nominees

Normally, only about half as many voters will turn out for a primary as for a general election.[19] If this smaller group of primary voters is not representative of those who will vote later, then it may select a weak candidate—one who, because of his or her issue stands or background, may not appeal to the broader voter turnout in the general election. In particular, party leaders fear that primary voters could choose a candidate who is more extreme than the party's electorate as a whole. Imagine the discomfort of Republican party leaders, for instance, when the controversial right winger Oliver North, who had been convicted on three felony counts for his role in a Reagan White House scandal, won the 1994 GOP nomination for senator in Virginia over a far more electable conservative. North went on to lose the general election. In another classic case, some Democratic Party leaders in southern California even felt the need to disown their own candidate when a former official of the Ku Klux Klan captured the Democratic nomination for Congress in a multicandidate primary race.

Another reason why primary voters might choose a weak candidate is that in a race in which all the candidates are of the same party, voters cannot use their party identification to select candidates, and many voters may not have any other relevant information available. They may choose a candidate because his or her name is familiar or may simply vote for the first name listed on the ballot (see "We Nominated . . . WHO?" on page 165). If the nominations were made by a party convention, it is often argued, convention delegates would know the prospective candidates better, so they would not be prone to these misjudgments.

Divisive Primaries

Primaries can create conflict that may open up old party wounds. As one observer described it, "a genuine primary is a fight within the family of the party and, like any family fight, is apt to be more bitter and leave more enduring wounds than battles with the November enemy."[20] A divisive primary election can have a number of effects on the party in the short term. Activists who campaigned for the losing candidate in the primary may sit out the general election rather than work for their party's nominee, although the excitement of the primary may bring in new activists to take their places.[21] Because this is a public fight, the wounds the candidates inflict on one another and on their followers

WE NOMINATED . . . WHO?

When voters choose a party's candidates in a primary election, sometimes the results are surprising. Voters in the 2002 Missouri primary, for example, selected Allen D. Hanson as the Republican candidate for state auditor, the office responsible for rooting out waste and abuse in the state budget. Hanson, it turns out, had spent nine months in a Minnesota jail for felony theft and swindling. He defeated Jay Kanzler, the general counsel of Washington University in St. Louis, who had been endorsed by several Missouri Republican leaders. Kanzler had raised $107,000 for his primary campaign. Hanson raised less than $500, but won about 65 percent of the vote. What was the secret of Hanson's success? Neither candidate was well known to the voters, and Hanson's name was listed first on the ballot. After the primary election, state Republican leaders urged Republican voters not to support this Republican candidate.

A columnist for the *St. Louis Post-Dispatch* warned that this lapse was not the only problem with Missouri elections. Two years earlier, the state had elected a dead man to the U.S. Senate (see page 209), and earlier in 2002, the state's other senator brought his 13-year-old springer spaniel onto the Senate floor to display the dog's voter registration card as proof that there was vote fraud in St. Louis. The columnist concluded, "They say that people get the kind of government they deserve. This is not a happy thought."

Sources: Kevin Horrigan, "Missouri Elections: 'Show Me' the Madness," *St. Louis Post-Dispatch,* August 11, 2002, p. B3; and Juliet Eilperin, "Mo. GOP: Felon's Win Is a Fluke," *Washington Post,* August 12, 2002, p. A4.

can take a long time to heal.[22] The charges raised by a candidate's primary opponent are often reused by the opposition in the general election, a source of free campaign help to the other party. Finally, if a bitter primary is expensive, it may eat up much of the money the primary winner would need to run an effective campaign in the general election.

These risks have increased recently. After the redistricting that followed the 2000 U.S. Census created so many U.S. House districts that were "safe" for one party, many ambitious candidates saw primary elections as the best and least expensive way to win a House seat. That attracted the attention, and the lavish spending, of dozens of national interest groups who wanted to change the ideological orientation of Congress. In 2002, there were more than 100 significant primary contests in House races, resulting in some bruising battles, especially in the races where redistricting had thrown two House incumbents into the same redrawn district.

The Democratic Party is famous for its internal disputes, but we can see just as much evidence of the effects of divisive primaries in the Republican Party, such as when candidates linked to the Christian Right challenge Republicans who are more moderate on social issues[23] (see the box on page 166). Other groups have also entered Republican primaries to try to unseat moderate incumbent Republicans. In 2003, the antitax group Club for Growth angered the White House and congressional Republican leaders by announcing that it would finance several intraparty fights, including a primary opponent to Pennsylvania Republican Arlen Specter, the only moderate in the Republican Senate leadership. Its purpose was to warn other Republicans to take the strictest antitax line

A CHRISTIAN RIGHT CHALLENGE IN ALABAMA

Divisions between the Christian Right and the more business-oriented wing of the party have become increasingly common in Republican primaries. One of the more colorful examples was the runoff after the 1998 Republican gubernatorial primary in Alabama, pitting incumbent Governor Forrest (Fob) James, an outspoken Christian Right leader, against a conservative businessman, Winton Blount. James was a two-term governor; he had served once as a Democrat in the 1970s and the second time, beginning in 1994, as a Republican. He was well known for his forceful support of teacher-led prayer in the schools and opposition to abortion and same-sex marriage. Blount placed his emphasis on economic development rather than on social issues.

The race was intense from the start. Blount criticized James's colorful antics, which included mimicking a monkey to ridicule a school textbook on evolution. James responded by calling Blount a "fat monkey" and referring to himself as a "God-fearing redneck." James supporter Jerry Falwell, a leader of the Religious Right, contended that James deserved reelection because he stood up to "liberal judges" who would deny children the right to pray in school.

Alabama's open primary allowed many Democrats to take part in the runoff between Republicans James and Blount. Their votes split; many blacks supported Blount while rural whites crossed party lines to vote for James. As often happens in a divisive primary, the bitterness between the two campaigns affected the general election. The two candidates spent so much money in fighting one another that James, the winner, had trouble raising funds for his general election race against Democratic Lieutenant Governor Don Siegelman. After Blount's defeat, many big business people threw their support to the Democrat. In the end, as in many other contests, the Christian Right candidate won the primary but lost the general election to the Democratic candidate.

Sources: Thomas B. Edsall, "In Tuesday's Vote, Bright Spots for Both Parties," *Washington Post,* June 4, 1998, p. A10; and Terry M. Neal, "In Alabama, a GOP Squabble," *Washington Post,* June 16, 1998, p. A1.

---

possible in their voting behavior.[24] "If you want to influence politics and policy, you really have to play in the primary game," said the Club president.[25]

Problems in Holding Candidates Accountable

When candidates are chosen in primaries rather than by party leaders, the party loses a powerful means of holding its candidates and officeholders accountable for their actions. In England, for example, if an elected official breaks with the party on an important issue, party leaders can usually keep him or her from being renominated. However, if the party cannot control or prevent the renomination of a maverick officeholder, then it has no way of enforcing loyalty. That, of course, is just what the Progressives had hoped. Thus,

- Primaries permit the nomination of candidates hostile to the party organization and leadership, opposed to the party's platform, or out of step with the public image that party leaders want to project.

- Primaries create the real possibility that the party's candidates in the general election will be an unbalanced ticket if primary voters select all or most of the candidates from a particular group or region.

- Primaries greatly increase campaign spending. The cost of a contested primary is almost always higher than that of a convention.

- Primaries extend political campaigns, already longer in the United States than in other democracies, to a length that can try many voters' patience.

THE PARTY ORGANIZATION FIGHTS BACK

Parties are clearly aware of the threats posed by primary elections, but they are just as aware that a direct attempt to abolish primaries would be futile. So party organizations have developed a range of strategies for trying to limit the damage primaries can cause. The success of these strategies varies; some local parties have neither the will nor the strength to try to affect primary election results, but others have been able to dominate the primaries effectively.

Persuading Candidates to Run (or Not to Run)

The surest way to control a primary is to make sure that the candidate the party favors has no opponent. Some party organizations try to mediate among prospective candidates or coax an attractive but unwilling candidate to run. If they have a strong organization, they may be able to convince less desirable candidates to stay out of the race by offering them a patronage position or a chance to run in the future, or they may threaten to block a candidate's access to campaign money. Even if they have little to offer or withhold, many party leaders have the opportunity to try to influence prospective candidates' decisions; researchers have found that almost 70 percent of nonincumbent state legislative candidates discussed their plans to run, before they announced their candidacy, with local party leaders.[26]

Endorsing Candidates

A number of state parties go beyond this informal influence on candidate selection and offer some form of preprimary endorsement to the candidates whom they prefer. In seven states, at least one of the parties holds a convention, with the blessing of state law, to formally endorse candidates for state office. Usually, a candidate who gets a certain percentage of the convention's vote automatically gets his or her name on the primary ballot. In several of these states, however, candidates who are not endorsed by the party can still be listed on the primary ballot if they file petitions that request it. In several other states, including Illinois, Ohio, and Michigan, party leaders meet informally to endorse some candidates.

How much influence do these endorsements have on the voters in primary elections? The record is mixed. Formal endorsements can often discourage other candidates from challenging the party's choice in the primary and can keep some interest groups from flooding a race with outside money in support of a nonendorsed candidate. Besides, the process of winning a formal endorsement usually involves the candidate in so many face-to-face meetings with party activists that the resulting visibility, and the resources that the endorsing party can provide, can give the endorsed candidate at least some vote-getting benefits.[27]

On the other hand, since 1980, when there has been competition in the primary, the endorsed candidate has won only about half the time—a big drop compared with the success rate of endorsed candidates in the 1960s and 1970s.[28] Some states have legal requirements that make the endorsement less valuable; the parties in Utah, for example, are required by state law to endorse two candidates for each office. Other states have passed laws to prevent parties from endorsing candidates in advance of the primary.

When the parties are restricted to offering informal endorsements before the primary, their effectiveness is even more limited. These informal endorsements are not listed on the primary ballot. As a result, only the most politically attentive voters are likely to know that the party is supporting a particular candidate and they are the ones least in need of the guidance provided by a party endorsement.[29]

Providing Tangible Support

If the party is not able to prevent a challenge to its preferred candidates, then it must fall back on more conventional approaches. It may urge party activists to help the favored candidates circulate their nominating petitions and leave the other candidates to their own devices (as John McCain learned in the 2000 New York primary). It may make party money and expertise available to the chosen candidates. It may publish ads announcing the party's endorsees or print reminders that voters can take right into the polling booth. On the day of the primary, the party organization may help to get party voters to the polls.

Party efforts to influence primary elections vary from state to state and within states. It is probably safe to say that the most common activity is the recruiting of candidates. Trying to clear the field for a favored candidate is less common. The parties' efforts are complicated by the fact that, in most parts of the country, parties are only one of a number of groups seeking out and supporting men and women to run for office. Local business, professional, farm, and labor groups; civic associations; ethnic, racial, and religious organizations; and other interest groups and officeholders may also be working to recruit candidates. The party organizations that seem best able to control candidate recruitment are generally the parties that also endorse and support candidates in the primary itself.

CANDIDATES AND VOTERS IN THE PRIMARIES

Two facts help make the primaries more manageable for the parties: often only one candidate files for each office in a primary and the vast majority of voters do not vote in them. The party may be responsible for one or both of these situations; there may be no competition in a primary, for example, because of the party's skill in persuading and dissuading potential candidates. No matter why they occur, however, the result is that nomination politics can be more easily controlled by aggressive party organization.

Many Candidates Run Without Competition

All over the United States, large numbers of primary candidates win nominations without a contest. Probably the most important determinant of the competitiveness of a primary is the party's prospects for victory in the general election; as mentioned earlier, candidates rarely fight for the right to face almost certain defeat. Primaries also tend to be less competitive when an incumbent is running, when parties have made preprimary endorsements, and when the state's rules make it harder to get on the ballot.[30]

The power of incumbency to discourage competition is another of the ironies of the primary. In an election in which voters cannot rely on the party label to guide their choices, name recognition and media coverage are important influences. Incumbents, of course, are more likely to have these resources than are challengers. To dislodge an incumbent, a challenger will often need large amounts of campaign money, but few challengers can raise large campaign budgets. By weakening party control of nominations through the direct primary, then, Progressive reformers may have unintentionally made it harder to defeat incumbents.

. . . And Voters Are in Short Supply

If competition is scarce in the primaries, so are voters. One important fact about primaries is that most people don't vote in them. One reason for the low turnout is that there is no competition in many primary races. Turnout tends to be lower in the minority party's primary, in primaries held separately from the state's presidential primary, and in elections in which independents and the other party's identifiers are not allowed to vote.[31] In addition, the fact that no one is elected in a primary probably depresses turnout; a race for the nomination lacks the drama inherent in a general election that is followed by victorious candidates taking office. (There are some notable exceptions, however; see "A Day in the Life" on page 170).

Because it is such a small sample of the eligible voters, the primary electorate is distinctive in several ways. Many primary voters are strong party identifiers and activists, which makes them more responsive to party endorsements of certain candidates. As would be expected, people who vote in primaries have higher levels of education and political interest. They are often assumed to hold more extreme ideological positions than those of other party voters. Although early studies of Wisconsin's open primary found little support for that assumption, other research suggests that it is accurate.[32] Even if the ideological positions of primary voters turn out not to be distinctive, the intensity of their ideological commitment may be.

Primary voters often make unexpected choices. Primary campaigns tend to get little media coverage, so the candidates are often not well known and the issues, if any, may be unclear. Thus, the voter's choice in a primary is not as well structured or predictable as that in a general election. Many voting decisions are made right in the polling booth. It is small wonder that parties are rarely confident about primary results and pollsters prefer not to predict them.

Southern primaries in earlier years were the one great exception to the rule that turnouts are low in primaries. Because winning the Democratic nomination in a one-party area was tantamount to winning the office itself, competition existed only in the Democratic primary, so turnout in the primaries was relatively high. As the Republican Party has become stronger and more competitive in the South, however, the Democratic primaries have lost their special standing. The result is that participation has declined in primaries, even at a time when the mobilization of blacks into Democratic Party politics should have increased competition within the party. Republican primaries are attracting more voters now because their candidates' prospects in the general election have greatly improved, but the GOP increase has not been large enough to compensate for the decrease in Democratic turnout. So turnout in southern primaries has become less and less distinctive.[33]

MORE THAN JUST "THE LESBIAN CANDIDATE FOR CONGRESS"

Soon after finishing law school, Tammy Baldwin won a seat on the county board of supervisors. At age 30, she moved on to the Wisconsin state legislature, where she was the youngest woman and the first openly gay person to serve in that body. Six years later, when the Republican U.S. Representative in her district announced his intention to retire, she entered the Democratic primary to replace him.

It was a long shot. The district's previous Democratic incumbent had endorsed another of the four candidates for the nomination. Even many Democrats considered Baldwin to be too liberal to win, although if elected, she would represent the city known to some as the People's Republic of Madison. She was forthright about her background and orientation, arguing that, as a woman, she would take on issues that most congressmen would not. In particular, she called for tougher environmental regulations, publicly financed day care, and long-term care for the elderly.

It was inevitable that Baldwin's sexual orientation would be an undercurrent in the campaign. By 1998, there were gay members of Congress, but all had gone public about their homosexuality *after* having been first elected to the House. Tammy Baldwin did not make an issue of her sexual orientation, but neither did she try to hide it. In fact, it offered one political advantage: She was able to raise a large campaign budget through her appeals to gay and women supporters. Antigay rhetoric was not common in the primary race, but stereotyping was; it took more than a month for her campaign manager to persuade newspapers to stop referring to the candidate as "Tammy Baldwin, the lesbian candidate for Congress."

Was she expecting to win? "Well, you know, throughout my political career," she says, "I've always been dealing with the skeptics and the cynics, who say, 'This isn't going to be our best candidate to win the primary.' And, you know, 'She's too progressive, she's too young, she's a woman, she's a lesbian.'. . . . Hey, folks, this is a democracy, and in a democracy the cynics don't decide who's elected to office unless you let them—unless they're the only ones who vote. We decide. And that's a message that pervaded the entire campaign—stop listening to those people who say, 'you can't, you shouldn't, it won't work,' and start deciding that we can do it." And she did; after narrowly winning the Democratic primary, Baldwin won the general election and went to Congress in 1999. She was reelected in 2000 by a narrow margin, and then won 66 percent of the vote in 2002.

Sources: Ruth Conniff, "Tammy Baldwin," *The Progressive,* http://www.progressive.org/baldwin9901.htm (accessed Aug. 15, 2003). See also David T. Canon and Paul S. Herrnson, "Professionalism, Progressivism, and People Power," in Michael A. Bailey, Ronald A. Faucheux, Paul S. Herrnson, and Clyde Wilcox, eds., *Campaigns & Elections* (Washington, DC: CQ Press, 2000), pp. 83–92.

THE IMPACT OF THE DIRECT PRIMARY

Americans have had nearly a century of experience with the direct primary. On balance, how has it affected us? Has the primary democratized nominations by taking them out of the hands of party leaders and giving them to voters? Has it weakened the party organizations overall? In short, have the Progressives' hopes been realized?

Has It Made Elections More Democratic?

It is true that more people take part in primaries than take part in conventions or caucuses. In that sense, the process has been made more democratic. But the democratic promise of primaries is cut short by the number of unopposed candidates and the low levels of voter turnout. If voters are to have meaningful alternatives, then there must be more than one candidate for an office. If the results are to be meaningful, people must go to the polls.

By its very nature, however, the primary tends to reduce participation. Would-be candidates are discouraged by the cost of an additional race, the difficulty of getting on the primary ballot, and the need to differentiate themselves from other candidates of the same party. The large number of primaries and the frequent lack of party cues reduce the quantity and quality of voter participation. If widespread competition for office and extensive public participation in the nominating process were goals of the primary's architects, then their hopes have not been realized.

The direct primary has not fully replaced party leaders in making nominations. Caucuses and conventions are still used, most visibly in presidential nominations, although they are more open than they used to be. And as we have seen, parties can influence the competition in primaries. If only 25 or 30 percent of registered voters go to the polls, then 15 percent will be enough to nominate a candidate. Parties count on the fact that a large part of that group will probably be party loyalists who care about the party leaders' recommendations. Thus strong party organizations—those able to muster the needed voters, money, activists, and organization—can still have a big influence on the results.

Even so, trying to influence primary elections is very costly and time-consuming, even for strong parties. The Jacksonian tradition of electing every public official from senator to surveyor means that party organizations need to deal with large numbers of contests. The time and expense force many parties to be selective in trying to affect primaries. Parties sometimes stand aside because picking a favorite in the primary might heat up old resentments or open new wounds. Of course, the greatest fear of party leaders is that if they support one candidate in a primary and the other candidate wins, they could lose all influence over the winning officeholder.

In some ways, then, the primary has been a democratizing force. In competitive districts, especially when no incumbent is running, voters have the opportunity for choice envisioned by the reformers. In all districts, the primaries place real limits on the power of party leaders. Parties, even strong ones, can no longer whisk just any warm body through the nomination process. The primary gives dissenters a chance to take their case to the party's voters, so it offers them a potential veto over the party leaders' preferences (as "A Day in the Life" shows).

How Badly Has It Harmed the Parties?

On the other hand, is it possible to say that the direct primary has strengthened democracy in the United States if it weakens the political parties? From the risk of divisive primary races to the added campaign funding and voter mobilization that they require, primaries strain party resources and create headaches for party leaders and activists.

Although we have seen the methods used by some state party organizations to maintain some control over their primaries by making preprimary endorsements or holding conventions to nominate some candidates, the bottom line is this: When a party organization cannot choose who will carry the party label into the general election, the party has been deprived of one of its key resources.

The direct primary has redistributed power within the parties. The Progressives' goal was to shift the power to nominate candidates from the party organization to the party in the electorate, but a funny thing happened along the way. Because candidates (especially incumbents) can win the party's nomination even when they defy the party organization, the idea of party "discipline" loses its credibility. Just as the direct primary undercuts the ability of the party organization to recruit candidates who share its goals and accept its discipline, it prevents the organization from disciplining partisans who already are in office. The primary, then, empowers the party's candidates and the party in government at the expense of the party organization. This sets the United States apart from many other democracies, in which the party organization has real power over the party in government.

Primaries also contribute to the decentralization of power in the American parties. As long as the candidates can appeal successfully to a majority of local primary voters, they are free from the control of a state or national party and its leaders. In all these ways, the direct primary has influenced more than the nominating process; it has helped to reshape the American parties.

Is the Primary Worth the Cost?

How party candidates should be nominated has been a controversial matter since political parties first appeared in the United States. It raises the fundamental question of what a political party is. Are parties only alliances of officeholders—the party in government? That seemed to be the prevailing definition in the early years when public officials selected their prospective colleagues in party caucuses. Should the definition be expanded to include the party's activists and leaders? The change from a caucus to a convention system of nominations, in which the party organization played its greatest role, reflects this change in the definition of party.

Should we extend the idea of party well beyond the limits accepted by most other democracies and include the party's supporters in the electorate? If so, which supporters should be included: only those willing to register formally as party loyalists or anyone who wants to vote for a party candidate in a primary election? The answer has evolved over the years toward the most inclusive definition of party. Even though the Supreme Court insists that the parties' freedom of association is vital, the "party," especially in states with an open or blanket primary and, in practice, in semiclosed primary states, has become so permeable that its boundaries are hard to define.

The methods that we use to nominate candidates have a far-reaching impact. The Jacksonians promoted the convention system in order to gain control of the party from congressional party leaders. Progressives used their preference for the direct primary as a weapon with which to wrest control of the party and, ultimately, the government from the party organization regulars. Because of the importance of nominations in the political process, those who control the nominations have great influence on the political agenda and, in turn, over who gets what in the political system. The stakes in this debate, as a result, are extremely high.

CHAPTER 10

Choosing the Presidential Nominees

The system that Americans use to nominate a president is unique. It takes almost a year, costs hundreds of millions of dollars, and differs from the way in which every other democratic nation chooses its executive. In fact, it differs from the process by which candidates for almost every other major office are selected in the United States. Understanding this process takes us a long way toward understanding the relationship between the parties and the presidency itself.

In a formal sense, each of the two major parties nominates its candidate for president at the party's national convention, held every four years. In reality, the convention delegates simply ratify the choices that have actually been made months before the convention's opening gavel, by voters in their states' delegate selection events (see the box on page 174). The great majority of states use primary elections, the benefits and drawbacks of which were explored in the last chapter, for that purpose.

THE MOVE TO PRESIDENTIAL PRIMARIES

It took decades for primaries to become established in the presidential nominating process. Florida adopted the first presidential primary in 1904 and many other states quickly followed. Within a decade, a majority of states were using this method of nomination. The use of primaries soon faded, however. Advocates may have lost faith in the effectiveness of primaries; opponents probably worked hard to get rid of them and restore party leaders' control over nominations. By 1936, only 14 states were still holding primaries to choose their delegates to the national conventions that select the parties' presidential candidates. That number had hardly changed by 1968.[1]

In most states during this time, then, the state parties regained the power to choose the delegates to the national conventions. Party leaders dominated the process and often even hand-picked the state's delegates. The selection was usually done in a series of party-controlled caucuses, or meetings, beginning at the local level and culminating in statewide party conventions. Even in many states that held primaries, voters could take part in only a "beauty contest" to express their preferences about presidential candidates;

173

HOW A PRESIDENTIAL CANDIDATE IS CHOSEN

Step 1: *Assessing Their Chances.* Many people who think they might have public support—governors, senators, House members, people who are well-known in another field—consider running for president. They take private polls to see how much backing they would have and how they are viewed by the public. They contact consultants, fund-raisers, and people with money to donate to assess their chances of getting the resources they'd need and to get the most well-respected consultants to commit to the campaign. They campaign for congressional candidates in order to win their loyalty.

Timing: At least a year, and often several years, before the presidential election.

Step 2: *Entering the Race.* Those who feel they would have a good chance—and some who want to run for president even if they are sure to lose—formally declare their candidacy and work to get on the ballots of all fifty states. They set up political action committees or foundations to raise money. They travel often to states with early primaries and caucuses and where large fund-raising events can be held.

Timing: Typically in the summer or fall of the year before the election year.

Step 3: *Primaries and Caucuses.* Voters cast a ballot in their states for the candidate they want their party to nominate for president. Most states hold primary elections for this purpose; a few use participatory caucuses and state conventions. Delegates are chosen to represent each state and to vote in the party's national convention for the candidates selected by the voters.

Timing: Between late January and early June of each presidential election year.

Step 4: *National Nominating Conventions.* The delegates vote in the two major parties' conventions to ratify the choice of presidential candidate made by the voters in the nominating season (Step 3) and the candidate's choice of a vice-presidential nominee and to adopt a party platform.

Timing: By tradition, the party that does not currently hold the presidency has its convention first, usually in July; the other party's convention is held in August or early September.

Step 5: *General Election.* The two major parties' candidates run against one another.

Timing: The first Tuesday after the first Monday in November.

---

the delegates who went to the national convention and chose the candidates were selected elsewhere. A fascinating story began to unfold in 1968, however, in which the national Democratic Party took control of the delegate-selection process away from the state parties and gave new life to the movement toward presidential primaries.

Turbulence in the Democratic Party

The 1968 Democratic convention was a riotous event. Struggling with the painful issues of civil rights and American involvement in the Vietnam War, the convention nominated the party leaders' choice, Vice President Hubert Humphrey, as the Democratic presidential candidate. Insurgent forces within the party protested that Humphrey's nomination violated the wishes of many Democratic activists. To try to make peace with their critics, the national party leaders agreed that the next convention's delegates would be selected in a more open and democratic manner.

A commission chaired by Senator George McGovern of South Dakota (and later by Representative Donald Fraser of Minnesota) recommended, and the Democratic National Committee and the next Democratic convention approved, major changes for the 1972 nominating process. One of the striking elements of this story is the remarkable ease with which Democratic Party leaders accepted rule changes that greatly reduced their influence on the awarding of the party's greatest prize, the presidential nomination.[2]

In trying to comply with the complicated new rules imposed by the national Democratic Party, many states stopped using caucus-convention systems and re-instituted primaries.[3] The few caucuses that remained were guided by strict party rules requiring delegates to be selected in open and well-publicized meetings. Techniques formerly used by state party organizations to control the caucuses were outlawed. In the process, not only were the delegate selection rules radically changed, but also the principle was established that the national parties, not the states or the state parties, make the rules for nominating presidential candidates.

Once the reform genie was let out of the bottle, it was hard to contain. The Democrats tinkered with their presidential nomination process in advance of almost every election for the next 20 years. First, they used national party leverage to make the process more open and more representative of women, blacks, and young people. Then, the Democrats "fine-tuned" the rules so that voter support for candidates was more faithfully represented in delegate counts; ever since 1992, candidates who win at least 15 percent of the vote in primaries or caucuses are guaranteed a share of the state's delegates proportional to their vote total. To bring party leaders (and their "peer review" of candidates) back into the process, many elected and party officials were guaranteed a vote at the convention as uncommitted "superdelegates" (to be discussed later).

The result has been a stunning transformation of the process by which the Democrats select their presidential nominees. Many state legislatures responded to the new Democratic requirements by changing state election laws for both parties. When states decided to run a primary for one party, for example, they typically did it for both. Thus, the Republicans became the unwilling beneficiaries of the Democratic reforms. Republicans have preserved their tradition of giving state parties wide latitude in developing their own rules, however, which has kept the national party out of much of the rules debate. So even while being swept up in the movement toward primaries, state Republican parties have tended to stay away from proportional representation; instead, they have retained statewide winner-take-all primaries. In addition, the Republicans have not followed the Democrats' lead in reserving delegate seats for party and public officials or developing affirmative action programs for women or minorities.

Presidential Primaries Today

Presidential primaries are now used in about two-thirds of the states, including most of the largest (see Figure 10.1). Because the decision to use primaries or caucuses is made by states and state parties, these numbers fluctuate from one presidential election to the next. In 2004, for instance, the number of primaries dropped when seven states decided to cut their budgets by eliminating their presidential primaries.

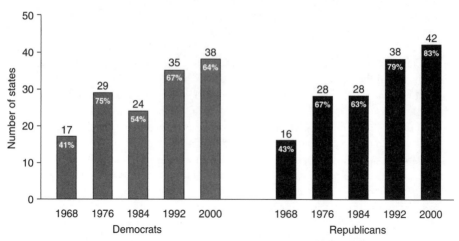

FIGURE 10.1   Change in the Number of Presidential Primaries: 1968–2000.
Note: The number above each bar is the number of states that held primaries to select delegates (not primaries that were purely advisory) in that year; inside the bar is the percentage of convention delegates elected in those primaries. All fifty states plus Washington, D.C., are included, but not the territories (American Samoa, Guam, Puerto Rico, Virgin Islands) or Democrats Abroad. Delegate percentages include Democratic superdelegates.
Source: Michael G. Hagen and William G. Mayer, "The Modern Politics of Presidential Selection," in William G. Mayer, ed., *In Pursuit of the White House 2000* (New York: Chatham House, 2000), pp. 11 and 43–44. Figures for 2000 were kindly provided by Mayer.

In the primaries, the popular vote determines how the state's delegates are apportioned among the presidential candidates. In earlier years, primary voters in some states were permitted to select only the convention delegates themselves, without any assurance as to which presidential candidates these delegates supported. Now, however, the names of the presidential candidates normally appear on the ballots, and the candidates, or their agents, usually select the members of their own delegate slates. This all but guarantees that the popular vote for candidates will be faithfully translated into delegates committed to the respective candidates at the national convention, even though there are no laws requiring delegates to support the popular vote winner in their state.[4]

Most party leaders prefer some form of closed primary (see Chapter 9). Democratic Party reform commissions have tried several times to ban open primaries, which allow non-Democrats to have a voice in selecting party candidates. However, the open primary has survived these assaults. After a long struggle, the national party allowed Wisconsin to return to its cherished open primary in 1988 and the other states that hold open primaries need no longer fear a veto by the national party.[5]

In fact, in the 2000 nominating season, even the closed primaries did not look very closed. In the rush to move their presidential primaries to the early weeks of the nominating season, as we will see later, several states separated their presidential primary from the rest of their primary elections. This helped state parties to protect their favorites for lower level offices from the crossover voters attracted by presidential contests.

Some Party Caucuses Remain

States that have not adopted presidential primaries use a longer process that begins with precinct caucuses. These are very different experiences than primaries for their participants; they involve face-to-face debate among voters who gather in local schools and other public buildings, often for several hours. Their purpose is to choose delegates to higher level caucuses, typically at the county, congressional district, and then the state level. It is only at the higher-level conventions where the final delegate slate for the national convention is determined. The much publicized Iowa caucuses, for example, began with precinct meetings in January 2004, but Iowa's national convention delegates were not chosen until the district and state conventions in April and June.[6]

The selection of delegates in the caucus states attracted little media coverage until 1976, when a virtually unknown Democratic governor, Jimmy Carter, made himself a serious presidential candidate by campaigning intensively in Iowa and winning an unexpected number of delegates. When caucuses do not get much media attention, party leaders have an easier time controlling their outcomes. But when a state's caucuses attract controversy, more people participate in them and the party leaders' influence fades. A classic case occurred in 1986, when Michigan GOP leaders scheduled their precinct caucuses two years before the 1988 state convention in order to boost the influence of their brand of moderate Republicanism in national nomination politics. Their efforts backfired when supporters of Pat Robertson, a leader of the Christian Right, flooded the local caucuses and threw the state's nomination process into turmoil for the next two years.

THE RACE TO WIN DELEGATE VOTES

To a presidential candidate, the marathon of primaries and caucuses is do-or-die; no recent presidential candidate who did poorly in the nominating season has been resurrected by his party's national convention. Every presidential nomination in both parties since 1956 has been won on the convention's first ballot, and since 1968, that first-ballot nominee has always been the winner of the most delegates in the primaries and caucuses. How does a candidate get to that coveted spot?

The "Invisible Primary"

It takes years to prepare for a presidential race. Almost all serious candidates begin at least two years before the election to take polls, raise money, identify active supporters in the states with early primaries, and compete for the services of respected consultants. Their aim is to win a place for themselves in the group of candidates who are described by the media as "front-runners."

Even before the first convention delegates are selected, at a time when the coming presidential race is not yet even on the radar screen for most Americans, journalists try to get the scoop on who will eventually win the nomination. Because money and organization are so crucial to a candidate's chances, media people tend to pick a likely winner by tracking the various candidates' fund-raising success in the year before the election. This process has become so important to the eventual result that it has come to be called the "invisible primary" or the "money primary."[7]

By July of 2003, for example, several Democrats—Senators John Kerry and John Edwards and former Vermont Governor Howard Dean—had been called front-runners by virtue of having raised more than $10 million for the 2004 nomination race, and President Bush had collected over $34 million. Prospective candidates who don't raise as much money as prominent observers expect them to, or perform poorly in media interviews or public opinion polls, are likely to be winnowed out of the nomination race well before Iowa and New Hampshire voters choose their convention delegates. "Every time I think it can't begin earlier," said *Newsweek* reporter Howard Fineman about the speeding up of the nomination race, "it does."[8]

Candidates' Strategic Choices

Those who are still considered serious candidates by the middle of the "invisible primary" must make endless strategic choices in preparing for the early delegate selection events. They need to decide how much effort and money to put into each state and which of their many issue stands and personal qualities to emphasize. As the dynamics of the race change, they will probably reconsider these choices many times.

The most important factor to be weighed in making these choices is the candidate's standing relative to the opposition. Someone who comes into the nominating season as a front-runner, for example, normally has to demonstrate overwhelming support in the early delegate selection events. Otherwise, his or her supporters' and contributors' confidence may be so badly undermined that the candidate's hopes for the nomination fade. George W. Bush entered the nomination season in January 2000 with more campaign money than any other candidate in American political history—$67 million—and the widespread expectation that he would coast to the Republican nomination. After he lost the very first primary in New Hampshire to Senator John McCain, his advisers were forced to rethink his approach. And McCain's brief success after New Hampshire shows how a candidate with less initial support can improve his or her chances for the nomination simply by exceeding expectations in an early and heavily reported contest.

All these decisions must take into account the rules of the process as set down by the parties and the states. Only a few presidential candidates—Bush is the most notable example, followed by Howard Dean and John Kerry in 2004—have been able to raise enough money to resist the lure of federal matching funds for their campaigns (see Chapter 12). The others must follow the rules that can give them access to those funds. First, they must build nationwide campaign organizations in order to qualify for the federal money and then they must decide how to allocate their funds and personnel. Public funding will not cover (or permit) full-blown campaigns in every state. The early primaries and caucuses necessarily attract the greatest candidate spending, but candidates must then set priorities; legal restrictions on the federal funds prevent candidates from raising money quickly from a few sources, as they were used to doing in the years before the reforms.

Other rules matter as well. A candidate who expects to do especially well among independents will need to concentrate resources in states with open primaries, in which independents and other partisans can vote, as John McCain did in 2000 (see box on page 179). These rules of the game differ from party to party. Because Democrats require a "fair reflection" of candidate strength in the selection of delegates, a candidate with significant support will not be shut out in any state. The Republican Party permits winner-take-all primaries, however, and many state Republican Parties hold them, so it is still

A TALE OF TWO PRIMARIES

In politics, as in everything else, the rules affect the results. Consider the rules that governed primary elections in the race for the 2000 Republican presidential nomination. Michigan's Republican contest is an *open primary* in which voters do not have to declare a party affiliation to take a Republican ballot. In fact, in an exit poll conducted by Voter News Service, only 47 percent of the voters in the Republican primary were Republicans! George W. Bush got the votes of Republicans by a margin of more than two to one, but Arizona Senator John McCain won enough independent and Democratic votes to win the primary.

New York held a *closed primary* two weeks later. There, 72 percent of the Republican primary voters were Republicans, according to the exit poll, and almost all the others called themselves independents. Eighty-four percent of the Bush voters said they were Republicans; 34 percent of the McCain voters were independents. Bush won the primary and clinched the nomination that day.

Source: R. W. Apple, Jr., "On a Rocky Road, the Race Tightens," *New York Times*, Feb. 23, 2000, p. A1 (on Michigan), and http://www.nytimes.com/library/pol (on New York; accessed Feb. 24, 2000).

possible for a Republican candidate to win 49 percent of the votes in a state and come away without a single delegate.[9]

Win Early or Die

The strongest imperative is the need to win early. Victories early in the nominating process create momentum; they bring the resources and support that make later victories more likely. Early successes attract more media coverage for the candidate and, in turn, more name recognition among voters. The candidate looks more and more unstoppable, so it is easier to raise money. The other candidates in the race fall further and further behind.

The early front-runners have gotten even more of a boost in recent elections because the nomination process has become highly "front-loaded." Many states have moved their primaries forward in the election calendar in order to benefit from the attention attracted by these early delegate selection events, not to mention the campaign spending that comes with it. The stampede among states to occupy an early position in the 2000 election calendar was so intense that both the Democratic and Republican nominations were wrapped up in the first six weeks of a five-month nominating season. Between late January and March 14, thirty-four states held their primaries or caucuses in at least one party, and 75 percent of the delegates had been selected by the end of March (see box on page 180).[10] The nominating calendar was even more front-loaded in 2004, as a result of a rules change by the national Democratic Party.

What Is the Party's Role?

The party organizations' interests in this process are not necessarily the same as those of the aspiring presidential candidates. State and local parties want a nominee who will bring voters to the polls to support the party's candidates for state and local offices; a weak

FRONT-LOADING THE NOMINATION PROCESS

In the 2000 presidential nomination race, the Democratic and Republican nominees had been effectively decided by March 7. By the end of that day, almost 40
percent of the Democratic convention delegates and 45 percent of the Republicans had been selected.

It's called the "front-loading" of the nomination race. The first of the state
delegate-selection events in 2000 were held in late January. Although the primaries and caucuses would continue until early June, more and more states
wanted to position their delegate-selection events close to the beginning of the
process, when they would get more media coverage, bring in more money from
campaign advertising, and give the state's voters more of a chance to influence
the choice of their parties' nominees. In 2004, the march to the front continued;
many states' primaries and caucuses were moved up by as much as a month.

So what? Does it matter that both major parties' nominees were selected fully
eight months before the general election? Front-loading has had important
implications for the nomination process. For one, it increases the importance to
candidates of raising money early. George W. Bush, for example, had raised $67
million before the first caucuses were held in 2000. In the 2004 race, he raised
$130.8 million by the time of the first caucuses, and he had no opponent for the
Republican nomination!

Front-loading gives an extra advantage to the candidates who were front-runners during the "invisible primary." When there are only a few days or weeks
between the earliest primaries and the rest, there is not enough time for a long-
shot candidate to get enough of a boost from an early primary win to raise the
money needed to compete in California or New York, and the cost of a strategic
mistake in these early events could be very high. This "rush to judgment," as two
political scientists call it, makes the nominating system "less deliberative, less
rational, less flexible and more chaotic."

Source: Michael G. Hagen and William G. Mayer, "The Modern Politics of Presidential
Selection," in William G. Mayer, ed., *In Pursuit of the White House 2000* (New York:
Chatham House, 2000), p. 40.

---

presidential candidate may hurt their chances. Party leaders also generally prefer early
agreement on a presidential candidate; a hotly contested race often heightens conflict
within local and state parties, which can weaken the party effort in the general election.

Historically, the state parties protected their interests by selecting delegates uncommitted to any candidate and then casting the state's delegate votes as a bloc for a particular nominee or platform plank. The ability to swing a bloc of delegates to a candidate
could increase the state party's influence at the convention. But the current nominating
system prevents the state parties from sending an uncommitted delegation. In most primary states, it is the candidates who set up their delegate slates, so the delegates' first
loyalty is to the candidate. In caucus states, delegates committed to a candidate simply
have greater appeal to caucus participants than do uncommitted delegates.

Party leaders, then, have a harder time protecting the party's interests in a nominating
process that is dominated by the candidates and their supporters. The Democrats tried to
enhance the party's role in 1984 by setting aside delegate seats at the national convention

for elected and party officials. These *superdelegates*—all Democratic governors and members of Congress, current and former presidents and vice presidents, and all members of the Democratic National Committee—were meant to be a large, uncommitted bloc totaling almost 20 percent of all delegates, with the party's interests in mind. But because the nomination race has concluded so quickly in recent years, superdelegates have not been able to play an independent role in the nominating process.[11] Presidential candidates, then, owe their nomination largely to their own core supporters, rather than to the party organization. That limits the party organization's influence on the president, once he or she has been elected.

VOTERS' CHOICES IN PRESIDENTIAL NOMINATIONS

The move to primaries has greatly increased citizen participation in the process of nominating a president. What determines the level of voter participation and what guides the voters' choices in these contests?

Who Votes?

Turnout varies a great deal from state to state and across different years in any one state. The first caucuses (Iowa) and the first primary (New Hampshire) usually bring out a relatively large number of voters because of the media attention to those early contests. More generally, turnout tends to be higher in states with a better-educated citizenry, higher percentages of registered voters, and a tradition of two-party competition—the same states where there is higher turnout in the general election. The nature of the contest matters too. Voters are most likely to participate in early races that are closely fought, in which the candidates spend more money and the excitement is high, all of which increase voter interest in the election.[12]

Are Primary Voters Typical?

However, turnout is lower in primary than in general elections, especially after the parties' nominations have been largely wrapped up. Are the people who turn out to vote in the primaries—and who therefore choose the nominees for the rest of the public—typical of other citizens? Critics of the reforms have charged that they are not and, thus, that candidates are now being selected by an unrepresentative group of citizens.

We can explore this question in several ways. When we compare primary voters with nonvoters, we find that those who vote in primaries are, in fact, better educated, wealthier, and older—but then, so are general election voters. A more appropriate comparison is with party identifiers because primaries are the means by which the party electorate chooses its nominees. Using this comparison, there are not many important differences. Just as is the case with primary voters more generally, voters in presidential primaries tend to be slightly older, better educated, more affluent, better integrated into their communities, and less likely to be black or Hispanic, but their positions on key policy issues are similar to those of other party identifiers.[13] So there is not much support for the argument that presidential primary voters are less representative of the party than are other groups of voters.

Do Voters Make Informed Choices?

Another criticism of the primaries is that voters do not make very well-informed decisions. Compared with voters in the general election, primary voters have been found to pay less attention to the campaign and to have less knowledge about the candidates. Especially in the early contests, voters are influenced by candidate momentum, as bandwagons form for candidates who have won by a large margin, or even just exceeded reporters' expectations. Candidates' personal characteristics influence voters in the primaries, but issues often have only a minor impact. The result, so this argument goes, is a series of contests decided mainly on the basis of short-run, superficial considerations.[14]

Most analysts think that this is too strong an indictment of the primaries. They feel that voters respond with some rationality to the challenge of having to choose among several candidates in a short campaign without the powerful guidance provided by party labels. Primary voters make decisions based on candidates' chances of winning, personal and demographic characteristics, and whatever inferences can be drawn about their policy positions.[15]

Is it rational for voters to be drawn to a presidential candidate who is gathering momentum in the primaries? Some would say yes—that party voters do not always see many big differences among their party's candidates and just want to pick the candidate who has the best chance of winning the nomination and the presidency. Momentum seems to matter especially when voters are being asked to sort through a pack of candidates about whom they know little,[16] and when there is no well-known front-runner.[17] Even then, the candidates who move to the head of the pack are usually subjected to more searching evaluations, which give voters more reasons to support or oppose them. Momentum probably matters the least in the campaigns of incumbent presidents and vice presidents; because they are better known, their candidacies are less likely to be affected by the ups and downs of the polls, unless their chances of winning decrease substantially.

In short, even though primary voters often base their decisions on less information than do general election voters, their choices are not necessarily irrational. In contests that pit a party's candidates against one another, issue differences among candidates are likely to be minor. It should not be surprising, then, that other factors, including candidates' characteristics and issue priorities, as opposed to issue positions, would become important. The basis for voters' decisions in primaries may not differ very much from those in caucuses or general elections.[18] Besides, the questions raised about the quality of voter decision making in primaries could be raised just as easily about the judgment of the party leaders who selected candidates under the earlier caucus-convention system.

Do Primaries Produce Good Candidates?

Both the current primary-dominated system and the earlier caucus-convention system have attractive and unattractive qualities. Talented and engaging candidates have been nominated by both, and so have less distinguished candidates. The earlier nominating system tended to favor mainstream politicians, those who were more acceptable to the party's leaders and activists, including some candidates who had earned their nomination through party loyalty rather than through either their personal appeal or their skills at governing. Primaries are more likely to give an advantage to candidates whose names are well known to the public and those who have the support of issue activists and ideological extremists.[19]

One clear result of the reforms is that the politics of choosing delegates has become more open and more similar in all states, whether they use primaries or caucuses and conventions. As the media coverage of nominations has become national in scope and the delegate selection is more open, candidates are forced to run more nationalized campaigns. The television ad run by a candidate in New York may well be reported to television viewers in South Dakota; it is harder for candidates to tailor their appeals to specific local areas. The quiet agreements once made to swing an uncommitted delegation have been replaced by the public promises designed to sway voters in a primary.

Because of this very openness, a primary's results confer a lot of legitimacy on the winning candidates. Primary victories may be just as important to candidates for their symbolic value, then, as for the delegates whom they award. Primaries give candidates a chance to demonstrate their public support, raise more campaign money, and demonstrate their stamina to a greater extent than they could in the older party-dominated system. Candidates' performance in the primaries may not be a good indicator of their likely competence in the White House, but they do give voters at least some measure of the candidates' ability to cope gracefully under pressure.

ON TO THE NATIONAL CONVENTIONS

Once the states have chosen their delegates in primaries and caucuses, the Democrats and Republicans assemble as national parties in conventions. These mass meetings bring together the party organization and activists and the party in government, but the main purpose of the convention—to select the party's presidential nominee—has already been accomplished in those primaries and caucuses. Aside from formally approving the candidates who have won the most delegates, what is left for the convention to do?

Roots of the Conventions

The national party convention is an old and respected institution, but it began, at least in part, as a power grab. In 1832, the nomination of Andrew Jackson as the Democratic-Republican candidate for president was a foregone conclusion, but state political leaders wanted to keep Henry Clay, the favorite of the congressional caucus, from being nominated as vice president; they preferred Martin Van Buren. So these leaders pushed for a national convention to make the nominations. In doing so, they wrested control of the presidential selection process from congressional leaders. By the time the Republican Party emerged in 1854, the convention had become the accepted means through which major parties chose their candidates for president and vice president. The GOP held its first convention in 1856. Ever since then, the two major parties have held national conventions every four years.

What Conventions Do

Months before the convention, its major committees begin their work (see box on page 184). What these committees decide can be overruled by the convention itself, which acts as the ultimate arbiter of its own structure and procedures. Some of the most famous battles on the floor of the convention have involved disputes over committee recommendations. The convention warms up with the keynote address by a party "star," tries to maintain momentum and suspense as it considers the platform, and reaches a dramatic peak in the nomination of the presidential and vice-presidential candidates. This general format has remained basically the same for decades.

KEY COMMITTEES OF THE NATIONAL PARTY CONVENTIONS

The national conventions have four important committees:

Credentials deals with the qualifications of delegates and alternates. In earlier years, fierce battles sometimes took place over the seating of delegations, for example, in the 1964 Democratic convention, when the all-white Mississippi delegation was challenged as being unrepresentative of Mississippi Democrats. Now, the state procedures are regularized, so this committee is no longer as crucial.

Permanent Organization selects the officials of the convention, including the chair, secretary, and sergeant at arms.

Rules sets the rules of the convention, including the length and number of nomination speeches. Disputes can occur over procedures for future conventions.

Platform (or Resolutions) drafts the party's platform for action by the convention. Because internal party battles focus increasingly on issues, this committee takes on special importance.

Approving the Platform   In addition to nominating candidates, the convention's main job is to approve the party's *platform*—its statement of party positions on a wide range of issues. The platform committee begins public hearings long before the convention opens, so that a draft can be ready for the convention. The finished platform is then presented to the convention for its approval.

Party platforms don't always get much respect. Even party leaders sometimes ignore them; the 1996 Republican presidential nominee, Senator Bob Dole, admitted that he had not read his party's platform. Because they are approved in nominating conventions whose main purpose is to choose a presidential candidate, platforms have usually reflected the candidate's views—or the bargains that the candidate has been willing to make to win support or preserve party harmony.[20] So a platform tends to look like a laundry list of the preferences of various groups in the party's (and the candidate's) supporting coalition. Platforms are also campaign documents, intended to help the party's candidates win their races.

Yet platforms are much more than just a laundry list of promises. They often define the major differences between the parties, as the leading scholar of party platforms shows.[21] As a result, they can provoke some spirited battles in the convention because many delegates care deeply about this single statement of the party's beliefs. In recent conventions, for example, struggles over the abortion issue have taken place or have been threatened. The completed Democratic and Republican platforms have presented voters with clearly differing sets of stands on a number of issues, most notably abortion, taxes, gun control, racial policy, deficit spending, and American involvement in the world (see Chapter 15).

Formalizing the Presidential Nomination   The vote on the party's candidate for president begins with nominations made by delegates, shorter seconding speeches, and brief but passionate demonstrations by the candidate's supporters. These events are low key compared with the rambunctious conventions of earlier years. The presence of media coverage encourages party leaders to aim for a carefully crafted picture of the party's strength and vision; this tends to deprive conventions of much of the sense of carnival and drama that was central to their tradition.

Once the nominee has been presented, the secretary calls the roll of the states (and other voting units), asking each delegation to report its vote. The result in recent times has taken only one ballot—far from the days when, in 1924, the Democrats plodded through 103 ballots in sultry New York's Madison Square Garden, before John W. Davis won the majority needed for the nomination. Yet a convention that requires more than one ballot to choose the nominee is still possible—especially for the Democrats because of their use of proportional representation in the primaries and caucuses.

In the past, when a convention had more than one candidate for the nomination and the first ballot did not produce a majority, intense negotiations would follow. The leading candidates would need to protect their image as likely winners by keeping other candidates from chipping away their supporters and by negotiating for the votes of delegates who had come committed to minor candidates. It is hard to imagine how these negotiations could work in conventions today because the delegates are tied to candidates rather than to state party leaders. If no candidate had a majority, it might be that uncommitted superdelegates could broker a victory for one candidate.

Approving the Vice-Presidential Nominee   The day after the presidential nominee is chosen, delegates vote again to select the vice-presidential candidate. This process, too, is ceremonial; presidential nominees normally choose their own running mates, and conventions routinely ratify their choice.[22] This method of selecting vice-presidential candidates has drawn criticism—not so much because they are handpicked by the presidential nominee as because the decision is often made by a tired candidate and then sprung, at the last minute, on convention delegates. George H. W. Bush's nomination of Senator Dan Quayle in 1988 was attacked on these grounds. But without any viable procedure to replace it, this choice will remain in the hands of the party's presidential nominee.

Launching the Presidential Campaign   The final business of the conventions is to present their party's presidential choice to the American voters. The nominating speeches and the candidates' own acceptance speeches are the opening shots of the fall campaign. Most nominees generally get a boost in public support (a "convention bounce") from this campaign kickoff. For the winning candidates, then, the most important role of the convention is as a campaign event.

WHO ARE THE DELEGATES?

Convention delegates are among the most visible of the party's activists. They help to shape the public's image of the two parties. Who are these delegates?

Apportioning Delegates Among the States

It is the parties that determine how many delegates each state can send to the convention. The two parties make these choices differently. The Republicans allocate delegates more equally among the states; the Democrats weigh more heavily the size of the state's population and its record of support for Democratic candidates.

These formulas affect the voting strength of various groups within the party coalitions. The GOP's decision to represent the small states more equally with the large states has been an advantage to its conservative wing. In contrast, by giving relatively more weight to the larger states with stronger Democratic voting traditions, the Democrats have favored the more liberal interests in their party. Even if these delegate allocation formulas have only marginal effects on the balance of forces within the parties, many nominations have been won—and lost—at the margin.

How Representative Are the Delegates?

The delegates to the Democratic and Republican conventions have never been a cross section of American citizens or even of their party's voters. White males, the well educated, and the affluent have traditionally been overrepresented in conventions. Reflecting their different coalitional bases, since the 1930s, Democratic delegations have had more union members and African Americans, and Republican conventions have drawn more Protestants and business entrepreneurs.

Demographics   Since the nomination reforms, the delegates of both parties, but especially the Democrats, have become at least somewhat more representative of other citizens. The Democrats used affirmative action plans after 1968 to increase the presence of women, blacks, and, for a brief time, young people; since 1980, they have required that half of the delegates be women. The percentage of female delegates at Republican conventions has gone up somewhat during this period as well but without party mandates. The Democratic National Committee has urged its state organizations to recruit more low- and moderate-income delegates, but the low political involvement levels of these groups and the high price of attending a convention stand in the way. So conventions remain meetings of the wealthy and well educated (see Table 10.1). In 2000, for instance, 23 percent of Republican delegates and 12 percent of Democrats said they were millionaires.[23]

Political Experience   We might assume that delegates would be recidivists, making return appearances at convention after convention. But that was not the case even before the reforms; even then, a comfortable majority of delegates at each convention were first timers. With the move to primaries, the percentage of newcomers jumped to about 80 percent before declining. The decline became more marked when the Democrats granted convention seats to politically experienced superdelegates.

Even if many delegates are new to conventions, however, the great majority are long-time party activists. In 2000, for example, most of a random sample of convention delegates reported that they had been active in their party for at least 20 years, and a majority said they currently hold party office.[24] In spite of the high turnover, then, these national party meetings still bring together the activists of the state and local party organizations and the leaders of the party in government.

Issues and Ideology   Another way in which convention delegates differ from the average party voter is that the delegates are more aware of issues and more ideologically extreme. Democratic delegates are more liberal than Democratic voters and much more liberal than

TABLE 10.1 How Representative Were the 2000 Democratic and Republican Convention Delegates?

	Dem. Delegates	Dem. Voters	All Voters	Rep. Voters	Rep. Delegates
Gender					
Female	48%	57%	54%	52%	35%
Race					
Black	19%	17%	10%	2%	4%
White	64	74	81	90	85
Hispanic	12	6	*	*	6
Education					
HS graduate or less	6%	50%	46%	40%	4
Some college	19	27	28	29	19
College grad	25	14	16	18	31
Postgraduate	49	10	11	11	46
Household income					
Under $25,000	3%	35%†	29%†	21%†	s2%
Over $75,000	57	15	19	25	57
Religion					
Protestant	47%	48%	53%	63%	63%
Evangelical or Born-again††	12	24	*	37	27
Catholic	30	28	25	19	27
Jewish	8	2	1	0	2

*Data not available. †Under $30,000. ††Asked in a separate question, so percentages for "religion" do not add up to 100 percent.

Source: Data on convention delegates are from a CBS News/New York Times poll in June–August 2000. Voter data are from a CBS News poll conducted from July 13–17, 2000; data were kindly provided by Kathleen Frankovic and Jinghua Zou of CBS News.

the average voter; Republican delegates tend to be further to the right than either their party voters or voters generally. The distance between delegates and their party's voters varies from issue to issue. As Table 10.2 shows, Democratic delegates in 2000 came closest to the views of Democratic voters (and all voters) in favoring environmental protection and trigger locks on handguns but were at least about 20 points more liberal on a number of other big issues. Republican delegates were most similar to Republican voters, as well as all voters, in their support for the death penalty and opposition to abortion and to prescription drug coverage under Medicare but scored well to the right on other questions.

The degree to which delegates hold more extreme views than party voters bears on a long-standing debate about the nominating process. Democrats who promoted the 1970s reforms were motivated, in part, by the argument that the old caucus-convention system, dominated by party leaders, did not represent the views of grassroots party supporters. In turn, the critics of the reforms contend that the delegates selected under the new rules are even more out of step ideologically with party voters and the electorate in general.

TABLE 10.2 Views on Issues: Comparing Delegates and Voters in 2000

	Dem. Delegates	Dem. Voters	All Voters	Rep. Voters	Rep. Delegates
Government should do more to solve national problems	73%	44%	33%	21%	4%
Abortion should be permitted in all cases	63	34	26	16	10
Death penalty for murder	20	46	51	55	60
Require gun manufacturers to put child safety locks on handguns	94	91	84	76	48
Favor affirmative action to remedy past discrimination	83	59	51	44	29
Medicare should cover prescription drugs for the elderly	58	39	37	36	34
Must protect the environment even if jobs in your community are lost	63	72	64	57	32
Tax-funded vouchers to help parents pay tuition for private/ religious schools	10	41	47	53	71
Individuals should be allowed to invest a portion of their Social Security taxes on their own	23	44	53	61	89

Note: Figures are the percentage of each group who agreed with the statement.
Source: Same as in Table 10.1.

The reality is that the reforms have not made the conventions more representative of the views of party identifiers. Prior to 1972, it was the Republican conventions whose delegates appeared to be more ideologically out of step with party voters and even more compared with the general voting public.[25] The Democratic reforms first seemed to reverse that pattern. Democratic delegates in 1972 were more ideologically distant from their party identifiers than Republican delegates were and even farther away from the public, and some charged that the reforms were at fault.[26] These disparities on issues seem to have been reduced in later Democratic conventions.[27]

The real effect of the reforms has been to link the selection of delegates more closely to candidate preferences. As a result, when an ideologically committed candidate does well in the primaries and caucuses, more ideologically oriented activists become convention delegates. At those times, conventions may be less representative of the party in the electorate. However, they may offer clearer choices to voters.

Amateurs or Professionals?   The reforms were also expected to result in delegates with a different approach to politics. Using the terms described in Chapter 5, some convention delegates can be described as amateurs, others as professionals. Amateurs are more attracted by issues, more insistent on internal party democracy, less willing to compromise and less committed to the prime importance of winning elections. Professionals, in contrast, are more likely to have a long-term commitment to the party and to be more willing to compromise on issues in the interest of winning the general election.

There is some evidence that the Democratic Party's reforms had, as intended, reduced the presence of party professionals between the 1968 and the 1972 conventions.[28] As we have seen, however, the party later moved to reverse this trend, particularly by adding superdelegates. Research shows that even after the reforms, delegates have remained strongly committed to the parties and their goals.[29] It may be that for both professionals and amateurs, involvement in this highly public party pageant strengthens delegates' commitment to the party's aims.

Who Controls the Delegates?   It would not matter how representative delegates are if they act as pawns of powerful party leaders. In fact, for most of the history of party conventions, that is exactly how the state delegations behaved. State party leaders and big-city mayors had a commanding presence, especially at Democratic conventions.

Now, however, strong party leaders no longer control the convention by dominating their state delegations. When the Democrats eliminated their long-standing unit rule in 1968, through which a majority of a state delegation could throw all the delegation's votes to one candidate, they removed a powerful instrument of leadership control. Perhaps the most powerful force preventing state party leaders from controlling the conventions is the fact that so many delegates in both parties now come to the conventions already committed to a candidate. That makes them unavailable for "delivery" by party leaders. If anyone controls the modern conventions, then, it is the party's prospective nominee for president, not leaders of the state parties.

HOW MEDIA COVER CONVENTIONS

In addition to all these changes in the convention's power centers and delegates, media coverage of conventions has changed significantly. On one hand, conventions have been reshaped and rescheduled to meet the media's needs.[30] On the other, ironically, media attention to the conventions has declined sharply in recent years.

Beginning with the first televised national party conventions in 1948, TV journalists and politicians found ways to serve one another's needs. In the early days of television before the convenience of videotape, networks were desperate for content with which to fill broadcast time. So they covered the party conventions live, from gavel to gavel. For television news, the convention became a major story, like a natural disaster or the Olympics, through which it could demonstrate its skill and provide a public service. Reporters swarmed through the convention halls, covering the strategic moves of major candidates, the actions of powerful figures in the party, and the complaints of individual delegates. Even the formerly secret work of the platform committee came to be done in the public eye.

For party leaders, television coverage offered a priceless opportunity to reach voters and to launch the presidential campaign with maximum impact. So they reshaped the convention into a performance intended as much for the national television audience as for the delegates. Party officials gave key speaking roles to telegenic candidates, speeded up the proceedings, and moved the most dramatic convention business into prime-time hours. More and more, the aim of the convention shifted from the conduct of party business to the wooing of voters.

These two sets of goals, however—the networks' interest in a good story and the parties' interest in attracting supporters—increasingly began to conflict. Once the nomination reforms took effect, the choice of the parties' presidential candidates was settled before the convention started. That took most of the drama and suspense out of the conventions. To keep their audience, media people searched the conventions for new sources of excitement, such as potential conflicts. But party leaders had no interest in making their disputes public; that would interfere with the positive message they were trying to convey. As the conventions' audience appeal continued to decline, the major networks reduced their coverage to broadcast only the most significant events. Although convention "junkies" still can turn to C-SPAN, MSNBC, or other cable sources for comprehensive convention coverage, the number of hours of coverage on ABC, CBS, and NBC decreased from about 60 per convention in 1952 to little more than an hour a night in 2000.[31]

Media coverage, of course, is not always a boon for the parties. Television's capacity to dramatize and personalize can make a convention come to life for its audience, as it did in covering the struggles in the Democratic convention hall and streets of Chicago in 1968, which led to the nomination reforms. However, the sight of bloody demonstrators and angry delegates did not help the Democratic Party to attract voter support for its candidates that year. Television cameras can encourage some participants to use the convention as a podium to advance their own causes even if they risk undermining the party's interests. For better or worse, the televised conventions of 2004 had become a shadow of their former selves, in which a shrinking audience watched snippets of roll-call votes, shots of people wearing funny hats, and intense discussions among media commentators.

DO CONVENTIONS STILL HAVE A PURPOSE?

Since the nomination reforms, then, conventions have greatly changed. They are no longer the occasions when the major parties actually select their presidential nominees. That happens in the primaries and a few caucuses; the conventions simply ratify the results. The national conventions have lost much of their deliberative character and independence; genuinely brokered nominations and last-minute compromises seem to belong to the past.

In another way, however, the conventions have become more significant. Because candidates must mobilize groups of activists and voters in order to win primaries and caucuses and because many of these groups are concerned with particular policies, the nomination reforms have made issues all the more important in convention politics. Many delegates arrive at the convention committed not only to a candidate but also to a cause. Ideological factions and their aims, then, have become new centers of power in the conventions. The pressures exerted by Christian conservatives at Republican conventions in the 1990s and 2000s on behalf of such causes as school prayer and opposition to abortion and homosexuality are a good illustration.

In spite of all these changes—or perhaps because of them—the national conventions are living symbols of the national parties. They provide a unique occasion for rediscovering common interests, and for celebrating the party's heroes and achievements. Conventions motivate state and local party candidates, energize party workers, and launch presidential campaigns. They give new party candidates some time in the media spotlight. They may not win Emmy awards for compelling viewing, but they frequently remind party activists, and even some party identifiers, why the party matters to them.

SHOULD WE REFORM THE REFORMS?

The reforms of the presidential nominating system are part of a time-honored pattern in American politics: efforts by reformers to break up concentrations of party power. As we have seen, however, the reforms have had many unintended effects as well. Primaries can create internal divisions in state party organizations that may not heal in time for the general election. The low turnouts in primaries and caucuses may increase the influence of well-organized groups on the ideological extremes: the right wing of the Republican Party and the left wing of the Democrats. The results of a few early contests in states not very representative of the nation have a disproportionate effect on the national outcome.[32] Candidates must invest such an enormous amount of time, energy, and money before the presidential campaign has even begun that the ultimate winner can arrive at the party convention personally and financially exhausted. And by the time most voters know enough about the prospective nominees to make an informed choice, the nominations have already been decided.

But there is no going back to the old system. As the reformers charged, it was usually controlled by state and local party leaders who were often out of touch with the electorate. It kept many party voters and even party activists out of the crucial first step in picking a president. It violated the desire for a more open, democratic politics, and it did not help presidential candidates learn how to prepare for the most powerful leadership job in the world.[33]

What Could Be Done?

Could the reforms' drawbacks be fixed by more reforms? One possibility is to create regional nominating events, in which the states in a given region would all schedule their primaries on the same day. That might bring more coherence to the welter of state contests by limiting the number of dates on which they could be held and reducing the enormous strain on the candidates.

For a time in the late 1980s and 1990s, one regional primary existed; most southern states chose to hold their primaries early in March on a date referred to as Super Tuesday. The aim of these states was to draw greater attention to southern concerns and to encourage the nomination of moderate candidates acceptable to the South. By 1996, New England states also scheduled their primaries on this date. In 2000, six southern and southwestern states attempted another southern primary, but the front-loading of other states' events reduced its impact.

Regional primaries, however, have drawbacks, too. Which region would go first? Even if the order were rotated from one election to the next, the first region to vote, with its peculiarities and specific concerns, would have a disproportionate effect on the nominations. Regional primaries could still produce all the complaints listed above, from internal party divisions to low turnouts. Given the fact that the only major war fought on American soil was a regional dispute—the Civil War—some might ask whether it is wise to encourage regional divisions.

Another option might be to hold a national primary in which all the states' delegate selection events were held on the same day. But this would serve the interests of neither the parties nor the states. States would lose their chance of becoming key players in the nomination race. The parties would lose control over presidential selection, throwing the contest for the presidency wide open to any candidate who could mobilize a national constituency (and a great deal of money). A national primary could be accomplished only by ending the long tradition of state and party control over the presidential nomination process—and even after all the reforms that we have seen in recent decades, there is little chance that will happen.

CHAPTER 11

The General Election

The world of campaigning has been transformed in the past two decades. Now, if you plan to run for statewide or national office (or even local office in many areas), you would expect to hire a long list of professional consultants, ranging from pollsters to media specialists, direct mail experts, Web page designers, fund-raisers, accountants, and others. They will do the work—for a fee, of course—that would have been done for free (or at least for no monetary payment) in the days when state and local party organizations were the main planners and managers of campaigns.

It would be easy to assume, as a result, that the traditional grassroots party organization has become technologically obsolete and has been replaced by independent consultants and the newer, more efficient, and powerful campaign techniques that they offer. But the party organizations are highly adaptable. Throughout their history, the Democratic and Republican Parties have adjusted to changing circumstances; that helps account for their long lives. Instead of relegating the parties to the sidelines, then, we need to examine their current role in campaigns.

Earlier chapters have discussed important parts of the campaign environment: the parties' organizational strength, political activists, party loyalties, voter turnout, and the rules governing party nominations. We begin this chapter by looking at the "rules" by which elections are run. Then we will examine the decisions that candidates can make to take advantage of those rules.

ELECTIONS: THE RULES AFFECT THE RESULTS

The rules in politics, as well as everything else, are never neutral. Each rule of the electoral process, for example, how votes must be cast or when elections must be held, not only limits a campaign's choices but also affects different parties and candidates differently. For example, if polling places close at 6:00 P.M. (as they do in Indiana and Kentucky), so that factory and office workers find it hard to get to the polls on time, then the Democratic Party may lose a disproportionate number of votes. If the state makes it easy to vote absentee, then any local party well organized enough to distribute absentee ballots to its supporters will benefit. Over the years, reformers have worked hard to change the rules in order to weaken the parties, and party leaders have tried to tinker with the rules to gain strength. The reformers have won these rules battles more often than the parties have. Here are some prominent examples.

The Secret Ballot

American elections did not always use secret ballots. In the early nineteenth century, in many areas, voters simply told the election officials which candidates they preferred. Gradually, this "oral vote" was replaced by the use of ballots printed by the parties or candidates. The voter brought the ballot of a particular candidate or party to the polling place and put it in the ballot box. The ballots of different parties differed in color and appearance, so observers could tell how an individual had voted. That was not accidental; if party leaders had done a favor for a voter in exchange for a vote, they wanted to be sure they had gotten their money's worth.

To discourage vote buying, a new ballot system came into widespread use in the 1890s. Called the Australian ballot after the country where it originated, these ballots were printed by the government and marked by the voter in secret. By the early twentieth century, its success was virtually complete; only South Carolina waited until 1950 to adopt it. Because the ballot is administered and paid for by the government, this reform involved the government in running elections, which opened the door to government regulation of the parties. It also enabled voters to split their tickets—to vote for the candidates of more than one party on the same ballot.[1]

The Format of the Ballot

The *format* of this secret ballot varies from state to state, however, which makes a difference in the role of the parties.

Office-Bloc Ballots.   In earlier years, most states used a party-column ballot, in which the candidates of the same party are grouped together so that voters could see them as a party ticket. That encourages straight-ticket voting (i.e., voting for all of a party's candidates on the ballot). More and more, however, states have adopted an office-bloc ballot form, which groups the candidates according to the office they seek. This ballot format makes split-ticket voting more likely.[2]

The Order of Candidates' Names.   Other aspects of the ballot format can affect a candidate's chance of winning. It is a curious fact that some voters are more likely to select the first name on a list of candidates than they are to select a name listed later.[3] So some states randomly assign the order in which candidates' names appear on the ballot or rotate the order among groups of ballots; in other states, incumbents' names or the candidates of the majority party appear first. The decision to list incumbents first increases their already substantial electoral advantages. The order of the candidates' names probably matters most in primaries and nonpartisan contests, when voters can find no information about the candidates on the ballot itself.

IF WE CAN COUNT CRATERS ON MARS, WHY CAN'T WE COUNT VOTES ACCURATELY?

Here is some of what we learned from the 2000 elections about voting systems used in the United States:

- In a nation where the latest hand-held computer is considered a staple of many professions, almost one-third of all voting in the United States in 2000 was done on punch-card machines, where voters must punch out a perforated rectangle (called a "chad") next to the candidate's name. Sometimes, however, the chad doesn't fall out or is pushed back in as the voter moves down the ballot. When that happens, the voter's choice can't be read by the voting machine. That's called an "undervote," and the voter may as well have stayed home.

- In some counties, the ballot format was confusing enough that some voters, whether intentionally or not, cast ballots for more than one candidate ("overvotes"). Those votes couldn't be counted either.

- New York City used pull-a-lever voting machines so old that they aren't made any more. The 900-pound machines each have 27,000 parts and must be pulled on and off trucks to get to the polls. Not surprisingly, they break down. Similar machines in Louisiana can be rigged using pliers, a screwdriver, a cigarette lighter, and a Q-tip. The late Louisiana Senator Earl Long used to say that he wanted to be buried in Louisiana so he could keep voting.

- Indiana's voter registration lists included hundreds of thousands of people who were ineligible to vote because they were dead, were felons, or had registered more than once. Alaska had more registered voters than people of voting age.

Sources: Robin Toner, "For Those Behind the Scenes, It's Old News That Elections Are Not an Exact Science," *New York Times,* Nov. 17, 2000, p. A23; David S. Broder, "In Need of an Overhaul," *Washington Post,* Dec. 6, 2000, p. A35; Times Staff Writers, "A 'Modern' Democracy That Can't Count Votes," *Los Angeles Times,* Dec. 11, 2000, p. A1.

The Long Ballot   Another important "rule" is that American voters are asked to elect large numbers of state and local officials who would be appointed in other democracies. In many areas, voters also cast ballots on issues. In an exhausting example in 2002, San Francisco voters faced 19 ballot questions on everything from parental leave to whether the city should grow its own marijuana. Voters also received a 300-page booklet of citizens' and groups' opinions about these ballot measures plus a 112-page guide to other ballot questions and candidates for state office.

   Citizens would need to process a lot of information (and have a lot of patience) to cast a meaningful vote in such an election. Many people consider this an invitation to stay away from the polls. Those who do vote may choose to cast ballots for some offices but not others. This partial voting, called roll-off, is most often seen on minor offices and referenda in which as many as 20 or 30 percent of the voters abstain.[4] The voter fatigue caused by the long ballot leads people to use various shortcuts to make their choices; party identification, of course, is one.

Voting Systems

Most of us assume that, even if a ballot is long, it is easy enough to understand: You choose a candidate, push a button or pull a lever, and that candidate gets your vote. At least, we *would* have made that assumption until the aftermath of the 2000 presidential race. Recounts prompted by the closeness of the vote showed that on 1.5 to 2 million ballots (about 2 percent of all those cast), the counting machines found no presidential vote or votes for more than one candidate; these voters' ballots, then, were not counted. Some of these "undervotes" or "overvotes" could have been intentional, but studies showing that these problems occurred much more frequently in some types of voting machines (such as punch-card systems) than in others suggest that the voting system itself may have been the culprit (see box on page 194).[5]

In other cases, analysts charged that confusing ballot layout, such as the so-called "butterfly ballot" used in Palm Beach County, Florida, led many voters to cast their ballot for a different candidate than they had intended (see Figure 11.1). This was an especially worrisome issue in Florida, which decided the election for Bush by a margin of

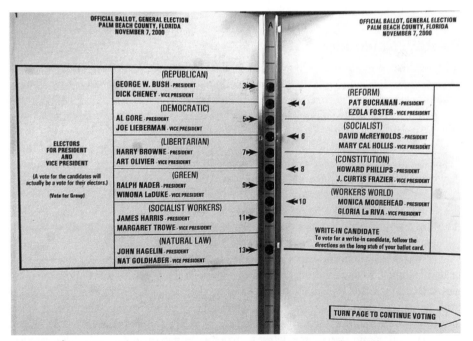

FIGURE 11.1 The Famous Palm Beach, Florida, "Butterfly Ballot."
This ballot format was designed by a Democratic official in Palm Beach County to make it easier for visually challenged older voters to read. As shown in this graphic by Daniel Niblock of the South Florida *Sun-Sentinel* (showing the angle at which most voters would have seen the ballot), the problem was that the punch card holes did not always line up with the candidates' names, so in order to vote for Al Gore, whose name was second on the list of candidates, voters had to punch the *third* hole.
Source: http://www.sun-sentinel.com/graphics/news/ballot.htm. Reprinted by permission of the *South-Florida Sun-Sentinel*. Photograph by Susan Stocker.

only 537 votes. There were other problems as well, such as voters turned away from polling places or misinformed about voting procedures, malfunctioning voting machines, and outright fraud.

Why does this happen? There are about 191,000 voting precincts in the United States. They contain about 700,000 voting machines tended by almost 1.5 million poll workers who are typically poorly paid, lightly trained partisan volunteers.[6] Simple human error is as likely to occur in running elections and counting votes as it is in any other large-scale activity. Because elections are decentralized, voters in one state, even in one county, may well be treated differently from voters in another. In particular, counties differ in their ability to pay for the most reliable (and costly) voting systems. The result is that error-prone systems are more likely to be found in poorer counties, which tend to vote Democratic.

In the wake of these revelations, Congress and state legislatures worked to modernize voting systems. Congress set minimum federal standards and provided almost $4 billion to help cash-starved states to upgrade their procedures. However, the problems have not vanished, as Floridians learned when many voters were unable to cast ballots in the 2002 primaries because not all poll workers had been trained to use the newly purchased, upgraded voting machines.

Election Calendars

Even a feature so seemingly trivial as when elections are held can have important consequences for the candidates and the parties. Since 1845, federal elections have almost always been held on the first Tuesday after the first Monday in November of the even-numbered years. To save money, many state and local elections were traditionally held at the same time.

Scheduling elections for various offices at the same time on the same ballot links the electoral fates of their candidates. A voter's decision on one contest can affect his or her other choices on the same ballot. This is termed a *coattail* effect: the ability of candidates at the top of the ticket to carry into office "on their coattails" other candidates on the same party ticket.[7] As a result, candidates for lesser offices have an incentive to want the strongest possible candidates at the top of the party ticket to ensure that those coattails are long and sturdy.

Parties often prefer to enhance this linkage because it encourages party cohesion. Progressive reformers worked to weaken it, using devices such as office-bloc ballots and nonpartisan elections. Some incumbents and other candidates have also found it preferable to insulate their campaigns from the powerful forces present in federal contests. Most states now elect governors in the second year after a presidential election. Local elections are usually scheduled at some other time, when no federal offices are on the ballot. This practice of insulating elected officials from one another limits the possibilities for coattail effects; it also tends to reduce the cohesiveness of the party in government.[8]

Even the fact that elections are held on a regular schedule, rather than at a time of the government's or the opposition party's choosing (as happens in parliamentary democracies), affects the issues discussed in campaigns. Californians had voted to reelect Governor Gray Davis in November 2002. Just eight months later, a conservative Republican enraged by the state's huge budget deficit and tax increases mounted a petition drive to recall the governor. The recall election was held about two months later. Because the time between the petition drive and the election was so short, the issues that prompted the drive were at the forefront of media coverage and, as polls showed, most voters' minds. Davis lost to actor Arnold Schwarzenegger. If this governor's race had been held three years later, at the expected time, the budget shortfall and the tax increases might have been changed or forgotten, and Davis could have had a better chance of setting a different agenda for the campaign.

Legislative Redistricting

Some types of candidates—legislative incumbents—have the opportunity to influence the size and shape of the election districts that they represent in order to benefit themselves. Every ten years, after the U.S. Census, state legislatures are asked to redraw the boundaries of congressional and state legislative districts in order to take account of changes in population size and distribution. How these opportunities have been turned to political advantage is a continuing story of the creativity and resourcefulness of American politicians.

Two methods have traditionally been used to turn redistricting opportunities into political gains. The first and most obvious has been simply to ignore population changes. Many states used this tactic for most of the 1900s by refusing to shift legislative districts and thus political power, from the shrinking rural and small-town populations to the growing cities. By the 1960s, many state legislatures and the U.S. House of Representatives better represented the largely rural America of 1900 than the urban nation it had become. Such *malapportionment* worked to the disadvantage of Republicans in the South and Democrats elsewhere and of the needs of cities everywhere. In a series of decisions in the 1960s, the Supreme Court ended these inequities by requiring that legislative districts be of equal population size and by applying this "one person, one vote" rule to all types of legislatures.[9]

It is still very possible, however, to *gerrymander*—to draw district lines in a way that maximizes one party's strength and disadvantages the other party. That can be done by dividing and thereby diluting pockets of the other party's strength to prevent it from winning office. Alternatively, if the other party's strength is too great to be diluted, then a gerrymander can be created by consolidating that party's voters into a few districts and forcing it to win elections by large, wasteful majorities.

The party in power when it is time to redistrict is probably always tempted to gerrymander. Its ability to do so has been enhanced by using computers to draw districts that yield maximum partisan gain and by the increasing party polarization, which has given state legislators the will to try. After the 2000 U.S. Census, only twelve U.S. House seats moved from one state to another because of changes in population, but the redrawing of House districts within each state offered ample opportunity for partisan gain. For instance, Republicans controlled the redistricting process in Florida, Michigan, and Pennsylvania in 2001, and the GOP won six more seats in those states in the 2002 elections than they had in 2000.[10]

After the 2000 redistricting had been completed, House Majority Leader Tom DeLay spurred an unprecedented second round of redrawing congressional district lines. DeLay urged Republicans in several states, including Colorado and Texas, to take advantage of their newfound state legislative majorities and take another cut at redistricting to improve their prospects for the 2004 elections. The Texas saga, in which minority Democratic legislators fled the state to keep the re-redistricting from passing, made headlines all over the world (see the box on page 198).

THE TALE OF THE TEXAS 62

First, 51 Democratic state representatives from Texas slipped quietly across the border to Oklahoma under cover of darkness. Then, the Republican governor dispatched state police to arrest them and bring them back. The U.S. Department of Homeland Security went looking for them. Republican legislators pasted the faces of the missing Democrats on milk cartons. The Democrats, hunkered down at a Holiday Inn in Ardmore, finally returned. Two months later, eleven Senate Democrats decamped for Albuquerque.

What was going on here? In 2003, Republicans took control of both houses of the Texas state legislature for the first time in 130 years. In a session that was termed "extraordinarily venomous" and partisan, the new Republican majority proposed to redraw the lines of the state's U.S. House districts. Texas' congressional district lines had already been redrawn following the 2000 U.S. Census. However, Republicans saw the chance, in a rare second redistricting, to bring the partisan composition of the state's House delegation more in line with what they perceived to be citizens' current party preferences. The proposal, drawn up by U.S. House Majority Leader Tom DeLay, was expected to result in big Republican gains.

Democratic legislators called the proposal a "power grab." Outnumbered, most of the Democrats decided to fight it by leaving town, thus depriving the legislature of a quorum (the minimum number of legislators who must be present to do business). The state Republican chair called the Democrats "cowards" and "betrayers of the people of Texas." Democratic lawmakers agreed to come home when Republican leaders, who could not pass any other legislation (including the state budget) without a quorum, promised to drop the redistricting proposal.

But the Republican governor then called a special legislative session, in which the state House passed the pro-Republican plan. Now it was the Senate Democrats who left town. When one Democrat broke ranks and came back, however, the battle was over. The redistricting plan, which was expected to cost Democrats at least half a dozen seats in the U.S. House, passed the state legislature and was signed into law by the governor and upheld by the U.S. Supreme Court.

Sources: Lee Hockstader, "Democrats Take Flight to Fight Tex. Redistricting," *Washington Post,* May 13, 2003, p. A1; Lee Hockstader, "Texas Democrats Trying Fight, Not Flight, Over Districts," *Washington Post,* July 1, 2003, p. A4.

Gerrymanders, however, do not always work the way that they were intended. California Democrats reaped major advantage from a gerrymander in the 1980s, but an equally notorious redistricting in Indiana designed to benefit Republicans had a short-lived effect. In 2002, two of four open House districts in Georgia, drawn carefully by the state legislature's Democratic majority in order to elect Democrats, went Republican instead. So the effects of redistricting are not always substantial, especially after the first few years.[11]

CAMPAIGN STRATEGY

Taking account of these "rules," candidates and their consultants and staff members must make a very large number of strategic choices.[12] They have the same goals as did candidates in the times when voters came to the polls on horseback: to identify the candidate's likely supporters, add to them, and get them to the polls to vote. But the methods used to do that now are much more sophisticated than they were even ten years ago.

Campaigners must consider a number of important variables in designing a strategy: the nature of the district and its voters, the type of office being sought, the candidate's skills and background and those of the opponent, the availability of money and other resources, and the party organizations and other organized groups in the constituency. Once they have identified their campaign's likely strengths and weaknesses, they must choose how to spend their scarce time and money in order to get the greatest possible harvest of votes. If the candidate's party is in the majority in a district where party voting is common, the campaign can spend most of its resources on appeals to party voters and get-out-the-vote drives. If that is not the case, they must figure out how to attract independents without losing their base of party identifiers.

The most important factors affecting the campaign's decisions are incumbency and the competitiveness of the race. Incumbents have enormous advantages in running for reelection, even in times of great cynicism about government.[13] Congressional incumbents, as we have seen in Chapter 2, have enormously high reelection rates. Incumbents of any office are greatly advantaged by having put together a successful campaign for that office at least once before. Part of that campaign organization is likely to remain in place between elections, some of it perhaps employed as members of the incumbent's office staff. Incumbents normally have greater name recognition, more success in attracting media coverage, and greater appeal to campaign contributors than do most of their potential competitors.

In painful contrast, most challengers, especially if they have not won any political office before, do not start with an experienced organization, proven fund-raising skills, or the other incumbent advantages. In the days when party organizations dominated campaigns, this might not have been a problem. Now it is. One obvious answer might be to purchase an experienced campaign organization by hiring political consultants, but most challengers do not have the money to do that. Thus, the predictable cycle begins: the challenger lacks an existing organization and enough money to attract the interest of well-known consultants and buy media time, so he or she cannot reach many voters; and without these vital resources, the challenger will not raise enough money to be able to afford either one.

Candidates for open seats (those for which no incumbent is running) are more likely to have competitive races. Those who choose to run for the most visible offices—governorships, the U.S. Senate, the presidency, major city offices—typically start with considerable name recognition, which increases because of the attention given to the race. They can usually raise enough money for extensive media campaigns. Their major challenge will be to spend their money effectively and to succeed in defining themselves to the voters before their opponents get the opportunity to define them.

HOW CAMPAIGNING HAS CHANGED

Within less than a generation, American political campaigning has been revolutionized. Campaigns have found effective ways to apply advances in polling, media use, and computer technology. They have done so with the help of a burgeoning industry of professional campaign consultants: specialists in an ever-widening range of political skills whose services are available to candidates who can afford the price.

Professional Consultants

Professional campaign consultants come from a variety of backgrounds. Some have been involved in party or other political work since they were old enough to pick up a phone. Others got their start in university graduate programs. Not only have they prospered in American politics, they have also exported their campaign expertise to the rest of the democratic world. Pollster Stan Greenberg, for instance, signed on to Al Gore's presidential campaign in 2000 after having worked on campaigns for prime minister in England in 1997, Germany in 1998, and Israel in 1999.[14]

Consultants contract to deliver a variety of services. Some are general consultants, similar to the general contractors who oversee the construction of a home; others concentrate on the details of mailing lists or Web page design. Some are experts in the development of media messages and others in how and where to place media ads. Some can provide organizational skills; they can organize rallies, coffee parties, and phone banks. Others provide lawyers and accountants to steer the campaign away from legal shoals and to handle the reporting of campaign finances to state and federal regulators. Some are publicists who write speeches and press releases; some sample public opinion and others are skilled in raising money.

Professional consultants typically work for several different campaigns during the same election cycle. It is not uncommon for a consulting firm to handle a collection of U.S. Senate, House, and governors' races in a given election year. As "hired guns," they work independently of the party organizations, yet they almost always work with clients from only one of the parties—some consultants restrict themselves even further to one wing, or ideological grouping, within the party—and they normally maintain a cooperative relationship with that party's leaders and organization. In fact, national party committees often play an important matchmaking role in bringing together consultants and candidates.

Sources of Information

Computers   Experienced candidates develop a picture of their constituency in their minds. As the result of years of contact with constituents, they know what kinds of people support them and how they believe that they can trigger that support again. In past years, this "theory" of the campaign would have guided the candidate's strategy, even if the beliefs were inaccurate or the constituency had changed.

Computer technology now provides a much more sophisticated check on the candidate's beliefs. Computerized records can produce much faster and more accurate answers to questions about voter behavior than even the most experienced party workers can, that is, if anybody is available to compile the information. A local party can computerize reports from canvassers so that they can quickly generate lists of voters to contact on Election Day. Fund-raisers can merge mailing lists from groups and publications whose members may be predisposed to favor their candidate and then produce targeted mailings within hours. Using computerized records, "oppo" researchers can locate statements made by the opponent on any conceivable issue.

Polls   No new avenue to political knowledge has been more fully exploited than the public opinion poll.[15] Candidates poll before deciding whether to run for an office to assess voters' views and to probe for weaknesses in the opposition. When the campaign begins, polls are used to determine which issues are uppermost in voters' minds and how the candidate's first steps are affecting his or her "negatives" and "positives." Polls can be used to decide whether the campaign ads should emphasize party loyalties or ties with other party candidates. Close to the end of the race, *tracking polls* can follow the reactions of small samples of voters each day to measure immediate responses to a campaign event or a new ad.

Not all candidates have access to poll data. The expense of sophisticated polling puts it beyond the reach of many candidates. Recent efforts by the national party organizations (reviewed in Chapter 4), however, have made some poll data available even to low-budget campaigns.

Methods of Persuasion: The Air War

Because of the large size of most state and federal election districts, the main means of persuasion are the broadcast media: television, radio, newspapers, and the Internet. Even older style communications are pursued with the media in mind: a candidate takes the time to address a rally largely in the hope that it will be covered by local television news. Early in the campaign, candidates fight to buy choice broadcast time for the weeks just before the election.

Television Television often consumes most of the campaign's money. In the early and inexpensive days of television, candidates bought large chunks of time for entire speeches that were carried nation- or statewide. Now, however, because of television's increased cost and voters' decreased attention spans, campaign messages are compressed into 30- or 60-second spot ads that can be run frequently. The writing, producing, and placing of these spots (after the pro football game? before the evening news?) has become a central focus of campaigns, as have the fund-raising activities needed to pay for them. What was once a long, stem-winder of a speech by the candidate in a sweaty hall is now a few carefully crafted visual images and a very simple text put together by professionals.[16]

Because of the high cost of network television, candidates and consultants look for alternatives. The cost of advertising on cable TV is often lower than on the networks and may also be more efficient for local campaigns, whose constituencies are too small to warrant buying time in major media markets. Many cable stations have more specialized "niche" audiences than do the major networks, for example, BET (Black Entertainment Television) and radio stations aimed at Spanish-speaking listeners.[17] This permits campaigns to target their messages (called ***narrowcasting***).

In addition, it makes good sense for campaigns to maximize their exposure on the *free media* of television newscasts and newspaper columns. When newscasts provide coverage of a candidate, the information may seem more credible and "objective" than if it is conveyed through the campaign's own spot ads. Some candidates do a masterful job of attracting free media coverage that transmits the images that they want voters to see. John McCain, for example, who began a run for the Republican presidential nomination in 2000 in relative obscurity, gained flattering media coverage by remaining almost constantly available to reporters aboard his "Straight-Talk Express" campaign bus. Unaccustomed to such a refreshing degree of candor, television and print reporters transmitted positive images of McCain's personal history and political stances that probably helped the candidate become the chief alternative to the front-runner, George W. Bush.

To get this free media coverage, campaigns need to provide material that the media want. In particular, the campaign's activities must meet the media's definition of what constitutes "news."[18] If "news" is that which is dramatic, controversial, and immediate, then a candidate is not likely to earn media coverage with yet another rendition of a standard stump speech. Dave Barry offers this illustration: "Let's consider two headlines. FIRST HEADLINE: 'Federal Reserve Board Ponders Reversal of Postponement of Deferral of Policy Reconsideration.' SECOND HEADLINE: 'Federal Reserve Board Caught in Motel with Underage Sheep.' Be honest, now. Which of these two stories would you read?"[19] Candidates who depend on free media need to stage campaign events that make for good television, using the tamer, political equivalent of the underage sheep: dramatic confrontations, visually exciting settings, or meetings with well-known or telegenic people.

The Internet   The newest means of campaign persuasion is the Internet, first used by candidates and consultants in 1996. By now, every major campaign has a Web site, as do many local races. Many Web sites ask visitors to register, which allows the campaign to contact them later using e-mail. Campaigns can also load their spot ads online and distribute them nationally through the Internet, without the cost of buying TV time. Because not all voters have ready access to the Internet, however, online campaigning is more likely to benefit candidates who seek the voters most likely to be "wired": young, highly educated, more affluent people. Its use is also limited by its audience's interests; only about one-fourth of the likely voters among these Internet users have searched online for information about candidates.[20]

The uses of online campaigning are regularly upgraded. In the 2004 Democratic nomination race, the big innovator was former Vermont Governor Howard Dean. His campaign used the Web site Meetup.com to organize meetings in hundreds of local communities during 2003. Dean raised most of his funds—millions of dollars—through his Web site, expanding the pioneering use of the Web for that purpose by John McCain in 2000. President Bush had an even larger investment in on-line campaigning and an e-mail list ten times the size of Dean's.

The Ground War: "Under the Radar"

The broadcast media have long been the Holy Grail of well-funded campaigners because they are an efficient way to reach large numbers of citizens. Their greatest strength, however, the breadth of their reach, is also one of their greatest weaknesses. (The other is their high cost.) If you were running for office, you would want to target different messages to different kinds of people, so that you could speak to each individual about the issue that concerns him or her the most. A prolife activist would probably be most interested in your views on abortion, whereas someone concerned mainly about terrorism might find a TV ad about your position on abortion to be irrelevant or, worse, evidence that you didn't view homeland security as a priority.

The value of broadcast advertising in campaigns has been reduced by other trends as well. The major networks have lost viewers; more and more TVs are tuned to videotapes and videogames. In many election districts, television stations are swamped with political ads during a campaign, and viewers now have the technology—from the "mute" button to more sophisticated programming tools—to screen out candidates' commercials.

Increasingly, then, candidates are turning to more carefully targeted appeals than the broadcast media can offer. These are known collectively as the ***ground war***: nonbroadcast activities such as house-to-house canvassing, computer-targeted mailings, and mass phone calls that go "under the radar" and therefore permit communication with selected groups of people. Especially since 1998, these ground-war techniques, some of them time tested, but constantly updated, have been used to get out the vote, particularly in competitive races.

Direct Mail   By merging mailing lists of people who are of special interest to a campaign, consultants can direct personalized letters to millions of people who might be inclined to respond to a particular campaign appeal. A candidate who wants to appeal to progun voters, for example, could send computer-generated letters to people on mailing lists of the National Rifle Association (NRA), donors to other progun candidates, and subscribers to hunting magazines. Because these messages are designed to be read by sympathetic individuals in the privacy of their homes, direct mail appeals can be highly emotional and even inflammatory, appeals that would not work well in the "cool" medium of television.

As the advantages of targeted communication become clearer, huge amounts of direct mail have been aimed at especially competitive races. Consider the 2002 South Dakota Senate race, for example, the most expensive race in the state's history. The margin of victory was only 524 votes. Some voters reported receiving six to ten pieces of campaign mail *a day*, at times containing harsh personal attacks that would not have withstood the broad exposure that TV provides.[21]

E-Mail   Like direct mail, e-mail can be targeted precisely. Beginning in the 2000 elections, for example, the Republican National Committee developed a computerized version of a phone tree, in which a core group of Republican supporters each created an e-mail distribution list to send campaign information to other supporters, who in turn spread the information more widely and, of course, almost simultaneously. E-mail has the great advantage that it is cheaper than regular mail. Its drawback is that it appeals to a limited audience; its use is widespread among college students and young professionals, but it is not as common among other groups.

Canvassing and Phone Banks   In recent years, organized labor has reminded the parties of a lesson from their past: the effectiveness of personal contact to identify and mobilize support on Election Day. For decades, labor unions have used their large memberships to phone or visit the homes of people who might support union-backed candidates. Recently, that effort has become much more sophisticated. Using phone banks, it is possible for volunteers or computers to dial thousands of phone numbers and convey a campaign appeal.

Like direct mail, these appeals can be carefully targeted to people who have been identified as concerned with a specific issue. In 2002, for example, South Dakotans received up to five phone calls a day from the U.S. Senate campaigns, playing recorded messages from people ranging from President Bush to the candidate's mother. Many South Dakotans opposed to gun control received tape-recorded phone messages from Charlton Heston, then president of the NRA, urging them to support the Republican candidate for Senate. In fact, some phone bank efforts are programmed to play only when an answering machine picks up, giving the impression that the political "star" has called them personally. Canvassers for the Democratic candidate in the South Dakota race carried nine different scripts, each with a particular issue message, so the canvasser could choose the appropriate script for the demographic characteristics of the occupants of each house.

The two major parties emphasize different aspects of the ground war. Door-to-door canvassing often makes better sense for Democrats because their core support tends to be geographically concentrated in cities, where canvassers can reach many prospective Democratic voters in a short time. Where Republican support is more rural, canvassing is not very efficient. So Republican campaigns put greater emphasis on phone banks, as they did in the 2002 and 2004 campaigns. Both parties are stepping up their use of these techniques; although only about one-third of poll respondents in 2000 reported having been called or canvassed by a party, that was the largest percentage reported in decades.[22]

Traditional campaign techniques are certainly not obsolete. Shaking constituents' hands at factory gates is still a common campaign activity, even when the television cameras do not show up. The old ways are very much alive. The new campaign technologies have simply layered on a sophisticated set of tools that demand expert knowledge and a great deal of money.

Negative Campaigning

All these techniques can be used to deliver negative as well as positive messages. It has become a staple of political consulting that, when a candidate is falling behind in the polls, one of the surest ways to recover is to "go negative" and attack the opponent. Negative campaigning is nothing new; politicians since the earliest days of the Republic have been the focus of vicious attacks. Concern about negative campaigns has increased recently, however, because they can be spread much more quickly and widely now; rumors about a candidate's personal life that were once circulated mainly within political circles can now be accessed on the Internet in Honolulu and Fairbanks. The greatly increased role of outside money in competitive campaigns has underscored these problems because outside funders (interest groups and party organizations) are more likely than the candidates themselves to use negative themes in their ads and direct mail.[23]

Does negative campaigning work? The findings are mixed. Some researchers find that negative ads are particularly memorable and that a negative campaign drives down turnout because it increases voter cynicism. Others find no advantage in effectiveness and no evidence of turnout decline.[24] One of the biggest challenges in tracing the impact of negative ads is the difficulty of defining "negative"; what one person considers an attack ad is helpful, "comparative" information to another. However, there are campaigns, such as the 2000 presidential primary in South Carolina in which a smear campaign of leaflets, e-mails, and phone calls referred to John McCain's "black child," a girl whom the McCains had adopted from Bangladesh, that few people would have trouble characterizing as negative.

The 2002 and 2004 Campaigns

These forms of campaigning were very visible in the 2002 elections, but especially in a small group of competitive races. In past elections, parties had spread their efforts widely, providing money and other resources even to secure incumbents. Because the two parties were so evenly matched in the U.S. House and Senate in 2002 and because redistricting and other forces had done such a good job of protecting the great majority of House incumbents, the parties and many interest groups ignored most congressional races and focused their resources on fewer than 50 competitive seats.

As a result, the residents of these districts were exposed to a virtual hurricane of campaign advertising. In addition to a huge volume of broadcast ads, an unprecedented amount of effort went into the ground war. In 1998 and 2000, Democrats had mounted major get-out-the-vote drives, especially among blacks, that had helped reelect several U.S. House members and governors. So the national Republican Party started early in the 2002 election cycle to try to neutralize the anticipated canvassing and get-out-the-vote drives by organized labor and the Democrats.

After a series of experiments to find out how best to reach voters, the GOP developed programs to flood precincts in competitive states with Republican volunteers and paid staffers. These campaigners would use door-to-door canvassing and phone calls to reach known Republican supporters and urge them to go to the polls. One, the "72-Hour Project," focused its efforts on the closing 72 hours of the campaign. National Republican officials felt that this personal contact increased Republican turnout by about 3 percent.[25] Other observers also judged these efforts to be effective; voter turnout was up by 2 percent compared with 1998, and Republicans won most of the close contests for the Senate and House.[26]

In the end, Republicans maintained control of the House in 2002 and narrowly regained control of the Senate. The Republican gains were widely touted because this was only the third time since the Civil War that the president's party had gained House seats in a midterm election. In actuality, the results were not so dramatic; the president's party had gained seats in the 1998 midterm as well, and in 2002, a net of only eight seats switched from Democratic to Republican control. Yet, the traditional expectation that the president's party would lose seats contributed to the sense that the Republicans had won a major victory.

There were several reasons for the GOP gains in Congress. One of the main reasons was the role played by President Bush. Before the race, Bush spent a lot of time raising money for Republican House and Senate candidates and, along with other party notables, persuading attractive candidates to run. Once the campaign began, Bush himself was an effective campaigner. Although he began his presidency with relatively low poll ratings, his approval ratings skyrocketed in the wake of the terrorist attacks of September 11, 2001, and remained high in 2002. When Bush campaigned for candidates in 15 states during the five days before the election, an almost unprecedented choice by a president to put his reputation on the line in a midterm election, his popularity probably helped the Senate and House candidates whose districts he visited.

On the Republican side, the campaign was a textbook example of a successful effort to set the campaign agenda. Polls showed that voters were most concerned about the economy, but the Bush administration's continuing stress on the dangers of terrorism and the need for military action against Iraq made it difficult for the Democrats to draw public attention to the weak economy and other Democratic issues. In addition, the House redistricting that moved several seats to Sunbelt states, where Republicans tend to do especially well, benefited the GOP. In all, eight of the twelve new districts created by reapportionment went to Republicans.

As so often happens in campaigns, party officials and consultants drew the lesson from Republican successes in 2002 that they needed to follow the Republican model in 2004. Activists in both parties emphasized the need for well-planned, large-scale get-out-the-vote drives. A full year before the 2004 election, the Bush campaign had put together plans for a massive ground-war campaign and was already training thousands of volunteers to recruit canvassers for the last few days before the election. Because the president had no opponent for the Republican nomination, the full force of his enormous campaign budget ($130.8 million as of January 2004) could be focused on the general election.

Democratic leaders were looking at a bleaker landscape. None of the contenders for the Democratic presidential nomination seemed likely to beat President Bush and there were more Democratic Senate incumbents up for reelection than Republicans, including several in states that Bush had won in 2000. Nevertheless, the Democratic campaigns and organized labor were hoping that an astute combination of television and the ground war could hold their losses to a minimum.

DO CAMPAIGNS MAKE A DIFFERENCE?

With so much money, energy, and professional advice invested in campaigns, it is easy to assume that they have a great impact on voters' choices. If they didn't, why would candidates bother? Yet, some researchers find that election results can usually be predicted pretty well from conditions that existed before the campaign began, such as the distribution of party loyalties in the district, economic conditions, and the incumbent's poll ratings. That doesn't leave much room for the events of a campaign to help to determine the outcome. Instead, it seems to suggest that, at most, campaigns simply remind voters of these longer lasting conditions and, in this way, help them move toward a largely preordained outcome.[27]

How can we determine how much influence campaigns have? Did George W. Bush win the presidency in 2000 because of preexisting factors such as voters' disgust with President Clinton's ethics or because of the tax cut that Bush proposed during the campaign or the strategic decisions that his staff made about advertising and voter contact? Observers' answers often depend on the observer's own agenda (see box on page 207). Researchers have used a variety of methods to measure campaign impact, and, not surprisingly, they have come up with a variety of conclusions.

The Argument That Campaigns Matter

A long line of evidence suggests that one form of campaigning, party canvassing, has a small but meaningful effect on both turnout and voters' choices,[28] as the parties acknowledged in 2002. Canvassing probably has more influence in local elections than in presidential races because there are fewer alternative sources of information in local contests. Researchers find that personal contacts activate voters more than mailings do, and door-to-door canvassing has more influence than telephone calls.[29] In particular, meeting a candidate face to face affects voters' knowledge about and attitudes toward candidates.[30] With regard to the voters' other decision—their choice of candidates—we find that where a party is active, its vote share can increase by at least a few percentage points, which could be the critical margin in a close race.[31]

Television news and advertising—and the money that pays for it—may have an even greater influence on voters' decisions. Since the early 1960s, television has been citizens' most important and most trusted source of political news.[32] The nature of TV has changed over time; a poll in 2000, for instance, found that almost one-half of 18 to 29 year olds said that they got information about the presidential campaign from late-night talk shows and more than one-fourth from comedy shows such as *Saturday Night Live.*[33] Despite

WHY DID GEORGE W. BUSH WIN?

Many conservative Republicans argued: Bush won because he was so clearly associated with conservative principles, such as personal morality and individual responsibility.

To many moderate Republicans: Bush won because he ran as a *compassionate* conservative, stressing issues such as education and health care, rather than as a right winger.

To moderate Democrats: Bush won because Al Gore moved too far to the left, emphasizing a populist appeal, rather than the more centrist message of budget discipline and responsibility.

To liberal Democrats: Gore led in the polls only when he linked himself to traditional liberal Democratic programs, such as Social Security and Medicare and to "the people, not the powerful." When he abandoned these themes, voters could not distinguish him from Bush.

Or . . . In fact, it was Gore who won the popular vote. It was the electoral college and a Supreme Court decision stopping further hand recounts in Florida that decided the election for Bush.

Sources: Charles Babington, "Democrats Split on What Went Wrong," *Washington Post,* Jan. 25, 2001, p. A6; Carter Eskew, "The Lessons of 2000," *Washington Post,* Jan. 30, 2001, p. A17; and David S. Broder, "Party's Fault Lines Likely to Surface," *Washington Post,* Jan. 21, 2001, p. A22.

(or perhaps because of) these changes, TV has supplanted the parties in providing campaign information. Although only 36 percent of a national sample reported being contacted by either party during the 2000 campaigns, 82 percent of the respondents paid at least some attention to television news about the campaign.[34]

This widespread exposure to TV news and ads can make a difference, especially when they give viewers new information about a candidate.[35] Campaign debates, to which most voters are exposed only through television, have been found to affect election results under some circumstances.[36] All these sources of campaign information, taken together, seem to improve citizens' knowledge and increase voter turnout. In 2000, for instance, residents of so-called battleground (highly competitive) states were more likely to be contacted by a campaign and to hear about it in the media and were also more likely to vote, to report having thought about and followed the campaign in the news, and to know candidates' issue positions.[37] Different kinds of campaign events—debates, conventions, TV ads—affect some voters differently from others, depending on the voter's party identification, level of interest in politics, and feelings about the current president. Independents, undecided voters, and people who are leaning toward a candidate of the opposite party are most likely to be affected by these campaign events.[38]

The Argument That They Don't

Even so, there are several reasons why even televised campaigning may have only a limited effect. First, television news, ads, and "ground war" activities offer viewers a wide range of conflicting messages about candidates—positive, negative, and neutral information and opinions, all mixed together. The inconsistency of these messages makes it harder for a campaign to change viewers' minds about candidates.[39] We know that voters pay selective attention to media and other campaign communications, just as they do to most other experiences. People usually see events through a filter of stable, long-lasting orientations, the most stable of which is party identification. They surround themselves with friends, information, and even personal experiences (such as rallies and meetings) that support their beliefs and loyalties.[40]

So even though most voters are exposed to campaigns on TV, they may pick and choose among the mix of differing messages and ignore those that conflict with their existing beliefs and opinions. Most campaign communications, then, probably have the effect of activating and reinforcing the voter's existing political inclinations, as they always have. That can explain why so much campaign effort is directed at getting people out to vote—to act on whatever opinions they already hold—rather than at trying to change their voting decision.[41]

However, news coverage of campaigns can have a more subtle influence. By the kinds of issues and events that they emphasize, the media affect what people come to consider important in a campaign; this process is known as *agenda setting.* In directing viewers' attention in this way, media coverage "primes" viewers to look for some qualities in candidates rather than others.[42] In addition, the way in which media coverage characterizes a candidate can affect voters' perceptions of him or her. Because of time constraints, coverage must inevitably simplify its presentation of a candidate. So rather than reflect a nuanced portrayal of each candidate, coverage usually pays attention to a limited number of themes or "frames," which then come to drive later coverage.[43] News coverage of the 2000 presidential race, for example, focused intently on Al Gore's boasts and exaggerations rather than on those of George Bush and on Bush's slips of the tongue rather than those of Gore.[44] This kind of media influence is indirect and thus hard to measure, but its effects on election results could be profound.

Some Tentative Answers

There is much left to learn about the effects of campaigns on voters. It seems clear that canvassing and media coverage have some impact on voter turnout and voters' decisions. As a rule, campaign communications are most effective in bringing weak partisans back into the fold when they have had doubts about their party's candidate.[45] Now, in the information-rich environment of current campaigns and among the large numbers of independents, the potential for campaigns to shape voters' perceptions may be higher than it has ever been. There are times when dramatic events during a campaign may actually decide the outcome (see "A Day in the Life"). The impact of campaigns, however, will continue to be limited by the same forces that have always constrained it: voters' tendency to pay attention to the messages with which they already agree, and their ability to tune out most political messages altogether.

CANDIDATE-CENTERED OR PARTY-CENTERED CAMPAIGNS?

The new campaign techniques that we have explored in this chapter have affected the balance of power in campaigns. Until about the middle of the 1900s, party organizations provided much of the money and volunteers for campaigns, just as they do now

A DAY IN THE LIFE

HOW DO YOU RUN AGAINST A DEAD MAN?

The campaign was a "clash of the titans," according to University of Missouri political scientist Rick Hardy. Republican U.S. Senator John Ashcroft had previously served as Missouri's governor and attorney general; he had never lost a race. In 2000, he was running for reelection against the state's current governor, Democrat Mel Carnahan. Like Ashcroft, Carnahan "had politics in his blood." He had been Missouri's treasurer and lieutenant governor and came from an old political family. The race was close—and bitter—but by mid-October, Ashcroft was beginning to pull ahead in the polls.

Everything changed on October 16. Carnahan's campaign plane crashed. The governor, his son, and his top aide were killed. As the shock receded, Missourians faced a novel challenge. It was too late in the campaign for the state Democratic Party to nominate another candidate, so Carnahan's name would stay on the ballot. If Carnahan got a majority of votes, the Democratic lieutenant governor announced, he would appoint Carnahan's widow, Jean, to fill the seat. In a poignant announcement from her home, Mrs. Carnahan said that she would accept.

Imagine that you are John Ashcroft. You have three weeks left to campaign before Election Day. Democrats are urging voters to "keep the fire lit" by voting for Carnahan so that his widow can take his place. Continued Republican control of the Senate could hinge on the outcome of this race. How will you respond? A negative campaign is out of the question; it's not good form to attack a dead man. But how can you run any kind of campaign when media coverage of the race is concentrating entirely on the tragedy of Carnahan's death?

"John Ashcroft was in a political straightjacket," said Hardy. "He had to put his campaign in abeyance. If he had continued campaigning, he would have come off as the 'heavy'; it would have been tacky. So he laid low. But politics abhors a vacuum." The media zoomed in on Jean Carnahan's losses and her unique campaign. Soon, her dead husband was moving ahead in the polls. "Ashcroft wasn't running against Mel Carnahan anymore," Hardy noted. "He was running against a martyr, against Mrs. Carnahan, and against the media. Mel Carnahan became more popular in death than he had been in life."

Ashcroft's frustrated supporters finally took some steps. A respected former senator, Republican John Danforth, reminded Missourians to look at Ashcroft's record and accomplishments. That hardly made a dent. Then, a week before the election, Hardy says, "Ashcroft took a statewide bus tour with other Republican 'heavyweights' to speak about his record. He was surrounded by hordes of media people—but all they were asking (and reporting) was whether he had called Mrs. Carnahan yet. He couldn't control the agenda. And when a politician can't control the agenda. . . ."

Ashcroft narrowly lost the election. If you had been in his shoes, would you have run those last three weeks of your campaign differently?

in most other democracies. Since then, American campaigning has become more **candidate centered,** focusing on the actions and strategies of the candidates rather than on the parties.

It is the candidates and their advisers, not the parties, who make the strategic decisions in most campaigns. Candidates have their own headquarters and staffers rather than using the party's facilities. Candidates communicate directly with voters rather than having to rely on the party organization as an intermediary, and, as a result, voters see candidates differently, and often as more moderate on issues, than they see the candidate's party.[46] Interest groups and other political organizations can work directly with candidates to support their campaigns. Campaign finance laws (see Chapter 12) have put limits on party spending comparable with the limits on nonparty groups. Party organizations, rather than running campaigns, work instead to enhance the appeal of individual candidates, and they compete with consultants, interest groups, and others for the chance to do so.

Many of the nation's electoral rules make it easier for campaigns to be candidate centered. The American electoral process has few institutions, such as parliamentary-cabinet government or proportional representation, that would encourage voters to see elections as contests between parties for control of government. Instead, rules ranging from the office-bloc ballot to the separate scheduling of national and state elections encourage candidates to run as individuals, not as members of a party ticket, and even make it hard for parties to coordinate the campaigns of several candidates. Progressive reforms strengthened this tendency; the direct primary, for example, allows candidates to run without the party organization's approval.[47]

Campaign technologies can also help candidates to resist party influence. Broadcast media, in their quest to get and keep an audience, tend to focus on individual personalities rather than institutions such as parties. Because tools such as direct mail and TV advertising are available to any candidate who can pay for them, these technologies let candidates communicate with voters without the party's help. If the American parties had been as strong organizationally as those in many other nations when these technologies developed, then they might have been able to monopolize the use of TV and other media for campaign purposes. In fact, as we have seen, the American parties have always struggled to maintain their power in a political culture hostile to their functioning.

Party Influence in Competitive Campaigns

The parties, however, are fighting back. The large sums of money that have flowed into the national parties in the past two decades have helped them to assist individual campaigns with money and other services.[48] As Chapter 4 noted, soft money enabled the party organizations to pour millions of dollars into campaign ads in a few battleground states in 2002, such as the Senate races in Iowa, Missouri, and South Dakota. The two parties in the close 2000 Montana Senate race ran more ads than their candidates did.[49] Republican parties, in particular, have worked to recruit experienced candidates and to increase their voter turnout and vote shares.[50]

As a result, the national parties have become more visible to candidates at all levels, especially in highly competitive races. Although party-funded ads generally follow the lead of the candidate's own advertising, sometimes they do not. Consider the comment of then-National Republican Congressional Committee Chair Tom Davis about party-run ads in the House campaign of Republican Melissa Hart in Pennsylvania: Hart "doesn't have any say about what we do in the race. . . . We have to protect our candidate whether she likes it or not."[51] Clearly, in these few highly competitive races, the parties have a shot at taking control of the campaign away from the candidate.

Yet the nature of this expanded party role, relying on money and sophisticated technology, is not likely to result in a more effective grassroots party organization. The parties' greater efforts take place within a much different political environment from the mid-1900s: an environment of stronger and more independent incumbents who have the freedom to accept or reject their party's help.

The Continuing Struggle Between Candidates and Parties

An expanded party role in campaigns can make economic sense. Party organizations can distribute literature for a number of candidates at the same time and mount voter registration drives to help the entire ticket. Parties can buy media advertising and consultants' services for use by several candidates at cost-effective prices. Party organizations can coordinate Election Day activities for all the party's candidates: providing poll watchers to oversee the voting, offering cars to get people to the polls, and checking voter lists to alert nonvoters late in the day.

This efficiency, however, would be bought at the cost of limiting each candidate's independence. In the competitive races that were the target of party soft-money spending in 2002, party-funded ads and those funded by interest groups often stressed messages different from those that the campaign itself wanted to emphasize, and, frequently, more negative messages than the campaign's own advertising.[52] Because voters rarely pay attention to the source of any particular message, candidates got blamed for negativity and claims that they had not made.

Party organizations and candidates do not always have the same goals. Although the party organization would like to stimulate party loyalty in voters, not all candidates find this helpful to their own chances of winning, especially when they are running in districts dominated by the other party. The first commitment of any candidate is to win his or her own race, no matter how dismal its chances are. The party, in contrast, takes a broader view. It wants to spend as few of its scarce resources as possible on the races that it considers hopeless.

The result is a continuing struggle between party organizations and candidates—the party in government—for control of campaigns. If they are going to have a role in campaigns now, party organizations have to earn it. In most elections, the candidates are winning the fight. Even if the parties have more to offer candidates than they did just a few years ago, party organizations still contribute only a fairly small percentage of candidates' overall campaign spending in all but the most competitive races. In contrast, European parties often provide more than half the funding used by most candidates.

This central role of the candidates and their staff members and consultants in most American campaigns has an important effect on governing. When they control their own campaigns, winning candidates can develop ties with their constituents that are free of party loyalty and party organizational control. By running their own campaigns, candidates are free to form alliances with political action committees, single-issue groups, and other nonparty organizations, which enhance the ability of these groups to influence public policy. In short, candidate-centered campaigning underscores the power of the party in government relative to that of the party organization. It also poses an important question: If strong party organizations can help to hold elected officials accountable for their actions, then how much accountability do voters get from a candidate-centered politics?

CHAPTER 12

Financing the Campaigns

Candidate George Washington was known to be a big spender. When Washington ran for the Virginia House of Burgesses in 1757:

> he provided his friends with the "customary means of winning votes": namely 28 gallons of rum, 50 gallons of rum punch, 34 gallons of wine, 46 gallons of beer, and 2 gallons of cider royal. Even in those days this was considered a large campaign expenditure, because there were only 391 voters in his district for an average outlay of more than a quart and a half per person.[1]

Washington was, by all accounts, a very well qualified candidate, yet he still felt that he needed to spend freely in order to win. Two and a half centuries later, fund-raising is a much bigger job; television advertising, after all, costs much more than 50 gallons of rum punch and takes more specialized training to prepare. Money has never been more important in American elections than it is today. As candidates have come to depend on paid professionals and television, money has become key to mobilizing the resources needed for a viable campaign. So candidates, especially for statewide and national office, are not likely to be taken seriously unless they start with a big campaign budget or a proven talent for raising funds.

Until the campaign finance reforms of the 1970s, much of the money used in campaigns was collected and spent in secret. Candidates were not required to disclose how they raised funds, and contributors were often reluctant to make their names public. The few laws governing campaign contributions were full of loopholes and were regularly ignored. Large amounts of money could be raised and spent for many state and local contests without any public accounting at all.

As a result of the 1970s reforms, we now have a flood of data about campaign spending and contributions. The regulation is mind-boggling in its complexity. It is constantly under assault by candidates and contributors who are adept at finding loopholes through which they can pursue their aims. Despite all this change, the basic questions remain the same. How much money is spent to elect candidates to office and who spends it? Who contributes the money? What is the party's role in funding campaigns? How effective were the campaign finance reforms in limiting the power of money in politics and what are the challenges we still face?

HOW BIG HAS THE MONEY BECOME?

Total campaign spending at all levels, including both nominations and general elections, would seem to have exploded since 1960. Candidates at all levels of office spent a total of about $3.9 *billion* in 2000,[2] a twenty-twofold increase during these 40 years. When we adjust for inflation, which has reduced the purchasing power of the dollar during this time, the increase is not nearly as impressive. But the fourfold increase in *real* (inflation-adjusted) spending since 1960 is not trivial, and the ingenuity of campaigners, parties, and interest groups in finding new sources of campaign money may fuel an even bigger jump in the coming elections.

Presidential Campaigns

The most expensive political campaigns in the United States are those for the presidency (Table 12.1). In fact, total spending in the 2000 presidential race may be underestimated

TABLE 12.1 Total Spending by Candidates, Parties, and Groups in Presidential Elections: 1960–2000

	Expenditures (in Millions)		Percentage of Change Since Previous Election	
Year	Actual	Inflation adjusted	Actual	Inflation adjusted
1960	$30.0	$30.0	—	—
1964	60.0	57.3	+100.0%	+91.0%
1968	100.0	85.2	+66.7	+48.7
1972	138.0	97.8	+38.0	+14.8
1976	160.0	83.3	+15.9	− 14.8
1980	275.0	99.1	+71.9	+19.0
1984	325.0	92.6	+18.2	− 6.6
1988	500.0	125.4	+53.8	+35.4
1992	550.0	116.3	+10.0	− 7.3
1996	700.0	132.4	+27.3	+13.8
2000	1,050.0*	180.9*	+50.0*	+36.6*

*Includes FEC data on candidates' spending ($607 million) and estimates of interest group ($364 million) and party spending ($79 million). The latter are conservative estimates because money spent by interest groups and parties on issue ads, which became a much larger portion of total spending in 2000, is not reported to the FEC.

Note: Estimates are for two-year cycles ending in the presidential election years. Inflation-adjusted figures are computed by deflating the actual expenditures using the Consumer Price Index (with 1960 as the base year).

Sources: John C. Green, ed., *Financing the 1996 Election* (Armonk, NY: M.E. Sharpe, 1999), p. 19; Candice J. Nelson, "Spending in the 2000 Elections," in David B. Magleby, ed., *Financing the 2000 Election* (Washington, DC: Brookings, 2002), Table 2-1 (for candidates' spending); David B. Magleby, "Conclusions and Implications for Future Elections," in David B. Magleby, ed., *The Other Campaign* (Lanham, MD: Rowman & Littlefield, 2003), p. 229 (for interest groups); and Anthony Corrado, Sarah Barclay, and Heitor Gouvea, "The Parties Take the Lead," in John C. Green and Rick Farmer, *The State of the Parties,* 4th ed. (Lanham, MD: Rowman & Littlefield, 2003), p. 107 (for parties). Consumer Price Index deflator is based on Table 680 in the U.S. Bureau of the Census, *Statistical Abstract of the United States: 2002* (Washington, DC: U.S. Government Printing Office, 2002), p. 449.

CAMPAIGN SPENDING: TOO MUCH OR TOO LITTLE?

What will $3.9 billion buy in the United States?

■ About one-third of the cigarette advertising and promotion run in 2001

■ Less than a year's advertising (in 2002) for General Motors plus Proctor & Gamble

■ 5 percent of the amount spent in 2001 on all forms of gambling

■ One-third more than Americans paid for running and jogging shoes in 2002

■ All the political campaigns run at all levels of government by and for all candidates in 2000

Sources: http://www.smokefree.net/bg-announce/messages/246903.html (on cigarette advertising);http://www.tnsmi-cmr.com/news/2003/031003.html (on GM and Proctor & Gamble); http://grossannualwager.com (on gambling); http://www.sgma.com/press/2003/press1058880583-27268.html (on athletic shoes) (all accessed Sept. 15, 2003).

in this table. A great deal of party and interest group money was spent in 2000 on "issue advocacy" ads (to be discussed later in this chapter), whose funding does not have to be reported to any federal agency. So although we know that the candidates themselves spent $607 million in that election, the total figure also includes only a conservative estimate of party and interest group money.

The cost of presidential campaigns varies depending on the number of candidates running for each party's nomination and their willingness to refuse federal funding (and its accompanying spending limits) and raise all their campaign money themselves. George W. Bush, Howard Dean, and John Kerry did just that in the 2004 nomination race. Bush had pulled in more than $130 million in contributions even before the first primary or caucus was held, making his the richest campaign in American history.

Congressional Campaigns

Individual House and Senate races are run on much smaller budgets, although their collective cost has surpassed that of the presidential race in recent years. The total spending is higher in House contests simply because there are many more House races in a given year than there are Senate races. A look at inflation-adjusted figures shows that real spending in congressional races has gone down almost as often as it has risen during the past 30 years (Figures 12.1 and 12.2). Even after adjusting for inflation, however, campaign spending in 2002 was almost triple that in 1972, and the numbers would be higher yet in recent elections if all party and interest group spending on these races were reported. Campaign costs at the state and local levels have grown substantially as well.

These figures must be kept in perspective. Even with these large increases, the total cost of campaigns still doesn't match the amounts some large corporations spend each year to advertise soap and cigarettes (see box above). Although few would dispute the

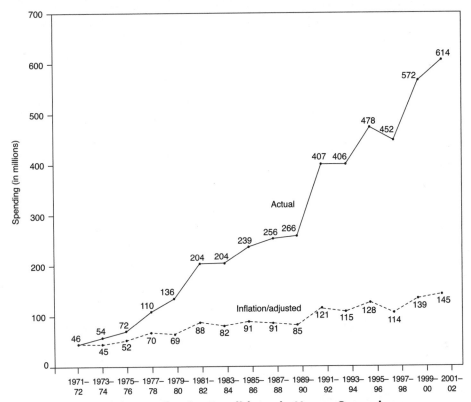

FIGURE 12.1   Total Spending by Candidates in House Campaigns, 1971–1972 to 2001–2002.

Note: Inflation-adjusted figures are computed by deflating the actual expenditures by changes in the price level as measured by the Consumer Price Index (yearly averages) using 1972 as the base year.

Source: John C. Green, ed., *Financing the 1996 Election* (Armonk, NY: M.E. Sharpe, 1999), Table 2.7, p. 23 for actual spending through 1995–1996; for 1997–2002, FEC news release June 18, 2003, on the Web at http://www.fec.gov/press/20030618canstat/20030618canstat.html (accessed Sept. 15, 2003). CPI deflator is the same as that listed for Table 12.1.

benefits of soap, our futures are affected more profoundly by the choices made in state and federal elections. So, to the extent that campaigns give us the chance to learn about the strengths and weaknesses of the people who would govern us, the amounts spent on campaign advertising could be considered a real bargain.[3]

WHO SPENDS THE CAMPAIGN MONEY?

In most other democracies, the parties do most of the campaign spending. In contrast, most campaign money in American elections is spent by the candidates' own organizations and by a variety of interest groups and individuals who flood the media with advertising. But parties play a growing part in campaign funding as well.

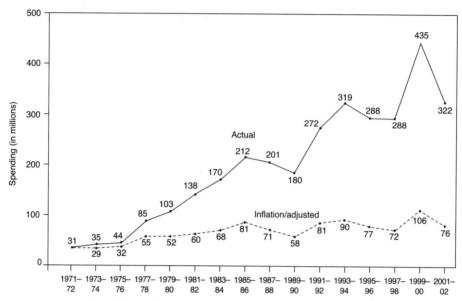

FIGURE 12.2   Total Spending by Candidates in Senate Campaigns, 1971–1972 to 2001–2002.

Note: Inflation-adjusted figures are computed as in Figure 12.1.

Source: Same as Figure 12.1.

Presidential Campaigns

Imagine that you are thinking about running for president. How much money would you need to raise? In 2000, it took hundreds of millions of dollars just to get started. Candidates spent a total of $326 million to run for their parties' nominations, including $224.7 million spent by Republican candidates and $88 million by Democrats prior to the parties' nominating conventions (see Table 12.2). Because Bush chose to forgo the federal money allowed for primary campaigns under campaign finance laws and, therefore, to avoid their spending limits, his campaign was able to spend $89 million of that total. Steve Forbes, a wealthy businessman, spent almost $48 million through the early Republican primaries (all but $10 million of that from his own pocket) in challenging Bush for the nomination. Al Gore, who ran for the Democratic nomination against former Senator Bill Bradley, accounted for just $42.5 million of the total nomination spending.

The price goes up in the general election (see part III in Table 12.2), but the candidates themselves get their campaign money mainly from federal tax dollars. Since 1976, every major party candidate has accepted public funds to run his or her general election campaign. (The story of these reforms is told later in this chapter.) To get the public money, candidates must agree to raise no other funds (except the money needed to pay lawyers and accountants to deal with federal campaign finance laws, called "compliance costs"). Thus, in 2000, the Bush and Gore general election campaigns were able to spend $67.6 million each, plus the compliance costs.

The money spent by candidates, however, is only a small part of the general election campaign's total cost. Most campaign communications are funded by groups and

TABLE 12.2 What It Cost to Nominate and Elect a President: 2000

	Amount (in Millions)	
I. Prenomination Receipts and Spending	Raised	Spent
All Republican candidates	$232.7	$224.7
Bush	94.5	89.1
Forbes	48.1	47.8
McCain	45.0	44.6
All Democratic candidates	95.9	88.0
Gore	49.2	42.5
Bradley	42.1	41.1
Third-party candidates	14.4	13.3
Independent expenditures by political action committees		1.2
Internal communication costs		3.3
Issue advocacy ads by interest groups, individuals, and parties		*
II. Conventions		
Public funding for party conventions		29.5
Private funding		*
III. General Election		
Public funding for major party candidates		$135.2
Public funding for Reform Party candidate		12.6
Compliance costs		18.6
Private funding for minor party candidates (mainly Nader)		5.7
Parties' coordinated expenditures		27.1
Parties' soft money, issue advertising (June 1 to Election Day)		at least 79*
Issue advocacy ads by interest groups and individuals (includes some primary spending)		at least 364*
Independent expenditures		14.7
Internal communication costs		10.2
Recount funds		11.2*

*Unreported or incompletely reported.

Source: Calculated from John C. Green and Nathan S. Bigelow, "The 2000 Presidential Nominations: The Cost of Innovation," in David B. Magleby, ed., *Financing the 2000 Election* (Washington, DC: Brookings, 2002), p. 55; and Corrado, Barclay, and Gouvea, "The Parties Take the Lead," in Green and Farmer, eds., *The State of the Parties,* p. 107.

individuals other than the campaigners themselves. The implications are important. The candidates' campaigns are (largely) under their own control; spending by other groups in the election is not and, thus, may emphasize appeals that the candidate would prefer to avoid. Even the "friendly fire" laid down by the parties' committees and supportive interest groups can pose a real problem for candidates, simply by diverting voters' attention from the campaign's own agenda.

Who are the other big spenders? The party organizations spend a great deal in the general election on advertising, consultants, and other services to support their party's candidate. In addition, party organizations, individuals, and political action committees (PACs) can spend as much as they choose to support or oppose a candidate; under the law, this spending must be done without the knowledge or cooperation of any candidate. These *independent expenditures* vary greatly from election to election.

"Internal communication costs" in Table 12.2 are the funds spent by groups to urge their members to vote for a particular candidate; labor unions account for most of this money. Unions, corporations, and membership associations also spent millions on "nonpartisan" voter mobilization—mainly in programs to register voters and get them to the polls on Election Day. Again, labor unions were the big spenders here.[4]

Congressional Campaigns

Candidates for Congress in 2000 spent a total of a little over $1 billion in the primaries and general elections, a major increase over the two previous congressional races. Total spending dropped a little in 2002 to $936 million because fewer of the large states had Senate seats up for election. The candidates themselves are the biggest spenders in most congressional contests, so we focus primarily on them.

One of the cardinal rules of modern campaign finance is that incumbents vastly outspend their challengers in campaigns for Congress. In the 2002 elections, incumbents spent $2.30 for every dollar spent by challengers. But the partisan direction of this advantage has changed. Until 1994, most congressional incumbents in most election years were Democrats, so Democratic candidates were normally able to outspend Republicans. However, in 1994, the Republican Party won majorities in both the House and Senate for the first time since 1954. Their status as the majority party gave the Republicans an increasing financial advantage going into the next two congressional elections. In 2000 and 2002, when the two parties' prospects looked more equal, the Republican edge decreased or disappeared.

Looking beneath these totals, we find a great deal of variation. The biggest spender in the 2000 Senate races was New Jersey Democrat Jon Corzine, a former investment banker and multimillionaire who won an open seat after spending $63 million, $34 million of it in the primary (at a reported $141 per vote). All the candidates in the unusual New York Senate race between former First Lady Hillary Rodham Clinton and Representative Rick Lazio spent a total of $92 million, of which Clinton and Lazio's campaigns together accounted for more than $70 million. There were fewer big-spending Senate races in 2002; even so, the average Senate candidate spent $3.6 million in the 2002 general election, the same as in 1998[5]—about what it would cost to buy fifty-one new BMW coupes.

The average 2002 House general election campaign, by contrast, cost "only" about $666,000, way up from about $493,000 in the last midterm election in 1998. A growing number of House candidates are running million-dollar campaigns, and in 2000, the House race between incumbent James Rogan and Democrat Adam Schiff, which cost $18.5 million, of which the candidates raised and spent $11.5 million, set the all-time record.

The candidates are not the only important spenders in congressional campaigns. In addition to the money that they gave directly to candidates, the two parties spent $20.4 million on behalf of their candidates in 2001–2002; Republican committees outspent the Democrats. Corporations, labor unions, and other groups also invest money directly in trying to mobilize their members on behalf of certain candidates.[6]

State and Local Campaigns

Much less is known about spending practices in the thousands of campaigns for state and local office, mainly because there is no central reporting agency comparable with the national Federal Election Commission (FEC). The range in these races is enormous. Many local candidates win after spending a few hundred dollars. On the other hand, in 2001, Michael Bloomberg spent $69 million of his own money to become mayor of New York, about $68.7 million more than the job's annual salary.[7]

Campaigns for governor in large states often cost as much as, or more than, races for the U.S. Senate; California typically sets the records. The major candidates in the bizarre 2003 election to recall California Governor Gray Davis managed to spend a total of $83 million in only 77 days. Winning a state legislative race in a large state can require more than $100,000. Again, the most expensive contests are usually found in California; by 1998, it cost an average of $500,000 to win a seat in the lower house of the California legislature.[8] Even state supreme court elections are becoming big-spending contests; the average candidate for a state supreme court seat in 2000 raised almost half a million dollars, much of it from trial lawyers who have a big stake in the judges' rulings.[9]

WHAT IS THE IMPACT OF CAMPAIGN SPENDING?

Money does not buy victory—but it certainly doesn't hurt either. In the general election for president, both sides have enough money to reach voters with their messages, so the candidate with the largest war chest does not gain an overwhelming advantage. Money matters more in the nomination race for president, especially in buying the early visibility that is so vital to an underdog. Nevertheless, a big budget did not make Steve Forbes a front-runner, and candidates who qualify for federal matching funds have at least a shot at competing effectively.

In fact, in some unusual races, candidates have won major offices with relatively little spending. Recall the case of Jesse Ventura, a former professional wrestler, who ran as the Reform Party candidate for governor of Minnesota in 1998. Ventura won the three-way race after spending only $400,000 on his campaign, while his Democratic and Republican rivals spent more than $4 million between them. Among other factors, Ventura's forceful personality and the novelty of his campaign brought free media attention that helped to make up for a small campaign budget.

In congressional elections, however, where we have the most evidence of the impact of campaign spending, most researchers find that money does make a real difference. The more that challengers can spend when they run against incumbents, the better their chances are of victory. The same is not always true for incumbents. Gary Jacobson found that the more incumbents spend, the worse they do in the race.[10] It is not that incumbent spending turns voters off but rather that incumbents tend to spend a lot when they face serious competition. A big budget for an incumbent, then, signals that he or she has (or expects) an unusually strong challenger.

Other researchers disagree and report that when incumbents spend more, they do get a return in terms of votes. The dispute turns on thorny questions about the proper way to estimate the impact of spending, but there is general agreement on three points. First, House incumbents rarely face a serious challenge for reelection. Second, challengers need a lot of money to have a chance of beating an incumbent. Third, when they do have a strong opponent, incumbents may not be able to survive the challenge by pouring more money into their reelection effort.[11] For political scientists, measuring the effects of particular types of campaign spending is a challenging task. For candidates, the answer is simpler: more is better.

WHERE DOES THE MONEY COME FROM?

Candidates raise their campaign funds from five main sources: individual contributors, PACs, political parties, the candidates' own resources, and public (tax) funds. There are no other sources from which candidates can raise large amounts of money. Campaign finance reform, then, cannot do much more than mandate a different mix among these five or try to eliminate one or more of these sources altogether.

Individual Contributors

It is one of the best kept secrets in American politics that individuals, not parties or PACs, dominate campaign finance—at least in the form of contributions to candidates (see Table 12.3). Although public funding has reduced the role of the individual donor in presidential general elections, individuals still fund most of the nomination races, both by their contributions and through the federal matching funds that they generate. Individuals also donate the largest portion of congressional campaign funds. In the 2002 races, individuals accounted for 50 percent of the contributions to House candidates and 66 percent of the money given to Senate candidates. Data on state elections are harder to obtain, but individual givers probably provide the majority of funds here as well.[12]

The nature of the individual contributor has changed, however. Before the 1970s campaign finance reforms, congressional and presidential candidates were allowed to take large sums of money from individuals. For example, insurance magnate W. Clement Stone and multimillionaire Richard Mellon Scaife donated a total of $3 million to President Nixon's reelection campaign in 1972. Well-supported fears that these "fat cats" were getting something in return for their money—preferential treatment ranging from tax breaks to ambassadorships—led Congress to pass the *Federal Election Campaign Act (FECA)* of 1974, which limited an individual's donation to any federal candidate to $1,000.

For the next two decades, these limits seemed to work. Because of the reforms, congressional campaigns were financed not by a handful of big givers, but by large numbers of people making small donations. That was also true of the nomination phase of presidential campaigns. These small contributors are not very representative of the American electorate; they tend to be older, more involved in politics, more conservative, and wealthier than the average American.[13] But they resemble the typical American voter much more closely than the Stones and the Scaifes did.

The $1,000 limit meant that campaigns had to learn new ways to separate prospective donors from their money. When the "fat cats" were the preferred funding source, they were wooed by star-studded dinners and personal visits and phone calls with the candidate. The small contributors, however, are usually found and solicited by mail and now by e-mail. With computerized mailing lists and the technology to personalize letters, direct-mail consultants can often raise a lot of money; mailing lists of dependable donors have become one of the most treasured resources in modern campaigning. In contrast to earlier elections, when individual donors had typically been more generous to

TABLE 12.3 **Sources of Campaign Funds for Presidential and Congressional Candidates (in Millions)**

	Presidential, 1999–2000					
	Democrats		Republicans		Total	
	Nomination	General	Nomination	General	Nomination	General
Individuals	$66.6	$0	$157.4	$0	$235.0	$5.7
Candidates	>0.1	0	43.0	0	52.3	0
PACs	>0.1	0	2.0	0	2.0	0
Party coordinated	0	13.5	0	13.2	0	26.7
Public funds	29.0	67.6	24.5	67.6	53.5	147.8
Legal, accounting, Recount	0	11.1	0	7.5	0	29.8
Total	$95.9	$92.2	$232.7	$88.3	$342.8	$210.0

	Congressional, 2001–2002						
	Democrats		Republicans		Total		Grand
	House	Senate	House	Senate	House	Senate	Total
Individuals	$151.9	$114.0	$168.7	$99.9	$322.5	$214.3	$536.8
Candidates							
Contributions	6.7	0.5	2.4	0.2	9.2	0.8	10.0
Loans	37.0	13.2	34.4	14.8	72.0	28.1	100.2
PACs	106.8	26.4	107.2	33.8	214.1	60.2	274.3
Party	1.7	0.5	2.4	2.0	4.2	2.6	6.8
Party coordinated*	2.9	2.1	5.7	9.7	8.7	11.8	20.4
Public funding	0	0	0	0	0	0	0
Other receipts†	10.1	8.3	11.2	12.0	21.3	20.1	41.4
Total	$314.2	$162.9	$326.3	$162.7	$643.3	$326.1	$969.5

*Party coordinated expenditures are spent on behalf of the candidate rather than given to the campaign, so they are not included in the totals at the bottom of the table.

†Includes money earned in interest and other receipts.

Note: Candidate loans are personal loans by the candidate to her or his campaign. The total columns include funds for Democratic, Republican, and other candidates.

Source: For the presidential campaign, FEC data calculated from David B. Magleby, ed., *Financing the 2000 Election* (Washington, D.C.: Brookings, 2002), pp. 55, 62, 70, 89, 93; for Congress, http://www.fec.gov/press/20030618canstat/01all2002.pdf (accessed Sept. 15, 2003).

Democratic congressional candidates than to Republicans, the GOP has maintained the edge since it took over control of Congress in 1994.

These small contributors remain very important to campaign fund-raisers, but with the rise of soft money and issue advocacy ads, as we will see shortly, the fat cats were back. From the late 1970s through 2002, campaign finance loopholes allowed wealthy donors to funnel large sums into campaigns via the party organizations. As a result, the influence that they could exert over candidates was revived as well.

Political Action Committees

PACs are political groups, other than party organizations, whose purpose is to raise and spend money to influence elections. Most PACs have been created by corporations, labor unions, or trade associations; these "parent" groups can support a PAC as it begins its work of raising money. Others have no sponsoring organizations; these so-called **nonconnected PACs** are most likely to be ideological groups of the right or the left. PACs can give money directly to candidates and party organizations. Some, especially the ideological PACs, also use it on independent expenditures or issue ads (see below).

Only 608 PACs existed in 1974, but by the end of 2002, there were about 4,600. The number of corporate and nonconnected PACs has grown the most. Corporate PACs increased from 15 percent of the 1974 total to 38 percent by 2000, and nonconnected PACs grew from 0 to 30 percent during this same period. There have also been big recent increases in "leadership PACs"—those set up by incumbents to distribute money to other candidates. Members of Congress contribute to other candidates to gain their support in elections for party leadership positions in Congress or because their Hill committee has insisted that they "share the wealth."[14]

A number of factors account for PAC growth. Most important was the reform legislation of the post-Watergate years. FECA stated that PACs could donate up to $5,000 per candidate while individuals could give only a maximum of $1,000; that made it more efficient for campaigns to raise money from PACs than from individuals. The new law also explicitly permitted corporations doing business with government to have PACs. Federal court decisions and the FEC confirmed the legality of PACs and the right of sponsoring organizations to pay their overhead expenses as long as the PAC's political funds are collected and kept in a separate fund; the sponsoring organization cannot use its regular assets and revenues to make political contributions. Once their legality was clarified and their fund-raising advantages became obvious, their numbers exploded.

Although PACs are an important source of campaign contributions, they are not always the big spenders that they may seem. In presidential general election campaigns, the candidates get most of their funding from federal tax money. PACs can contribute to presidential candidates during the nominating season, but these contributions have been modest in recent years ($2.6 million in 1999–2000). PACs can also make independent expenditures for or against presidential candidates. They did so to the tune of $6.1 million in the 2000 election— a big increase over their independent spending in 1996. They can air issue ads as well.

The bulk of PAC contributions, however, goes to congressional candidates. PACs gave a total of $274.3 million to House and Senate candidates in 2001–2002 (Table 12.3), a 12 percent increase over the prior election cycle. In the 2002 election, the largest amounts came from corporate PACs (33 percent) and PACs of trade associations (26 percent; most of these are business related as well). Nonconnected PACs added 16 percent, and labor PACs gave 19 percent. Even these large numbers, however, accounted for only one-fourth of all the money received by congressional candidates in 2001–2002 (28 percent).

Another limit on their power is that PACs are not monolithic; the several thousand PACs represent diverse and even competing interests. Although corporate PACs are the largest PAC givers overall, often donating almost twice as much to Republicans as to Democrats, there are both business and labor PACs among the biggest PAC spenders (see Table 12.4). Further, because labor PACs give almost all their money to Democrats, they help to compensate for the Republican edge in corporate contributions. Other types of groups also specialize; in 2000, for example, environmental groups gave more than 93 percent of their federal donations to Democrats, while 85 percent of progun groups' money went to Republicans.[15]

TABLE 12.4   The Top Ten (Plus Two) List of the Biggest PACs (in Contributions to Federal Candidates, 2001–2002)

Rank	PAC	Contributions to Federal Candidates		
		Total (in millions)	% to Democrats	% to Republicans
1	National Association of Realtors	$3.6	47%	53%
2	Laborers Union*	2.8	88	12
3	Association of Trial Lawyers	2.8	89	11
4	National Auto Dealers Association	2.6	34	66
5	American Medical Association	2.5	39	61
6	American Federation of State, County and Municipal Employees*	2.4	96	3
7	Teamsters Union*	2.4	86	14
8	United Auto Workers*	2.3	99	1
9	Electrical Workers*	2.2	96	4
10	Carpenters & Joiners*	2.2	77	22
11	Machinists & Aerospace Workers*	2.2	99	1
12	National Beer Wholesalers	2.1	21	79

*Labor union PACs. Totals do not always add up to 100 percent due to rounding error.

Source: FEC data on the Internet at http://www.opensecrets.org (accessed Sept. 12, 2003).

Candidates and parties work hard to get PAC money. Both parties' congressional and senatorial campaign committees connect their candidates with PACs likely to be sympathetic to their causes. Campaigners also seek PAC help directly, assisted by directories that list PACs by their issue positions, the size of their resources, and their previous contributions. Incumbent Congress members invite PACs or the lobbyists of their parent organizations to fund-raising parties in Washington. PACs take the initiative as well. Unlike most individual donors, they are in the business of making political contributions and they don't necessarily wait to be asked.[16]

What do PACs buy with their donations to congressional campaigns? Most PAC money is intended to gain access for the giver: the assurance that the legislator's door will be open when the group needs to plead its case on a bill. The result is that most PAC contributions go to incumbents—in 2002, about three-fourths of all PAC spending. Challengers get only a small share of the PAC dollars; there is little advantage, after all, in getting access to a likely loser. PAC money, like individual donations, therefore flows to the party with the most incumbents, and since the 1994 elections, that has been the Republicans. Party competition in the 2002 House and Senate races was so close, however, that only a bare majority of PAC money at the federal level went to Republican candidates.

It seems likely that PAC contributions do help them get access to lawmakers. What elected officials will slam the door shut on representatives of interests that donated money to their campaigns? It is harder to determine, however, how intently they listen and whether the PAC's concerns will influence their legislative behavior. There is not much evidence that PAC contributions affect the recipients' roll call votes,[17] but legislators who receive PAC money do seem to become more active on congressional committees on behalf of issues that interest their PAC donors.[18]

There are many reasons why PAC money rarely "buys" votes. Because most PACs give much less than the $5,000 maximum per candidate, many PACs could be considered small contributors. PACs give most of their money to incumbents, who normally have an easy time raising other campaign funds. PACs generally support legislators who have shown that they already favor the PAC's interests. That limits the opportunity for PAC money to change legislators' votes.

In some cases, their limited success may be due to their structure as organizations. Many large PACs are set up as federations; their local members, who provide most of these PACs' money, may want to support local incumbents even when those incumbents are not helpful to the national PAC.[19] PAC influence is also limited because they have so much competition—from party leaders, constituents, and other PACs—for the ear and the vote of a legislator. Their influence tends to be greatest when they represent powerful interests in the legislator's constituency, when they are not in conflict with his or her party's position, and when the benefit that they want is of little concern to anyone else (such as a small change in the tax laws that gives a big break to a particular corporation).

Party Organizations

At the time of the 1970s reforms, the party organizations' role in campaign finance could easily have been overlooked. However, party money, or, more accurately, money raised by the party organizations from individuals, PACs, and other interests, now plays an increasingly important role in campaigns. The two parties raised a whopping $1.2 billion in the 2000 election cycle and almost matched that amount in 2002, even with no presidential candidates on the ballot.[20] Especially in the past decade, they injected large sums of "soft money" into campaigns.

In congressional races, the parties' direct contributions are only a small part of the candidates' campaign budgets. In the 2002 races, for example, Republican committees gave $4.5 million directly to candidates and Democrats contributed $2.3 million. More substantial are the two parties' *coordinated spending*—the funds that they spend on behalf of their candidates, typically for services such as television and radio ads and polling. Federal law limits the parties' coordinated expenditures in each race: in the 2000 House campaigns, each party was permitted to spend $33,780 per election, except in states with only one House district, where the limit was $67,560. The state party can spend the same amount or transfer its spending authority in an "agency agreement" to the national party. In Senate campaigns, the limit varied with the size of the state's voting-age population: from $135,120 in Delaware to $3.3 million in California. Counting direct contributions by the party's national committee, the relevant congressional campaign committee, and the state party, plus the national and state shares of coordinated spending, each party could put almost $100,000 in direct and coordinated spending into a House race and much more into a Senate race.

Overall, in the 2002 congressional elections, the two parties' coordinated expenditures were about three times greater than their direct contributions. Coordinated spending is useful to the party because party committees have more control over how the money is spent than they do in making direct contributions to candidates, but even these coordinated expenditures amounted to only about 2 percent of the candidates' total spending in 2002.

The largest portion of the party money spent in 2000 and 2002 was sent to the state parties, combined with "soft money" (to be described below), and then used to fund issue advertising in congressional and presidential campaigns under the national party's direction. When they began to raise soft money in a big way in 1996, both national parties almost doubled their fund-raising compared with their 1992 totals, and the money kept increasing through 2002.

The Candidates Themselves

Candidates have always spent their personal wealth on their campaigns, and that has been especially true in recent years. Take the example of Jon Corzine: FEC reports show that he invested as much of his own money in his New Jersey Senate campaign ($60 million of his $63 million budget) as Ross Perot spent in seeking the presidency in 1992. (A placard held by a supporter of Corzine's primary opponent, referring to Corzine's reputed $400 million fortune, read "Make him spend it all!") In 2002, congressional candidates bankrolled their campaigns to the tune of $10 million plus $100 million in loans, representing 11 percent of all their campaign money (Table 12.3), much less than in 2000, when 19 House candidates each contributed at least half a million dollars to their own campaigns. The averages can be greatly inflated by a few wealthy candidates, however. In 1993–1994, for example, just one candidate, Michael Huffington of California, accounted for almost one-fourth of the total personal contributions and loans.

Public Funding

Finally, public funding is available for presidential campaigns if the candidate wishes to accept it, and, thus, to accept the spending limits that come with it. Congress voted in the early 1970s to let taxpayers designate a dollar (now $3) of their tax payments to match small contributions to candidates for their party's presidential nomination and to foot most of the bill for the major-party nominees in the general election campaign. The intent was to reduce corruption by limiting the role of private funds. In 2000, public matching funds in the nomination race and the general election campaign totaled $208.3 million. Public funds comprised the majority (62.5 percent) of Al Gore's spending in the nomination race and the general election, but only 35 percent of George Bush's funds, although the public funds spent by both candidates were clearly overshadowed by parties' and interest groups' spending on issue ads. Congress has chosen not to extend public funding to its own races.

MONEY IN STATE AND LOCAL CAMPAIGNS

State campaigns generally follow a pattern similar to those at the national level. Individual donors are the most important source of candidates' campaign funds, followed by PAC contributions, and then, at greater distance, by party and personal funds. There are, of course, exceptions; in an increasing number of states, parties' legislative leaders and caucuses are donating to state legislative candidates. Individual donors are even more important in local campaigns because parties and PACs play a lesser (although expanding) role at this level.

Also following the national example, several states and even some cities (such as New York) were providing public funding for candidates by the early 2000s. Some set campaign spending limits that were not much higher than the public funding to restrict the role of private money in these campaigns. In other states, the public funding covers only a small portion of the campaign's costs and often goes to parties rather than candidates. But public support for these programs, as seen by taxpayers' willingness to direct their tax money to these funds, has declined sharply.[21]

REFORM OF THE CAMPAIGN FINANCE RULES

For years, American campaign finance laws were a flimsy structure of halfhearted and not very well integrated federal and state statutes. Reformers tried periodically to strengthen legal controls over the raising and spending of campaign money. A new episode of reform was under way in the early 1970s when the Watergate scandals broke. The revulsion caused by these fund-raising scandals produced the most extensive federal law on the subject in U.S. history—the FECA amendments. The Supreme Court invalidated some of these reforms in 1976. Congress then revised the law and did so again in the late 1970s. The resulting legislation put limits on federal campaign contributions and spending and set up a system of public funding for presidential campaigns.

Contribution Limits

The law limited the amounts of money an individual, a PAC, and a party organization can give directly to a candidate in each election (primary or general) in a given year. Legislation passed in 2002 raised the limits for the first time in almost 30 years (see Table 12.5). These limits apply only to federal campaigns—those for president and Congress. Corporations and labor unions are not allowed to contribute directly, but they may set up PACs and pay their overhead and administrative costs. The money contributed under these regulations is called *hard money*—contributions that fall under the "hard limits of the federal law."

TABLE 12.5   Limits on Campaign Contributions Under Federal Law

	Limit on Contributions		
	Individual	Political Action Committee	Party Committee
To candidate or candidate committee per election	$2,000	$5,000*	$5,000*
To all candidates combined, per 2-year cycle	37,500	No limit	No limit
To a national party committee per year (An individual's total contribution to all national party committees and PACs per 2-year election cycle is limited to $57,500.)	25,000	15,000	—
To a state or local party committee per year	10,000	5,000	—
Total per 2-year election cycle	95,000	No limit	No limit

*If the political action committee or the party committee qualifies as a "multicandidate committee" under federal law by making contributions to five or more federal candidates, the limit is $5,000. Otherwise the committee is treated as an individual with a limit of $2,000. Party committees can contribute up to $17,500 to U.S. Senate candidates per election.

Note: These are the limits on so-called hard money contributions. Individual limits are indexed for inflation; PAC limits (and individual limits to PACs and state parties) are not.

Source: The Campaign Finance Institute.

Spending Limits

FECA also limited spending by presidential candidates. Those who accept federal money in the race for their party's nomination must also accept spending limits in each of the 50 states. These limits are set according to the state's voting-age population and, in 2000, ranged from a high of $13.1 million in California to a low of $675,000 in the smallest states. In the general election, presidential candidates who accept federal subsidies can spend no more than the law permits.

Congress tried to limit spending in House and Senate campaigns as well, but the Supreme Court would not agree. The Court's majority accepted the arguments of a group of strange bedfellows, including conservative New York Senator James Buckley, liberal Democratic Senator Eugene McCarthy, and the New York Civil Liberties Union; they contended that the law's restrictions on campaign spending infringed on the right to free speech. Therefore, in *Buckley v. Valeo*,[22] the Court ruled that Congress could limit campaign spending only for candidates who accepted public funding. Congress could apply spending limits to its own campaigns, then, only as part of a plan for subsidizing them. That would mean subsidizing their challengers' campaigns as well. For congressional incumbents who are normally quite capable of outspending their challengers, that was not an attractive prospect.

Public Disclosure

A vital part of the FECA reform was the requirement that campaigns had to publicly disclose their spending and the sources of their contributions. Reformers assumed that if voters had access to information about the sources of candidates' cash, they could punish greedy or corrupt campaigners with their ballots. All donations to a federal candidate must now go through and be accounted for by a single campaign committee; before the reforms, candidates could avoid full public disclosure by using a complex array of committees. Each candidate must file quarterly reports on his or her finances and supplement them with reports ten days before and thirty days after the election. All contributors of $200 or more must be identified by name, address, occupation, and name of employer.

Earlier legislation had tried and failed to achieve this goal. Required reports were sketchy at best and missing at worst. The new legislation improved the quality of reporting by creating the FEC to collect the data and make them available. Some members of Congress still try to undercut the disclosure of campaign finance data by regularly threatening to reduce the FEC's funding, but the commission's public files, available on the Internet (at http://www.fec.gov), have provided a wealth of campaign finance information for journalists and scholars.

Public Funding of Presidential Campaigns

Although Congress has not yet been willing to fund its own challengers from the public treasury, since 1976, it has provided public funding for presidential candidates. To get the money, a candidate for a party's presidential nomination must first raise $5,000 in contributions of $250 or less in each of 20 states, as a way of demonstrating broad public support. After that, public funds match every individual contribution up to $250. In return, candidates must limit their spending in each primary and overall; the limit for 2004 is about $45 million.[23] In addition, the Democratic and Republican parties each received $14.6 million in public funds to help pay for their 2004 national conventions. Then each major party's candidate gets public money to pay for his or her general election campaign. The figure rises every year with increases in the Consumer Price Index; it reached $74.4 million in 2004.

Minor parties fare less well. They receive only a fraction of that total and then only after the election if they have received at least 5 percent of the vote. Once they have reached that milestone, however, they have qualified to receive their payment before the next presidential election. Because Ross Perot won 8 percent of the vote as the Reform Party's presidential candidate in 1996, the party's candidate in 2000 was guaranteed to receive $12.6 million in advance of that campaign. That clearly enhanced the attractiveness of the Reform Party's nomination. No other minor party, however, has ever qualified for public funding. Because of the need to pay cash for many campaign expenses, this provision of FECA adds to the difficulty of financing even a modest third-party campaign.

THE LOOPHOLES THAT ATE THE REFORMS

This set of reforms was far-reaching. Yet, not long after the legislation was passed, those affected by it began to find and exploit loopholes in its provisions. Seeds were planted by FECA amendments in 1979 and by FEC and Supreme Court action, which have steadily eaten away at the framework of the FECA reforms.

Independent Spending

If an interest group or individual runs a campaign ad in support of a candidate and works with the campaign in doing so, then the law treats that ad as a campaign contribution. But as long as the individual or group does not coordinate its advertising with a candidate's campaign, it is regarded by the Supreme Court as *independent spending,* and the group is permitted to spend unlimited amounts of money on it. The Court majority's logic in *Buckley v. Valeo* was that free speech is fundamental to democracy and since "free" speech normally costs money to disseminate through radio, television, and other media, Congress cannot limit the amount that groups or individuals can spend on campaign ads that are run independent of a candidate's campaign. In 1996, the Supreme Court said that political parties could spend independently in campaigns as well.

Independent spending poses many challenges. For one, it can encourage irresponsible campaign attacks. If a *candidate* launches an outrageous attack, voters can protest by voting for his or her opponent. However, if an independent spender runs an outrageous ad, who can be held responsible? The independent spender can't be punished at the polls; he or she isn't running for anything. And because independent spenders, by definition, are not supposed to be coordinating their efforts with a candidate, is it fair to punish the candidate for the offensive ad? Therefore, independent spenders are free to say whatever they wish and the candidate whom they favor can't be held accountable.

From a regulator's perspective, the problem is to determine how independent the spending really is. The 2000 presidential race was beset with an unusually heavy volume of these ads, on issues ranging from abortion to gun control. A high-tech executive put more than a million dollars into newspaper and Internet ads lambasting Bush on education,[24] and a wealthy Bush supporter spent about $2.5 million on an ad praising Bush's environmental record. These sky-high expenditures were legal because they claimed to be independent of the presidential candidates' campaigns—but were they? Short of an admission of guilt, how would you prove collusion between an independent spender and a presidential campaign?

Soft Money

As a means of strengthening state and local parties, Congress amended FECA in 1979 to exempt from federal regulation any money raised and spent by state and local parties for party building, voter registration, and get-out-the-vote activities, even though these activities would inevitably bring out voters who could then cast votes in presidential and congressional elections. This came to be called *soft money,* or, because it was exempt from federal law, *nonfederal money*.

The law was interpreted to allow unlimited contributions not only to be donated to state and local parties but also to pass through national party committees on their way to the state parties. So although FECA permitted individuals to give no more than $1,000 each to a federal candidate per election, citizens could also give unlimited amounts of money to party organizations as soft money. These funds could not be spent directly on federal campaigns, but they could pay for any nonfederal portion of a campaign effort and they had a tendency to migrate wherever they were needed.

In effect, then, soft money became a way for individuals and PACs to launder large contributions through a party organization. The parties pushed hard to get the money. In a letter made famous by a Supreme Court case, for example, then-Republican National Chair Jim Nicholson sent a draft of the party's health care legislation to the drug company Bristol-Myers Squibb and asked for any suggested changes—and a $250,000 contribution to the Republican National Committee.[25] Fat cats, in short, had reentered the building. It was not the law's stated intention for soft money to become an end run around the limits on hard money, but the difficulty of monitoring the uses of these funds made it so. In most states, soft money could be raised not only from individuals and PACs but from corporations' profits and labor union dues as well—funds that could not be donated directly to federal candidates under FECA.[26]

Tremendous sums flowed through the soft-money conduit from the early 1990s until 2002, when it was banned at the federal level. In 1999–2000, for example, the major national party committees raised $495 million in soft money, almost twice the amount raised in the last presidential election cycle. In the 2002 election cycle, the national parties' last-ditch drive to beat the deadline for soft money resulted in an intake of $496.1 million, an unprecedented take in a midterm election. Soft money had become so attractive a source of funding, especially for the Democrats, who do not have as many hard-money donors, that in 2002, it comprised more than half of the Democratic Party's receipts and more than one-third of those of the Republicans (see Figure 12.3).

Issue Advocacy Ads

Soft money has been used to fund a number of different campaign efforts: for example, to pay some of the party organization's overhead expenses and for registration and get-out-the-vote drives or to be transferred to state and local parties for their use. Most soft money, however, has been used to fund *issue advocacy ads*. These are campaign

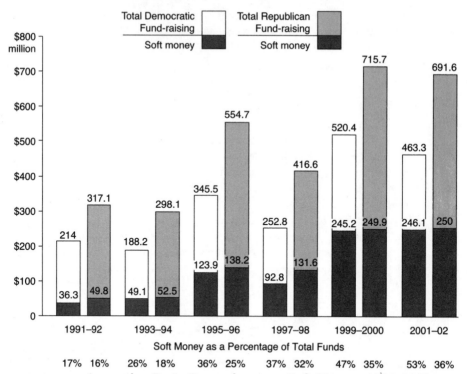

FIGURE 12.3   Increasing Party Dependence on Soft Money: 1991–2002.
Note: Bars represent total party fund-raising and the portion of it received in the form of soft money for each election cycle.
Source: FEC data, from http://www.fec.gov/press/20030320party/demfederalye02.xls,
http://www.fec.gov/press/20030320party/repfederalye02.xls,
http://www.fec.gov/press/20030320party/demsoftye02.xls, and
http://www.fec.gov/press/20030320party/repsoftye02.xls (accessed Sept. 13, 2003).

ads that do not include the terms "elect," "vote for," "support," or "oppose." As long as an ad does not use these "magic words," the courts define it as "issue advocacy" instead of election advertising. Therefore, it falls under the First Amendment's right to freedom of expression and cannot be regulated by FECA. The Democratic National Committee was the first to exploit this loophole to support President Clinton's reelection in 1996.[27]

Here are two examples of ads that met the definition of "issue advocacy" in 1996 and 2000. Thus, they could be funded with unlimited amounts of soft money and fully coordinated with the candidate's campaign, with no need for the sponsoring organization to disclose its receipts or spending:

> "Congresswoman Andrea Seastrand has voted to make it easier to dump pollutants and sewage into our water. Fact is, it's time to dump Seastrand, before she dumps anything else on us" (sponsored by the Sierra Club).[28]

(Video: pictures of babies, one wearing a Yankee ball cap), "In New York, all babies like these have something in common. They've lived here longer than Hillary Rodham Clinton" (sponsored by the American Conservative Union).[29]

These certainly sound like campaign ads. But because they don't use the "magic words," they give these groups, as well as corporations, unions, party organizations, and big individual donors a perfectly legal way around the spending limits imposed by FECA (see Figure 12.4). Why does this make sense? The Supreme Court has ruled that the right of individuals and groups to express their ideas freely carries more weight than concerns about campaign corruption. The result is that in some campaigns in 2000 and 2002, the volume of issue ads funded by interest groups and parties threatened to drown out the voices of the candidates.

From the candidate's perspective, that can be a mixed blessing. Just as is the case with independent spenders, the issue ads run by outside groups may convey different messages than the campaign would prefer. In a close House race in Colorado in 2002, for instance, a TV ad run by the national party showed a grainy image of the opponent, with a narrator asking, "What kind of person works for a group that wants to force people to pay rent in a nursing home up to ninety days after they die?" The ad concluded by asking viewers to call the opponent and ask, "What kind of person are you?" The candidate's campaign manager conceded that many of these ads were "pure, harsh hate."[30] Similarly, after the National Rifle Association spent $600,000 in 2000 on issue ads on behalf of Republican Senate candidates Spencer Abraham of Michigan and George Allen of Virginia, the candidates' poll numbers declined.[31] In 2000, pro-Democratic groups spent about as much on issue ads as did pro-Republican groups, but in 2002 campaigns, the spending shifted heavily to the Republican side.

"527" Groups ("Stealth" PACs)

In recent years, almost 2,000 political groups have formed to take advantage of a provision in tax law (which gave them their name: the "527s") allowing them to raise and spend unlimited amounts of money on campaigns without losing their tax-exempt status as long as they do not expressly call for the election or defeat of specific candidates and are not directly affiliated with federal candidates or parties. In the 2002 congressional campaigns, these groups, including the antitax Club for Growth and the Sierra Club Voter Education Fund, were estimated to have raised more than $115 million to spend on issue ads, direct mail, and phone banks.[32]

Some of these groups are traditional PACs whose campaign advertising is easy enough for voters to identify. Others carry such generic labels as Citizens for Better Medicare, a group formed by drug companies. This group spent an estimated $40–65 million in 2000, including $8 million on ads opposing prescription drug coverage under Medicare, yet it did not have to disclose its contributors or its spending under Internal Revenue Service rules. Another group, called the Republican Leadership Coalition, spent almost $2 million on ads encouraging Democrats to vote for Ralph Nader for President rather than Al Gore; the group's executive director explained, "I don't think he [Bush] could have gotten away with it the way we did."[33]

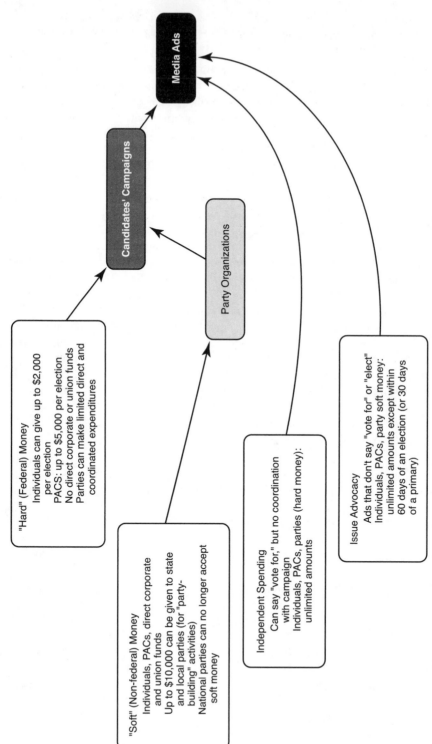

Media Ads

Candidates' Campaigns

Party Organizations

"Hard" (Federal) Money
Individuals can give up to $2,000
per election
PACS: up to $5,000 per election
No direct corporate or union funds
Parties can make limited direct and
coordinated expenditures

"Soft" (Non-federal) Money
Individuals, PACs, direct corporate
and union funds
Up to $10,000 can be given to state
and local parties (for "party-
building" activities)
National parties can no longer accept
soft money

Independent Spending
Can say "vote for," but no coordination
with campaign
Individuals, PACs, parties (hard money):
unlimited amounts

Issue Advocacy
Ads that don't say "vote for" or "elect"
Individuals, PACs, party soft money:
unlimited amounts except within
60 days of an election (or 30 days
of a primary)

FIGURE 12.4   How Money Flows into Federal Campaigns.

Source: Adapted from "Types of Contributions," *Congressional Quarterly Weekly Report (CQ Weekly),* May 13, 2000, pp. 1086–1087; and "The Bill at a Glance," *Washington Post,* March 21, 2002. This is the status of the regulations beginning November 6, 2002.

Congress voted in 2000 to require such groups to disclose their contributors and expenses. Soon after, some of these groups reorganized themselves as for-profit organizations or nonprofit organizations under different provisions of the tax code to avoid the need for disclosure.

WHAT HAVE THE REFORMS ACCOMPLISHED?

With loopholes this size, there was reason to wonder, by the end of the 2000 campaign, if the federal regulation actually regulated anything. Public funding and money raised under the limits of FECA had been swamped by massive quantities of issue advertising, paid for largely by unregulated soft money. As one expert noted, "In the world we live in today, practically speaking, there are no limits on what you can give to a campaign."[34] So—have the reforms accomplished anything?

Intended and Unintended Effects

At first, the FECA reforms seemed to achieve *most* of their goals. They slowed the growth of campaign spending in presidential races, at least in spending by the candidates' own campaigns. Between 1960 and 1972, presidential campaign expenditures had tripled; from 1972 to 2000, however, real spending increased more slowly, and in three of the eight elections, spending actually declined. In the early days of the reforms, the contribution limits made small donations more valuable to candidates than ever, which broadened the base of campaign funding. The reforms also opened much of the campaign finance process to public scrutiny.

Like all reforms, however, the campaign finance laws of the 1970s have had some worrisome, unintended effects. One of the largest is the ever-expanding imbalance between hard money contributions to candidates, which are limited, and the unlimited spending that soft money, issue advocacy ads, and independent expenditures made possible. The cap of $1,000 on hard money contributions was not raised until 2002, although inflation had eroded its value during that time. These relatively low ceilings on individual contributions made soft money and independent spending all the more attractive to parties and interest groups. Both these forms of spending raise real questions of accountability and bring back the types of money—big money from individuals and corporate and union treasuries—that the sponsors of FECA had hoped to clean out of federal campaigns.

In the long run, then, the reformers' efforts have failed to meet one of their major goals: reducing the influence of "interested money." Currently, less than 5 percent of Americans give money to political campaigns, and only one-fourth of 1 percent give $200 or more.[35] All the rest of the money comes from groups—corporations, labor unions, and other organized interests—that want something specific from lawmakers. On a single evening in the spring of 2002, for instance, one Republican dinner raised a record-breaking $33 million; some of the biggest givers, including drug and telecommunications companies, had a major interest in pending legislation, and Democrats were working hard to do the same.[36]

Effects on the Parties

For the first two decades after FECA was passed, the prevailing view was that the reforms had harmed the party organizations. By limiting parties' direct contributions to presidential and congressional candidates, FECA treated the parties as no more privileged in the campaign process than were PACs or other groups. In addition, the public funding of presidential campaigns goes to the candidates themselves, not to the parties, as it does in most other democracies. That creates more distance between the party organization and the presidential campaign.

Since 1996, however, the loopholes in the reforms, particularly the provisions for soft money and issue advocacy, have given the national parties the means to raise and spend much more money than ever before. In fact, in 17 of the most competitive House and Senate races in 2000, party organizations spent more on TV and radio advertising than the candidates did.[37] Most of this party advertising was paid for by soft money. So were the beefed-up voter mobilization programs so prominent at the conclusion of the campaign.

State and local parties, energized by money received from the national parties and by their own fund-raising success, have become more actively involved in campaigns as well. Some have put major effort into the labor-intensive grassroots work that was the staple of party organizations in an earlier era. Soft money, then, allowed the parties to play more of a role in the most competitive races than had been the case in more than half a century. Party organizations used some of these new riches to invest in long-term state and local party building.[38]

Not all the news has been good for the party organizations, however. Very little of the party-funded issue advocacy even mentions the party labels, so it is not helping to strengthen the parties' ties with voters.[39] And it is not yet clear whether the new party money has given the state and national party organizations more control over most campaigns or more of a voice in how their members of Congress vote on legislation. If it did, that would change the balance of power within the parties, but the end of this story is not yet in sight.

State Regulation and Financing

Even more complicated than this tangled federal reform are the 50 different sets of state regulations. The Watergate scandals triggered a reform movement in many states during the 1970s. The wave of new campaign finance laws focused mainly on requiring public disclosure; there was little effort at that time to limit campaign contributions or to restrict the fund-raising practices commonly used in the state.

Since that time, the movement has broadened. As the federal government has pushed a number of conflict-filled issues (abortion policy, for example) back to the states, interest group activity and PAC formation at the state level have increased as well. More state legislatures have regulated the size of campaign contributions. As of 1998, 38 states limited campaign contributions by individuals—a right upheld by the Supreme Court in 2000. About the same number either prohibited or limited union and PAC donations, and even more regulated corporate contributions.[40] Some states have even limited contributions from the candidates themselves—a step that the Supreme Court would not let Congress take in federal elections. More than half of the states limit party contributions to campaigns.

A growing number of states, now nearly half, have ventured into public funding for state elections. In 11 of these states, the payments go to the political parties, which can spend the money on behalf of candidates. Another ten give the funding directly to the candidates, and in three states, public funding goes to both the parties and the candidates. The amount of the funding provided is not large, however, and is not typically accompanied by limits on campaign spending.[41] In most states, as at the federal level, the agencies designed to enforce these rules are small and poorly funded.

Continuing Efforts at Reform: The Bipartisan Campaign Reform Act and Beyond

The unintended effects of the 1970s reforms—and some of the intended effects as well—created pressures for new reforms. They also led to cynicism about the chance for genuine reform; when respondents were asked in a Fox News poll in 1997 whether they were more likely to see Elvis or to see real campaign finance reform, Elvis won, 48 percent to 31 percent.[42]

Nevertheless, in 2002, thanks to the dogged determination of its sponsors, Senators John McCain (R-AZ) and Russ Feingold (D-WI), and another set of fund-raising scandals, Congress passed *the Bipartisan Campaign Reform Act* (known as *BCRA*), pronounced BICK-ra).[43] This act banned soft-money contributions to national parties and capped contributions to state and local party organizations (at $10,000 to each state, district, and local party committee per donor per year), beginning right after the 2002 elections. It also banned issue advocacy ads funded by soft money within 60 days of a general election and 30 days of a primary. The BCRA increased the individual contribution limit to $2,000.

The immediate result, of course, was to set off an unprecedented drive by both national parties to soak up every possible drop of soft money before the November 2002 deadline. Democratic leaders were particularly worried that their party's fundraising would be seriously undercut once BCRA took effect. For decades, Republicans have been much more successful than Democrats in raising hard money; many more of the individuals able to contribute $2,000 to a campaign are Republicans. In recent elections, Democrats narrowed the fund-raising gap to some extent by raising soft money from big donors such as labor unions and some wealthy individuals. A ban on soft money (ironically, promoted by Democrats in Congress) would increase the Republican advantage in fund-raising. In fact, at the beginning of 2004, the Republican National Committee, with its extensive hard-money donor base, had three times as much cash on hand as did the Democratic National Committee.

The ink on the legislation was barely dry, however, when new loopholes had been created. Unregulated money could still be given to state parties under less restrictive state rules. Unlimited amounts of soft money could also be donated to groups that can give directly to candidates, including PACs, "527" groups, and special committees created by the national parties specifically to receive these funds.

The new law also had the effect of encouraging increased use of an older practice known as *bundling*. An individual or interest group can ask a lot of people to make hard-money contributions to a candidate and then combine ("bundle") these checks to be delivered to the candidate by the individual or group. Each individual check is limited to the BCRA maximum of $2,000, but if a group bundles together thousands of checks, the total amount can be substantial. Groups such as the prochoice EMILY's List and the conservative Club for Growth have delivered donations totaling hundreds of thousands of dollars to a single candidate. Because these are hard-money donations, they can be used for almost any purpose in campaigns.

The 2004 Bush reelection campaign took bundling to new heights. Supporters were asked to solicit friends and co-workers for donations of up to $2,000; those who raised at least $200,000 were termed "Rangers," after the Texas Rangers, the baseball team once owned by Bush. Most of the Rangers are corporate CEOs, lobbyists, doctors, and corporate lawyers, who, like other big donors, have interests in the policies being set by the federal government. Although bundling is a clear end run around the effort to limit contributions, it has not been ruled illegal.

Has BCRA harmed the parties by limiting soft money? If most of the soft money had been used to beef up the party organizations' capabilities, then its loss would be very painful for the parties. However, most of the time, the parties have been little more than a pipeline by which big soft-money contributions have moved from the givers to the candidates. A complicated ruling by Federal District Court judges struck down the soft-money ban for a time in 2003, but a sharply divided Supreme Court reinstated it and other key parts of BCRA, ruling that even the appearance of corruption justified the restrictions.

MONEY IN AMERICAN POLITICS

Money plays a bigger role in American elections than in those of many other democracies. The sheer size of many constituencies in the United States tempts candidates to buy expensive mass media. The large number of elected officials combined with frequent primary and general elections has produced a year-round election industry. Fund-raising occupies a great deal of the candidates' time, even after they are elected, which raises public suspicions of corruption (see box).

Campaign finance in Britain works very differently. British election campaigns run for only about three weeks, and candidates and parties cannot buy TV and radio time for ads during this period. Instead, British parties get free time on the government-run BBC network. British campaigns are organized around their national party leaders, but there is considerable integration between the local parliamentary candidate and the leader rather than the largely separate campaigns of American congressional and presidential candidates. Because the average constituency in the House of Commons has less than one-fifth as many people as the average American congressional district, smaller sums of money are spent, generally under the control of the party organizations.

The fact that candidates dominate the fund-raising in American campaigns gives them a lot of independence from their party organizations once they take office. Even the parties' fund-raising organizations at the national and state levels, the legislative campaign committees, for example, are controlled by elected officeholders rather than party leaders. The 1970s reforms gave the parties some tools to expand their influence; soft money is a good example. But even a return to large-scale, party-controlled soft money would not be enough to establish strong parties with power over their candidates and elected officials.

The story is broader than the struggle between these two segments of the American parties, however. More generally, the limited results of the reforms remind us that money will always have an important impact on elections. Campaign finance reforms designed to limit and channel that impact often seem like sandcastles in the face of big waves. The most foolproof restrictions become challenges for the resourceful campaigner and contributor to overcome. Reformers are often able to alter the flow of money, at least temporarily, although sometimes in ways that they did not anticipate or want, but they will never be able to eliminate it.

A FORMER CONGRESSMAN VIEWS THE MONEY CHASE

When I first ran for the House in 1964, my total campaign budget was $30,000; my final campaign, in 1996, cost $1 million. The current system of financing congressional elections is a problem, and a serious one, for a variety of reasons.

Members of Congress must spend an enormous amount of time fundraising. Raising $4 million for an average Senate campaign, for example, means raising $15,000 every week over the Senator's six-year term. The money chase distorts the political process, crowding out other activities like writing laws, thinking about public policy, or meeting with ordinary voters. Incumbents know that the way to scare off competition is to raise a lot of money, and it has become a chief campaign tactic.

Many who contribute money are concerned about a "shakedown" atmosphere. They often feel they cannot get their views across unless they contribute generously to politicians they may dislike. The rising flood of money that flows into campaigns also undermines general public trust in the political system.

Changing the campaign finance system is terribly difficult. The blunt fact is that most members of Congress and both political parties prefer the system under which they were elected . . . It is a system they know how to work for their advantage, and under which they have risen to the top. Moreover, it is very difficult to devise a system that will reduce the disproportionate influence of money in politics and still not trample on constitutional rights to express political views.

Source: Excerpted from Lee Hamilton, "Comments on Congress," Center on Congress, Indiana University, Sept. 26, 2002. Used with permission.

PART 5

The Party in Government

In the spring of 2003, President George W. Bush had an advantage that few other recent presidents have enjoyed: His party was in the majority in both houses of Congress. With unified party control of both the White House and the legislative branch, it should have been a slam dunk for Bush to get his legislative proposals through the House of Representatives and the Senate. Yet when Bush asked his House Republican colleagues to soften the image of his proposed tax cuts by providing a larger child tax credit to low-income families, House Republican Majority Leader Tom DeLay had a concise response: "Ain't going to happen."[1]

Bush and DeLay are both important members of the Republican *party in government.* As you recall from Chapter 1, the party in government includes *any elected or appointed public officials* who see themselves as belonging to that party. They are vitally important to the party as a whole because it is the members of the party in government who pass and enforce laws; they, rather than the party organization or the party electorate, are the people who can legislate the party's proposals on college student loans, pornography, and gun control.

So if Bush and DeLay are part of the same party in government, why did they disagree on this bill? The Republican Party in government, like its Democratic counterpart, is a very diverse group. In addition to the party in Congress, which consists of everyone elected to the House or the Senate as a Republican, and the Republican president, the Republican Party in government includes Republicans who work for federal, state, and local administrative agencies; Republican governors and state legislators; Republicans who serve in local elective and appointive office; and even judges (and Supreme Court Justices) who see themselves as Republicans. The 23-year-old Republican city council member in a small town in Michigan is likely to have a different perspective from the Supreme Court justice who identifies as a Republican and the middle-aged Republican woman who works for the FBI.

The design of the American political system works against a unified party in government. Because members of Congress are elected separately from the president, they do not need to act as a single Democratic or Republican "team." State and local officeholders, too, have been elected as individuals. They are not chosen to run by their party

239

organization; rather, they become the party's candidates by winning voter support in primary elections. They deal with different constituencies and different pressures, so they may have very different ideas from one another as to what their party in government should be doing. Federalism and the separation of powers, then, fracture the party in government and keep it from setting the administration on a single, coherent policy path.

For decades, reformers have dreamed of an alternative. One of the most discussed is the idea of *party government*, or *responsible parties*. The argument is that American democracy would be strengthened if the parties were to offer clearer and fuller statements of their proposed policies, nominate candidates pledged to support those policies, and then see to it that their winning candidates enact those programs.[2] The parties, then, would let voters choose not only between candidates but, more importantly, between alternative sets of policies and be assured that the winning set would be put into effect. That would greatly strengthen the parties' role in American politics. Parties would be unified at all levels of government; they would become the main link between citizens and the uses of government power. Voters, the argument goes, would be better able to hold their government accountable.

Several European parties do behave more like responsible parties. In Britain, for example, the parliamentary system encourages the kind of legislative party unity that the advocates of responsible parties have in mind. The House of Commons selects the government's chief executive, the prime minister, from its own ranks; he or she must keep a legislative majority in order to stay in office. That creates a powerful incentive for party government. The party in government then tries to carry out a program that was adopted with the help of party leaders, activists, and members at party conferences.

Could this work in the United States? Probably not. The design of the American system is not likely to change. Because of the separation of powers, Republicans can hold a majority in Congress while a Democrat sits in the White House, or one party can dominate the House while the other controls the Senate. In fact, in recent years, divided control of government has been the norm at the national level and in most states. That makes it difficult for a party to implement all its preferred policies; instead, legislation is likely to involve compromise. Even at times when one party controls both Congress and the presidency, the legislative party might not always be in perfect agreement with its colleague in the White House, as the story of Bush and DeLay shows. The party organization can't guarantee that all the party's candidates, selected in primary elections in differing constituencies across the nation, will run on the party's platform. And the party electorate is still only loosely connected with the party organization.

However, even though the American system stands in the way of the full implementation of this reform, the Democrats and the Republicans have been acting a bit more like responsible parties in recent years. More and more citizens are being attracted to party work because of particular issues that concern them, so pressure builds for greater party responsibility. Congress and state legislatures now divide more along party lines than they have in decades. Partisanship has a major influence on the staffing of top executive offices and the appointment of judges.

As a result, government policies change depending on the makeup of the party in government because the party winning the presidency is usually able to carry out much of its platform.[3] After Republicans won majorities in both the House and Senate in 1994, for instance, an Associated Press analysis showed that there was a movement of federal spending from some areas of the nation to others, reflecting the priorities of the newly dominant Republicans. Cuts in public housing grants, food stamps, and child care programs took money away from poor rural and urban areas. On the other hand, increases in business loans and farm subsidies gave more federal spending to suburbs and farm areas. These are real, tangible indicators of a shift in priorities associated with the change in party control.[4] It would be too strong to call the result an American twin of British party government, but we are probably safe in describing it as a distant cousin.

Why have these changes occurred? What does this party polarization mean for American politics? The chapters in Part Five address these questions of party influence in government. Chapters 13 and 14 examine the roles of the parties in the organization and operation of the legislature, the executive branch and the courts. Chapter 15 looks at the degree to which party government can be said to exist in American politics.

CHAPTER 13

Parties in Congress and State Legislatures

Christopher Shays had crusaded for years to reform campaign fund-raising. Shays, a Republican U.S. House member from Connecticut, cosponsored a campaign finance bill to limit soft money even though his party's leadership in the House opposed the bill. Shays was about to step into a position of power in the House; as the most senior Republican on the Government Reform Committee, he expected to be named the committee's chair. But Shays was passed over for the job. The party's leaders gave the position instead to another Republican more willing to go along with the leadership, another case, reporters wrote, of House party leaders "cracking down on wayward members . . . centralizing power and demanding discipline."[1]

As Shays's experience shows, party is central to the workings of Congress and most state legislatures, even more today than it was for most of the 1900s. Congress and state legislatures are organized by party. Each of the four congressional parties—the House Democrats, House Republicans, Senate Democrats, and Senate Republicans—is more unified internally, and legislative voting is more intensely partisan now than it has been for decades. There are sharp differences on important issues between the congressional Republicans and their Democratic colleagues. Even so, there are still party "mavericks," legislators who vote against their party's position, sometimes even on big issues, who continue to be reelected by their constituents, and who manage to live with their party leaders' disapproval.

The parties' recent increase in strength has not come easily; to be effective, they must fight an uphill battle against the system's design. One of the most basic rules of American politics, the separation of powers, undermines efforts at party unity. In a political system without a separation of powers—a parliamentary regime, such as that of Great Britain—a majority party in the legislature must unite to support the issue positions of its leaders in the government. When those leaders cannot muster a majority in parliament on big issues, either the governing cabinet must be reshuffled or the legislature must be dissolved and its members sent home to campaign for their jobs again. This creates powerful pressures for the legislative party to remain united.

American legislators do not face these pressures. They can reject the proposals of a president, a governor, or a legislative leader of their own party without bringing down the government and having to face a new election. Their constituents probably will not punish them for doing so. Yet, in Congress and many state legislatures in the early 2000s, several forces are encouraging members of each legislative party to hang together.

How is this happening, even though the institutional rules don't require it? To some analysts, these increasing levels of party unity don't reflect the power of *party* in legislative life at all. Rather, they suggest, legislators rely on their own preferences on issues when they vote, and it happens that legislators from the same party tend to agree on their policy preferences.[2] However, there is ample evidence that party leadership, organizational reforms, and changes in the parties outside of Congress have expanded the roles of the legislative parties and that parties structure the action in most state legislatures as well.[3] Let us begin with changes in the legislative leadership.

HOW THE LEGISLATIVE PARTIES ARE ORGANIZED

Almost all members of Congress and state legislators are elected as candidates of a major party.[4] Once they take office, however, there are enormous differences among the legislative parties that they create. In a few states, the legislative party hardly exists; in others, it completely dominates the legislative process. The parties in most state legislatures and in Congress fall somewhere in between these extremes.

Party Organization in Congress

At the beginning of a new congressional session, the members of each party come together in both houses of Congress. These party meetings (called *caucuses* by the Democrats and *conferences* by the Republicans) select the leadership of the party (the leaders, whips, and policy committees; see the box on page 245). They also structure the chamber itself by nominating candidates for its presiding officer (the Speaker of the House of Representatives or president pro tempore of the Senate) and setting up procedures for appointing party members to congressional committees. In this way, the organization of the two parties is closely interwoven with the organization of the House and Senate as a whole.

The majority party dominates the organization of both houses. Its elected leader becomes Speaker of the House, the top office in the House of Representatives. The vice president of the United States is the formal presiding officer of the Senate, but it is the majority party that manages floor action, to the degree that floor action can be managed in that highly democratic institution. The majority party chooses the chairs of all the committees in both houses. It hires and fires the staff of these committees and of the chambers. Most of each committee's members come from the majority party, by a margin that is usually larger than the majority's margin in the chamber.

The majority party, in short, controls the action in the committees and on the floor. From the early 1950s until 1994, the Democrats held this position in the House; since then and for much of the period since 1980 in the Senate, the Republicans have been in charge. This system was sorely tested in 2001 when, in what was justifiably called "uncharted territory," the Senate split 50-50 between the two parties. After a few months' experience with power sharing under a Republican "majority" (because Republican Vice President Dick Cheney had the power to break any tie votes), one Republican senator

PARTY LEADERSHIP POSITIONS IN THE HOUSE AND SENATE

Each party creates its own leadership structure in each house of Congress; the individual leaders are elected by the entire party membership of the chamber. At the top of the hierarchy is the party leader (called the **majority** or **minority leader**, depending on whether the party controls the chamber). In the House of Representatives, the **Speaker** ranks above the majority leader as the true leader of the majority party. These party leaders have assistants called **whips** and **assistant whips** who tell members the party's position on bills, try to convince them to vote the way the party leadership wants, and keep a head count of each bill's supporters and opponents.

Each congressional party also has several specialized leadership positions. There is a **caucus** or **conference chair** to head the meeting of all party members. Other chairs are selected for the **Steering Committee** (among all but the Senate Republicans, where it is called the Committee on Committees), which assigns party members to committees; the **Policy Committee**, which identifies the party's position on proposed legislation and issue priorities; the **Campaign Committee**, which provides campaign support to the party's congressional candidates; and any other committees the legislative party may create.

renounced his party ties and became an independent. That gave control to the Democrats—the first time in American history that party control of a house of Congress switched in the middle of a legislative session. Republicans regained the majority in 2002.

Changes in the Power of House Party Leaders

The power of congressional party leaders has varied a lot over time. Much of the change reflects differences in the degree to which a party's members in Congress are willing to accept strong leadership; because party leaders in Congress are chosen by the votes of all members of their legislative party, their power is, in effect, delegated to them by their party caucus (or conference) and they serve subject to its approval.[5] In addition, party leaders have differed in their styles of exercising power.

The Revolt Against "Czar" Cannon   Years ago, power in the House of Representatives was highly centralized in the hands of the Speaker. In the first decade of the 1900s, powerful Speaker Joe Cannon chaired the Rules Committee, the "traffic cop" through which he could control the flow of legislation to the floor. He appointed committees and their chairs, putting his chief supporters in the key positions, and generally had the resources and sanctions necessary to enforce party discipline.[6] In 1910, however, dissidents from within his own party combined with the minority Democrats to revolt against "Czar" Cannon. For decades after that, Speakers were not able to muster the kind of power that Cannon commanded. Instead, they had to operate in a much more decentralized House in which party discipline could be maintained only through skillful bargaining and strong personal loyalties. Successful Speakers during this era, such as Sam Rayburn and Tip O'Neill, were skilled compromisers rather than commanders.[7]

Growing Party Coordination   Party coordination has increased more recently, however, especially in the House. The Republicans took a small step in this direction in the late 1960s, by giving rank-and-file party legislators more opportunity to influence party policy through the party conference. In the 1970s, the Democrats, under the prodding of the reform-minded Democratic Study Group and the wave of liberals elected in the wake of the Watergate scandals of 1974, took more serious steps toward the same goal by strengthening both the party caucus and the party leadership.

Next came a direct assault on the party leaders' main competitors for power in the House: the chairs of the standing committees that deal with proposed legislation. These committee chairs were selected using the *seniority rule,* which directed that the most senior member of the majority party on a committee automatically became its chair. Because of this rule, members of the majority party could win a chairmanship simply by being reelected to Congress over and over again, even if they did not support their party leadership's position on issues—in fact, even if they voted with the *other* party more often than with their own. That gave experienced party members a base of power in Congress independent of the party leaders. Committee chairs could, and often did, use that power in an autocratic manner.

In order to enhance its own power and to give rank-and-file Democrats more rights on their committees, the Democratic caucus revised the seniority rule in the mid-1970s. The caucus gave itself the power to challenge and even oust committee chairs by secret ballot. Soon after, some chairs were, in fact, challenged in the caucus and a few were defeated and replaced by the caucus's choice, who was not always the second most senior party member.[8] This change increased the party leaders' authority by reducing the power of the committee chairs. That fundamentally changed the structure of authority within the Democrat-run House.

The power to assign members to committees was vested in the new Steering and Policy Committee chaired by the Speaker. The Speaker was also allowed to choose, with the caucus's approval, the chair and other Democratic members of the Rules Committee, whose independence had formerly been a real thorn in the side of the party leadership. Thus, the Speaker gained more power over the careers of other party legislators and over the fate of the bills that they wanted to pass. The whip system, a set of deputies responsible for informing their party colleagues about the party's stands and for finding out how many members are supporting those stands, was enlarged and made more responsive to party leaders as well.[9]

Policy Leadership   These reforms gave the legislative party in the House, with its strengthened leadership, the ability to use its new power to promote certain policy goals. Individual party members in the House were becoming more willing to use the party caucus to achieve these goals. One main reason is that both parties in the House became more ideologically homogeneous during the 1970s and 1980s.[10] Southern voters were leaving the Democratic Party in increasing numbers, and fewer conservative southern Democrats were being elected to Congress. Democratic House members, then, were more cohesively liberal than had been the case in earlier decades. Because of the committee reforms, the remaining conservative southerners were losing their strongholds of committee power. Congressional Republicans had become more ideologically unified as well and were energized by the conservative policy leadership coming from the White House under Ronald Reagan in the 1980s.

When a party is ideologically cohesive, it is easier for the party caucus to agree on a unified position on legislation. The members of each of these ideologically cohesive parties could better trust that their leaders would share their policy concerns and protect their reelection interests. In addition, at this time, the two congressional parties were more at odds with one another on issues than they had been for some time. So parties became more willing to grant power to their legislative party leaders, including the power to pressure straggling legislators to fall in line, in order to pass the party's legislation.[11]

Even with these changes, some party leaders were more willing than others to make use of the new opportunities for power. Speaker Jim Wright, during his brief tenure as party leader in the late 1980s, did take advantage of the changes to become one of the most assertive Democratic leaders in decades. His successor, Thomas Foley, was not as inclined to aggressive partisanship; Foley returned to a more collegial style before being defeated for reelection in the Republican surge of 1994.

The Gingrich Revolution

Ironically, given that the Democrats in the House had been the agent of stronger legislative party leadership during the 1970s and 1980s, it was a Republican who brought party leadership to its recent position of strength. The Republican minority had been bystanders to the Democratic procedural reforms of the 1970s and 1980s, but the 1994 election produced landmark changes. Republicans won a majority of House seats that year, after a campaign centered on their "Contract with America," a set of comprehensive, conservative policy pledges made most visible by the party's leader in the House, Representative Newt Gingrich.

The election of a number of new conservative members made the House Republicans even more cohesive. Most of these newcomers had gotten campaign help from Gingrich, and, together with their more senior colleagues, credited him with engineering their party's takeover of the House—the first Republican House majority in 40 years. However, the Republicans had only a slender majority in the House and they faced a Democrat, Bill Clinton, in the White House. In order to fight for the goals of the Contract, GOP members were willing to accept strong party leadership and discipline.[12] They elected Gingrich Speaker and gave him unprecedented authority to push the Republican agenda.

One of the most important tools given to the Speaker by the House Republican conference was the power to set aside the seniority rule; instead, the Speaker could pick committee chairs on the basis of their commitment to bringing the desired legislation to the floor. Gingrich was very willing to exercise that power. Why did the committee chairs, the chief losers in this extraordinary usurpation of committee power, agree to it? The new Republican majority was so uniformly conservative that the change may well have reflected their dedication to the party's policy agenda, the chairs' personal loyalty to Gingrich, or perhaps even fear for their political careers if they resisted. It was a giant step in the expansion of party power in the House, and Gingrich became the strongest Speaker in modern times.[13]

The result was a level of party discipline with which "Czar" Cannon would probably have felt comfortable. When the ten sections of the Contract with America came to a vote in the House, out of a possible 2,300 Republican voting decisions (ten provisions times 230 Republican House members), there were a grand total of only 111 "no" votes; 95 percent of the Republican votes supported the party leadership's position. To a greater extent than had been seen in almost a century, the party discipline was directed toward achieving the congressional party's policy goals.

. . . and Its Aftermath

Later in 1995, however, Gingrich's aura of invincibility started to crumble. When a stand-off on the national budget between President Clinton and the House Republicans led to a shutdown of the government, Gingrich and his colleagues got the blame. The Speaker was dogged by charges of ethics violations and declining popularity ratings. House Republicans were frustrated by his uneven leadership style. An aborted effort to oust him from the Speakership in 1997 had quiet help from some other Republican leaders. Then, when the GOP lost a net of five House seats in the 1998 election, there were widespread demands among House Republicans for new leadership. Gingrich resigned three days later; many wondered whether he had been better suited to lead a contentious minority than to manage the day-to-day demands of a majority.

Gingrich's successor, Dennis Hastert, did not begin by demanding unshakable party discipline, and his party colleagues, in 1999, were not as inclined to give it. Although committee chairs have been allowed to take the lead on most legislation, the Republican Party leadership has maintained control over the chairs' selection. The Gingrich reforms included a six-year term limit on committee chairs. Those who hoped to head committees after the first term-limited chairs had to step down in 2001 were in the unusual position of having to submit to interviews by Hastert and other party leaders as well as to the judgment of the party's backbenchers before the appointments were made.

After the Republicans made gains in the 2002 elections, the leadership strengthened its hand with further changes. The term limit on the Speaker was eliminated, seniority rules were undercut even more in order to move loyal leadership allies into powerful subcommittee chairs, and party leaders cracked down on Republican colleagues who refused to follow the party's lead.[14] The Republican leadership dedicated itself wholeheartedly to enacting President Bush's conservative economic and social agenda into law.

Parties in the "Individualist" Senate

Clearly, the job of a House party leader is challenging. But the work of the Senate's party leaders is more like herding cats. By the mid-1970s, Barbara Sinclair explains,[15] the U.S. Senate had moved from an institution governed by elaborate "rules" of reciprocity, specialization, and apprenticeship, in which powerful committees dominated the legislative work, to a much more individualistic body. Increasingly, and with avid media attention, members of the Senate established themselves as national spokespersons on various policy questions. Once they had become political "stars," these senators expected to participate more fully in the Senate's work, on their way to, many hoped, greater glory and higher office.

By the late 1980s, that individualism had led to a big increase in use (or the threat) of the peculiar Senate institution of the filibuster—the right of extended debate, used to talk a bill or a nomination to death if the votes were not available to defeat it in any other way. Senators are also able to plaster a bill with nongermane amendments (those not pertinent to the bill) as a means of stalling it or getting other favored bills through. By the same time, changes in southern politics had led to greater party polarization in the Senate, just as they had in the House.

The combination was potentially explosive. Issues reaching both houses of Congress were often contentious. Add to this a more partisan Senate and a set of rules that permitted any member to tie up the work of the institution for an indefinite period, and the result is a desperate need for a legislative traffic cop. Increasingly, it has been the party leadership in the Senate that has tried to direct the traffic. The Senate's rules do not allow the centralization of power in the party leadership that was seen in the House in the 1990s, however.[16] So the Senate's majority and minority party leaders consult extensively with their party colleagues, rather than command them, to build the unanimous consent agreements that allow bills to be brought to a vote without risking a filibuster by an unhappy senator.

That has been an extremely difficult job. Small, organized groups of partisans intent on blocking a bill have become the main obstacles to these unanimous consent agreements. In fact, a central element in the minority party's strategy since the 1990s was its ability to use the Senate's elaborate rules to take control of the legislative agenda from the majority party. In this polarized atmosphere, individual senators have come to depend on their party leaders to promote the legislative party's interests, both inside and outside the Senate chamber.

Parties in the State Legislatures

As in Congress, the legislative parties organize the legislatures in almost every state.[17] They structure everything from the legislative leadership to its committees. The power of the legislative parties varies, however, depending in part on the legislature's rules and on the personal skills and resources of the party leaders. In a few state legislatures, daily caucuses and strong party leadership make for a party every bit as potent as the Republicans in the 2003 U.S. House. In others, especially the traditionally one-party states, party organization is weaker than it was in Congress before the reforms of the 1970s. There are states, for example, in which a majority party's caucus has split, either because of ideological differences or personal rivalries.

More typically, however, state legislative party leaders have a lot of power over the day-to-day workings of the legislature. They do not usually have to defer to powerful steering committees or policy committee chairs; the party leaders can appoint the members as well as the chairs of these committees, often without having to consider the members' seniority. So party leaders can choose committee chairs and members on the basis of their support for the party leader personally, or for their views on issues that the committee will consider. Even so, party leaders increasingly feel the need to consult with other legislators as they exercise their power. Members of state legislatures have become less tolerant of autocratic leadership, so the job of party leader is now "more complex and more challenging than in the past."[18]

Party leaders exercise their influence, in part, through the party caucus. Caucuses can be used for a number of purposes. In many states with strong two-party systems, party leaders call caucus meetings to give members information about upcoming bills, learn whether their membership is united or divided on an issue, and encourage legislators to support the party's position. Leaders in a few of these states even try, occasionally, to get the caucus to hold a "binding" vote on some important issues, a vote that calls on all members to support the party's position. Where the state parties are not as strong, it is more common for the party caucus simply to offer information or allow leaders to hear members' opinions but not to try to build consensus.[19]

In sum, although the parties' legislative organizations look similar across the states—their party leadership positions are fairly uniform—they differ in their behavior. The power of state party leaders varies substantially, even between the two houses of the same state legislature, as do the influence and effectiveness of the party caucus.[20]

METHODS OF PARTY INFLUENCE

How do legislative parties and their leaders exercise their power? What resources can they use to influence their members' behavior?

Carrots and Sticks

Congressional party leaders have a variety of tools available to try to shape the behavior of their party colleagues. They tend to rely more on incentives than on punishments because the most effective punishments are limited in their use and occasionally have been known to backfire. The most powerful punishment would be to remove a maverick legislator from his or her seat in the House or Senate. Except in rare cases, however, such as that of Ohio Democrat James Traficant, who was in jail at the time the House expelled him in 2002, party leaders do not have that power. Only the legislator's constituents can do that, and they are not likely to serve as the agents of the congressional party leadership. So representatives and senators can normally vote against their party's leadership or against major bills proposed by their party's president, without fear of losing their jobs.

Even the in-your-face disloyalty of supporting the other party's presidential candidate in the general election has not been punished consistently in Congress. In 1965, the House Democratic caucus stripped committee seniority from two southern Democrats who had supported the Republican presidential candidate, Barry Goldwater, the year before. In 2000, however, a conservative southern Democrat, Representative Ralph Hall from Texas, endorsed Republican George W. Bush for president and faced no sanctions from his party.

Perhaps the most famous example of the weakness of party penalties is the story of Phil Gramm, elected as a Democratic representative from Texas. The House Democratic leadership gave Gramm, a conservative, a seat on the prestigious House Budget Committee in return for his promise to cooperate with party leaders. But in 1983, members of the Democratic caucus were outraged to learn that Gramm had leaked the details of secret Democratic Party meetings on the Reagan budget to Republican House members. The caucus took away Gramm's seat on the Budget Committee.

Gramm did not accept his fate quietly, however. He resigned from the House and then ran—as a Republican—in the special election held to replace him. His constituents reelected him to the House and later to the Senate as a Republican. In fact, he was soon back on the House Budget Committee, courtesy of the Republican leadership! As long as legislative party leaders cannot keep a party maverick from being renominated and reelected and in districts where voters are not impressed by a legislator's party loyalty, party influence will be limited. So this step is taken only rarely. Several of Gramm's southern Democratic colleagues had voted for the Republican budget in 1983 but were not disciplined in any way. Republican Speaker Newt Gingrich made veiled threats in 1995 to remove some GOP committee chairs from their positions when they stood in the way of action on the party's Contract with America. His maneuver worked; the chairs became more compliant. If it had not, Gingrich would have had to call on an unusual level of party conference support in order to make good on his threats.

In sum, the House and Senate party leaders have a fairly short list of punishments at their command when trying to unify their parties. In addition, using these punishments might do more harm than good. There is always the risk, especially when the two parties are closely matched in numbers, that punishing a legislator will cause him or her to defect to the other party or will give the party leadership a bad public image.

So the party organizations in Congress are more likely to rely on incentives to gain their members' loyalty. Party leaders can offer or withhold desirable committee assignments, help in passing a member's bills, or even provide additional office space in order to cultivate party support. They can promote pork barrel projects in the member's district. They can offer members useful information, for example, about the status of a bill on the legislative schedule. Some researchers find that junior members of Congress are more likely to vote with their party than are more senior members, perhaps because the newer legislators have greater need for the information or other resources that party leaders can provide.[21]

Party leaders have other persuasive resources as well. They can use their personal relationships with party colleagues to cajole them through careful listening and dialogue or through more hard-edged persuasion. On a recent House vote on school vouchers, for example, a *Washington Post* reporter describes House Republican leaders surrounding a Kentucky Republican who had opposed the leadership on this bill the week before. A senior Democrat, "Rep. David R. Obey (D-Wis.) took to the microphone. 'Is anyone from the office of the attending physician present?' he deadpanned. 'I understand someone's arm is being broken.'" The Republican did decide to vote for the bill.[22]

By using their control of floor activities, party leaders can set the agenda so as to maximize party unity on important matters.[23] They can also provide campaign help by giving speeches and raising money for a member's reelection effort. The parties' congressional campaign committees, with their newfound riches and services, have been a major factor in promoting party cohesion in Congress.[24]

PARTY INFLUENCE ON LEGISLATIVE VOTING

How effective is this party influence? The first place to look is at the votes cast by Congress members on proposed bills. Roll-call votes are not the only important actions Congress members take. Yet the public nature of the roll-call vote makes it a good test of the party's ability to persuade its members.

A party can influence legislators' votes in two ways: through the direct impact of party leaders' persuasion and as a result of the ability of a member's partisanship to structure issues and create loyalties within his or her own mind. In both senses, party has a lot of competition in trying to influence legislators' votes on any given issue. There may be contending demands from organized interests and financial contributors back home as well as from friends in the legislature. In a broad sense, there may be constituency pressure. The wishes of a president or governor may be pressed on the legislator, and he or she is likely to have personal experiences with, and beliefs about, policies. Increasingly, on many issues, all or most of these pressures point in the same direction. When they don't, party loyalty may give way.

How Unified Is Each Legislative Party?

Researchers use several measures to determine the impact of party on roll calls. The first, *party unity voting* (or, more simply, *party voting*), is the proportion of roll calls on which most Democrats vote one way on a bill and most Republicans vote the other way. The second, *party unity scores* (or *party support*), is the degree to which legislators vote with their party's majority on these party votes.

Party Voting   One way to measure party voting is to use the toughest test: any legislative roll call in which at least 90 percent of one party's members vote yes and 90 percent or more of the other party vote no. By such a strict test, party discipline appears regularly in the British House of Commons and the German Bundestag, but not as often in American legislatures. Under Czar Cannon, about a third of all roll calls in the House met this standard of party discipline. From 1921 through 1948, that had dropped to only 17 percent,[25] and it declined steadily to about 2 to 8 percent in the 1950s and 1960s. During approximately the same period in the British House of Commons, this striking party division occurred on almost every roll call.

Since the 1990s, there has been a notable increase in "90 percent votes." In 2003, for example, both houses were dramatically divided by party on President Bush's proposal for a $350 billion tax cut (see Figure 13.1) and other issues such as environment, health care, and the budget deficit. Republicans were more likely to reach this 90 percent level than were Democrats; as an example, look at the party division in Figure 13.1 on banning so-called "partial birth abortion." In fact, in the first three months of 2003, the House Republicans voted *unanimously* 44 percent of the time, and their Democratic counterparts did so on almost one-fourth of all roll calls; both these figures were a clear increase over the 2002 session.[26] In a system of separated powers, this is a remarkable level of party polarization.[27]

The 90 percent standard is too strict, however, for a look at the American legislative experience over time. So researchers have focused on a less demanding measure: the *party unity vote*, or the percentage of roll calls in which the *majority* of one party opposed a majority of the other. By this measure, the early 1990s produced the highest levels of congressional party voting in many years.

Let us start where senators think we should—with the Senate. During the late 1960s and early 1970s, a majority of Democrats opposed a majority of Republicans in only about one-third of all Senate roll-call votes.[28] By 1995, the figure was up to 69 percent, the highest recorded in the Senate since these measurements started in 1954. That dropped to between 45 and 55 percent beginning in 2000, but not because the two parties were less unified. Rather, the Senate was so closely divided that party leaders avoided bringing highly partisan issues to a vote unless they felt confident of winning. When these issues *did* come to a vote and a majority of Republicans opposed a majority of Democrats, the former voted with their party's position 84 percent of the time in 2002, compared with 83 percent for the Democrats.

Party voting has been even more prevalent in the House at times. In the 1800s, congressional party voting was substantial (although still far below that of the British Parliament). This was a time when the parties were competitive in most congressional districts, party leaders wielded considerable legislative authority, and Congress was a much less professionalized institution. After 1900, following a decline in the party-based link among candidates for different offices and the development of a more professional-ized Congress,[29] party voting decreased dramatically. The New Deal realignment of the 1930s increased the frequency of party voting for a time, before it fell again to twenti-eth-century lows in 1970 and 1972 (27 percent).

Then the rise began. By the mid-1980s, party voting in the House reached levels not seen since the partisan divisions over New Deal legislation (Figure 13.2). Again, in the late 1990s and early 2000s, for reasons we will discuss shortly, these figures rose to their highest levels in modern times.[30] In the rancorous 1995 session, party voting hit a 50-year high of 73 percent in the House. Those levels could not be sustained after 1995; the figure was down as low as 43 percent in 2002. However, as was the case in the Senate, on votes in which a majority of Republicans did oppose a majority of Democrats, a full 90 percent of Republicans voted with their party, as did 86 percent of Democrats.

In state legislatures, there is a lot of variation in levels of party voting, both across the states and within a given state from one political generation to the next. We are most likely to see party voting in states where the two parties are closely balanced in strength in the legislature, so both parties feel they have a chance to get their bills passed. It is also more common where the two parties represent distinctive groups of voters, for exam-ple, in urban, industrialized states where Democratic strength is concentrated among union members and blacks in the big cities, and Republican state legislators tend to rep-resent suburban and rural districts that are largely white and conservative. As is the case in Congress, state legislative parties are more likely to accept strong party leadership when the parties are highly polarized. Party voting in southern states, then, such as Texas and Florida, has been increasing in the 1990s.[31]

Party Support   To what extent do legislators support their party on party votes? In the 1960s and 1970s, conservative southern Democrats often crossed the aisle to vote with Republicans in the House and Senate, and their defections were tolerated by the decentralized party leadership of that time. This cross-party alliance, known as the *conservative coalition,* came together to oppose civil rights bills and Democratic labor and education proposals.

However, the Democratic Party's supporting coalition in the South was in the process of being reshaped in the 1960s and 1970s, as we have seen. The Voting Rights Act, bring-ing southern blacks into the electorate, was resulting in the election of fewer conserva-tive southern Democrats to Congress and more moderate and liberal Democrats. The policy disagreements between northern and southern Democrats were starting to fade. So the conservative coalition of northern Republicans and southern Democrats grew weaker, leaving the Democratic Party more cohesive than it had been in decades.[32] Party cohesion continued to increase during the Clinton and Bush presidencies, especially among the Republicans once they took control of Congress in 1995 (see Figure 13.3).

As a result, there are very clear—and often bitter—differences on issues between the House Democrats and the House Republicans (see box on page 257). When the Amer-icans for Democratic Action (ADA), a liberal group, examined how often legislators voted with the ADA's position on 20 key votes, the median score for Democratic sena-tors in 1999 was 100 percent and that of the Republicans was zero. The House pattern was almost as stark.[33] In addition, the organizational reforms discussed earlier in the chapter, which reduced the power of committee chairs and strengthened the power of

Case 1: Cut taxes by $350 billion over 11 years?

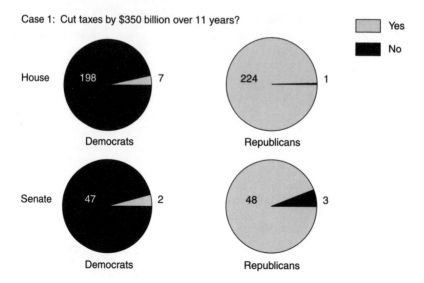

House

198 | 7

Democrats

224 | 1

Republicans

Senate

47 | 2

Democrats

48 | 3

Republicans

Yes
No

Case 2: Increase spending on environmental programs by $12.4 billion over 10 years
(cost to be offset by reducing the planned Bush tax cuts)?

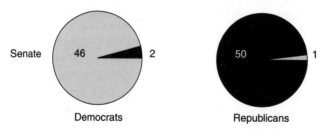

Senate

46 | 2

Democrats

50 | 1

Republicans

Case 3: Ban the late-term abortion procedure termed "partial birth" abortion by
its opponents?

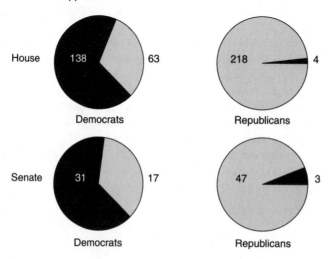

House

138 | 63

Democrats

218 | 4

Republicans

Senate

31 | 17

Democrats

47 | 3

Republicans

FIGURE 13.1   Party Unity and Disunity in the 2003 Congress.

Note: The figure shows the numbers of Democrats and Republicans in the Senate and House casting "yes" and "no" votes on the bills named. Rep. Bernard Sanders (I-Vermont) and Sen. James Jeffords (I-Vermont) are counted as Democrats because they caucus with the Democrats. *Source: CQ Weekly,* May 24, 2003, p. 1245 and May 31, 2003 p. 1342 (on taxes: conference report); Mar. 29, 2003, p. 783 (environment), and http://clerk.house.gov/cgi-bin/vote.exe?year=2003rollnumber=530 and http://www.senate.gov/legislative/LIS/roll_call_lists/roll_call_vote_cfm.cfm?congress=108session=1vote=004 02#top (on abortion: conference report) (accessed Oct. 21, 2003).

party leaders, made it easier for the Democratic leadership to unify its party and to fend off Republican appeals to more conservative Democrats.[34]

Conservative Democrats are still at least an occasional force in both the House and Senate, however; when the Democrats do split, it is the remaining conservative southerners who are the main source of disunity within the party. Even the highly unified Republicans struggle to deal with a small, mainly northeastern group of moderates within their ranks. The influence of these tiny minorities in both parties has been magnified by

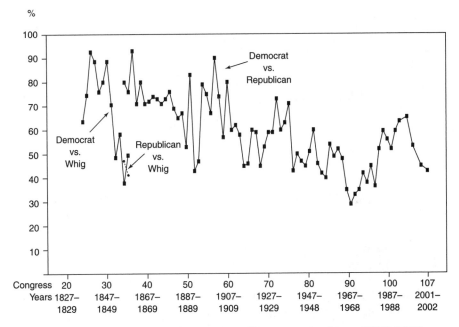

FIGURE 13.2   Party Voting in the House of Representatives: 1835–2002.

Note: Entries are the percentage of roll-call votes on which a majority of one party opposed a majority of the other party. Because party voting tends to decrease in the even-numbered years, as an election approaches, the data are averaged across the two sessions of each Congress. *Source:* For 24th through 36th Congresses, Thomas B. Alexander, *Sectional Stress and Party Strength* (Nashville, TN: Vanderbilt University Press, 1967). For 37th through 93rd Congresses, Jerome B. Chubb and Santa A. Traugott, "Partisan Cleavage and Cohesion in the House of Representatives, 1861–1974," *Journal of Interdisciplinary History* 7 (1977), 382–383. More recent data are from *CQ Weekly,* reported in December or early January issues.

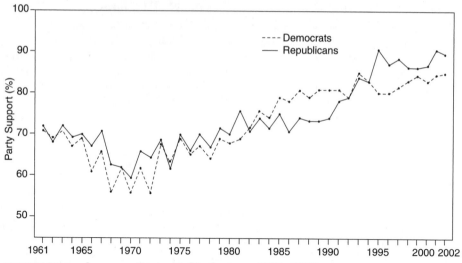

FIGURE 13.3   Average Party Unity Scores: 1961–2003.

Note: Entries are the average percentages of members voting in agreement with a majority of their party on party unity votes—those in which a majority of one party voted against a majority of the other party. Figures for the House and Senate are combined.

Source: CQ Weekly, Dec. 14, 2002, p. 3281.

the close party division in Congress, especially in the Senate. During Senate debate over President Bush's tax cut proposals, for example, two moderate Republicans, just enough to swing the close vote, were able to force a reduction in the size of the cut, from the $726 billion proposed by Bush to $350 billion, by threatening to vote against the bill if the cut was not made.

When Are the Parties Most Unified?

Students of Congress and state legislatures find that three types of issues are most likely to prompt high levels of party voting and party support: those touching the interests of the legislative party as a group, those involving support of or opposition to an executive program, and those concerning the issues that divide the party voters.

On Issues That Touch the Interests of the Legislative Parties   These are the issues that tend to produce the greatest party unity. Among the clearest examples are the basic votes to organize the legislative chamber. In Congress, for example, it is safe to predict 100 percent party unity on the vote to elect the Speaker of the House. In 2001, when the 107th Congress began, Republican Dennis Hastert got all the Republican votes for Speaker and only one Democratic vote (from a hopeful Rep. Traficant, prior to his move to a federal prison).

The parties also tend to be very unified on issues affecting their numerical strength. In a 1985 vote on whether to award a congressional seat to Democrat Frank McCloskey or Republican Richard McIntyre after a disputed Indiana election, for instance, House Democrats voted 236 to 10 to seat McCloskey and Republicans voted 180 to 0 for McIn-

THE DARK SIDE OF PARTISANSHIP: A LACK OF CIVILITY

With partisanship at a recent high in both the House and the Senate, it would not be surprising if the elaborate rituals of respect that characterized Congress decades ago had begun to fade. After some glimmers of bipartisan cooperation in 2001, particularly after the terrorist attacks of September 11, one observer had this to say about the events of one week in February 2002: "Capitol Hill is breaking down into fierce, partisan encampments . . . all thought of a bipartisan, working relationship in Congress has been wiped aside by bitter, incendiary language and incriminating gestures of contempt and disparagement.

"In short, it's back to business as usual."

Then things got worse. In July 2003, the House Ways and Means Committee met to discuss a lengthy bill to revise the pension system. Democratic committee members objected to Republican chair Bill Thomas's effort to substitute his own version of the bill for the bipartisan draft under consideration. After some taunting remarks by the chair, outraged Democrats left the room and gathered in a nearby library. The chair demanded that the Capitol Police remove the migrating Democrats. A police commander, reluctant to arrest House members for milling around in a library, declined to handcuff or evict them. Thomas later apologized on the House floor.

The incident was simply a more dramatic version of the heavy-handed use of majority power that has characterized the Congress in recent years, under both Republican and Democratic majorities.

Sources: David Rapp, "Editor's Notebook: The Comity Is Over," *CQ Weekly,* Feb. 9, 2002, p. 346; and Juliet Eilperin and Albert B. Crenshaw, "The House That Roared," *Washington Post,* July 19, 2003, p. A1.

---

tyre. Discipline runs high in state legislatures over issues such as laws regulating parties, elections, and campaigning; the seating of challenged members of the legislature; and the creation or alteration of legislative districts, all issues that touch the basic interests of the party as a political organization.

On the Executive's Proposals   Legislators often rally around their party's executive or unite against the executive of the other party, and in recent years, this partisanship has been increasing. Figure 13.4 traces the support that each legislative party has given to the president on issues that he clearly designated a part of his program. In the late 1960s, on average, members of a president's party in Congress voted for his program about 60 percent of the time; by the early 2000s, that support had increased dramatically to more than 85 percent. In fact, in 2002 Republicans in the Senate supported President Bush's program a remarkable 89 percent of the time, and their party colleagues in the House did so 82 percent of the time.

Conversely, the opposition party's support for a president's program has decreased steadily.[35] During the 1990s, the opposition supported the president's proposals only about one-third of the time, on average, although this support increased in the wake of the September 11 attacks. The Clinton presidency is an excellent example of this party

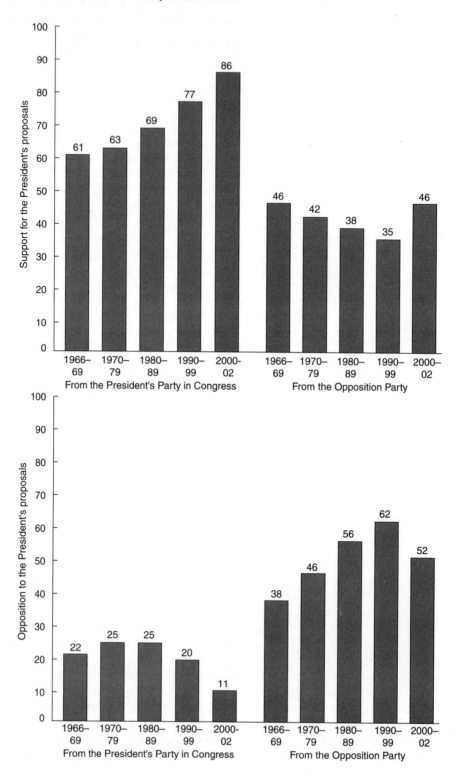

FIGURE 13.4   Party Support of the President in Congress: 1966–2002.

Note: Entries are the percentages of the time, averaged by decade, that members of each party supported the announced position of the president.

Source: CQ Almanac.

polarization. In the early years of Clinton's first term, Democrats' support for their president was higher than it had been since the mid-1960s and Republicans' support was relatively low. The president became an even more powerful partisan trigger in 1998, when Clinton was impeached by the House for lying about his sexual relationship with a White House intern. Sparked by strongly antagonistic congressional party leaders on both sides of the aisle, the House vote to impeach and the Senate vote to acquit Clinton were close to being party-line votes. As an expert observer puts it, "On what everyone claimed was a conscience vote, 98 percent of Republican consciences dictated a vote to impeach the president, while 98 percent of Democratic consciences dictated the opposite."[36] In 2000, Clinton's last year as president, there was a difference of almost 50 percentage points between Republicans' and Democrats' support of the president's position.

Media coverage often highlights cases when legislators go against a president of their party. Republican Senator John McCain's commitment to campaign finance reform, forged before he ran against George W. Bush for the presidential nomination in 2000, led him to press for a vote that his chief executive did not want on that issue, and we have seen that Senator James Jeffords left the Republican Party in 2001 after expressing his belief that Bush and his party were not paying attention to moderate Republican voices. But even though the legislative party's disloyalty to its president can be a major embarrassment to the president and a source of tension between the White House and Capitol Hill, it does not carry the threat of a new election or a new leader as it does in a parliamentary system.

On Policies Central to the Party System   Legislative parties are especially unified on issues that fundamentally divide the parties in the electorate—the "label-defining" issues.[37] At the time of the Civil War, the questions of slavery and Reconstruction generated the greatest party conflict and internal party cohesion. These issues were displaced by conflicts between agrarian and industrial interests in the realignment of 1896. Now, the parties are most cohesive on the issues of the welfare state—the role of government in the economy and in people's personal lives—that have dominated the party system since the 1930s.

In many state legislatures, for instance, an attempt to change the rules governing the hiring of teenagers by local businesses will pit one unified party against another, with the legislators' prolabor or promanagement stands reinforced by their roots in their home districts and by their own values. Other such issues include Social Security, welfare, environmental issues, the rights of women and minority groups, and aid to agriculture and other sectors of the economy. In Congress, a similar set of issues—social welfare, government management of the economy, and agricultural aid—has produced the most cohesive partisan voting over the years.[38]

Because these issue divisions are particularly sharp in the early years of a new party system, we might expect to see the greatest party cohesion at times when a realignment has reshaped the fault lines of American party politics.[39] The trend line in Figure 13.2 confirms that party voting in the House has generally peaked during party realignments. These realignments focus attention on national rather than local issues, so they overcome the inherent localism of Congress. Realignments promote party unity on the issues most central to the new party system and thereby permit a degree of party discipline that is unusual in American politics. The new majority party then has a chance to enact major policy changes.[40]

Does Party Competition Promote Party Unity?

The amount of competition between the two parties has an interesting relationship with party voting. At the level of the individual legislator, those from marginal districts, where the two parties have relatively equal shares of the electorate, are less likely to vote with their legislative party than are those from "safer" districts. Two characteristics of marginal districts encourage a legislator to be highly sensitive to the constituency at times when constituency opinion conflicts with the party's position on an issue. In many marginal districts, the groups that support Democrats or Republicans differ from those more typically associated with the party. And both parties in marginal districts often have strong organizations and appealing candidates. Where constituency and party point in different directions, most legislators remember that their constituents, not their party leadership, gave them their job.

At the level of the legislature as a whole, however, close party competition tends to increase party voting. When there are clear differences between the parties on issues, closely competitive parties feel the need to hold on to every legislative vote. In contrast, when a party dominates a legislative body, it can become flabby and vulnerable to squabbles among regional or personal cliques. That was true of many legislative parties in the South during the period of one-party Democratic rule. It is true today in state legislatures in which one party has a lopsided majority, such as the Republicans in the Idaho and Kansas state legislatures.[41]

WHEN CONSTITUENCY INTERFERES WITH PARTY UNITY

We have seen that forces within the constituency affect party voting and cohesion in Congress and state legislatures. When party voters in a district hold different views from the national or state party on a big issue, a representative will usually need to bend to constituency wishes in order to get reelected, even if that means opposing his or her legislative party's position. Party leaders often don't insist on the member's party loyalty in such situations; they would rather have a legislator who will at least vote for the party's candidate for Speaker than a totally loyal legislator who is defeated for reelection because his or her constituents do not want what the national party is selling. Racial issues have been good examples; U.S. House members during the late 1950s did not stray far from their constituents' preferences on civil rights, especially in the South where constituency pressures were intense.[42]

In the current Congress, small groups within both parties resist the influence of their legislative party leaders and cling to more moderate positions "because they are convinced that is what their constituents want."[43] Within the Democratic Party, a dominantly southern group of about 30 conservative House Democrats calling themselves the "Blue Dogs" often votes with the Republicans on tax and many social issues, a milder version of the old conservative coalition. On the Republican side, several moderates, many of them from the Northeast, often break with their party on environmental, fiscal, and social issues. As long as the American parties cannot protect legislators from constituency pressures and as long as what it means to be a Democrat in Alabama is not the same as what it means to be a Democrat in Alaska or New York, then party cohesion will suffer.

COMPARING PARTY POWER IN CONGRESS AND STATE LEGISLATURES

These constituency pressures exist within state legislatures too. Yet parties in some state legislatures are at least as disciplined and cohesive as the parties normally are in Congress. Based on what we know about the role of parties in the U.S. House and Senate and the state legislatures, we can draw some conclusions about the conditions most likely to produce strong legislative parties and the places where they are likely to appear.

Party Polarization   We have seen that legislators are more likely to accept strong party leadership if there are clear differences between the parties: if the two parties represent different sets of interests in the state. So legislative party strength has long flourished in northeastern states, such as Connecticut, New York, and New Jersey, where the two parties have quite different bases of support. The increasing party polarization at the national level has been associated with an increase in party strength in Congress as well, and especially in the House, whose rules permit greater control by the leadership.

Greater Interparty Competition   When the two parties in a legislature are relatively evenly balanced numerically, "the majority party must stick together to get legislation passed, and the minority party has some realistic chance of winning if it can remain cohesive."[44] Close party competition gives both parties an incentive to remain unified, as do situations in which a governor has been elected from the minority party, which sees the opportunity to pass the governor's program if it stays together. Party cohesion in the U.S. House and Senate has increased during recent years in which the two houses have been closely divided by party.

No Competing Centers of Power   The more independent a legislature's committees are, for example, when committee influence comes from seniority or some criterion other than party loyalty, the less they owe to parties and their priorities. In Congress, when seniority was the only criterion for becoming a committee chair, the chairs became centers of power independent of the legislative party leaders.

In the typical state, on the other hand, seniority is used much less often as a basis for appointing legislators to powerful positions. Party leaders are better able to appoint their party loyalists to committee chairs, so the committees usually operate as instruments of party power. In this way, Congress, since 1995, may be coming to resemble the patterns of power in many state legislatures or the Congress of the late nineteenth and early twentieth centuries.

Other Needed Resources   Where the party organizations have more to offer a legislator, he or she will be more inclined to follow the organization's lead in legislative voting. In the past, party leaders in the stronger state parties probably had an advantage over their congressional counterparts in affecting their members' behavior, but the advantage has likely been reduced.

Party leaders in many state legislatures control resources that are vital to their colleagues. Through their power over the legislative agenda, they can help a member get a desired bill passed. Pork barrel projects in the member's home district can be moved up or down on the agenda by legislative party leaders to help to maintain the loyalty of their party colleagues, as happens in Congress and in at least some parliamentary democracies.[45] In some states, these material rewards, which also include patronage and other forms of governmental preference, are more abundant than in the national government.

The party organizations outside the legislature can also influence legislative voting if they control important resources. Just as in Washington, the leaders of many state parties have become more active in recruiting candidates for the legislature, and some may be able to convince local activists and voters to oppose the renomination of candidates disloyal to the party (although that ability can always be undermined by primary elections). Further, it is not as rare in the states, as it is in Washington, where serving in Congress is a full-time job, for state and local party leaders to *be* legislative leaders as well.

State and local parties are also important to state legislative candidates because of the campaign money that the parties can provide. Many states place no ceilings on party contributions to campaigns, so parties can make substantial investments, if they wish, as they were able to do at the federal level through the use of soft money. The parties' legislative campaign committees help out in most states, and legislative party leaders' personal political action committees help in some.[46] Given the shortage of campaign funds at this level, many candidates look beyond the legislative campaign committees to the state parties themselves for campaign money and services. The state parties are better prepared to respond now than they have been in the past.

Lesser Legislative Professionalism   Congress has evolved into a highly professional legislative body. Each member controls a sizable and well-paid personal staff and a considerable budget, which are used to meet the member's legislative and reelection needs. Congress now meets almost continuously, and the office has become a full-time job with high pay (an annual salary of $154,700 in 2003) and good benefits.

State legislatures have become much more professional in recent years, but very few provide ordinary members with levels of support that even approach those in the Congress. Staff and budget resources are usually minimal. Most state legislators are lucky to have as much as a private office and a personal secretary. Many state legislatures meet for only part of the year and pay so little that most members must hold other jobs and live only temporarily in the capital. With such limited personal resources, state legislators in most states welcome additional help in performing the tasks of legislative life. Party leaders can often provide such help. When a state legislator depends on the party leadership for needed resources, he or she has a greater incentive to listen when a leader calls for party discipline.

Styles of Individual Leaders   Just as party leaders in the U.S. House and Senate have varied in their leadership styles and in their willingness to take up the tools of strong leadership, so do legislative party leaders in the states. Their experiences and abilities interact with the situation of their party, whether it is a powerful majority, a competitive minority, or a weakened minority, to determine whether they function effectively in uniting their party members and getting their bills passed.

LEGISLATIVE PARTIES: FIGHTING FOR POWER

The story that this chapter tells is complex. On the one hand, parties are at the very center of the legislative process. Some even view them as "legislative leviathans" that dominate the business of Congress in order to benefit their individual members.[47] Party affiliation does more to explain the legislative behavior of state legislators and Congress members than any other single factor in their environment. There has been an increase in party unity and polarization in recent years in both the U.S. House and Senate.

Yet even now, most American legislative parties are only moderately unified when compared with those of other nations. The legislative party leaders must compete with the efforts of big givers, single-issue groups, powerful state and local leaders, and, in some cases, committee chairs for the ability to organize legislative majorities. So although the legislative parties in Congress and the states have been strengthened, the primary relationship in American legislatures is between representatives and their constituents rather than between legislators and their party leaders or party organizations (see "Which Would You Choose?").

This is another instance in which the fragmenting institutions of American government have left their mark. Because of the separation of powers, there is no institutional need for a party to remain internally unified, as there is in parliamentary systems.[48] Under certain conditions, in particular, times when the party's legislative constituencies are more alike in their preferences and more different from those of the other party, the legislative parties will be more unified and party voting will be common. That has been strikingly true in the U.S. Congress and many state legislatures in recent years. However, at other times, when greater localism and sectionalism have existed, the legislative parties have been weak and fractured.[49]

Even at times when American legislative parties have been very cohesive, their unity is in support of *legislative* party policies to a greater extent than "party policy" more broadly; these policies are more likely to flow from the members' reelection needs than from the party's national platform. The reason is inherent in the nature of the American parties: the party in government has only limited ties to the party organization. The parties in Congress and the state legislatures are not controlled by—or always even in contact with—the party's national, state, or local party committees. The legislative parties control most of their own rewards and punishments in the form of party campaign help and legislative carrots and sticks. So when the legislative parties are able to muster some degree of discipline, it is usually on behalf of a set of proposals that originated in the executive or within the legislative party itself rather than in the party organization.

SHOULD YOUR SENATOR OR CONGRESS MEMBER LISTEN MORE CLOSELY TO THE PARTY OR TO THE CONSTITUENTS?

To the constituents: This sounds like a no-brainer. If we elect members of Congress, they ought to represent the interests of their constituents, right? We have a single-member district system with candidate-centered campaigns; that encourages us to focus on the qualities of individual candidates rather than on the party's platform or plans. We vote for a candidate, and he or she goes to Washington and is then supposed to do whatever we ask. Why should the legislator listen to the party leadership?

To their party: This constituent-centered approach sounds good, but it isn't realistic. How are members of Congress supposed to know what each of their 650,000 constituents wants? Isn't it better for the two major parties to offer competing answers on issues, press their legislative party colleagues to pass these policies, and then let voters decide whether they like the results? That asks less of us as voters and probably corresponds more to the (minimal) time that we are willing to spend on politics. Besides, by taking a longer view, the parties can look beyond local concerns to a broader national interest.

To both: As we have seen, when the various constituencies that a party's legislators represent become more similar in views and more different from the constituencies of the other party, then most legislators don't have to choose between constituents and party. At these times, members can vote with their party colleagues and also speak for the interests and the voters who, in their view, sent them to the legislature. So party and constituency are not necessarily in conflict.

CHAPTER 14

The Party in the Executive and the Courts

By December 7, 2000—a full month after Election Day—the United States still didn't know whom it had elected president. That decision would be made by the courts. First, the Florida Supreme Court, all of whose members had been appointed by Democratic governors, ruled in favor of Democratic candidate Al Gore, who had argued that a hand recount of ballots in Florida should be allowed to continue. However, the U.S. Supreme Court followed with a ruling that shut down the recount, thus handing the presidency to George W. Bush. All five of the Supreme Court justices who voted to support Bush, a Republican, had been appointed to their posts by Republican presidents.[1]

This looks suspiciously like partisan behavior—but how could that be, in high courts that most Americans prefer to see as nonpartisan? Could it have been a remarkable coincidence? Or is it time to set aside the notion that the courts are "above party politics?"

In fact, as we see in this chapter, American presidents, governors, and judges have been drawn into party politics since the nation's earliest years. Presidents and governors are often viewed as party leaders—and some have accepted the role with enthusiasm. Even though the writers of the Constitution designed an independent federal court system with lifetime appointments, hoping that it would be protected from the bruising battles of partisanship, it has never been possible to design judges who are free of party identification. The high-stakes conflicts today over the nomination of federal judges clearly show that the courts are at the center of heated partisan confrontations.

In many ways, partisanship has penetrated more deeply into the executive and judicial branches in the United States than it has in other Western democracies. As Chapter 2 showed, the push for popular democracy led to the election of public officials who would be appointed to their jobs in most other nations, such as state school superintendents, local judges, and even coroners. When judges and administrators are elected to office, the door is open to party influence in their elections. In addition, the extensive use of patronage in earlier years encouraged the use of party ties as a criterion for appointment to administrative offices. These tendencies have remained, even though reformers have tried to insulate judges and bureaucrats from partisan pressures.

What difference does it make if partisanship reaches into administrative agencies, courtrooms, and executive offices? If partisanship affects the selection of these office-holders, does it also influence the ways in which judges and administrators use their powers? Do Democratic voter registration officials make different decisions from their Republican brethren? If you go to court as a criminal defendant, will you get a different ruling from a Democratic judge than you would from a Republican? If so, does this result from efforts by party organizations to affect the behavior of executives and judges in order to promote the party's views? Or is it simply that people who consider themselves Democrats tend to share similar attitudes toward political issues, whether they are voters, county surveyors, or Supreme Court justices, and the same is true of those who identify as Republicans?

PRESIDENTS AND GOVERNORS AS PARTY LEADERS

American presidents were not always the dominant figures that they are today. In the 1920s, it was possible for President Calvin Coolidge to sleep for ten or eleven hours every night, followed by a three-hour afternoon nap; government and politics went on without him. But as the United States' role as a world power grew and Franklin D. Roosevelt expanded the federal government to bring the nation out of the Great Depression, presidents were pulled into the public spotlight.

The spread of television and radio into almost every American home further elevated the presidency. These media naturally focus on individual personalities such as presidents and governors; it is harder for the media to tell an interesting story about more faceless institutions such as Congress and the courts. Presidents, in particular, have become leading public figures, capable of arousing the most passionate loyalties and hatreds. This increase in personal leadership can be seen even in nations with parliamentary systems, whose election campaigns increasingly center on the potential prime ministers.[2]

As the most visible members of the party in government, presidents often come to personify their party at the national level, just as many governors do within their states. As a senior House Democratic aide commented about the national executive, "The president becomes the face of your party."[3] When presidents and governors are central to their party's public image, then their successes and failures can affect their party's fortunes in elections.

Presidents don't normally serve as formal party leaders, although they do choose the leadership and shape the functioning of their party's national committee. In recent years, however, several presidents have involved themselves extensively in party organizational efforts by helping to recruit party candidates, campaigning with them, and raising money for the party. These efforts have helped to strengthen the bond between presidents and the party colleagues in Congress for whom they campaign. Especially in the current polarized atmosphere in Washington and in many state capitals and when the party division in the legislature is close, executives have good reason to nurture their ties with their party's legislators in order to get the votes necessary to pass their policies.

The President as Campaigner-in-Chief

Recent presidents have invested a lot of energy in their party's campaign activities. Presidents are normally a big draw on the fund-raising circuit; George W. Bush, who has broken all campaign finance records in his own presidential races, has proven to be an unparalleled fund-raiser for the Republican Party. After headlining a record-breaking $33 million fund-raiser for the Republican National Committee in May of 2002, the president appeared at campaign events for a variety of Republican candidates.[4] In all, Bush was credited with raising $140 million for Republican House and Senate candidates in the 2002 elections.

Presidents can do a great deal more for their party organizations as well. They are, for example, persuasive recruiters of candidates. The state or national party organization often finds itself in the difficult position of trying to convince a reluctant but attractive prospect to run for office or to ask a House member to give up a safe seat in order to challenge a potentially vulnerable opposition senator. When the unwilling target of the party's affections is invited to dinner at the White House to hear how important the race is to the president of the United States, the party's job gets easier.

Take the example of the South Dakota Senate race in 2002. To have a chance of regaining control of the U.S. Senate, the national Republican Party needed a highly effective candidate to run against Democrat Tim Johnson. Party leaders set their sights on Republican John Thune, a popular House member. Thune had planned to run for governor that year, a race he was expected to win easily. After repeated conversations with Bush and top Republican strategists, Thune gave up the "easy" governor's race and ran against Johnson instead. (Thune lost this very close contest.)

The president remained deeply involved in recruiting Republican candidates for the 2004 elections. One such prospect, former North Dakota Governor Ed Schafer, was invited to a White House briefing in 2002; after he told Bush that he was reluctant to run, the president reportedly responded, "That's fine, but your country needs you. . . . .Don't make a decision about this until we get a chance to sit down and talk about it." A Republican official explained, "Clearly, any White House wants to make sure there are senators elected who share the president's priorities."[5]

White House leverage is also useful in clearing a path for the party's preferred nominees. In 2001, for instance, Vice President Dick Cheney persuaded a Minnesota Republican to give up a bid for the state's 2002 Senate nomination—just 90 minutes prior to the scheduled press conference at which he was to announce his candidacy—to clear the way for a candidate the party regarded as stronger. "I was de-cruited," explained the suddenly retired candidate.[6] In other cases, a Bush fund-raiser was scheduled more than a year before the election to give the Republican favored by the White House an early fundraising lead and thus to scare off potential opponents.

In the 2002 congressional campaigns, with party control of the Senate on the line, the president took frequent trips to states where Republican House and Senate candidates were in highly competitive campaigns. During the week before the election, he visited up to five states a day to increase Republican turnout. One was Georgia, where Rep. Saxby Chambliss was running behind incumbent Democratic Senator Max Cleland in the polls. Chambliss, who had been recruited to run by the White House, asked for Bush's help; "There's only one guy who can juice" potential Republican voters, said Chambliss' aide.[7] Three days later, Chambliss upset Cleland.

The President as the "Top of the Ticket"

Even when the president doesn't actively campaign for other candidates, presidents' successes and failures in office, and those of governors as well, affect the electoral fates of other candidates of their party. For example, Ronald Reagan's victory in 1980 and landslide reelection in 1984 were accompanied by higher than normal levels of success for other Republican candidates. Republicans gained control of the Senate in 1980 for the first time since the 1952 election, and Republican House candidates won a higher percentage of the votes cast in 1980 and 1984 than in the preceding and following midterm elections, when Reagan was not on the ballot.

Coattail Effects   This link between presidential success and party victories is traditionally explained by the metaphor of *coattails*. Presidents ran "at the top of the ticket," the explanation goes, and the rest of the party ticket came into office clinging to their sturdy coattails. (Nineteenth-century dress coats did have tails.) This coattail effect was very common in the nineteenth century when the parties printed their own ballots, so a voter was limited to casting a ballot for an entire party ticket.

Coattail effects have declined since World War II.[8] Members of Congress have gotten extremely good at cultivating their constituency by attending closely to its interests and providing services to individual constituents; this helps to insulate them from outside electoral forces, including the president's popularity.[9] Incumbents have also gained impressive advantages over their challengers in fund-raising and other campaign resources, especially in House races.

Nevertheless, presidents can develop coattails in particular races even now.[10] At times, presidential coattails have extended beyond House races to some Senate elections, in spite of the high visibility of most Senate candidates. Coattail effects can even reach into nonfederal races; from 1944 through 1984, when a president ran strongly in a state, the president's party typically did better in state legislative contests on the same ballot.[11] As a result, many states decided to move their state legislative elections to years when the presidency was not on the ballot to insulate state elections from presidential politics.

Coattails Even Without the Coat   In fact, presidential leadership is so prominent in voters' eyes that a president can sometimes influence election results for other contests even when he is not on the ballot. During the period leading up to a midterm congressional election and in the midterm elections themselves, voters' approval of the president's job performance is closely related to their support for candidates of the president's party.[12] Drops in President Clinton's approval rating at the time of the 1994 midterm election coincided with big Democratic losses in the House and Senate. Clinton's public approval was on the upswing in time for the 1998 congressional elections, and Democratic congressional candidates reaped some of the benefit.

Most often, however, presidents' public approval has dropped by the midpoint of their terms and analysts find that the president's party has almost always suffered a decline in its share of House seats in the next midterm election.[13] It may be that the president's declining popularity has dragged down congressional candidates of his party; there is evidence that citizens who disapprove of the president's performance vote in larger numbers in midterm elections than those who approve and that their disapproval leads them to vote for the other party's candidates.[14] It may be that voters have learned more since the presidential election about the capabilities or policies of the president's party.[15] Or it may suggest that, just as an initially popular presidential candidate can boost the chances of his party's candidates in the presidential year, his absence from the ticket may deprive them of this advantage at midterm.

This pattern of midterm losses by the president's party didn't hold in the 1998 and 2002 elections. Just as the Democrats gained seats in 1998 during President Clinton's second term, Republicans expanded their House majority and won a slim Senate majority in 2002. In both cases, voters' approval of the president was either holding steady or increasing. Although President Bush had begun his first term with fairly low approval ratings, his popularity soared to almost 90 percent after the September 11 terrorist attacks. His approval ratings remained consistently above 60 percent as the 2002 election approached. Observers reported that his 90 percent approval among Republicans, in particular, made a difference in close campaigns.[16]

A Broader Perspective on Electoral Influence   In short, there are several ways in which a president is the electoral leader of his party. Presidential coattails vary in strength, but at least some voters seem to be influenced by the president's performance when they cast ballots for other offices. That happens especially if the candidates emphasize their connection with the president in their advertising and if the president campaigns actively for them, as was the case in 2002. So candidates for other offices take the president's approval ratings into account as they plan their campaigns.[17]

Even if the president's popularity accounted for only small percentage shifts in the congressional vote, these small shifts can make a big difference in party strength in Congress. From 1952 to 1970, each shift of 1 percent in the popular vote added or subtracted about eight seats in the House of Representatives.[18] House seats have become less responsive to popular vote changes since then, but the close competition between Democrats and Republicans in both the House and Senate means that even a small change in seats can have a big impact on legislation.

Limits on Presidential Leadership

The bond between presidents and their party, however, is not always close. Some presidents and governors have preferred to remain "above" party politics and to keep their distance from their party organization and its people. President Jimmy Carter was a good example; he ran for office in 1976 as a political outsider and was repaid by a marked lack of cooperation from Democrats in Congress. Even those who are comfortable with a party leadership role find that the inevitable differences in perspective between the executive and the legislative branches can strain party ties.

Nevertheless, presidents usually dominate their party in government, just as most governors do in their state parties.[19] An especially attractive president can add luster to a party's public image for years by making a big positive impression on young adults who are just entering the electorate, as Ronald Reagan seems to have done for the Republican Party. No other leader can compete with presidents and governors in representing the party to the public, in commanding a broad range of tools of influence or in enjoying as much legitimacy as the center of party leadership. What, then, do presidents do with their leadership of the party in government?

PARTY LEADERSHIP AND LEGISLATIVE RELATIONS

Presidents aim to get their programs passed by Congress. To do so, they often draw on the capital they can generate as leader of the party in government: their command of the media, the coattails that they may have provided, and whatever public approval they may have at the time. They appeal to their shared party ties with members of their party in the House and Senate. They refer to whatever lingering patronage or preferments that they can command (a judicial appointment here, a government project there). Members of the president's party know that if they make him look bad, they might also make themselves and their party look bad; that can encourage them to rally around the president on important votes, even if they would prefer to vote differently.

Legislative Support for Executives

Popular support is a valuable resource for the chief executive in getting Congress to go along with his programs. Bush's public popularity after September 11 helped him to gain considerable success on the Hill, just as President Clinton's unpopularity in 1993 made it harder for him to steer health care reform through a Democratic Congress.

Even when a president is riding high in public opinion, however, there are times when Congress can be stubbornly resistant to presidential leadership. As Figure 14.1 shows, presidential success rates have dropped a bit during the past five decades, through the administration of Bill Clinton. The weakening of presidential coattails during that time probably helped to dilute presidents' influence in Congress. Recent presidents have not always been able to win congressional approval of their proposals even in years when their party controlled both houses of Congress. President Carter had only about a 75 percent success rate with a Democratic Congress, and President Clinton scored only about 10 percent higher during his first two years in office, when Democrats held majorities in both the House and Senate.

President Bush has been an exception to this pattern. He matched Clinton's high initial levels of success with Congress even after Democrats regained control of the Senate in mid-2001. In addition to the impact of the September 11 attacks, the Bush administration's legislative strategy also helped to increase the president's success rate in Congress. Bush focused on a fairly short list of legislative proposals, modified them when necessary, and then endorsed what he felt Congress was likely to approve, which of course increased his success rate. He also benefited from the remarkable party unity among congressional Republicans (see Chapter 13).

However, within two months of the start of a unified government in 2003—with Republicans in control of the House and Senate as well as the White House—the more customary strains between presidents and Congress were surfacing. Some congressional Republicans made it clear that they didn't like the big increase in the federal budget deficit accepted by the Bush administration in its effort to cut taxes. Others were nervous about the president's intention to restructure Medicare, a vital concern of senior citizens. As we saw in the Introduction to Part V, although President Bush was stunningly successful in getting Congress to pass two enormous tax cuts and many other bills, he was turned down cold by the House Republican Majority Leader on a bill involving child tax credits. Even with high public approval and party majorities in both houses, presidents cannot coast to legislative success.

Divided Control of Government   Presidents get much less support, of course, when Congress is in the hands of the opposing party. Unhappily for modern presidents, divided government has been the rule, not the exception, in the past three decades. During the same period, almost all of the states have also experienced

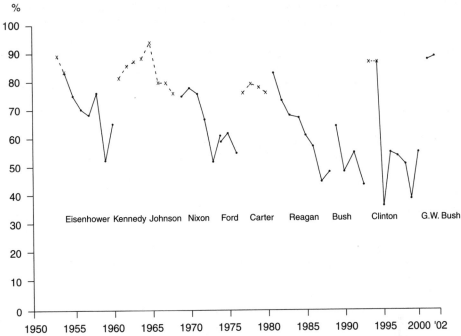

FIGURE 14.1   Presidential Success in the U.S. Congress: 1953–2002.

Note: The entry for each year is the percentage of time members of both the House and the Senate voted in support of the announced position of the president. Years in which the president's party controlled both houses of Congress are indicated by an "x" and connected by dotted lines. Years in which the opposition party controlled at least one house of Congress are indicated by a "." and connected by solid lines.

Source: CQ Weekly, Dec. 31, 1994, 3654, and, for 1995–2002, other end-of-the-year CQ Weekly issues.

divided party control of the legislature and the governorship. (The next chapter has more to say about divided government.)

In times of divided government, it can be risky for presidents and governors to rely heavily on partisan appeals. Because of the close party division in many legislatures and the unreliability of some legislators of their own party, executives must also curry favor with some legislators in the opposing party. That requires them to walk a fine line, using partisan appeals to legislators of their own party and nonpartisan, or bipartisan, appeals to those in the opposition. There are times when especially effective presidential leadership can get even a Congress controlled by the other party to go along with what he wants. Bill Clinton deftly used the veto and threats of the veto to get the Republican Congress to accept many of his initiatives after 1995,[20] and we have seen Bush's success rate with a divided Congress in 2001–2002. However, American presidents have never been able to gain as much support in Congress as prime ministers naturally enjoy in parliamentary systems.

Governors, on the other hand, can often exercise greater party organizational power over the legislators of their party. In the many state legislatures that do not use seniority rules, governors can take an active part in selecting committee chairs and party floor leaders when the legislative session begins. A few governors lead powerful state party organizations; legislators who cross them may risk undermining their legislative career as well as their ambitions for higher office. In short, the average governor has greater control over party rewards and incentives than a president does. On the other hand, governors are not as visible as presidents, so their coattails and prestige are normally less influential than those of presidents.

PARTY INFLUENCE IN EXECUTIVE AGENCIES

The president is the tip of an iceberg. Below the surface, huge and powerful, lies the rest of the executive branch. The bureaucrats who work there in cabinet-level departments such as Defense and Transportation and in other agencies such as the Environmental Protection Agency (EPA) are charged by the Constitution with carrying out the laws Congress passes. In spite of a burst of deregulation in the 1980s and 1990s, these executive agencies still regulate vast areas of the economy, food safety, prescription drugs, and pollution, for example, under congressional mandates that require a lot of interpretation. The bureaucrats who implement these laws, therefore, must make important decisions on public policy; they shape policy by applying it. It is they, for example, who determine whether the beef that you ate last week was inspected for disease and whether your next car will need side air bags. Because of their power, we need to ask whether presidents and governors are able to hold these administrators responsible for implementing a party program—or any program at all.

Bureaucrats Have Constituents Too

Perhaps the biggest problem executives face in enforcing party discipline on their subordinates is the same problem faced by legislative party leaders: constituency pressure. Just as individual legislators try to meet the needs of their constituents, administrators deal with demands from a variety of groups. Top-level administrators know that their best political protection is the support of their client groups. The EPA, for instance, works very closely with the industries that it regulates as well as a variety of professional and citizen groups. If its rulings in applying the Clean Air Act enrage automobile manufacturers and oil companies or if they outrage big environmental groups, the EPA will be in the political hot seat. Party loyalties do not compete very well with the power of these constituencies; in the executive as well as the legislative branch, the party has less to give and less to take away than the constituency does.[21]

Many other factors limit an executive's ability to unify an administration and hold it accountable for achieving a party's policy goals. Several of these limits were put in place by Progressive reforms aimed at crippling party power:

- Legislatures can protect top-level bureaucrats from presidential influence (and, through the president, party influence) by giving them terms of office longer than that of the president, by limiting the president's (or governor's) power to remove them, or by requiring that they be chosen through a merit system rather than a political appointment process.

- Legislatures can prevent party control of an administrative agency by requiring that its leadership include members of both parties. The Federal Election Commission board, for example, must be composed of three Democrats and three Republicans—and at least *four* board members must agree to investigate any suspected campaign finance abuse. (This, of course, is as much a guarantee of inactivity as it is of bipartisanship.)

- Top administrators in many states are elected. So voters may choose, say, a Republican for governor and a Democrat for state treasurer to work together in an uneasy alliance. Even if both officials are of the same party, their offices are often politically and constitutionally independent.

- Most American executives are term limited; presidents can run for only two terms and most governors can serve only one or two consecutive terms. As the end of their term approaches, their authority over other officeholders lessens.

- Finally, executives must often share power with others. The practice of senatorial courtesy gives the U.S. Senate a say in presidential appointments.

Holding Bureaucrats Accountable

Some high-level administrators are easier to hold responsible for promoting a party program than others. The people appointed to head cabinet departments—the biggest and best-known parts of the executive branch, such as State, Health and Human Services, and Defense—have often had a long history of party activity, so they are likely to feel some degree of commitment to the party's goals and programs. All but one of President Bush's cabinet appointees in 2001 had been active in Republican Party politics: a Republican state party chair, the wife of a Republican House member, a former director of the National Republican Senatorial Committee, two Republican governors, two other Republican elected officials, four political appointees in previous Republican administrations—and, as the lone exception, a Democratic House member.

So party remains a source of talent for modern administrations. Presidents are no longer as explicitly partisan as they once were in making cabinet appointments; they no longer use these positions as rewards for loyal *party* service. Instead, they look for individuals with experience in the areas of policy that they will administer and loyalty to the president's *own* aims. Nevertheless, most presidential appointees have been active partisans whose values and political careers have been shaped to a significant degree by their party.

Just below this top level, however, appointees are less likely to have party and governmental experience. These officials are most often chosen for their administrative skills and experience and only secondarily for their political credentials. The party organization's role in their selection may extend only to verifying that they are politically acceptable (that is, not offensive) in their home states. Yet they continue to come largely from the party of the president, and the party link can produce a commitment to a common outlook.

Modern presidents can make only about 3,500 political appointments, however—fewer appointed positions than some governors have—to try to gain control of an executive branch employing several million civilian employees. Many of these appointees are novices with little time to "learn the ropes" and little hope of gaining the necessary support of career bureaucrats. As Hugh Heclo has shown, together they comprise "a government of strangers": a set of executives whose limited familiarity and interaction with one another keep them from acting as an effective team and who are therefore likely to be overwhelmed by a huge, fragmented, and more or less permanent bureaucracy.[22]

It is a difficult task, then, to establish political control over the executive bureaucracy, especially at the national level.[23] Not surprisingly, recent presidents, and especially Republican presidents, have relied more and more on their immediate White House staff and the Office of Management and Budget when they try to mobilize the executive branch to achieve their policy goals.[24] Party can help in organizing an administration, serving as a recruitment channel for executive talent and a common bond between the executive and top bureaucrats, but it does not have the power to hold the executive branch responsible for carrying out a party program.

Changing Political Outlooks in the Federal Bureaucracy

Even though the executive's party is not able to enforce party discipline, the federal bureaucracy (and many state bureaucracies) does show some responsiveness to partisan forces over the long run. As the federal government expanded in the 1930s, President Roosevelt drew people into the career bureaucracy who were committed to his programs. They then became a bulwark against later efforts to weaken these programs, especially as these dedicated New Dealers were promoted to more and more senior positions in their agencies.

This pro-Democratic slant could still be seen in the federal bureaucracy decades later. By 1970, Joel Aberbach and Bert Rockman found that nearly a majority of these career bureaucrats said that they normally voted Democratic and only 17 percent usually voted Republican. In federal social service agencies, even the administrators who were not Democrats said that they favored liberal policies. So Republican President Richard Nixon, in office at that time, faced a federal bureaucracy that had little sympathy for his conservative agenda. His administration spent a lot of time trying to control the bureaucracy by appointing Nixon loyalists to top bureaucratic positions.[25]

By 1992, however, the bureaucratic environment had changed. In the intervening two decades, Republicans had held the White House for all but four years. When Aberbach and Rockman returned to interview career administrators in comparable positions to those they interviewed in 1970, they now found slight Republican pluralities, although the career executives were still much more Democratic and liberal than the Reagan and Bush political appointees. As older civil servants retired, a new generation, less committed to New Deal and Great Society programs, had been recruited into senior executive positions. Changes in civil service laws further allowed positions formerly reserved for career employees to be filled by political appointees who could be carefully screened by the White House. The bureaucracy was no longer as unsympathetic to Republican initiatives, but the inherent difficulties of controlling even a sympathetic bureaucracy remained.[26]

In sum, although there is party influence in the executive branch, most presidents and governors use their party leadership role to promote their own programs and their own reelection, not the programs of their party. To the extent that the executive's goals are similar to those of their party, of course, the party's program benefits. Many governors do use some patronage appointments purely to boost their state party, and presidents may use some cabinet appointments to recognize various groups within their party. For most American executives, however, the goals and interests of their party organization are secondary to their own policy goals and political careers.

TRACES OF PARTY IN THE COURTS

Courts and judges are affected by party politics as well. Most American judges—even most Justices of the U.S. Supreme Court—are political men and women who took office after careers that involved them in some aspect of partisan politics (see the box below). Although reformers have tried to insulate the judicial system from party politics, the selection of judges continues to be shaped by partisanship in elections and through appointments. Because of the nature of the judiciary, however, the influence can be subtle.

THE PARTISAN BACKGROUNDS OF U.S. SUPREME COURT JUSTICES

Justices Appointed by Republican Presidents

William H. Rehnquist (Chief Justice, appointed by President Nixon) was a Republican Party official in Phoenix. He was later appointed Assistant Attorney General in the Republican administration of President Nixon.

John Paul Stevens (Ford) is a registered Republican, although he was never active in Republican Party politics.

Sandra Day O'Connor (Reagan) was a Republican Party committeewoman and legislative district chair in Phoenix. She served two full terms as a Republican state senator in Arizona and became Republican Majority Leader in the State Senate.

Antonin Scalia (Reagan) was named General Counsel for the Office of Telecommunications Policy in the Republican Nixon administration and then Assistant Attorney General under Republican Gerald Ford.

Anthony Kennedy (Reagan) was a Republican activist and campaign donor in California and then became a legal adviser to Reagan as governor.

David H. Souter (G. H. W. Bush) was never active in party politics but was appointed Deputy Attorney General and then Attorney General in New Hampshire, in both cases by Republican governors.

Clarence Thomas (G. H. W. Bush) served on the staff of Missouri's Republican Attorney General and as Assistant Secretary for Civil Rights and Director of the Equal Employment Opportunity Commission in the Republican Reagan administration. Thomas's wife is a senior aide to the House Republican Majority Leader.

Justices Appointed by a Democratic President

Ruth Bader Ginsburg (Clinton) had no formal party positions or appointments prior to her nomination to the Court.

Stephen G. Breyer (Clinton) was a special assistant to the Assistant Attorney General under Democratic President Lyndon Johnson, assistant special prosecutor in the Watergate investigation, and Special Counsel and then Chief Counsel to the Democratic-led Senate Judiciary Committee.

Judicial Voting Along Party Lines

Hints of party influence appear when we examine the voting in American appellate courts. Several studies show that judges split into partisan blocs on several types of cases. Judges appointed by Democratic presidents tend to be more liberal than those appointed by Republican presidents on issues such as civil liberties, labor issues, and regulation.[27] In a study of state and federal courts, in comparison with Republican judges, Democratic judges were found to decide more often in favor of the defendant in criminal cases, for the government in tax cases, for the regulatory agency in cases involving the regulation of business, and for the claimants in workers' compensation, unemployment compensation, and auto accident cases.[28] These are the kinds of differences that we might expect to find when comparing the views of Democratic and Republican activists outside the courtroom.

Similarly, in recent redistricting cases, U.S. District Court judges have tended to uphold plans enacted by their party more than those enacted by the opposing party.[29] That was often the case in 2001 when state legislatures deadlocked over redistricting plans, which were then kicked to the courts. Judges show much less party cohesion than members of legislatures do, and it appears only in certain types of cases. Yet it does appear; Democratic judges rule differently under some circumstances than their Republican colleagues.

What Causes Partisan Behavior on the Courts?

Very little of this apparent partisanship is due to active efforts by Democratic and Republican Party leaders to influence court decisions. It does happen occasionally, for example, in the case of a local judge who continues to be deeply involved in party politics even after being appointed to the bench. A judge who is closely tied to the local party may provide some patronage for the party organization through guardianships, receiverships in bankruptcy, and clerkships that can be given to party loyalists who are attorneys. In most areas, however, openly partisan activity by a judge or pressure by a party leader to decide a case in a certain way would now be seen as violating the norms of the court system.

A much better explanation for the impact of party on judges' behavior is simply that judges, like most other well-educated people, hold party identifications and bring these partisan frames of reference to their work on the court. Just as the two parties reflect different sets of values, so do their identifiers, including those who become judges. Two judges might vote together on the issue of regulating business because of the values that they share about the proper role of government in the economy. Those values may have led them to join the same party years earlier or were developed out of experience in that party. In other words, it is not usually the external pressure from a party organization or leader but rather the party *in* the judge that leads judges with similar partisan backgrounds to make similar decisions. (See "A Day in the Life," on page 277.)

Those who appoint judges to their positions are well aware of the importance of judges' value systems. They know that judges often have discretion in deciding cases and that the choices that they make may reflect, at least in part, their own experiences and beliefs. So the selection of judges, especially for the higher courts that receive the most challenging cases, has traditionally taken into account the values and attitudes of the possible nominees.

CAN PARTISAN ELECTIONS PRODUCE IMPARTIAL JUDGES?

"Many of us joked that we went to law school because we watched 'Perry Mason' on TV when we were children," says Circuit Court Judge E. Michael Hoff. "The role of a lawyer was an attractive role; I wanted to be a lawyer for a long time. But I had never thought about becoming a judge.

"While I was practicing law, I served occasionally as a judge pro tem—a kind of 'substitute judge' in cases where the juvenile court magistrate had previously been involved as a deputy prosecutor and so had to recuse herself. That got me interested in the process.

"I was also involved at that time as an active member of the local Democratic Party. I worked in several elections as an election official, went to candidates' fund-raising events, and served as a volunteer attorney for the party, in one instance representing a candidate in a recount. I knew a lot of people who were local officials. Then a friend who was also active in the local party told me that a group of people was trying to recruit candidates and asked if I'd consider running for judge. The occupant of the judgeship had retired. So the party was essential in my selection.

"Beginning in February, I started campaigning door-to-door, talking to people who were likely voters in the Democratic primary. Running for office is an exciting experience, but not an easy one. It's very hard to go up to a group of people and start introducing yourself; it didn't come naturally to me. But I went knocking on doors almost every day after work until it got dark, and I won the primary in May and then beat a very good Republican candidate in November.

"Does my political affiliation affect me on the bench? On one hand, a lot of the decisions you have to make as a judge don't have much to do with partisan matters: for example, when you decide where a child ought to be placed or how to interpret a contract. On the other hand, judges do have a lot of discretion in many of the decisions they make. Someone's personal philosophy will inevitably influence him or her in exercising this discretion—for instance, in cases where you have to decide: should I enforce this lease and evict a tenant in mid-January? Decisions on sentencing criminals can certainly be related to someone's philosophy. This is not, however, the same thing as a judge making a certain decision *because* the judge is a Democrat, or a Republican, or a Libertarian. Any good judge would avoid that like poison, and the judges I know care about their jobs and want to do them well.

"Should judges be elected to office? I think they definitely should. I don't see any reason why judges shouldn't be elected by the people they serve. Supreme Court and appeals judges are different; I can see the logic in having commissions appoint them. For other judges, however, although I believe that they should be elected, I can see the argument for electing them on nonpartisan ballots. It's a little strange to require that judges run on partisan ballots and run along with other people who have to make strictly political decisions, and then ask judges to behave on the bench in a completely nonpartisan manner."

Party Considerations in Judicial Appointments

Parties can affect the selection of judges in several ways. In many states, party organizations have the opportunity to recommend or at least to advise on the nominations of prospective judges. That gives them a means to advance party goals by encouraging the appointment or election of judges who believe in the party's values. It also permits them to further the careers of lawyers who have served the party loyally. Even when party organizations don't have that opportunity, the nomination of judges by a governor or a president permits the influence of the party in government on judicial appointments.

Federal Judges   Presidents nominate candidates for federal judgeships; the Senate has the right to confirm or deny them. Because prospective judges' party and ideology are important indicators of their attitudes and, thus, can affect their decisions in some kinds of cases, every American president during the twentieth century has made at least 80 percent of his judicial appointments from within his own party (see Table 14.1). The average is higher than 90 percent.

The Reagan and first Bush administrations took special care to screen candidates for their dedication to conservative principles. In fact, since 1980 the Republican platform has pledged to nominate only prospective judges who believe in the sanctity of human life—in other words, those who oppose abortion. These administrations modified the tradition of allowing the presidential party's senators to select candidates for district and appellate judgeships; senators were asked to submit three names for consideration and the administration made the final choice.[30]

As a result, Reagan and Bush appointees were even more ideologically distinctive (as well as more likely to have been active in party politics) than average among recent presidents. By contrast, the Clinton administration gave a larger role to Democratic senators and other party leaders in suggesting judicial nominees and was less concerned with

TABLE 14.1 Partisan Appointments to Federal District and Appellate Courts: Presidents Grover Cleveland to George W. Bush

	Percentage from the President's Party		Percentage from the President's Party
Cleveland	97.3	Eisenhower	95.1
Harrison	87.9	Kennedy	90.9
McKinley	95.7	Johnson	94.5
T. Roosevelt	95.8	Nixon	92.8
Taft	82.2	Ford	81.2
Wilson	98.6	Carter	88.8
Harding	97.7	Reagan	92.7
Coolidge	94.1	G. H. W. Bush	88.6
Hoover	85.7	Clinton	87.1
F. Roosevelt	96.4	G. W. Bush	82.8
Truman	93.1		

Source: Harold W. Stanley and Richard G. Niemi, *Vital Statistics on American Politics 1999–2000* (Washington, DC: CQ Press, 2000), Table 7.6, p. 278; and Sheldon Goldman, Elliot Slotnick, Gerard Gryski, and Gary Zuk, "Clinton's Judges: Summing Up the Legacy," *Judicature* 84 (2001), pp. 244 and 249. Data for the Bush administration were kindly provided by Sheldon Goldman.

ideological screening. Clinton also appointed a slightly lower percentage of federal judges from his own party than most of his predecessors did and was less inclined to choose judges with records of party activity.[31]

Senate action on the president's nominations to federal judgeships has become increasingly partisan during the past two decades. The first shots were fired in the 1980s and early 1990s, when Senate Democrats and their allies waged major battles over the confirmation of two conservative nominees to the Supreme Court: Robert Bork and Clarence Thomas. (In fact, the former case gave rise to a new verb: when an intense, usually partisan campaign has been mustered against a nominee, he or she is said to have been "Borked.") By the end of the Clinton administration, the level of partisan animosity over judicial appointments was so high that Republican Senate leaders were refusing to schedule debate on some of the president's nominees. In one especially dramatic case, Clinton nominated an African-American lawyer to the Fourth Circuit Court of Appeals, regarded as the most conservative circuit court in the nation. To avoid the threat that the Senate would stall the nomination indefinitely, Clinton appointed his nominee while the Senate was not in session.[32]

Examples of bare-knuckles partisanship continued in 2001, when the situation was reversed and the Senate's Democratic leaders sat on the judicial nominations of the Republican president.[33] The atmosphere surrounding judicial appointments became more and more acrimonious as the parties came to see the battles over the nomination of federal judges as a way to mobilize their core support in the electorate.[34] President Bush was forced to withdraw some nominations of federal judges when Senate Democrats filibustered. In one case, a conservative group ran newspaper ads accusing opponents of an appeals court nominee of displaying anti-Catholic bias, which led a senator to charge that "something very ugly has been injected" into the judicial confirmation process.[35]

State Court Judges State court judges are selected in a very different manner. Methods of selection can vary even within a single state. In sixteen states, candidates for at least some types of judgeships must run in partisan elections. At times, however, both parties will endorse the same candidate, who is often the choice of the state bar association. Twenty states try to take partisanship out of the selection process by electing at least some of their judges on a nonpartisan ballot. (In some of these states, it is common for each party to endorse its own slate of candidates publicly, so the "nonpartisanship" is a sham.) In eleven states, at least some judges are appointed to their posts, either by the governor or the state legislature. Nineteen states use the merit, or "Missouri," plan for some courts, in which judges are first selected (usually by the governor) from a list compiled by a nonpartisan screening committee and then must run in a retention election within several years of their appointment.[36]

Most of these alternatives leave room for partisan influence. Even when the voters do the choosing, in practice many of the candidates will be incumbents who were appointed to their posts by a partisan official. Judicial terms tend to be long, often as long as ten years. Those elected to them are typically middle aged or older. When an elected judge leaves the bench because of death or illness, the governor normally fills the vacancy until the next election, in which the appointee, with the advantage of even a brief period of incumbency, usually wins a full term. Of course, the security of a long term and a high probability of reelection can free judges from party pressures. But these pressures are so often already internalized in the judge's values that a long-term judgeship merely allows them to flourish.[37]

So the selection process is one reason why we see party differences in judges' rulings. Another major reason is that in the American system, there is no special training process for judges—no exam to take, no advanced degree in "judgeship." Any lawyer can be a judge if he or she can win the election or appointment to the job. In many European countries, on the other hand, someone prepares to be a judge through study, apprenticeship, and then by scoring well on a special exam. That makes it much harder for party organizations to influence the selection of judges. Even so, those who become judges will still have political preferences, many of which will have been shaped by their party identification and their earlier partisan experiences.

THE PARTY WITHIN THE EXECUTIVE AND THE JUDGE

When we talk about party influence on executives and judges, then, the best explanation for this influence is that executives and judges are people who hold political beliefs, and those beliefs tend to differ according to the individual's party affiliation. Democrats tend to hold different views about government and the economy than Republicans do, and Democratic judges and bureaucrats, similarly, hold different views from Republican judges and bureaucrats. These party differences are reinforced by partisan elements in the process by which presidents and governors, top executive officials, and most judges are chosen. However, we rarely see much evidence of direct influence by the party organization on bureaucrats and courts; the parties don't have the means to enforce party discipline in the executive or judicial branches.

Efforts have been made, including the use of the merit system to appoint officials, to wring partisan considerations out of the selection process. There is good reason to do so. When judgeships are elected, candidates can receive campaign money from private interests, just as other candidates can. In elections from 1994 to 1998, as one example, judges who won seats on the Texas Supreme Court raised about $11 million in campaign contributions; more than one-third of the money came from corporate law firms, many of whom try cases before that court.[38] When people suspect that partisan forces are active, as some inevitably believed about the case that opened this chapter, public confidence in courts and administrative agencies can be undermined. However, there is no way to eliminate individuals' beliefs and values, including their partisanship, from their selection as administrators or judges or from their behavior in administrative agencies and in court.

CHAPTER 15

What the Parties Stand For

Political parties play so central a role in Germany that its political system is described as a "party-based democracy."[1] British parties have been called "the heart of the political system," with the ability to enact most or all of their preferred policies when they are in the majority.[2] In Australia, "the hallmark of Australian politics is the dominance of party."[3]

And in the United States? Well . . .

It's a puzzle. On the one hand, in earlier chapters, we've seen evidence of renewed party activity at all levels, from higher levels of party voting in Congress to state party effort at recruiting candidates and raising money. Even when party leaders and organizations are nowhere to be seen, large numbers of voters rely on party labels when choosing among a series of unfamiliar names on the ballot, and judges' and bureaucrats' decisions often reflect their partisan backgrounds.

On the other hand, although parties are ever present in American politics, they have less power over the functioning of government than do parties in many European nations. In the United States, even when a party has won a majority in government, it still can't guarantee that its promises to the nation—the pledges that it has made in its platform—will be carried out. Unified Republican control of Congress and the White House in the early 2000s brought the tax cuts pledged by the Republican platform but not the promised oil exploration in the Arctic National Wildlife Refuge or the right to invest part of an individual's Social Security taxes in the stock market.

Parties are among the best means available to citizens for controlling their government. If the American parties are not strong enough to hold elected officials accountable, then doesn't that put American democracy at risk?[4] A series of observers believe that it does. Bolstered by an early report from some leading academic experts on political parties,[5] they argue that the answer is to create a system of more "responsible" parties. The governing party in this system would translate a coherent political philosophy into government action and would then be held responsible for the results. That, they argue, would improve the American system of governance.

Others see a more limited problem with party politics. For decades, the American parties have been criticized for being too much alike in their platforms, too centrist, and not clear and specific enough on major issues. Conservative Republican activists in 1964 pleaded for a platform that would be "a choice, not an echo" of the Democrats. In his third-party candidacy in 1968, George Wallace scoffed that there was "not a dime's worth of difference" between the major parties. John McCain and Ralph Nader campaigned for president in 2000 on the charge that both parties were tied to the demands of moneyed special interests, just as Ross Perot had claimed in 1992 and 1996.

These two sets of critics—the scholars who favor party government and the ideologically oriented activists—have different perspectives, but at heart they make the same point. They both want the parties to offer clearer and more specific platforms and they want the winning party to put its principles to work in public policy. To some extent, their complaints have been answered. Both parties have become more distinctive in their stands on important issues in the past two decades. The Democratic Party is more uniformly liberal now, after many southern conservatives moved away from their traditional Democratic allegiance and into the Republican Party, and the Republicans have followed a more clearly conservative path. Have they become more like "responsible" parties, and does that make them better able to serve the needs of a democracy?

THE CASE FOR RESPONSIBLE PARTY GOVERNMENT

The idea of *party government*, or *responsible parties*, offers a vision of a democracy very different from the traditional American commitment to limited government and the equally traditional American hostility to powerful political parties. Champions of party government believe that we need a strong and decisive government to solve social and economic problems. Our political institutions, they feel, may have been well suited to the limited governing of the early years of American history but do not serve us well today, when we need more vigorous government action.

However, this strong government must be held accountable to the public. The current system doesn't permit that, they charge. Individuals rarely have the time or the information to play an active political role or even to find out what their elected representatives are doing, so they depend on parties to present them with coherent alternatives and to hold elected officials accountable for their actions. When parties are unable to do that, voters drift from one meaningless decision to another.[6] In a system of candidate-centered politics in which power in government is often divided between the parties, there can be no genuine public control. The result, they argue, is that well-financed minorities—corporations, labor unions, single-issue groups—find it easy to step in and get what they want from government.

How Would Party Government (Responsible Parties) Work?

The best way to deal with this problem, party government advocates say, is to restructure the American parties. The parties would then play the primary organizing role in government and would, in the process, reinvigorate the other institutions of popular democracy. The process of party government would work like this:

- Each party would draw up a clear and specific statement of the principles and programs that it favors. It would pledge to carry out those programs if the party won.

- The parties would nominate candidates loyal to the party program and willing to enact it into public policy if elected.

- Each party would run a campaign that clarifies the policy differences between the two parties, so voters would grasp these differences and vote on that basis.

- Once elected, the party would hold its officeholders responsible for carrying out the party program. Voters could then determine whether they approved of the results and decide whether to keep or throw out the governing party at the next election.

In this system of responsible parties, then, the party's main focus would be on the set of policies that it has pledged to put into effect. Winning elections would not be an end in itself. Nominations and elections would become no more—and no less—than a means to achieve certain public policy goals.[7] For this to happen, all the elected branches of government would have to be controlled by the same party at a particular time. The party would bind the divided institutions of government into a working whole, as happens in parliamentary democracies.

What qualifies the party to play this crucial role? In the words of a prominent party scholar, it is because

> the parties have claims on the loyalties of the American people superior to the claims of any other forms of political organization . . . the parties are the special form of political organization adapted to the mobilization of majorities. How else can the majority get organized? If democracy means anything at all it means that the majority has the right to organize for the purpose of taking over the government.[8]

So parties would hold a privileged position in politics compared with interest groups, their major rivals as intermediaries between citizens and government.[9]

Those who argue for party government do not always agree on the purposes that they feel a strong, decisive government should serve. Many conservatives, once suspicious of a powerful central government, grew to like it better when conservative Presidents Reagan and Bush used their power to try to make Congress eliminate liberal programs. Similarly, liberals who were frustrated by the separation of powers developed greater enthusiasm for the principle when Congress proved capable of checking some of Reagan's and Bush's initiatives. It is much easier to like party government, apparently, when your party is in charge. In any case, proponents of party government feel that a central government pulled together by strong parties would give the public a bigger voice in politics.

THE CASE AGAINST PARTY GOVERNMENT

The advocates of party government are persuasive, but most American political scientists and political leaders remain unconvinced. Their concerns about party government and responsibility take two forms. One is the argument that party government would not produce desirable results. The other is that it simply would not work in the American context.[10]

It Would Increase Conflict

First, these skeptics fear that the nature of party government—its dedication to providing clear alternatives on major issues—would stimulate more intense and conflict-filled politics. Compromise would become more rare. Legislators, they say, would be bound to a fixed party position and would no longer be free to represent their own constituents and to negotiate mutually acceptable solutions. That would weaken the deliberative character of American legislatures.

Critics of party government also fear that a system that makes parties the primary avenue of political representation could undercut or destroy the rich variety of interest groups and other nonparty organizations. Without these other means of representing the nation's diversity, the two major parties might be seriously overloaded. Minor parties would be likely to pop up, which would further fragment the American system. In short, critics fear that politics and legislatures would be dominated by a number of doctrinaire, unyielding political parties unable to resolve problems.

It Wouldn't Work in American Politics

The second major argument against responsible parties is that the idea could not take root in the United States because it is not compatible with American political culture. The biggest problem here is the design of the American government itself. The principles of separation of powers and federalism were intended to prevent tyranny by dividing constitutional authority among the various levels and branches of government. The separation of powers, for example, allows voters to give control of the executive branch to one party and the legislative branch to the other. Elections for Congress take place on a different schedule from presidential elections, so congressional candidates can try to insulate themselves, although they don't always succeed, from presidential coattails. Federalism permits different parties to dominate in different states. Any change in these basic principles, for example, a switch to a parliamentary system, which would give the party a powerful reason to remain united in the legislature, would require major revision of the Constitution.

In recent years, American voters have made enthusiastic use of the separation of powers. Until 1950, the president's party controlled both houses of Congress most of the time. However, since then, *divided government* has prevailed: A president or governor faces at least one house of the legislature controlled by the other party. As you can see in Table 15.1, there have been only four years since 1980 when control of the federal government *wasn't* shared by the two parties. Divided party control has existed in most state governments as well since the early 1980s.[11]

Until the 1950s, the rare instances of divided government at the federal level usually resulted from very close elections or times when the president's party lost control of one or both houses of Congress in a midterm election. In more recent decades, the main cause of divided government has been split-ticket voting. At the national level, many voters have been willing to split their votes between Republican presidential candidates and Democratic candidates for Congress, most of them incumbents seeking reelection. For a time in the 1990s, the pattern was reversed; voters chose a Democratic president and Republicans for the House and Senate, but the result was a federal government just as divided. Ticket splitting has also been a cause of divided control of government in the states.[12]

Divided government makes responsible party government impossible. By giving control of different branches of government to opposing parties, it requires agreement between the parties for successful policy making. The alternative is gridlock, as New Yorkers have so often seen in their state legislature, in which Republicans have controlled the state Senate and Democrats have dominated the state Assembly for decades. Nego-

TABLE 15.1 Party Control of Government at the National Level, 1951–2004

Year	Party in control of the President	House	Senate	Divided Government
1951–1952	D	D	D	
1953–1954	R	R	R	
1955–1956	R	D	D	X
1957–1958	R	D	D	X
1959–1960	R	D	D	X
1961–1962	D	D	D	
1963–1964	D	D	D	
1965–1966	D	D	D	
1967–1968	D	D	D	
1969–1970	R	D	D	X
1971–1972	R	D	D	X
1973–1974	R	D	D	X
1975–1976	R	D	D	X
1977–1978	D	D	D	
1979–1980	D	D	D	
1981–1982	R	D	R	X
1983–1984	R	D	R	X
1985–1986	R	D	R	X
1987–1988	R	D	D	X
1989–1990	R	D	D	X
1991–1992	R	D	D	X
1993–1994	D	D	D	
1995–1996	D	R	R	X
1997–1998	D	R	R	X
1999–2000	D	R	R	X
2001–2002	R	R	D*	X
2003–2004	R	R	R	

*The Senate was Republican-controlled for the first five months of 2001 until Senator James Jeffords left the Republican Party and the Democrats gained majority control.

Note: D, Democratic control; R, Republican control; x, president, House, and Senate controlled by different parties.

Source: Updated from Harold W. Stanley and Richard G. Niemi, *Vital Statistics on American Politics 1999–2000* (Washington, DC: CQ Press, 2000), pp. 34–38.

tiation and bargaining are necessary in any democratic system. However, when both Democrats and Republicans have their fingerprints on every major piece of legislation, voters find it difficult to figure out which party is responsible for bad policies. Without that ability, voters can't throw out the guilty party and replace it with the opposition—the most effective tool for controlling government.

To party government advocates, the prevalence of divided government helps to explain why the federal government has failed to respond effectively on a number of major concerns from health care to campaign finance. The critics disagree. They contend that unified party government doesn't necessarily produce more significant legislative accomplishments, that the federal government has a lot of practice in coping with shared party power,[13] and even that American voters prefer it that way.[14] The jury is still out regarding some aspects of this question. However, it is clear that divided government is a big problem for those who would like to see responsible parties.

The Gingrich Experiment: A Temporarily Responsible Party

Americans did get at least a whiff of party responsibility in the mid-1990s. In a move spearheaded by House Republican minority leader Newt Gingrich, the great majority of Republicans running for House seats in 1994 signed a statement they called a "Contract with America." In it, they pledged that if the voters would give the Republicans a House majority, they would guarantee a vote on each of ten pieces of legislation, all embodying conservative principles, within the first one hundred days of the next Congress. The statement concluded, in words that would gladden the hearts of party government advocates: "If we break this contract, throw us out. We mean it."

The Republicans did win a majority of House seats in 1994. They delivered on their promise; once in office, the new Republican leadership used its iron control of the House agenda to vote on each of those bills before the self-imposed deadline. Levels of party cohesion on these bills were higher than they had been in decades. That, however, is when party government stalled. The Senate Republican majority had not committed itself to the Contract with America and it did not feel bound to consider these bills promptly or to pass them when they came up. The House Republicans' efforts were further stymied by divided government; a Democratic president had the power to veto any legislation that made it through both houses.

What can we learn from this experiment? As we have seen, the separation of powers is a mighty roadblock in the path of party government. Even the commitment of a legislative party to a set of clear and consistent principles is not enough to produce responsible party government, as long as the president and the other house of Congress are not willing to go along. There is reason to doubt, as well, that most voters appreciated the experiment; although Republicans kept their House majority in the next elections in 1996, so did the Senate Republicans who had not signed the Contract with America, and the Democratic president was reelected as well.

There are many other obstacles to achieving party government in the United States. Because party candidates are chosen by voters in primary elections, parties lack the power to insist on their nominees' loyalty to the party program. Even legislators who often buck their party's leaders or its platform are able to keep their jobs as long as their constituents keep voting for them. Changes in campaign finance have given candidates even greater freedom from their party organization, which makes it harder to create and promote a unified party "team" in elections. Critics of the responsible parties model have also argued that:

- American voters are not issue oriented enough to be willing to see politics only through ideological lenses.

- The diversity of interests in American society is too great to be contained within just two platforms.

- The parties themselves are too decentralized to be able to take a single, national position on an issue and then enforce it on all their officeholders.

- Americans distrust parties too much, as seen by their frequent efforts to reduce party influence in politics, to be willing to accept increased party power.

The idea of a responsible governing party, in other words, seems to the critics to ask too much of the voters, the parties, and the institutions of American government.

THE SEMI-RESPONSIBLE PARTIES: PARTY COHESION AND IDEOLOGY

There is little chance, then, for genuine party government to emerge in the United States. Even so, it might still be possible to nudge the parties in the direction of greater account-ability. The challenge would be to unite the party organization with party voters and the party in government behind a clear and consistent party program—in short, to make the parties more cohesive. Perhaps the only feasible way for a party to grow into a more cohesive unit in modern American politics is if its various parts were to agree voluntar-ily on a party ideology or at least on a set of shared goals. Because their shared com-mitment to that program would be voluntary, it would not violate the separation of powers or require a basic change in the form of the federal government. What is the chance that more ideological parties could develop in American politics?

Are the American Parties Ideological?

An *ideological party* is one with clear and consistent principles on a wide range of ques-tions from the purpose of government to the pitfalls and possibilities of human nature. Good examples include European Socialist parties, the old-style Communist parties, and the Muslim fundamentalist parties that have arisen in Middle Eastern nations. The prin-ciples of an ideological party offer straight answers to questions such as these: What should the power relationships in the society look like? How should the society be gov-erned and what values should the government try to achieve? What are the appropriate means to achieve these values?

Throughout their histories, however, the American parties have tended to be pragmatic rather than ideological, focusing on concrete problems rather than on protecting the purity of their principles. Ever since their founding, each party has been a blend of its own origi-nal tradition (the egalitarian tradition of the Democrats and the Republican tradition of order and industrial capitalism) with those of other groups that associated with it because of per-sonal ties, geographic nearness, or simple expectations of political gain.[15]

Why have the major American parties been so free of ideology? Most important, there are only two of them to divide up a tremendous array of interests in American pol-itics. In a system with several parties, a party can cater to one particular ideological niche in the voting public and still hope to survive. In a diverse two-party system, with so many different interests and people to represent, such specialized appeals can be made only by minor parties—or by a major party intent on self-destruction.

Do They at Least Offer Clear Choices?

Even though the two parties are not as ideological as are many European parties, they do, nevertheless, differ clearly in their stands on specific policies. We can see these differences in the platforms they adopt every four years at their national conventions (see the box on pages 288–89), in their candidates' speeches, and in the policies they pursue when they win.[16] It would have been hard during the 2000 presidential campaign, for example, to mistake the tax-cutting proposals of Republican George W. Bush for the spending on social programs recommended by Democrat Al Gore. These differences, most notably the Democratic commitment to federal social programs and the Republican desire to limit them, have been central principles of the two parties since the New Deal.

WHAT THE DEMOCRATS AND REPUBLICANS STAND FOR: THE 2000 PARTY PLATFORMS

These selections from the 2000 platforms show some of the most important differences between the major parties.

Abortion

Democrats: "The Democratic Party stands behind the right of every woman to choose, consistent with *Roe v. Wade,* and regardless of ability to pay."

Republicans: "The unborn child has a fundamental individual right to life which cannot be infringed. . . . We oppose using public revenues for abortion and will not fund organizations which advocate it."

Civil Rights

Democrats: "We continue to lead the fight to end discrimination on the basis of race, gender, religion, age, ethnicity, disability, and sexual orientation. . . . We support the full inclusion of gay and lesbian families in the life of the nation."

Republicans: "We support the traditional definition of 'marriage' as the legal union of one man and one woman, and we believe that federal judges and bureaucrats should not force states to recognize other living arrangements as marriages. . . . We do not believe sexual preference should be given special legal protection or standing in law."

Defense

Democrats: "Ensuring peace and security for Americans today does not just mean guarding against armies on the march. It means investing in building the global peace. It means addressing the fact that more than 1 billion of the Earth's inhabitants live on less than $1 a day—inviting social dislocation, violence, and war."

Republicans: "A strong and well-trained American military is the world's best guarantee of peace."

Education

Democrats: "What America needs are public schools that compete with one another and are held accountable for results, not private school vouchers that drain resources from public schools and hand over the public's hard-earned tax dollars to private schools with no accountability."

Republicans: "Raise academic standards through increased local control . . . empower needy families to escape persistently failing schools by allowing federal dollars to follow their children to the school of their choice [including private and religious schools]."

Environment

Democrats: "The Republicans have tried to sell off national parks; gut air, water, and endangered species protections; let polluters off the hook; and put the special interests ahead of the people's interest. . . . We must dramatically reduce climate-disrupting and health-threatening pollution in this country."

Republicans: "We believe the government's main role should be to provide market-based incentives to innovate and develop the new technologies for Americans to meet—and exceed—environmental standards. . . . We will safeguard private property rights. . . . "

Guns

Democrats: "We should require a photo license I.D., a full background check, and a gun safety test to buy a new handgun in America."

Republicans: "We defend the constitutional right to keep and bear arms. . . . We oppose federal licensing of law-abiding gun owners and national gun registration as a violation of the Second Amendment."

Health Care

Democrats: "Instead of the guaranteed, universal prescription drug benefit that Democrats believe should be added to Medicare, Republicans are proposing to leave to insurance companies the decisions about whether and where a drug benefit might be offered. . . . "

Republicans: "We need to build on the strengths of the free market system, offer seniors real choices in coverage, give participants flexibility, and make sure there are incentives for the private sector to develop new and inexpensive drugs. . . . [N]o more governmental one-size-fits-all."

Labor

Democrats: "We must . . . protect workers' rights to organize into unions by providing for a more level playing field between management and labor during organizing drives, and facilitating the ability of workers to organize and to bargain collectively."

Republicans: "We therefore support the right of states to enact Right-to-Work laws [which would require that any workplace be open to non-union as well as union employees, even if the nonunion employees benefited from union negotiations without paying union dues]."

Privatizing Government Services

Democrats: "Democrats do not believe that privatization is a panacea. Some services are inherently public."

Republicans: "If public services can be delivered more efficiently and less expensively through the private sector, they will be privatized."

Taxes

Democrats: "The Bush tax slash . . . would let the richest one percent of Americans afford a new sports car and middle class Americans afford a warm soda. Democrats seek the right kind of tax relief—tax cuts that are specifically targeted to help those who need them the most."

Republicans: "We cheer [the Republican Congress'] lowering of the capital gains tax and look forward to further reductions. . . . To guard against future tax hikes, we support legislation requiring a super-majority vote in both houses of Congress to raise taxes."

You can find the full text of the platforms at http://www.democrats.org/about/platform.html (for the Democrats) and http://www.rnc.org/gopinfo/platform (for the Republicans).

Both major parties have become more concerned with issues in the past few decades and more cohesive as well. A major contributor was the issue of civil rights. As issues of racial justice emerged as an important focus of national policy, white southerners deserted the Democratic Party in increasing numbers and took with them their more conservative views on a variety of other issues as well. This lowered the biggest barrier to unity within the Democratic Party on several issues.[17] As Chapter 13 shows, the Democratic congressional party votes more cohesively now than it has in decades. The Republicans have also become more united on conservative principles. State parties tend to divide along issue lines as well, with Democratic parties more liberal, especially when there is real party competition in the state.[18]

A major step in this direction occurred with the election of Ronald Reagan in the 1980s. Reagan, a candidate strongly identified with the conservative wing of the Republican Party, demonstrated the appeal of a simple vision based on one major principle: less government regulation of business. The clarity of his message appealed even to voters who were not persuaded by its content. His principled assault on the role of government as it had developed since the New Deal gave a more ideological tone to American politics than had been seen in decades. Since then, more issue-oriented leaders have been selected in both parties—the House party leaders are an excellent example—and have gained a platform to pursue a more policy-driven agenda.[19] In the same sense, political ideas, or purposive values, have become more prominent in bringing people into party activism.

As a result, a change in party control can now make a noticeable difference in public policy. When Vermont Senator James Jeffords left the Republican Party in mid-2001 and caused the Republicans to lose their one-vote Senate majority, the agenda of the Senate changed very quickly. A patients' rights bill, for example, which was regarded as dead in the water under Republican control, went to the head of the legislative line after the Democrats took over, and several environmental measures took on new life as well.

But Internal Divisions Remain

Even these clear differences on major issues, however, do not add up to the kinds of sharply articulated, all-encompassing political philosophies that are found in genuinely ideological parties. Nor do the American parties insist that their elected officials and identifiers obey these principles faithfully. Party leaders and followers can be drawn into the party for whatever reasons they choose, without having to pass any kind of ideological "litmus test" to enter.

The result is that some internal divisions remain within each party. Economic conservatives in the Republican Party, for instance, stress reducing the size of government, while the party's social conservatives want greater government intervention to protect against pornography, abortion, and homosexuality.[20] A small group of Republican moderates in Congress has proved to be the Bush administration's biggest challenge in uniting Republicans in support of the president's program. Several Republican senators and House members, largely from the northeast, have parted with the president on environmental issues, abortion rights, and even forced a major reduction in Bush's proposed tax cut in 2003. Moderate Republican elected officials have organized the Tuesday Group in Congress and the Republican Main Street Partnership, which includes Congress members and some Republican governors, to increase their influence on the national party.[21]

The Democrats have at least as long a history of internal conflict. After the Democratic defeat in 2000, for example, some moderate Democrats blamed Al Gore's campaign, saying that he should have stressed more centrist themes, such as the economic growth that had taken place under the Clinton–Gore administration. Voices from the more liberal wing of the party strongly disagreed, arguing that Gore did best when he emphasized the liberal goals of defending Social Security, Medicare, and a higher minimum wage.[22] These recriminations reflected years of dispute between party moderates and liberals,[23] as could be seen in the struggles between Vermont Governor Howard Dean and former Vice-Presidential candidate Joe Lieberman to win the 2004 Democratic nomination. The conflicts occur in state parties as well, as in Idaho where rural, mainly Mormon Democrats split from urban liberals on abortion and Democrats from the logging and mining areas vote differently from urban Democrats on environmental issues.[24]

There is no doubt, however, that both parties have become more cohesive in recent years and their positions on issues have become more distinct, at least among party leaders and activists and members of the party in government. What about party voters? Is it true, as some ideologues have charged, that most Americans are committed to ideological principles and want the Democrats and Republicans to provide more clearly defined ideological alternatives? Or are party voters bored with, or even alienated by, the programmatic concerns of many party activists?

IDEOLOGY AND THE AMERICAN VOTER

Popular and media commentary often suggest that the American public is ideologically oriented. Reports of election results frequently use the terms "liberal" and "conservative" to describe voters' choices. It has been common, for example, to explain the Republican electoral successes since 1980 and the emergence of more moderate Democratic leaders as a response to what is regarded as a more conservative mood among American voters.

How Ideological Is the American Public?

Careful study of American political attitudes since the 1950s, however, raises serious doubt that most voters can be described as "ideological." An ideological voter, like an ideological party, would not just hold clear attitudes toward a variety of individual issues but would connect those attitudes into a coherent structure. However, since the early days of opinion research, analysts have found that individuals with conservative attitudes on, say, taxes may express moderate or liberal attitudes on other issues, such as foreign policy or the environment.[25] It has been one of the staples of American survey research that large numbers of respondents say that they want both a smaller government with lower taxes *and* a government that provides more services in areas such as defense, health care, environment, and education. These are understandable goals but not a likely foundation for ideological thinking.[26]

Most of us, researchers find, hold in our minds a mix of conflicting thoughts about politics in general and even about particular issues. We do not necessarily hold a set of fixed and unyielding stands, such as an unqualified "yes" on all forms of affirmative action and a firm "no" to tax breaks for business. Rather, we might feel that affirmative action can help those who need it *and* that it can give an unfair advantage. We can be pulled toward one of these views under some conditions and toward another view under other conditions. Thus, most people react to issues with a degree of ambivalence[27]—a sharp contrast with the more stable, predictable response of an ideologue.

Studies show that only a small (but growing) minority of the public spontaneously refers to liberal or conservative ideological principles in discussing their political views, although much larger numbers use those terms if a pollster includes them in the question. Even when people call themselves liberals or conservatives, the label they choose for themselves may have little to do with the positions that they take on specific issues or with their party choice. In a recent survey, for instance, only 55 percent of the Republicans called themselves conservatives and 54 percent of Democrats said they were liberals.[28]

Instead, for most Americans, politics revolves around concrete problems and pragmatic efforts to solve them. Even in the case of Ronald Reagan, who campaigned for president in 1980 as a principled conservative, voters' judgments turned more on their *retrospective evaluations* of presidential performance—their feelings as to whether the most recent presidency had turned out well—than on Reagan's issue positions. In fact, many voters supported Reagan in spite of his conservative positions rather than because of them; in both 1980 and 1984, most voters preferred the policy stands of Reagan's opponent.[29] In the 2000 presidential election as well, the drag of Bill Clinton's ethical lapses and the importance of such personal qualities as honesty and leadership also suggested a focus on the candidates' character, even for many survey respondents who said that they were mainly concerned about specific policy issues.[30]

Because voters' choices tend to be results oriented, retrospective evaluations, not ideological judgments, parties and candidates try to stitch together winning coalitions by appealing to a range of qualities—the candidates' personal characteristics, group interests, single issues, and feelings toward the party in power—but rarely by using ideological appeals. Even though Americans are more likely now to see a difference between the two parties on issues (see Figure 15.1) and Republican and Democratic identifiers are increasingly divided in their attitudes toward candidates and issues,[31] ideological thinking has not been common enough within the American public to provide a dependable foundation for responsible parties.

The more polarized parties in government may have helped to educate voters about the differences between the parties. That can make a voter's party identification an even more useful tool in guiding voting choices and may improve many voters' ability to approximate the demands of the responsible parties model.[32] It is possible as well that responsible party government may not require an ideologically oriented public. Even in nations that have ideological party systems, the political thinking of the average citizen is not typically as highly structured as that of political activists and leaders; it is the institutional arrangements and the leaders' perspectives that sustain party government.[33] In American politics, however, none of these supports for responsible party government is especially strong or stable.

Differences Among Voters, Activists, and Candidates

In recent years, then, an interesting gulf has opened up within the parties. Leaders, activists, and many voters seem to be increasingly concerned with policy questions, and both parties' leaders and activists appear to be more united and more polarized—the Democrats more liberal and the Republicans more conservative. Yet most voters remain more interested in practical questions and politicians' personal qualities.

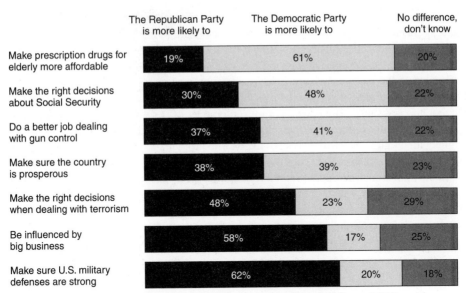

	The Republican Party is more likely to	The Democratic Party is more likely to	No difference, don't know
Make prescription drugs for elderly more affordable	19%	61%	20%
Make the right decisions about Social Security	30%	48%	22%
Do a better job dealing with gun control	37%	41%	22%
Make sure the country is prosperous	38%	39%	23%
Make the right decisions when dealing with terrorism	48%	23%	29%
Be influenced by big business	58%	17%	25%
Make sure U.S. military defenses are strong	62%	20%	18%

FIGURE 15.1 **Party Differences on Issues as Seen by Voters, 2002**

Source: New York Times/CBS Poll conducted October 27–31, 2002, at
http://www.nytimes.com/pages/politics/index.html, "Poll Watch, Previous Surveys, Perceptions of the
Parties" (accessed Nov. 6, 2003).

Party activists, for example, tend to take more extreme positions on many issues than do party voters. Studies of delegates to the two national parties' nominating conventions have consistently found Democratic activists on the liberal end of the liberal-conservative continuum and Republican activists on the conservative end, with both parties' voters much closer to the center. You can find a dramatic illustration of these patterns in Table 10.2, on page 188. The table shows that a full 83 percent of delegates to the 2000 Democratic National Convention favored affirmative action, for example, compared with only 29 percent of the Republican convention delegates. The parties' voters were in between; 59 percent of Democratic voters and 44 percent of the Republicans supported affirmative action.

A similar pattern appears on other major issues. Only 10 percent of the Democratic activists supported the idea of giving tax-funded vouchers to help parents pay for tuition at private or religious schools. Almost three-fourths of the Republican activists favored these vouchers. Again, the parties' voters were in the middle. In fact, in the case of vouchers, each party's activists were more distant from their own party's voters than the two parties' voters were from one another.[34]

A party's candidates and officeholders often find themselves caught in between: closer to the left or right than the party's voters but not as extreme as its activists. That can put candidates in a difficult position. If they try to muffle their conservative or liberal views, they risk alienating their party's activists. But if they express those views candidly, more moderate voters may choose not to support them in the next election.[35] It is no wonder that many candidates often prefer to remain ambiguous when asked about issues in their campaigns and resist the push toward clearer, more ideological commitments within the parties.

These differences between more ideological activists and more flexible candidates can aggravate the tensions among the party organization, the party in government, and the party's voters. The ideologues in both parties complain periodically about the moderation of at least some parts of the party in government. Liberal Democrats often objected to the more centrist policies of Democratic President Clinton, and although George W. Bush has done an effective job of calming the fears of social conservatives about his core values, right-wing groups (and moderates as well) remain watchful.

The dilemma of ideology, then, is not whether the American parties can become genuinely ideological parties. That is not likely. The problem is whether the increasing ideological commitment of their activists and of many of their officeholders can be sustained without alienating their more pragmatic supporters. The parties already face a deep well of public suspicion; much of the public feels alienated from the parties' vulnerability to organized interests, their affinity for negative campaigns, and their failure to keep their promises.[36] It is entirely possible that many Americans, whose tolerance for politics is low, will find these sharpened party differences to be more of a turnoff than an incentive to learn more.[37]

WHEN IS PARTY GOVERNMENT MOST LIKELY?

Responsible parties are hard to achieve. Even the British Parliament, so often cited as a model by proponents of party government, has not always had the cohesion and the binding party discipline that a "pure" responsible party government would require.[38] Under what conditions have the American parties come closest to the ideal of responsible parties?

When There Is Strong Presidential Leadership

At times, a strong president—George W. Bush and Ronald Reagan are good examples—has been able to push Congress to enact important parts of the platform on which he ran for office. That is especially likely, of course, when the president's party controls both houses of Congress. Strong party-oriented presidents can also draw voters' attention to party differences. But the result is likely to be "presidential government" rather than party government; voters are likely to respond to the president's performance rather than that of the party as a whole.

In Times of Crisis

At critical times in American history, the parties have divided in ways that were, if not truly ideological, at least determinedly policy oriented. In the 1936 presidential election, for example, the Democrats and the Republicans offered dramatically different solutions to a nation devastated by the Great Depression. The hardships of that economic collapse probably focused voter attention to an unusual degree on the possible remedies that government could provide. This, combined with a campaign centered on the pros and cons of the Roosevelt program for social and economic change, may well have produced something close to a mandate in the election for both the president and Congress. When strong presidential leadership is combined with crisis conditions, then a degree of responsible party government might be achieved, at least for relatively short periods.

During Party Realignments

American politics seems to have approached the requirements for party government most closely during party realignments. At these times, the parties have tended to divide more clearly on a single, riveting set of issues, and party leaders, activists, and voters seem to reach their highest levels of agreement with one another and their greatest differences with the other party (see Chapter 7). Realignments typically produce a unified federal government with the same party controlling both houses of Congress, the presidency, and a judiciary that, through the president's appointment power, comes to reflect the new majority. On only five occasions in American history has one party enjoyed control of Congress and the presidency continuously for more than a decade, and each time, this control was first established during a realignment.

Unified party control does not guarantee that the branches of the government will cooperate with one another. However, cooperation is certainly more likely when a president is dealing with a majority of his own party in Congress and especially if its members feel that they owe their positions to their party label, as often is the case during a realignment. Moreover, during realignments, party cohesion in Congress is especially high. So it is not surprising that major bursts of comprehensive policy change have typically followed realignments.[39] Realignments and the atmosphere of crisis and the strong presidential leadership that have accompanied them have brought the United States as close to responsible party government as we have been able to achieve.

Even at these times, however, the American version of party government has been a pale imitation of its European counterparts. The realignment of the 1930s, for example, produced a majority Democratic Party by linking a liberal northern wing, attracted to the party because it represented the hopes of disadvantaged groups and championed the developing welfare state, and a conservative southern wing that often opposed both of these goals. The president at the time, Franklin D. Roosevelt, had a congressional majority large enough to achieve many of his policy goals, but he faced opposition within his own party throughout his long career in the White House.

In short, even when they are most unified around a single political agenda during a realignment, the American parties contain differing interests and goals. They have never been sufficiently united in a set of common principles to be able to overcome the institutional forces, federalism and the separation of powers, that tend to disunite them.

PARTY GOVERNMENT AND POPULAR CONTROL

To many analysts, the idea of party government, or responsible parties, has continuing appeal. When parties stand for clear principles and voters are offered clear choices in elections, it is easier for citizens to hold government responsible for the policies it produces. That may make for a stronger and more vibrant democracy.

The major American parties are not ideological parties like many in Europe. But the congressional parties and, to some extent, the parties in the electorate have become more cohesive in the past two decades than they have been in a very long time. At the federal level and in many states, there is a great deal of conflict between the parties over basic principles of public policy. The national party committees never have been stronger than they are today nor more engaged in helping state and local parties and financing campaigns.

Yet if the parties are to become more accountable, more like responsible parties in a system of party government, clear differences on issues and greater organizational strength are not enough. There must be some set of basic principles or values that can connect different issues into a single logical structure for each party, some means by which voters and leaders are able to distill the large number of policy issues into one major dimension or a few, so that voters can easily understand and predict the party's stands and the party's supporting coalition remains constant from one issue to the next.

That much structure and coherence will be harder and perhaps impossible to achieve. Too many powerful forces stand in the way. Even if party organizations gain an enormous increase in resources, they still won't be able to choose their own candidates; prospective officeholders will still have to attract voter support in primary elections in order to become their party's standard-bearer. So candidates will still need to run their own campaigns and raise most of their own campaign money. Issue advocacy ads will still encourage voters to respond to candidates as individuals, not as parts of a party ticket. All these forces give candidates greater independence from their parties than the increase in party resources can counteract. And no amount of party money can buy an exception to the rules of federalism and the separation of powers.

It is not likely, then, that the American parties and the American voters can meet the demands of the responsible parties model. The party organizations have not grown into the central role that the reformers so valued—that of drawing up a party program and enforcing it on candidates and officeholders. Many would find that to be cause for celebration. Others would remind us that, in a system of government as fragmented as that of the United States, semi-responsible parties make it even harder to accomplish one of the basic tasks of a democracy: holding public officials accountable for their actions.

CHAPTER 16

The Place of Parties in American Politics

Three decades ago, the American parties appeared to be in decline. Because their troubles seemed to reflect long-term changes in American society, it was easy to assume that the decline was permanent. By the time their decay had become the central theme of books and articles about the parties, however, there were clear signs of resurgence. The parties have grown into different types of organizations than they once were, but in this changed form, they continue to be an important part of the American political landscape.

To conclude this look at the American parties, let's sum up these changes in relation to a simple, but profound truth: Political parties are powerfully shaped by the world around them. Parties affect presidents, legislatures, citizens, election rules, interest groups, and campaign finance, but they are also influenced by these forces. The changes in party power and functions over time can be better understood by looking at the relationships between parties and their environment.

PARTIES AND THEIR ENVIRONMENT

Political parties influence their environment in a variety of ways. They promote public policies in response to citizens' beliefs, demands, and fears. They recruit individuals into active roles in politics and government. Through their communications and performance, parties affect public attitudes about the Democrats and the Republicans and about politics more generally. Party organizations and the parties in government structure their own environment even more directly as well: They make the rules governing how the parties' candidates will be nominated and financed and who will have the opportunity to choose them.

In turn, their environment helps to shape the parties' nature, activities, and effectiveness. Three types of environmental factors have been especially important in influencing the American parties as well as those in other western democracies: the nature of the electorate, the nation's basic governmental institutions and rules, and the forces that mold the broader society (Table 16.1).[1]

TABLE 16.1 **How Their Environment Influences the American Parties**

Types of Influences	Examples
1. Nature of the electorate	Expansion of the right to vote, citizens' political interest and knowledge, social characteristics of the electorate (distributions of age, race, income, education)
2. Political institutions and rules	
(a) Institutions	Federalism, separation of powers, nature of the presidency, single-member districts
(b) Electoral processes	Direct primary, nonpartisan elections
(c) Laws and regulations	Laws governing campaign finance, structure of party organization, patronage
3. Social forces	
(a) National events and conditions	State of the economy, war, other national problems
(b) Other political intermediaries	Types of other organized interests, nature and importance of television and other media, independent consultants
(c) Political culture	Attitudes toward parties and politics

The Nature of the Electorate

The nature and concerns of the voting population are vital influences on a party system. The societal "fault lines" that divide the electorate into opposing groups—race is one of the best and most persistent examples in American politics—help to define the parties' issue agendas. So do the social characteristics that make some groups more likely to vote than others.

The right to vote has expanded enormously in the United States. From an extremely limited suffrage—the small proportion of white male adults who owned property—it now includes the overwhelming majority of citizens over the age of 18. Political information has expanded as well. Mass media and computers have made information about politics much more accessible, and more citizens have the advantage of higher education, which helps them find and understand the information. Voters have gained unprecedented opportunities to take part in political decisions through primary elections, referenda, recall elections, and e-mail access to public officials throughout the nation. Yet people's interest in politics and feelings of political effectiveness have not increased. So at the same time that these opportunities for participation have expanded, voter turnout has declined.

Turnout has not declined to the same degree among all groups in the population, however. There has been a steeper decline among lower income Americans than among those with greater wealth.[2] And as we saw in Chapter 8, the turnout rate of college-age Americans has dropped to slightly more than half the turnout rate of adults over 65. It should come as no surprise, then, that Social Security and Medicare are much more frequent campaign issues than are college loans; the social forces that help to determine who votes and who doesn't are powerful influences on which groups' concerns will dominate the political system.

Political Institutions and Rules

The second cluster of environmental influences on the parties includes the nation's basic framework of political institutions: whether the government is federal or unitary, whether it is parliamentary or has separated powers, and how its positions of power are structured. Then there are the laws that regulate the parties and their activities, ranging from state laws telling the parties when to hold their meetings to federal laws regulating campaign spending. We have discussed, for example, the effects of the separation of powers, the direct primary, and the use of plurality elections in single-member districts on the development and cohesion of the parties.

The American parties are regulated more heavily than are parties in other nations. The direct primary limits their role in the selection of candidates to a degree unknown in most other democracies, and American state laws defining the party organizations have no parallel in the democratic world. The effect of this regulation—and in most cases its aim—is to put limits on the party organization. An unintended effect is to boost the power of the party in government relative to that of the party organization. With the important exceptions of the direct primary and the secret ballot, however, these political rules have probably changed less dramatically over time than has the nature of the electorate.

Societal Forces

A third set of environmental influences refers to events and trends in the larger society that affect politics at a particular time. The horrors of the World Trade Center attack, the relocation of U.S. industries to Mexico and China, and the changes in women's roles and family structures have had powerful effects on the nation's agenda. Thus, they have become part of the parties' agenda as well and affect the parties' platforms, their campaign appeals, and their supporting coalitions.

Other societal forces include the number and character of organized interests in the nation, the types and behavior of the media, and other means of representing interests. If individuals find alternative ways to pursue their political goals that seem more effective than the parties, they will use them. If the "hot line" of a local newspaper is better able to track down a reader's Social Security check that has gotten lost in the bureaucracy or if an interest group is more vocal in opposing abortion or gay rights, then why should the individual try to achieve her political aims through a party? The nature of the parties at any given time, then, depends in part on the available alternatives to parties and the competition among them.

All these elements of their environment have contributed to the unique character of the American parties. Thus, as we summarize the dramatic changes that have occurred in the parties' structure, supporting coalitions, and strength during the past four decades, we will pay special attention to the effects of their environment and especially to changes in the electorate.

PARTY DECLINE IN THE 1960s AND 1970s

A basic feature of the American parties is that the three party sectors are bound together only loosely. The party organization has never been able to involve large numbers of party identifiers in its structure and activities, nor has it been able to direct the campaigns or the policy making of the party in government. The party decline that was becoming apparent in the 1960s affected the three sectors very differently.

The Parties in the Electorate

During a time of upheaval in many of aspects of American life, voters' loyalty to the parties weakened noticeably in the late 1960s and 1970s. More people began to think of themselves as independents rather than as party identifiers. Those who remained attached to a party no longer relied on that identification as much as they once did. The parties, then, found themselves with smaller numbers of less loyal identifiers.

One result was a surge in ticket splitting. By 1968, almost half of the respondents in national surveys said they had voted for more than one party's candidates in state or local elections, and by 1974 that figure topped out at 61 percent. At the aggregate level, the number of congressional districts selecting a presidential candidate of one party and a congressional candidate of the other party exceeded 30 percent for the first time in history in 1964 and had reached 44 percent early in the next decade.[3]

As education levels increased, some voters became more responsive to the increasingly issue-oriented candidacies of the time. The campaigns of Barry Goldwater in 1964, Eugene McCarthy and George Wallace in 1968, and George McGovern in 1972 spurred many people's awareness of political issues and events. As television came to be used more widely in campaigns, others were drawn to candidates' personalities and media images. The handsome faces and ready smiles that television screens convey attracted some of the support that party symbols once commanded.

Voters became more inclined, then, to respond to candidates as individuals rather than as members of a party. Independent candidates for president—McCarthy in 1976 and John Anderson in 1980—and for governor enjoyed some success. Because candidates and issues change far more frequently than parties, the result was a less stable and predictable pattern of voting.

Party Organizations

The last of the great party machines were fading in the 1960s and 1970s. The famous Daley machine in Chicago was ripped apart in a series of tumultuous struggles after Richard J. Daley's death in 1976. Party organizations could no longer depend on the patronage and preferments that once were so vital in recruiting party activists. Instead, more people were being drawn into party activism because of their commitment to particular issues. These were better educated people, and they demanded greater participation in the party's decisions. Some of these new activists felt that compromise was a dirty word; to them, standing for a set of principles was more important than winning an election. If their party did not satisfy their ideological goals, they stood ready to leave it for other groups—candidates' campaigns and single-issue organizations—that were more narrowly targeted to meet their needs.

Other aspects of the party organization were under stress as well. As the direct primary came to dominate presidential nominations, party organizations gave up their control over nominations to whoever chose to vote in the primary. By the time a primary season had ended, the party's presidential nominee had been determined, so its presidential nominating convention no longer had much of an independent role. As grassroots activists came to expect a bigger say within the party organization, its own internal decision making was no longer under the party leaders' control. This was particularly true of the Democrats, who in 1972 and 1976 nominated presidential candidates who were well outside the mainstream of their own party.

In addition to their declining influence over nominations, by the 1960s and 1970s the party organizations had lost their central role in campaigns more generally. Candidates now built their own campaign organizations, raised their own campaign money, and made their own decisions on how to spend it. The campaign assets that they once received from their local party organizations—information about public opinion, strategic advice, fund-raising, willing helpers—could now be obtained directly from pollsters, the media, issue-oriented activists, or campaign consulting firms that were, in effect, "rent-a-party" agencies. The campaign finance reforms gave candidates an incentive to try to raise nonparty money at a time when the technologies for doing so were becoming more widely available.

In fact, in comparison with independent consultants, the campaign skills that local party organizations could offer their candidates were fairly primitive. The national parties began to develop expertise in newer campaign technologies during the 1970s and to share their resources with state and local parties, but consultants and the other nonparty providers of campaign services had already established a beachhead. Even in the face of new vigor in the national committees, the party organizations in the 1970s remained much more decentralized than did life and politics in the United States. Voters were looking more and more to national political leaders and symbols, but the party organizations still tended to be collections of state and local fiefdoms.

The Party in Government

In the 1960s and 1970s, elected officials came to depend more than ever on direct appeals to voters. Officeholders had been freed from reliance on the party organization by the direct primary, their direct access to the media, and the money they could raise and the volunteers they could attract independent of the party's efforts. Because of split-ticket voting, candidates didn't even need to rely on party identification. Through personal style, personal appeals, and personal funds, they developed a "personal vote" independent of party.[4]

It became harder than ever before to unseat an incumbent, especially in Congress. The cycle perpetuated itself; because there was not as much chance of beating an elected official, serious challengers did not appear as frequently. When they did, party organizations were not vigorous enough to provide challengers with the campaign resources they so desperately needed. Holding public office became more of a profession—a lifetime career—even at the state and local level, where political professionals had formerly been rare.

As incumbents became more secure electorally, even though many did not feel that way, the congressional parties gained greater freedom from the party organizations. Even the legislative party leaders found it harder to marshal their troops on behalf of the legislative party's bills or the programs of the party's president. Party-line voting in Congress fell to an all-time low in the late 1960s and early 1970s. However, it was a perverse kind of freedom. Protected from the demands of party activists and party organizations, legislators were thus more exposed to other pressures, mainly from large numbers of organized interests.

With the legislative parties less cohesive and strong, presidents and governors began to exercise greater leadership. The parties, then, could be viewed as executive-centered coalitions during the late 1960s and 1970s. Presidents did not depend on their party organizations for much; in fact, with the help of federal campaign money after 1974, presidential candidates were able to run their campaigns free of obligation to the party organization at any level. By that time, however, divided government had become the norm. That undercut executives' power by permitting the opposition party to block their leadership.

Shifting Power Centers Within the Parties

These changes produced a major shift of power within the parties. From the decentralized party organization, power had flowed to the individual members of the party in government, especially the executives. The changes also accentuated a shift in influence away from the parties and toward rival political intermediaries, especially organized interests and the mass media.[5]

At the core of these changes was the increasing isolation of the party organization, not only within the parties but also in American politics more generally. The organizations' days of glory were over by the mid-1900s. Party organizations and their leaders became even more vulnerable to suspicions that they were run by bosses plotting in smoke-filled rooms. Visions of "boss rule" were as much alive at party conventions in the 1960s and 1970s as they were in the early 1900s, even though, ironically, the resources that the party organizations had in the early 1900s, which could have justified the charge of boss rule at that time, were largely eroded by the 1960s.

The result was a peculiar kind of political party. A party organization is the only sector of the party whose interests go beyond the winning of individual elections. It is the party organization that sustains the party when its candidates lose their races. It is the organization that links the party's officeholders and office seekers; it can call them to collective action of the type that parties were created to achieve. Without it, party candidates are individual entrepreneurs seeking individual goals in a political system that requires collective decisions. The decline of the party organizations was clearly a major force in the decline of the parties more generally.

PARTY RENEWAL

This marked decline was not the end of the story, however. The American parties responded to these challenges, just as they had adapted to changing circumstances at other times in the past. The steady decay of the parties was stopped and even reversed, but some of the changes that took place in the 1960s and 1970s have left their imprint even now. In some important ways, then, the parties have had to adjust to a new role in American politics.

Change in the Parties' Electoral Coalitions

The slow, steady change in the two parties' supporting coalitions, discussed especially in Chapter 7, has led to regularly recurring speculation that a party realignment has taken place. The symptoms that normally precede a realignment began to be present in the mid-1960s: lower voter turnout, more ticket splitting, greater support for third-party or independent candidates, less predictable elections, and divided government.

When Republicans won both the presidency and the Senate in 1980 and gained control of the House in 1994—the first time since 1954 that there was a Republican majority in both Houses of Congress—some concluded that the long-awaited realignment had finally taken place. There is no doubt that one condition of a realignment has been fulfilled. The party coalitions have clearly changed from those of the New Deal period; black Americans are now steadfastly Democratic, white southerners have moved into the GOP in large numbers, and religious conservatives, southern and nonsouthern, are now a distinctive force within the Republican Party. Other demographic categories have become partisan, such as the tendency of unmarried people to identify as Democrats. The most striking feature of this new alignment has been the decline of Democratic strength in the South (see Figure 16.1). In addition, the proportion of party identifiers has rebounded since the 1970s and there is much greater parity between the numbers of Republican and Democratic identifiers than there had been since the 1930s.

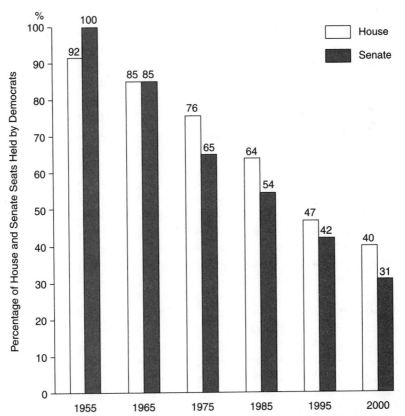

FIGURE 16.1   Eroding Democratic Strength in the South: U.S. House and Senate Seats, 1955–2000.

Note: Data points are the percentage of U.S. senators and House members from the thirteen 13 southern states who are Democrats.

Source: Data for 1955–1995 from *Congressional Quarterly Weekly Report*, Nov. 12, 1994: 3231. Data for 2000 calculated from Harold W. Stanley and Richard G. Niemi, *Vital Statistics on American Politics 1999–2000* (Washington, DC: CQ Press, 2000), Tables 5.10 and 5.11, pp. 213–238.

Yet if this is a realignment, it doesn't look like the realignment of the 1930s. Elections continue to be volatile. Republican House candidates went from great success in 1994 to panic in 1998 and back to success in 2002. The proportion of the public calling themselves independents remains high. New parties and independent candidacies have aroused public interest. Polls do not reveal any great public enthusiasm for the major parties or, for that matter, many other aspects of American politics. Even a full-fledged realignment, in a world of primaries, would not give back the party organizations' power to nominate their candidates. Lasting change in the parties' coalitions could not guarantee an end to the more candidate-centered electoral world that has resulted.

Whether or not they led to a realignment, the events of the 1960s and 1970s resulted in a continuing challenge to American party loyalties. Large numbers of voters now rely on sources other than the parties, such as the media and single-issue groups, for their political information. In earlier times, these sources may have helped to reinforce partisan views and loyalties; now, they often do not.[6] This variety of sources can encourage people to create their political commitments as they would a patchwork quilt—an issue from this group, a candidate from that party. Even with this formidable competition, however, parties remain important landmarks on most people's political map. Levels of party identification rebounded in the 1990s, and partisanship is at least as strong an influence on people's voting now as it was before the 1960s and 1970s.[7]

The Rise of More Cohesive Parties in Government

Well before the current revival of partisanship among voters—and thus a possible cause of it—the parties in government had begun a revival of their own. By the mid-1970s, the long decline in party cohesion in Congress had stopped and the organizational seeds had been sown for greater party strength. By the 1980s, with stronger and more assertive leadership, the congressional parties had become more cohesive than they had been since the early part of the century. As historically one-party areas became competitive, each of the congressional parties grew more homogeneous, which made it easier for them to offer distinctive alternatives on major issues. Recall the example of the House Republicans' Contract with America and the House Democrats' response to it. In a number of states, as well, legislative parties were becoming more unified and taking clearer positions on issues.

Parties also took on greater importance in the executive branch. The Reagan administration came into office in 1981 as the most ideologically committed and the most partisan in decades. Reagan's leadership placed conservative principles at the top of the GOP's agenda and solidified the hold of his brand of conservatives on the party. The Democrats, although more internally diverse, became more unified in response. By the mid-1990s, there was intense partisan warfare in Washington between a programmatically committed Republican majority in Congress and an activist Clinton White House. The battles continued in 2004 between a conservative Republican president and large Democratic minorities in the Senate and House.

The New "Service Parties"

The party organizations have revived in even more dramatic fashion. Facing an environment of candidate-centered campaigns, both parties retooled their national organizations to provide services to the party's candidates. They have used their increased funding and professional staffs to assist state and local parties, recruit candidates for office, provide them with more resources, and thus step up their role in campaigns, at least in comparison with the 1960s and 1970s. The infusion of resources is both timely and necessary; as two-party competition spreads, state and local parties need to become more effective just to keep up with the competition.

The new service party, however, differs a great deal from the grassroots organizations of earlier years. Because its main role is to support candidates, it is not very visible to voters, nor is it assured of making a major impact on campaigns. In the big-spending world of campaign finance, the party organizations do not bring enough money to the table to be able to dominate political campaigning or at times even to be heard very clearly. The service party is one of many forces, including campaign consultants and interest groups, trying to win the attention of candidates, influence elected officials, and mobilize citizens.

The party organizations, in short, are more vigorous now than they have been in years. They have adapted to new conditions and taken on a new form: that of the service party. However, as service parties, the party organizations are no longer as distinctive as they used to be in the sense of providing campaign resources that no other group could deliver.

THE FUTURE OF PARTY POLITICS IN AMERICA

These trends are vital to us because political parties are vital to us. Parties have the potential to do a great deal of good for a democracy. They enable political leaders to work together and to nurture a lasting set of shared interests. They can clarify political choices for the public, which helps voters to learn about politics at lower cost to themselves. They can bring voters to the polls, which helps to legitimize a democracy. Perhaps most important, parties organize majorities, which are necessary for governing. Interest groups can effectively represent intense minorities, but there are not many alternatives to the parties for organizing lasting and predictable majorities.

The problem is that although we need parties, we don't like them. We don't even like to admit that they influence us. When asked, most of us claim that issues and candidates' personal qualities have the biggest impact on our votes. Yet it's clear that partisanship is closely related to our attitudes toward issues and candidates and is the source of much of their influence.[8]

A Changing Intermediary Role

Elections require voters to make large numbers of choices, often on the basis of little information. Parties serve as an efficient guide. The value of the party label in elections is probably greatest when a mass electorate has just begun to develop and has serious need for information. As the electorate matures, its needs change. One explanation for American voters' decreased reliance on party loyalties in the 1960s and 1970s was that voters had become better educated and better informed than was the case 60 or 80 years earlier, so they might have been better able to sift through a broader range of political messages without the need for party labels as a guide.[9]

It is interesting, then, that although education levels have continued to increase since the 1960s, party identification has reasserted itself as an influence on many voters' choices. Why should partisanship help citizens who have so many other sources of information about candidates and issues? Perhaps *because* they are exposed to so much information. Without this simple guide, the blizzard of political communication could serve as more of a deterrent than a tool. At the same time, the fact that the two major parties have drawn farther apart from one another on important issues lends even more meaning to the party labels for politically engaged citizens. Added to the heightened party competition in the early 2000s and the resulting intensity of campaign advertising, changes in the political environment can make an individual's partisanship even more significant to him or her.

Granted, the parties' traditional dominance in politics has been eroded by competition from organized interests and the media. A century ago, someone concerned about environmental quality would probably have had to pursue his or her goals through a political party; not many groups focused specifically on resource conservation, much less pollution control. Now, however, along with the growing reach of government into most aspects of private life, a huge array of organized interests has developed that permit individuals to establish a "designer link" with the political system. If someone prefers to see politics entirely from the perspective of gun rights or gay rights, several groups exist to make that possible. There is no need to compromise or to support a coalition of other groups' needs and a range of candidate styles, as a party loyalty would require.

In this fractured world of political interests, parties become even more important as a means of broadening individuals' perspectives and improving their ability to hold elected officials accountable. The parties have long struggled with hostile environmental forces, from a system of separated powers that is inhospitable to strong parties to a political culture that regards parties with suspicion. However, as we have seen throughout this book, the parties are adaptable. They are not the intermediaries they were in 1900 or 1950, but for large numbers of Americans and for the process by which policies are made, the major parties remain the most important intermediaries.

The Need for Strong Parties

Democracy is unworkable without parties.[10] The United States has probably come closer to testing that principle than any other democracy; much of American local politics has been, at least officially, nonpartisan for some time. But it seems clear that when parties are reduced to playing a smaller role in politics, the quality of democracy is weakened.

In a society dominated by other intermediaries, most people would not be as well represented. Among the many links between citizens and government, only the parties have the incentive to create majorities in order to win a wide range of elections over a long period. That, in turn, gives the parties, to a greater extent than interest groups, political action committees, or even elected officials, a reason to pay attention to those citizens who are not activists or big campaign contributors. As political scientist Walter Dean Burnham has written, parties are the only devices that can "generate countervailing collective power on behalf of the many individually powerless against the relatively few who are individually—or organizationally—powerful.[11]

It is the parties that mobilize sheer numbers against the organized minorities who hold other political resources. The parties do so in the one political arena where sheer numbers count most heavily: elections. Because of that, parties traditionally have been the means by which newly enfranchised but otherwise powerless groups gained a foothold in American life. The old-style urban machines, for example, provided the instrument with which recent immigrants won control of their cities from the more established Anglo-Saxon Protestant elites.

In other periods of American history as well, the party has been the form of political organization most available to citizens who lack the resources to make a real impact on public decisions using other means. In a less party-driven politics, in which bargaining takes place among many more types of political organizations, the well-organized minorities with critical resources—money, insider knowledge, and technological expertise—would probably have even greater advantages than they do now. As we have seen from research on nonpartisan elections, for instance, the elimination of the party symbol and of the party as an organizer has probably helped wealthier and higher status groups of both the right and left to dominate these elections and has made it more of a challenge for citizens to hold their representatives accountable.[12] That may be one reason why participation has declined more sharply during the past few decades among lower status and less educated Americans; they may feel less represented by a politics in which the parties are no longer dominant.[13]

Finally, weakened parties would rob the political system of an effective means for creating governing coalitions. Without at least moderately strong parties, it becomes harder to mobilize majorities that can come together in support of policies. Individual candidates, freed from lasting party loyalties, would have to recreate majorities for every new legislative proposal. The result could be political immobility in which legislatures splinter into conflicting and intransigent groups. This can further undermine public confidence in democratic politics.

Laws and policies would continue to be made, but they would be made by shifting coalitions composed of interest groups, campaign contributors, bureaucrats, and elected officials acting as free agents. These coalitions would be less permanent and less identifiable to the public, and therefore much harder to hold accountable, than the parties have been and can be. In a diverse nation, the challenge is whether any of the alternatives could pull together the pieces of a fragmented politics and separated political institutions as effectively as the parties have done.

How to Make the Parties Stronger

Because parties bring so much value to American democracy, some analysts have considered ways to expand the parties' role in political life. The most potent solutions—abolishing the separation of powers, the direct primary, and the antiparty sentiment engrained into the political culture—are not on the table, of course. But there are a variety of less dramatic ways in which the parties might be strengthened.

Larry J. Sabato and Bruce Larson report that a majority of respondents in their recent survey would like the parties to be more active in helping people deal with government. They propose, among other ideas, that the party organizations could create "mobile units" to help citizens in areas where the U.S. (and perhaps the state) representative is from the other party. That would allow the party organization, not just the members of the party in government, to perform constituent service. They note that this idea was especially attractive to respondents who described their commitment to party as having declined in the past five years and who said they were not registered to vote, those, in short—more likely to be alienated from politics.[14]

The parties could help to build long-term loyalty among their activists by providing volunteers with such attractive nonpolitical benefits as low-cost health and life insurance and other money-saving services, as many interest groups do now.[15] This would make the American parties into organizations more like European-style mass membership parties. Another way for the parties to renew their connection with citizens is to air campaign ads that promote the party as a whole rather than just its individual candidates. In particular, such advertising could strengthen the meaning of party by stressing the link between the party's stands and individuals' daily lives. To this point, however, the bulk of both parties' money goes to fund ads that do not even mention the party itself.

The parties will likely benefit as well from the current movement by some cash-starved states to forgo their presidential primary elections and permit the parties to hold caucuses instead. The experience of taking part in a party caucus has brought many politically interested citizens and candidate activists into more active work for their party, which in turn allows the party organization to expand its canvassing and other forms of direct contact with voters.

CONCLUSION: THE PARTIES' PROSPECTS

The American parties have never lacked problems to solve. The electorate has become more and more varied. Traditional group ties have broken down. New groups, from antiabortion to animal liberation, are tilling the ground that the major parties once owned. The great majority of voters still identify with a political party, but they also respond to candidates and issues, stylistic changes, and national trends. The result is a more diverse, complicated politics that no single set of loyalties or political organizations can easily contain.

The parties can't meet every political need. They can't represent the individual agenda of each citizen while trying to build a majority coalition. It is very difficult for them to be pure in their issue stands while still making the compromises necessary to build coalitions and govern. They find it hard to offer policy alternatives in campaigns without engaging in the partisan conflict that many Americans find so distasteful. It is as difficult to mesh the needs and agendas of their candidates and officeholders as it is to satisfy every voter; it can be an impossible task for the parties to unite their elected officials and office seekers on a single agenda while giving candidates the independence to choose their own appeals and meet their own districts' needs. The parties can't provide party accountability to an electorate that wants to choose candidates individually.

We will continue to challenge the parties with these conflicting expectations. The American parties will continue to have to adapt to them while facing attack from a rich assortment of critics. The parties' distinctive character has sustained them longer than any other tool of democratic politics. For the sake of representation, effective policy making, and accountability in governance, even the most independent-minded citizens have a stake in sustaining vigorous party politics in the United States.

Party Politics on the Internet

The Web pages of the two major parties and a variety of minor parties can provide a fascinating glimpse into the world of each party's politics and can serve as the basis for some interesting assignments. Here are the main sites of the Democrats, the Republicans, and almost *twenty* American minor parties for you to explore. Later in this section, you'll find a listing of other sites on party politics and a number of sample assignments using these sites.

http://www.democrats.org

This is the official website of the Democratic National Committee (DNC). It contains party news, DNC ads, special reports about President Bush and Republican issue positions, and lists of special events. There are links to state and local Democratic Parties and the party's most recent national platform as well as information for various Democratic constituency groups (women, Latinos, and others). Visitors can find out how to receive e-mail updates from the DNC and register to vote. Job and internship opportunities at the DNC are listed.

http://www.rnc.org

The Republican National Committee's official website provides party statements and research reports about current events and issues, biographies of President and Mrs. Bush, and information about the party's history. Profiles of Democratic candidates are posted here at election time, and the site includes the party platform and a listing of allied groups, such as the College Republican National Committee. Links enable the visitor to contact state Republican organizations, donate money, and register to vote.

http://www.reformparty.org

This is the site of the dominant branch of the Reform Party, founded in the mid-1990s by Ross Perot. Perot has left the party, but it remains committed to campaign finance reform, restrictions on lobbying, term limits for elected officials, and a balanced budget. The party's main principles are posted here, along with a statement of party history and current party news. Visitors to the site can register to vote, contribute online, and join the party's e-mail lists. There are links to state Reform Parties.

http://www.americanreform.org

The American Reform Party is an anti-Perot group that split off from the main body of the Reform Party in 1997. The site contains a history of the organization, position papers, a party platform, profiles of party candidates, and links to state groups. You can get information on how to contribute online and join the party.

http://www.americanheritageparty.org

An explicitly Christian party, the American Heritage Party promotes the Bible as a blueprint for political action and opposes abortion, group-based civil rights, gun control, property taxes, and government welfare programs. Its website emphasizes its statement of principles and states its aim to establish voter clubs at the local level, in addition to its existing party organization in the state of Washington.

http://www.Constitutionparty.com

Formerly the U.S. Taxpayers Party, the Constitution Party favors limited government and opposes abortion, gun control, immigration, taxes, and gay rights. The site offers press releases, a list of party events, its platform, and a place to order campaign materials. There are audio clips, links to state party organizations in about half the states, and online opportunities to volunteer for the party and make contributions.

http://www.dsausa.org/dsa.html

The Democratic Socialists of America's site offers a statement of the party's principles and links to information about socialism in the United States and in other nations. There are reports about the activities of its approximately thirty local parties and an invitation for members to form other local parties, receive e-mail updates, and join Young Democratic Socialists.

http://www.greens.org/na.html

The Green Parties of North America post their platform, which emphasizes environmental issues, peace, and social justice, on this website. The site includes a series of party publications, e-mail services, listings of its election results since 1985, and, at election time, its current candidates. There are links to state Green Parties and to Campus Greens.

http://www.usiap.org

The Independent American Party wants smaller government and an emphasis on Christian values, patriotism, and property rights. It is prolife and favors a strong military and the free enterprise system. It began as a Utah party but now has contacts in about half of the states. The site contains the national platform, membership information, and a discussion of party history.

http://www.lcr.org

The Log Cabin Republicans are the largest national gay and lesbian Republican organization; their motto is, "Inclusion Wins." Their website includes legislative information, material about party conventions and Republican candidates, and a newsletter. Candidate endorsements are listed at election time. Links exist to various local chapters.

http://www.lp.org

The Libertarian Party believes in complete freedom from government and taxes. Its home page provides news about party candidates and party principles. There is a link to a quiz, "Are You a Libertarian?" You'll also find a list of state chapters. Interested visitors can sign up for the party's e-mail announcement list, register to vote and contribute online. The site includes a sample letter that sympathizers can send to their friends to encourage interest in the Libertarian Party.

http://www.natural-law.org

The Natural Law party says that it wants to "bring the light of science into politics" and espouses Transcendental Meditation and other new-age practices. The site includes the party platform, news and party events, information about issues such as genetic engineering, and a link to the Student Natural Law Party Club. You'll find links to party representatives in the states, recommended readings, and an opportunity to join the party's e-mail list.

http://www.newparty.org

The New Party is a progressive grassroots party concerned mainly with local elections in a variety of cities. It promotes "fusion," the listing of candidates on multiple party lines. The website features materials about the party's principles, including nondiscrimination, a living wage, and a reduction in military spending, and an opportunity to join its e-mail list.

http://www.prohibition.org

Founded in the mid-1800s to oppose the manufacture and sale of alcoholic beverages, the Prohibition Party has taken on a new life as a prolife, antigay, proprayer party. Its website discusses the party's 1999 national convention and its nomination of a presidential candidate. There are no links or mentions of any further activity.

http://www.cpusa.org

This is the home page of the Communist Party USA. Posted here are position papers stating the party's stands against joblessness, racism, and poverty and a list of party-related journals. There are e-mail addresses for joining the national party, contacting state parties, and donating money, listings of party events, and links to a variety of groups with similar aims.

http://www.sp-usa.org

The century-old Socialist Party USA stands for principles of democratic socialism, including full employment and an internally democratic party organization. It is an anticommunist socialist group, unlike several other socialist parties. Its website lists a variety of socialist publications and introduces its 2004 presidential candidate. Visitors can find information about joining, locating state parties, and participating in the party's e-mail list.

http://www.slp.org

The Socialist Labor Party bills itself as the original Socialist party in the United States, founded in the late 1800s. It no longer runs candidates for president but does take part in a few local races. Its website discusses its principles, contains links to a newsletter and other socialist writings, and provides e-mail links to several local chapters.

http://www.themilitant.com

The Socialist Workers Party broke away from the Communist Party decades ago and now espouses a pro-Castro and workers' rights viewpoint. It runs local candidates in some areas as well as a candidate for president. Its website is a newsletter presenting party views on current issues.

http://www.southernindependentparty.com

The Southern Independence Party argues for the sovereignty, and eventually the independence, of the southern states. It broke off from a similar party, the Southern Party, in 2000. Its website contains a party platform, material about the Civil War, links to state sites (including, interestingly enough, hopes for a future in Delaware, Nevada, and New Mexico), and a list of articles, speeches, and other publications.

http://www.wethepeople-wtp.org

The We the People Party views itself as a coalition of independents organized to take part in the 2004 presidential race. Its primary concern is campaign finance reform. The website contains newsletters, a statement of principles, a free membership application, and a page encouraging visitors to express their concerns as well as links to websites dealing with campaign finance. The creation of two founders, it is located in New Hampshire.

http://www.workers.org

The Workers World Party has a 45-year history in the United States since it split off from the Socialist Workers Party. It is an anticapitalist organization with a pro-Cuba, pro-China approach to communist politics. Its website contains news of issues that the organization finds interesting, events, and a listing of local parties.

Here are some other Internet websites on political parties, elections, and voting.

CAMPAIGN FINANCE

http://www.commoncause.org

Common Cause monitors a variety of political issues. You can research your own members of the U.S. House and Senate, get campaign spending data, and learn about campaign finance reform.

http://www.fec.gov

This is the Federal Election Commission's website. In addition to information about the Commission itself, it provides access to current and past campaign finance data in federal (presidential and congressional) races.

http://www.opensecrets.org

The Center for Responsive Politics, a nonpartisan research group, distributes information on money in politics. Its databases include presidential and congressional races, political action committees, soft money, lobbyists, and news links of various kinds.

POLITICS AND POLITICAL ISSUES

http://www.govote.com

This site has a wealth of information on elections, issues, and other political news. You can take part in surveys, compare your views with those of a variety of public officials, and track the voting record of your senator or House member on a range of issues.

http://www.heritage.org

The Heritage Foundation is a conservative think tank; its website provides current political news and detailed analyses of policy issues from a conservative perspective.

http://www.mojones.com

Mother Jones, a liberal publication that appears on the Web as well as in hard copy, covers American politics and issues and also contains a lot of international news.

http://www.nga.org

You can find information about every state governor at the site of the National Governors' Association as well as NGA positions on issues of interest to the states. Job opportunities are also listed here. The home page of the Council of State Governments (http://www.statesnews.org) has more information on state policy issues.

http://politics.com

This website has surveys to take, discussion groups, election results, information about state politics, and links to news stories about politics and to the websites of a variety of parties and other political groups.

http://www.rollcall.com

Roll Call is a newspaper that covers Congress and Capitol Hill. Its website contains news about current legislative action and "insider" information about Congress.

http://www.vote-smart.org

Project VoteSmart offers a wealth of information on federal and state candidates, including biographical data, interest group ratings, voting records, and candidates' responses to questions about their issue priorities. It contains data on campaign finance, tracks legislation in Congress, and tells website visitors how to register to vote.

POLLING

http://www.gallup.com

Here you'll find the most recent Gallup polls and links to reports on previous polls conducted by the Gallup organization.

http://www.people-press.org

The Pew Research Center for the People and the Press conducts polls about politics, policy, and public attitudes toward the media. Its website contains a lot of polling data and analysis by Pew and other groups.

http://www.tarrance.com/battleground.html

The Battleground Poll is a collaboration between Democratic pollster Celinda Lake and Republican strategist Ed Goeas. The website offers public opinion polling data and strategic analyses from both parties' perspectives.

http://www.umich.edu/~nes/

The National Election Studies, based at the University of Michigan, have been conducted since 1952 to provide information on public opinion, political participation, and voting behavior. Students can view and download survey data from current and earlier studies and look at research reports.

MEDIA SITES

http://www.cnn.com/ALLPOLITICS

Here are links to current and recent news stories from CNN and *Time* magazine.

http://cagle.slate.msn.com/politicalcartoons/main.asp

You'll find dozens of current political cartoons on this website from the United States and other nations.

http://www.Washingtonpost.com

Major national newspapers such as the *Washington Post* can be read on the Internet. The *Post* is notable for the excellence of its political coverage. See also the *New York Times* (http://www.nytimes.com) and the *Los Angeles Times* (http://www.latimes.com).

SAMPLE ASSIGNMENTS USING THESE WEBSITES

- Pick two political issues that interest you. Use the Democratic and Republican Parties' websites to determine where they stand on these issues. How clear are their stands and how much difference do you find between them? Do they offer you a real choice?

- Compare the positions of the two major parties with those of two minor parties. How easy is it to find out where the minor parties stand on the issues that interest you? How different are their stands from those of the Democrats and Republicans? What would be the advantages and disadvantages for American politics if these alternatives were more widely publicized?

- What can you learn from these websites about the parties' organizations? At what levels of government do the major parties have organizations? Where do the minor parties have chapters or branches, other than at the national level?

- What kinds of activities do the Democrats and Republicans sponsor? To what extent do minor parties offer similar activities to their sympathizers?

- Does a party's website show evidence that the party offers material rewards for activists or solidary or purposive rewards (see Chapter 5)? Which type of rewards seems to be most common? Do you find more emphasis on purposive rewards in the major parties' websites or in those of the minor parties? What about solidary rewards?

- Which do the Democrats' and Republicans' home pages stress most: their candidates' experience and personal qualities or the party's issue stands?

- Do the two major parties seem to be targeting particular groups in the population, such as women, Latinos, or others? Which ones? Do the Democrats and Republicans target the same groups or different groups?

- Are the statements on these websites predominantly positive, that is, presenting the party's own beliefs, or predominantly negative, in the sense of criticizing other parties' or groups' actions and views? Do you find the major parties' statements to be more positive (or negative) than those of the minor parties? The liberal parties' statements to be more positive (or negative) than those of the conservative parties?

- In comparison with the major parties, why is the universe of minor parties so splintered? There are, for example, five socialist parties listed here. How do they differ from one another, and how substantial are their differences? What about the differences among the several conservative minor parties? Do you find anything in these websites that helps to explain this proliferation?

- Are there any major issue positions or views of the world that you do *not* find represented by any party, major or minor? What are they, and why do you think no party espouses them?

- Using the American National Election Studies website, familiarize yourself with the results of survey questions on citizens' feelings about the parties. When you read a survey question, predict what you expect the responses to be. Compare your prediction with the actual data. Have the responses changed over time?

- Use this American National Election Studies website to create cross-tabulations: How do Democratic and Republican identifiers compare in their views on various issues? Are there big differences among strong identifiers, weak identifiers, and independent leaners? Which group expresses the greatest interest in politics? Would you have expected this finding?

- Using the Opensecrets website, check out the information on campaign contributions by various interest groups and corporations (see Chapter 12). Which types of groups would you expect to give the most campaign money? Compare your prediction with the actual data.

- Using the Federal Election Commission website, scroll down to "Candidate and PAC/Party Summaries" and follow the link. Find out how much the various candidates for federal office in your state have raised for their next campaign. How much have the incumbents received compared with the challengers and the candidates for open seats? How much have the Democrats raised compared with the Republicans? Have third-party candidates raised any money?

- What interest groups would you expect to give Democrats in Congress high ratings? Republicans? Go to the VoteSmart website and test your guesses against their findings.

- Using the *Washington Post*'s website (or that of any other major newspaper or broadcast media outlet), read articles, columns, and editorials about political issues. Are the major parties mentioned? If so, what aspects of the parties' activities are emphasized? Are political candidates mentioned more frequently than parties are or the reverse? Do you find any mention of minor parties?

Endnotes

PART ONE

1. This is the title of Harold Lasswell's pioneering book, *Politics: Who Gets What, When, How* (New York: McGraw-Hill, 1936).
2. E. E. Schattschneider, *Party Government* (New York: Rinehart, 1942), p. 1.
3. See Herbert Kitschelt, Zdenka Mansfeldova, Radoslaw Markowski, and Gabor Toka, *Post-Communist Party Systems* (New York: Cambridge University Press, 1999), and Timothy J. Colton, *Transitional Citizens* (Cambridge, MA.: Harvard University Press, 2000).
4. Austin Ranney, *Curing the Mischiefs of Faction* (Berkeley: University of California Press, 1975).

CHAPTER 1

1. These definitions come from Edmund Burke, "Thoughts on the Cause of the Present Discontents" (1770) in *The Works of Edmund Burke* (Boston: Little, Brown, 1839), vol. I, pp. 425–426; Anthony Downs, *An Economic Theory of Democracy* (New York: Harper & Row, 1957), p. 24; William Nisbet Chambers, "Party Development and the American Mainstream," in Chambers and Walter Dean Burnham, eds., *The American Party Systems* (New York: Oxford University Press, 1967), p. 5; John H. Aldrich, *Why Parties?* (Chicago: University of Chicago Press, 1995), pp. 283–284; and V. O. Key, Jr., *Politics, Parties, and Pressure Groups* (New York: Crowell, 1958), pp. 180–182. See also Leon Epstein, *Political Parties in Western Democracies* (New Brunswick, NJ: Transaction Books, 1980); and Gerald Pomper, *Passions and Interests: Political Party Concepts of American Democracy* (Lawrence: University of Kansas Press, 1992).
2. V. O. Key, Jr. used this "tripartite" conception to organize his classic text, *Politics, Parties, and Pressure Groups.* Key attributed the concept of party-in-the-electorate to Ralph M. Goldman, *Party Chairmen and Party Factions, 1789–1900* (Ph.D. diss., University of Chicago, Chicago 1951).
3. See Denise L. Baer and David A. Bositis, *Elite Cadres and Party Coalitions* (Westport, CT: Greenwood Press, 1988), pp. 21–50.
4. See Joseph A. Schlesinger, "The Primary Goals of Political Parties," *American Political Science Review* 69 (1975): 840–849.
5. State legislative elections in Nebraska are nonpartisan, although the candidates' partisan ties are obvious to many voters, and statewide officials (such as the governor and attorney general) are elected on a partisan ballot.
6. This image is Joseph A. Schlesinger's in "The New American Political Party," *American Political Science Review* 79 (1985): 1152–1169.
7. See William N. Chambers, *Political Parties in a New Nation* (New York: Oxford University Press, 1963); Chambers and Burnham, *The American Party Systems;* Everett C. Ladd, Jr., *American Political Parties* (New York: Norton, 1970); A. James Reichley, *The Life of the Parties* (Lanham, MD: Rowman & Littlefield, 2000); and John H. Aldrich, *Why Parties?*
8. See John H. Aldrich and Ruth W. Grant, "The Antifederalists, the First Congress, and the First Parties," *Journal of Politics* 55 (1993): 295–326; and John F. Hoadley, *Origins of American Political Parties 1789–1803* (Lexington: University of Kentucky Press, 1986).
9. Chilton Williamson, *American Suffrage: From Property to Democracy* (Princeton: Princeton University Press, 1960).
10. Neal R. Peirce and Lawrence D. Longley, *The People's President* (New Haven: Yale University Press, 1981).
11. See Aldrich. *Why Parties?* Chapter 4, and Reichley, *The Life of the Parties*, Chapter 5.
12. See Reichley, *The Life of the Parties*, Chapters 6–11.

317

13. See Moisei Ostrogorski, *Democracy and the Organization of Political Parties, Volume II: The United States* (Garden City, NY: Anchor Books, 1964, originally published in 1902).

14. On party reform, see Austin Ranney, *Curing the Mischiefs of Faction* (Berkeley: University of California Press, 1975); and Richard Hofstadter, *The Age of Reform* (New York: Vintage Books, 1955).

15. See Leon Epstein, *Political Parties in the American Mold* (Madison: University of Wisconsin Press, 1986), p. 155–199.

16. See The NES Guide to Public Opinion and Electoral Behavior, located on the Internet at http://www.umich.edu/~nes/nesguide/toptable/tab2b_2.htm

CHAPTER 2

1. Arend Lijphart, *Electoral Systems and Party Systems* (New York: Oxford University Press, 1994).

2. See John F. Bibby and L. Sandy Maisel, *Two Parties—Or More?*, 2nd ed. (Boulder, CO: Westview, 2003), p. 46.

3. Charles S. Bullock III, "It's a Sonny Day in Georgia," in Larry J. Sabato, ed., *Midterm Madness* (Lanham, MD: Rowman & Littlefield, 2003), p. 177.

4. Gregory L. Giroux, "Redistricting Helped GOP," *CQ Weekly,* November 9, 2002, p. 2934.

5. Interparty competition refers to competition between the parties, as opposed to competition within a particular party (termed "intra-party"). See Austin Ranney, "Parties in State Politics," in Herbert Jacob and Kenneth Vines, eds., *Politics in the American States* (Boston: Little, Brown, 1965), p. 65. For an alternative index based on state legislative races, see Thomas M. Holbrook and Emily Van Dunk, "Electoral Competition in the American States," *American Political Science Review* 87 (1993): 955–962.

6. See Malcolm E. Jewell and Sarah M. Morehouse, *Political Parties and Elections in American States* (Washington, DC: CQ Press, 2001), Chapter 2, and John F. Bibby and Thomas M. Holbrook, "Parties and Elections," in Virginia Gray and Russell L. Hanson, eds., *Politics in the American States,* 8th ed. (Washington, DC: CQ Press, 2003), Chapter 3.

7. Paul R. Abramson, John H. Aldrich, and David W. Rohde, *Change and Continuity in the 1996 Elections* (Washington, DC: CQ Press, 1998), Chapter 9. On state legislative races, see John M. Carey, Richard G. Niemi, and Lynda W. Powell, "Incumbency and the Probability of Reelection in State Legislative Elections," *Journal of Politics* 62 (2000): 671–700.

8. All the losing candidates in 1994 were Democrats, however, which suggests that party considerations were more important than incumbency. Data from 1994–1996 come from Abramson et al., *Change and Continuity,* and for 1998–2002 from *CQ Weekly* postelection figures. On the influence of incumbency on elections, see Gary C. Jacobson, *The Politics of Congressional Elections,* 5th ed. (New York: Longman, 2001), Chapter 3; Paul S. Herrnson, *Congressional Elections,* 3rd ed. (Washington, DC: CQ Press, 2000), Chapter 9; Stephen Ansolabehere, James M. Snyder, Jr., and Charles Stewart III, "Old Voters, New Voters, and the Personal Vote," *American Journal of Political Science* 44 (2000): 17–34; and Scott W. Desposato and John R. Petrocik, "The Variable Incumbency Advantage," *American Journal of Political Science* 47 (2003): 18–32.

9. Stephen Ansolabehere and James M. Snyder Jr., "The Incumbency Advantage in U.S. Elections," *Election Law Journal* 1 (2002): 315–338.

10. Gary C. Jacobson, "The Marginals Never Vanished: Incumbency and Competition in Elections to the U.S. House of Representatives, 1952–82," *American Journal of Political Science* 31 (1987): 126–141. See also Monica Bauer and John R. Hibbing, "Which Incumbents Lose in House Elections: A Response to Jacobson's 'The Marginals Never Vanished,'" *American Journal of Political Science* 31 (1987): 262–271.

11. Maurice Duverger, *Political Parties* (New York: Wiley, 1954). See also Octavio Amorim Neto and Gary W. Cox, "Electoral Institutions, Cleavage Structures, and the Number of Parties," *American Journal of Political Science* 41 (1997):149–174.

12. This used to be a frequent occurrence in the United States. In 1955, 58 percent of all state legislative districts were multimember; this number had declined to 10 percent by the 1980s. See Richard Niemi, Simon Jackman, and Laura Winsky, "Candidates and Competitiveness in Multimember Districts," *Legislative Studies Quarterly* 16 (1991): 91–109.

13. See A. James Reichley, *The Life of the Parties* (Lanham, MD: Rowman & Littlefield, 2002), p. 4.

14. Leon Epstein, *Political Parties in the American Mold* (Madison: University of Wisconsin Press, 1986), pp. 129–132.

15. V. O. Key, Jr., *Politics, Parties, and Pressure Groups*, 5th ed. (New York: Crowell, 1964), pp. 229ff.

16. See Louis Hartz, *The Liberal Tradition in America* (New York: Harcourt, Brace and World, 1955). However, this "consensus" is full of mixed feelings; see Stanley Feldman and John Zaller, "The Political Culture of Ambivalence," *American Journal of Political Science* 36 (1992): 268–307.

17. Marjorie Randon Hershey, "Like a Bee: Election Law and the Survival of Third Parties," in Matthew J. Streb, ed., *Election Law and Electoral Politics* (Boulder: Lynne Rienner, 2004).

18. Researchers have also found that nonpartisan elections reduce voter turnout and increase incumbents' chances of winning. See Brian F. Schaffner, Matthew J. Streb, and Gerald C. Wright, "Teams without Uniforms: The Nonpartisan Ballot in State and Local Elections," *Political Research Quarterly* 54 (2001): 7–30.

19. Gerald C. Wright and Brian F. Schaffner, "The Influence of Party: Evidence from the State Legislatures," *American Political Science Review* 96 (2002): 367–379.

20. J. David Gillespie, *Politics at the Periphery* (Columbia: University of South Carolina Press, 1993).

21. Holly A. Heyser, "Minnesota Governor: The End of the Ventura Interlude," in Sabato, *Midterm Madness,* pp. 233–245.

22. Associated Press, "Record Number of Libertarians Seeking Votes," *Hoosier Times,* November 3, 2002, p. B4.

23. Among the best books on American third parties are Steven J. Rosenstone, Roy L. Behr, and Edward H. Lazarus, *Third Parties in America*, 2nd ed. (Princeton: Princeton University Press, 1996); Paul S. Herrnson and John C. Green, *Multiparty Politics in America,* 2nd ed. (Lanham, MD: Rowman & Littlefield, 2002); and John F. Bibby and L. Sandy Maisel, *Two Parties—Or More?* 2nd ed. (Boulder, CO: Westview, 2003). Lisa J. Disch makes an argument in favor of third parties in *The Tyranny of the Two-Party System* (New York: Columbia University Press, 2003).

24. Joseph M. Hazlett II, *The Libertarian Party* (Jefferson, NC: McFarland and Company, 1992). Third parties' websites are listed in "Party Politics on the Internet," at the end of this book.

25. As evidence, almost all third-party presidential candidates since 1900 have received less support on election day than they did in pre-election polls; see Rosenstone, Behr, and Lazarus, *Third Parties in America*, p. 41.

26. Rosenstone, Behr, and Lazarus, *Third Parties in America*, p. 162.

27. See Paul R. Abramson, John H. Aldrich, and David W. Rohde, *Change and Continuity in the 1992 Elections* (Washington, DC: CQ Press, 1994).

28. James E. Campbell, "The 2002 Midterm Election," *PS* 36 (2003): 203–207.

29. See Lee Epstein and Charles D. Hadley, "On the Treatment of Political Parties in the U.S. Supreme Court, 1900–1986," *Journal of Politics* 52 (1990): 413–432, Richard Winger's *Ballot Access News* at http://www.ballot-access.org and issues of the *Election Law Journal.*

30. See Howard A. Scarrow, *Parties, Elections, and Representation in the State of New York* (New York: New York University Press, 1983).

PART TWO

1. See Alan Ware, ed., *Political Parties: Electoral Change and Structural Response* (New York: Basil Blackwell, 1987).

CHAPTER 3

1. Andrew M. Appleton and Daniel S. Ward, *State Party Profiles* (Washington, DC: CQ Press, 1997), Appendix.

2. A public utility is a government-regulated provider of services, such as an electric company or a water company. Leon Epstein, *Political Parties in the American Mold* (Madison: University of Wisconsin Press, 1986), pp. 155–199.

3. The cases are *Tashjian v. Republican Party of Connecticut,* 479 U.S. 1024 (1986); and *Eu v. San Francisco County Democratic Central Committee et al.,* 489 U.S. 214 (1989). See Clifton McCleskey, "Parties at the Bar," *Journal of Politics* 46 (1984): 346–368, and David K. Ryden, "'The Good, the Bad, and

the Ugly': The Judicial Shaping of Party Activities," in John C. Green and Daniel M. Shea, *The State of the Parties,* 3rd ed. (Lanham, MD: Rowman & Littlefield, 1999), pp. 50–65.

4. V. O. Key, Jr., *Politics, Parties and Pressure Groups* (New York: Crowell, 1964), p. 316.

5. Samuel J. Eldersveld, *Political Parties: A Behavioral Analysis* (Chicago: Rand McNally, 1964).

6. The organization of American political parties differs from what Robert Michels calls the "iron law of oligarchy"—that organizations are inevitably controlled from the top. See Robert Michels, *Political Parties* (Glencoe, IL: Free Press, 1949).

7. M. Craig Brown and Charles N. Halaby, "Machine Politics in America, 1870–1945," *Journal of Interdisciplinary History* 17 (1987): 587–612.

8. See David Mayhew, *Placing Parties in American Politics* (Princeton: Princeton University Press, 1986), pp. 19–21.

9. See Kenneth Finegold, *Experts and Politicians: Reform Challenges to Machine Politics in New York, Cleveland, and Chicago* (Princeton, NJ: Princeton University Press, 1995).

10. Steven P. Erie, *Rainbow's End: Irish-Americans and the Dilemmas of Urban Machine Politics, 1840–1985* (Berkeley: University of California Press, 1988); but see John F. Bibby, "Party Organizations 1946–1996," in Byron E. Shafer, *Partisan Approaches to Postwar American Politics* (New York: Chatham House, 1998), pp. 142–185.

11. Anne Freedman, *Patronage: An American Tradition* (Chicago: Nelson-Hall, 1994), Chapter 5.

12. Kenneth R. Mladenka, "The Urban Bureaucracy and the Chicago Political Machine," *American Political Science Review* 74 (1980): 991–998.

13. Michael Johnston, "Patrons and Clients, Jobs and Machines," *American Political Science Review* 73 (1979): 385–398.

14. Timothy B. Krebs, "The Determinants of Candidates' Vote Share and the Advantages of Incumbency in City Council Elections," *American Journal of Political Science* 42 (1998): 921–935.

15. See Raymond Wolfinger's "Why Political Machines Have Not Withered Away and Other Revisionist Thoughts," *Journal of Politics* 34 (1972): 365–398.

16. James L. Gibson, Cornelius P. Cotter, John F. Bibby, and Robert J. Huckshorn, "Whither the Local Parties?" *American Journal of Political Science* 29 (1985): 139–160.

17. Cornelius P. Cotter, James L. Gibson, John F. Bibby, and Robert J. Huckshorn, *Party Organization in American Politics* (New York: Praeger, 1984), pp. 49–53.

18. See Cotter et al., *Party Organization in American Politics*, p. 54, for 1964–1980. On 1984: James L. Gibson, John P. Frendreis, and Laura L. Vertz, "Party Dynamics in the 1980s," *American Journal of Political Science* 33 (1989): 67–90. On 1988: Charles E. Smith, Jr., "Changes in Party Organizational Strength and Activity 1979–1988," unpublished manuscript, Ohio State University, 1989. See also Samuel J. Eldersveld, "The Party Activist in Detroit and Los Angeles," in William J. Crotty, ed., *Political Parties in Local Areas* (Knoxville: University of Tennessee Press, 1986), pp. 89–119.

19. John Frendreis and Alan R. Gitelson, "Local Parties in the 1990s," in John C. Green and Daniel M. Shea, *The State of the Parties,* 3rd ed., pp. 135–153.

20. Carol S. Weissert, "Michigan," in Appleton and Ward, *State Party Profiles,* pp. 153–160.

21. L. Sandy Maisel, "American Political Parties: Still Central to a Functioning Democracy?" in Jeffrey E. Cohen, Richard Fleisher, and Paul Kantor, eds., *American Political Parties: Decline or Resurgence?* (Washington, DC: CQ Press, 2001), pp. 112–114.

22. Gary F. Moncrief, Peverill Squire, and Malcolm E. Jewell, *Who Runs for the Legislature?* (Upper Saddle River, NJ: Prentice Hall, 2001).

23. John J. Coleman, "The Resurgence of Party Organization? A Dissent from the New Orthodoxy," in Daniel M. Shea and John C. Green, eds., *The State of the Parties* (Lanham, MD: Rowman & Littlefield, 1994), pp. 282–298.

24. A. James Reichley, *The Life of the Parties* (Lanham, MD: Rowman & Littlefield, 2000), pp. 129–130.

25. Malcolm E. Jewell and Sarah M. Morehouse, *Political Parties and Elections in American States*, 4th ed. (Washington, DC: CQ Press, 2001), p. 4.

26. Jewell and Morehouse, *Political Parties and Elections,* p. 1.

27. See James L. Gibson, Cornelius P. Cotter, John F. Bibby, and Robert J. Huckshorn, "Assessing Party Organizational Strength," *American Journal of Political Science* 27 (1983): 193–222.

28. John H. Aldrich, "Southern Parties in State and Nation," *Journal of Politics* 62 (2000), p. 655.

29. Jewell and Morehouse, *Political Parties and Elections*, p. 52; Aldrich, "Southern Parties," 655–659.

30. Jewell and Morehouse, *Political Parties and Elections*, p. 211.

31. Anthony Gierzynski, *Legislative Party Campaign Committees in the American States* (Lexington: University Press of Kentucky, 1992).

32. Robert E. Hogan, "Candidate Perceptions of Political Party Campaign Activity in State Legislative Elections," *State Politics and Policy Quarterly* 2 (2002): 66–85.

33. Raymond J. La Raja, "State Parties and Soft Money," in John C. Green and Rick Farmer, eds., *The State of the Parties,* 4th ed. (Lanham, MD: Rowman & Littlefield, 2003), pp.132-150.

34. Sarah M. Morehouse and Malcolm E. Jewell, "State Parties: Independent Partners in the Money Relationship," in Green and Farmer, *The State of the Parties,* p.151. The budget estimates come from Robert J. Huckshorn and John F. Bibby, "State Parties in an Era of Political Change," in Joel L. Fleishman, ed., *The Future of American Political Parties* (Englewood Cliffs, NJ: Prentice-Hall, 1982), pp.70–100; Gibson, Cotter, Bibby, and Huckshorn, "Assessing Party Organizational Strength," and Aldrich, "Southern Parties," p. 656.

35. See Aldrich, "Southern Parties," pp. 656–657.

36. Aldrich, "Southern Parties," Table 7, pp. 656–657.

37. See Mildred Schwartz, *The Party Network* (Madison: University of Wisconsin Press, 1990) and Jonathan Bernstein and Casey B. K. Dominguez, "Candidates and Candidacies in the Expanded Party," *PS* 36 (2003): 165–169.

38. John H. Kessel, "Ray Bliss and the Development of the Ohio Republican Party During the 1950s," in John C. Green, ed., *Politics, Professionalism, and Power* (Lanham, MD: University Press of America, 1994), pp. 48–61.

39. Jewell and Morehouse, *Political Parties and Elections*, p. 36. See also Edward G. Carmines and James A. Stimson, *Issue Evolution* (Princeton: Princeton University Press, 1989); and Joseph A. Aistrup, *The Southern Strategy Revisited* (Lexington: University Press of Kentucky, 1996).

40. Charles Prysby, "North Carolina," and Anne E. Kelley, "Florida," in Appleton and Ward, *State Party Profiles*, pp. 234–243 and 62–64.

41. John F. Bibby, "State Party Organizations: Coping and Adapting," in L. Sandy Maisel, ed., *The Parties Respond* (Boulder, CO: Westview, 1994), pp. 36–43.

42. Walter Dean Burnham, *Critical Elections and the Mainsprings of American Politics* (New York: Norton, 1970), p. 72.

43. Alan Ware, *The Breakdown of the Democratic Party Organization 1940–80* (Oxford, England: Oxford University Press, 1985).

44. Jewell and Morehouse, *Political Parties and Elections*, p. 214.

45. John J. Coleman, "Party Organizational Strength and Public Support for the Parties," *American Journal of Political Science* 40 (1996): 805–824.

CHAPTER 4

1. Cornelius P. Cotter and Bernard C. Hennessy, *Politics without Power: The National Party Committees* (New York: Atherton, 1964). See also Ralph M. Goldman, *The National Party Chairmen and Committees* (Armonk, NY: M. E. Sharpe, 1990).

2. See Philip A. Klinkner, *The Losing Parties: Out-Party National Committees, 1956–1993* (New Haven: Yale University Press, 1994).

3. James W. Ceaser, "Political Parties—Declining, Stabilizing, or Resurging," in Anthony King, ed., *The New American Political System* (Washington, DC: American Enterprise Institute, 1990), p. 115. See also Sidney M. Milkis, *The President and the Parties* (New York: Oxford University Press, 1993).

4. Jo Freeman, *A Room at a Time* (Lanham, MD: Rowman & Littlefield, 2000).

5. Dan Balz, "On Heels of Election, Governors Seek Higher Profile Within Democratic Party," *Washington Post,* December 10, 2002, p. A16.

6. John C. Green, ed., *Politics, Professionalism, and Power: Modern Party Organization and the Legacy of Ray C. Bliss* (Lanham, MD: University Press of America, 1994).

7. See Austin Ranney, *Curing the Mischiefs of Faction* (Berkeley: University of California Press, 1975); William J. Crotty, *Decisions for the Democrats* (Baltimore: Johns Hopkins University Press, 1978); and Byron E. Shafer, *The Quiet Revolution* (New York: Russell Sage Foundation, 1983).

8. John F. Bibby, "Party Renewal in the Republican National Party," in Gerald M. Pomper, ed., *Party Renewal in America* (New York: Praeger, 1981), pp. 102–115.

9. See Paul S. Herrnson, "The Revitalization of National Party Organizations," in L. Sandy Maisel, ed., *The Parties Respond,* 2nd ed. (Boulder, CO.: Westview, 1994), pp. 45–68.

10. See Don Van Natta, Jr. and John M. Broder, "The Few, the Rich, the Rewarded Donate the Bulk of G.O.P. Gifts," *New York Times,* Aug. 2, 2000, p. A1; and Ceci Connolly, "In Final Funding Drive, Parties Eye 'Hard' Cash," *Washington Post,* Sept. 21, 2000, p. A16.

11. Jim VandeHei and Juliet Eilperin," For GOP, a High-Priced Pitch," *Washington Post,* June 16, 2003, p. A4.

12. Federal Election Commission at: http://www.fec.gov/press/20030320party/20030103party.html (accessed June 11, 2003).

13. Dan Balz, "GOP Aims for Dominance in '04 Race," *Washington Post,* June 22, 2003, p. A6.

14. F. Christopher Arterton calls them "service vendor" parties, and Paul Herrnson refers to them as "intermediary" parties. See Arterton's "Political Money and Party Strength," in Joel Fleishman, ed., *The Future of American Political Parties* (Englewood Cliffs, NJ: Prentice Hall, 1982), pp. 101–139; and Paul S. Herrnson, *Party Campaigning in the 1980s* (Cambridge, MA.: Harvard University Press, 1988), p. 47.

15. See David B. Magleby and Quin Monson, eds., "The Last Hurrah?", unpublished manuscript, Brigham Young University, 2003.

16. Mike Allen, "Bush Goes for 'Icing' in Louisiana," *Washington Post,* December 4, 2002, p. A1.

17. Daniel A. Smith, "Strings Attached: Outside Money in Colorado's Seventh Congressional District," in Magleby and Monson, eds., "The Last Hurrah?"

18. Howard Fineman, "How Bush Did It," *Newsweek,* November 18, 2002, pp. 32, 34.

19. Richard L. Berke, "G.O.P. Mobilizes to Help Hopefuls in Primary Races," *New York Times,* March 3, 2002, p. 26.

20. A. James Reichley, "The Rise of National Parties," in John E. Chubb and Paul E. Peterson, eds., *The New Direction in American Politics* (Washington, DC: Brookings Institution, 1985), pp. 175–200.

21. Timothy P. Nokken, "Ideological Congruence Versus Electoral Success," *American Politics Research* 31 (2003): 3–26.

22. Mike Glover, "Iowa Senate: Harkin's Best Yet," in Larry J. Sabato, ed., *Midterm Madness* (Lanham, MD: Rowman & Littlefield, 2003), pp. 78–79.

23. John J. Coleman, "The Resurgence of Party Organization? A Dissent from the New Orthodoxy," in Daniel M. Shea and John C. Green, eds., *The State of the Parties* (Lanham, MD: Rowman & Littlefield, 1994), pp. 311–328.

24. Leon D. Epstein, *Political Parties in the American Mold* (Madison: University of Wisconsin Press, 1986), p. 200.

CHAPTER 5

1. Peter B. Clark and James Q. Wilson, "Incentive Systems: A Theory of Organizations," *Administrative Science Quarterly* 6 (1961): 129–166; and James Q. Wilson, *Political Organizations* (New York: Basic Books, 1973), Chapter 6.

2. See A. James Reichley, *The Life of the Parties* (Lanham, MD: Rowman & Littlefield, 2000), pp. 72, 118, 128–130, 174–176, and Martin Shefter, *Political Parties and the State* (Princeton, NJ: Princeton University Press, 1994).

3. The 1976 case is *Elrod v. Burns,* 427 U.S. 347; the 1980 case is *Branti v. Finkel,* 445 U.S. 507; and the 1990 case is *Rutan v. Republican Party of Illinois,* 111 L. Ed. 2d 52.

4. On the case for patronage, see the dissenting opinions to the Supreme Court's *Elrod, Branti,* and *Rutan* decisions. The case against patronage is well put in Anne Freedman, *Patronage: An American Tradition* (Chicago: Nelson-Hall, 1994), Chapter 5.

5. Cornelius P. Cotter, James L. Gibson, John F. Bibby, and Robert J. Huckshorn, *Party Organizations in American Politics* (New York: Praeger, 1984), p. 42, and Robert J. Huckshorn, *Party Leadership in the States* (Amherst: University of Massachusetts Press, 1976), p. 37.

6. See William Crotty, ed., *Political Parties in Local Areas* (Knoxville: University of Tennessee Press, 1986) and Sidney Verba, Kay Lehman Schlozman, and Henry E. Brady, *Voice and Equality* (Cambridge, MA: Harvard University Press, 1995), pp. 112–121.

7. John C. Green, John S. Jackson, and Nancy L. Clayton, "Issue Networks and Party Elites in 1996," in John C. Green and Daniel M. Shea, eds., *The State of the Parties,* 3rd ed. (Lanham, MD: Rowman & Littlefield, 1999).

8. Samuel J. Eldersveld, "The Party Activist in Detroit and Los Angeles: A Longitudinal View, 1956–1980," in Crotty, *Political Parties in Local Areas,* Chapter 4.

9. Verba, Schlozman, and Brady, *Voice and Equality,* p. 121.

10. John A. Clark, John M. Bruce, John H. Kessel, and William Jacoby, "I'd Rather Switch than Fight," *American Journal of Political Science* 35 (1991): 577–597; Mary Grisez Kweit, "Ideological Congruence of Party Switchers and Nonswitchers: The Case of Party Activists," *American Journal of Political Science* 30 (1986): 184–196, and Dorothy Davidson Nesbit, "Changing Partisanship among Southern Party Activists," *Journal of Politics* 50 (1988): 322–334.

11. See M. Margaret Conway, *Political Participation in the United States,* 2nd ed. (Washington, DC: CQ Press, 1991), p. 61.

12. See Clark and Wilson, "Incentive Systems" and Wilson, *The Amateur Democrat.* Note that the term "professional," as used here, does not necessarily refer to someone who is paid for party work.

13. Walter J. Stone and Alan I. Abramowitz, "Winning May Not Be Everything But It's More Than We Thought," *American Political Science Review* 77 (1983): 945–956.

14. Michael A. Maggiotto and Ronald E. Weber, "The Impact of Organizational Incentives on County Party Chairpersons," *American Politics Quarterly* 14 (1986): 201–218.

15. Robert D. Putnam, *Bowling Alone: The Collapse and Revival of American Community* (New York: Simon & Schuster, 2000).

16. Verba, Schlozman, and Brady, *Voice and Equality,* Chapter 3.

17. American National Election Studies data, found at http://www.umich.edu/~nes/nesguide/toptable/tab6b_2.htm and _3.htm.

18. See Paul Allen Beck and M. Kent Jennings, "Updating Political Periods and Political Participation," *American Political Science Review* 78 (1984): 198–201; and Steven E. Finkel and Gregory Trevor, "Reassessing Ideological Bias in Campaign Participation," *Political Behavior* 8 (1986): 374–390.

19. See Verba, Schlozman, and Brady, *Voice and Equality,* pp. 15–16 and Chapters 9–14.

20. Henry E. Brady, Kay Lehman Schlozman, and Sidney Verba, "Prospecting for Participants," *American Political Science Review* 93 (1999): 153–168.

21. Verba, Schlozman, and Brady, *Voice and Equality,* pp. 135 and 139–144.

22. Verba, Schlozman, and Brady, *Voice and Equality,* Chapters 7 and 12, for campaign activists; Cotter, et al., *Party Organizations in American Politics,* p. 42, for local leaders; Ronald B. Rapoport, Alan I. Abramowitz, and John McGlennon, *The Life of the Parties* (Lexington: University of Kentucky Press, 1986), Chapter 3, for state convention delegates; and Chapter 10 of this book for national convention delegates.

23. Verba, Schlozman, and Brady, *Voice and Equality,* p. 190.

24. See Michael Margolis and Raymond E. Owen, "From Organization to Personalism," *Polity* 18 (1985): 313–328.

25. Malcolm E. Jewell and Sarah M. Morehouse, *Political Parties and Elections in American States,* 4th ed. (Washington, DC: CQ Press, 2001), p. 86.

26. Verba, Schlozman, and Brady, *Voice and Equality,* pp. 84–91.

27. Verba, Schlozman, and Brady, *Voice and Equality,* pp. 220–225.

28. Alan Abramowitz and Kyle Saunders, "Ideological Realignment in the U.S. Electorate," *Journal of Politics* (1998): 634.

29. See Morris P. Fiorina, "Extreme Voices: A Dark Side of Civic Engagement," in Theda Skocpol and Morris Fiorina, eds., *Civic Engagement in American Democracy* (Washington, DC: Brookings Institution Press, 1999), pp. 395–425.

PART THREE

1. See Angus Campbell, Philip E. Converse, Warren E. Miller, and Donald E. Stokes, *The American Voter* (New York: Wiley, 1960), Chapter 6.

2. Steven E. Finkel and Howard A. Scarrow, "Party Identification and Party Enrollment: The Difference and the Consequence," *Journal of Politics* 47 (1985): 620–642.

CHAPTER 6

1. This is happening in newer democracies such as Russia and the Ukraine as well, even in the face of over-whelmingly negative attitudes toward political parties more generally. See Arthur H. Miller and Thomas F. Klobucar, "The Development of Party Identification in Post-Soviet Societies," *American Journal of Political Science* 44 (2000): 667–685; and Ted Brader and Joshua A. Tucker, "The Emergence of Mass Partisanship in Russia, 1993–1996," *American Journal of Political Science* 45 (2001): 69–83.

2. John R. Petrocik, "An Analysis of the Intransitivities in the Index of Party Identification," *Political Methodology* 1 (1974): 31–47; and Herbert F. Weisberg, "A Multidimensional Conceptualization of Party Identification," *Political Behavior* 2 (1980): 33–60.

3. Paul Allen Beck and M. Kent Jennings, "Family Traditions, Political Periods, and the Development of Partisan Orientations," *Journal of Politics* 53 (1991): 742–763.

4. Paul Allen Beck, Russell J. Dalton, Steven Greene, and Robert Huckfeldt, "The Social Calculus of Voting," *American Political Science Review* 96 (2002): 57–73.

5. Richard G. Niemi and M. Kent Jennings, "Issues and Inheritance in the Formation of Party Identification," *American Journal of Political Science* 35 (1991): 970–988.

6. See William Clagett, "Partisan Acquisition vs. Partisan Intensity," *American Journal of Political Science* 25 (1981): 193–214.

7. James E. Campbell, "Sources of the New Deal Realignment," *Western Political Quarterly* 38 (1985): 357–376; and Warren E. Miller, "Generational Changes and Party Identification," *Political Behavior* 14 (1992): 333–352.

8. The seminal report of these studies is Angus Campbell, Philip E. Converse, Warren E. Miller, and Donald E. Stokes, *The American Voter* (New York: Wiley, 1960).

9. See Paul Allen Beck, "The Dealignment Era in America," in Russell J. Dalton, Scott C. Flanagan, and Paul Allen Beck, eds., *Electoral Change in Advanced Industrial Democracies* (Princeton, NJ: Princeton University Press, 1984), pp. 244–246.

10. Philip E. Converse and Gregory B. Markus, "Plus ça change . . . : The New CPS Election Study Panel," *American Political Science Review* 73 (1979): 32–49. See also Donald Philip Green and Bradley Palmquist, "How Stable Is Party Identification?" *Political Behavior* 16 (1994): 437–466.

11. Russell Dalton, "The Decline of Party Identification," in Russell J. Dalton and Martin P. Wattenberg, eds., *Parties without Partisans* (Oxford, UK: Oxford University Press, 2000), pp. 19–36.

12. Martin P. Wattenberg, *The Decline of American Political Parties, 1952–1994* (Cambridge, MA.: Harvard University Press, 1996), p. ix.

13. See James H. Kuklinski, Paul J. Quirk, Jennifer Jerit, and Robert F. Rich, "The Political Environment and Citizen Competence," *American Journal of Political Science* 45 (2001): 410–424; and Paul M. Sniderman, "Taking Sides: A Fixed Choice Theory of Political Reasoning," in Arthur Lupia, Mathew D. McCubbins, and Samuel L. Popkin, eds., *Elements of Reason* (New York: Cambridge University Press, 2000).

14. David G. Lawrence, "On the Resurgence of Party Identification in the 1990s," in Jeffrey E. Cohen, Richard Fleisher, and Paul Kantor, eds., *American Political Parties: Decline or Resurgence?* (Washington, DC: CQ Press, 2001), pp. 30–54.

15. The classic here is Bernard R. Berelson, Paul F. Lazarsfeld, and William N. McPhee, *Voting* (Chicago: University of Chicago Press, 1954), pp. 215–233.

16. Donald E. Stokes, "Some Dynamic Elements of Contests for the Presidency," *American Political Science Review* 60 (1966): 23.

17. "Stay or Go?" *Washington Post,* December 17, 2002, p. A8.

18. See Wendy M. Rahn, "The Role of Partisan Stereotypes in Information Processing about Political Candidates," *American Journal of Political Science* 37 (1993): 472–496.

19. Larry M. Bartels, "Partisanship and Voting Behavior, 1952–1996," *American Journal of Political Science* 44 (2000): 35–50.

20. Paul Allen Beck, Lawrence Baum, Aage R. Clausen, and Charles E. Smith, Jr., "Patterns and Sources of Ticket Splitting in Subpresidential Voting," *American Political Science Review* 86 (1992): 916–928.

21. See Barry C. Burden and David C. Kimball, "A New Approach to the Study of Ticket-Splitting," *American Political Science Review* 92 (1998): 533–544; and Malcolm E. Jewell and Sarah M. Morehouse, *Political Parties and Elections in American States* (Washington, DC: CQ Press, 2001), p. 277.

22. Beck, Baum, Clausen, and Smith, "Patterns and Sources of Ticket Splitting"; and Burden and Kimball, "A New Approach."

23. See Morris P. Fiorina, *Retrospective Voting in American National Elections* (New Haven; Yale University Press, 1981); and Michael B. MacKuen, Robert S. Erikson, and James A. Stimson, "Macropartisanship," *American Political Science Review* 83 (1989): 1125–1142.

24. Paul R. Abramson, John H. Aldrich, and David W. Rohde, *Change and Continuity in the 2000 and 2002 Elections* (Washington, DC: CQ Press, 2003), Chapter 6.

25. See Bartels, "Partisanship and Voting Behavior"; and Abramson, Aldrich, and Rohde, *Change and Continuity,* Chapter 8.

26. Overall turnout in 2000 among citizens of voting age was estimated at 51 percent. Reported turnout levels in the 2000 American National Election Studies survey are considerably higher for reasons specified in Chapter 8.

27. Abramson, Aldrich, and Rohde, *Change and Continuity,* pp. 178–189.

28. Sidney Verba and Norman H. Nie, *Participation in America* (Chicago: University of Chicago Press, 1987), Chapter 12.

29. See Bruce E. Keith, David B. Magleby, Candice J. Nelson, Elizabeth Orr, Mark Westlye, and Raymond E. Wolfinger, *The Myth of the Independent Voter* (Berkeley: University of California Press, 1992).

30. V. O. Key, Jr. (with Milton C. Cummings), *The Responsible Electorate* (Cambridge, MA: Harvard University Press, 1966).

31. See Paul R. Abramson, John H. Aldrich, and David W. Rohde, *Change and Continuity in the 1992 Elections* (Washington, DC: CQ Press, 1995), p. 245.

32. Data from the 1992 and 1996 American National Election Studies were made available by the Inter-University Consortium for Political and Social Research.

33. See Martin P. Wattenberg, *The Rise of Candidate-Centered Politics* (Cambridge, MA: Harvard University Press, 1991).

CHAPTER 7

1. See, for example, Edward G. Carmines and James A. Stimson, *Issue Evolution* (Princeton: Princeton University Press, 1989). On the social group "anchoring" of party ID, see Donald Green, Bradley Palmquist, and Eric Schickler, *Partisan Hearts and Minds* (New Haven: Yale University Press, 2002).

2. See V. O. Key, Jr., "A Theory of Critical Elections," *Journal of Politics* 17 (1955): 3–18; Walter Dean Burnham, *Critical Elections and the Mainsprings of American Politics* (New York: Norton, 1970); and James L. Sundquist, *Dynamics of the Party System* (Washington, DC: Brookings Institution, 1973).

3. For differing views, see Carmines and Stimson, *Issue Evolution*; Byron E. Shafer, ed., *The End of Realignment?* (Madison: University of Wisconsin Press, 1991); and Peter F. Nardulli, "The Concept of a Critical Realignment, Electoral Behavior, and Political Change," *American Political Science Review* 89 (1995): 10–22.

4. These events typically unfold over a period of time, but for convenience, the beginning of each party system is located in the year in which the new majority party coalition first took office.

5. Michael Holt, *The Rise and Fall of the American Whig Party* (New York: Oxford University Press, 2003).

6. The third party system actually contained two distinct periods. From the end of the Civil War in 1865 through 1876, Democratic voting strength in the South was held in check by the occupying Union army and various Reconstruction policies and laws. So to reflect the true party balance during this time, it is helpful to differentiate between 1861–1876 and the more representative 1877–1896 period.

7. A. James Reichley, *The Life of the Parties* (Lanham, MD: Rowman & Littlefield, 2000), p. 104.

8. Jeff Manza and Clem Brooks, *Social Cleavages and Political Change* (Oxford: Oxford University Press, 1999).

9. See Madison's *Federalist* 10.

10. See Paul R. Abramson, John H. Aldrich, and David W. Rohde, *Change and Continuity in the 2000 and 2002 Elections* (Washington, DC: CQ Press, 2003), pp. 113–115.

11. Jeffrey M. Stonecash, *Class and Party in American Politics* (Boulder, CO: Westview Press, 2000), pp. 13 and 139, and Chapter 4.

12. See Russell J. Dalton, Scott C. Flanagan, and Paul Allen Beck, eds., *Electoral Change in Advanced Industrial Democracies* (Princeton, NJ: Princeton University Press, 1984).

13. Henry E. Brady, "Trust the People: Political Party Coalitions and the 2000 Election," in Jack N. Rakove, *The Unfinished Election of 2000* (New York: Basic Books, 2001), p. 55.

14. Abramson, Aldrich, and Rohde, *Change and Continuity,* pp. 60–63.

15. Steven M. Cohen and Charles S. Liebman, "American Jewish Liberalism," *Public Opinion Quarterly* 61(1997): 405–430.

16. See Ted G. Jelen, *The Political Mobilization of Religious Belief* (Westport, CT: Praeger, 1991); and David C. Leege and Lyman A. Kellstedt, eds., *Rediscovering the Religious Factor in American Politics* (Armonk, NY: M. E. Sharpe, 1993).

17. "Stay or Go?" *Washington Post,* December 17, 2002, p. A8.

18. Abramson, Aldrich, and Rohde, *Change and Continuity,* pp. 97–100.

19. On black political behavior, see Katherine Tate, *From Protest to Politics* (Cambridge, MA: Harvard University Press, 1994). On racial differences in issue attitudes, see Donald R. Kinder and Nicholas Winter, "Exploring the Racial Divide," *American Journal of Political Science* 45 (2001): 439–453.

20. Dan Balz, "Strategists Prescribe No Rest for the GOP," *Washington Post,* November 24, 2002, p. A5.

21. "Most Hispanics Say They're Democrats," *Washington Post,* October 4, 2002, p. A8.

22. Karen M. Kaufman and John R. Petrocik, "The Changing Politics of American Men," *American Journal of Political Science* 43 (1999): 864–887.

23. Kira Sanbonmatsu, *Democrats, Republicans, and the Politics of Women's Place* (Ann Arbor: University of Michigan Press, 2002), Chapter 3; see also Christina Wolbrecht, *The Politics of Women's Rights* (Princeton: Princeton University Press, 2000).

24. Calculated from *CQ Weekly*'s "Special Report: Election 2002: New Senators, New Representatives," November 9, 2002, pp. 2948–2970.

25. David O. Sears, Richard R. Lau, Tom R. Tyler, and Harris M. Allen, Jr., "Self-Interest vs. Symbolic Politics in Policy Attitudes and Presidential Voting," *American Political Science Review* 74 (1980): 670–684; and Abramson, Aldrich, and Rohde, *Change and Continuity,* pp. 156–160.

26. Abramson, Aldrich, and Rohde, *Change and Continuity,* pp. 145–147.

27. Greg D. Adams, "Abortion: Evidence of an Issue Evolution," *American Journal of Political Science* 41 (1997): 718–737.

28. Quoted in Thomas B. Edsall, "Political Party Is No Longer Dictated By Class Status," *Washington Post,* Nov. 9, 2000, p. A37.

29. See Geoffrey C. Layman, *The Great Divide* (New York: Columbia University Press, 2001).

30. Harold W. Stanley and Richard G. Niemi, "The Demise of the New Deal Coalition," in Herbert Weisberg, ed., *Democracy's Feast* (Chatham, NJ: Chatham House, 1994), pp. 220–240.

31. Carmines and Stimson, *Issue Evolution.*

32. Kevin P. Phillips, *The Emerging Republican Majority* (New Rochelle, NY: Arlington House, 1969).

33. Helmut Norpoth, "Under Way and Here to Stay: Party Realignment in the 1980s?" *Public Opinion Quarterly* 51 (1987): 376–391; and Warren E. Miller, "Party Identification, Realignment, and Party Voting," *American Political Science Review* 85 (1991): 557–570.

34. See Earl Black and Merle Black, *Politics and Society in the South* (Cambridge, MA: Harvard University Press, 1987); Michael F. Meffert, Helmut Norpoth, and Anirudh V. S. Ruhil, "Realignment and Macropartisanship," *American Political Science Review* 95 (2001): 953–962; and Paul Frymer, "The 1994 Electoral Aftershock," in Philip A. Klinkner, ed., *Midterm: The Elections of 1994 in Context* (Boulder: Westview, 1996), pp. 99–113.

35. "Voting for the US House of Representatives 1984–1996: The Group Story," *The Public Perspective* (1997): 24.

36. See Martin P. Wattenberg, *The Decline of American Political Parties 1952–96* (Cambridge, MA.: Harvard University Press, 1998).

37. See Paul Allen Beck, "The Electoral Cycle and Patterns of American Politics," *British Journal of Political Science* 9 (1979): 129–156.

38. Burnham, *Critical Elections,* Chapters 4 and 5.

39. Thomas E. Patterson, *The Vanishing Voter* (New York: Alfred A. Knopf, 2002), p. 40.

40. Carmines and Stimson, *Issue Evolution.*

41. See Paul Allen Beck, "A Tale of Two Electorates," in John C. Green and Rick Farmer, eds., *The State of the Parties,* 4th ed. (Lanham, MD: Rowman & Littlefield, 2003), pp. 38–53.

CHAPTER 8

1. Because of the difficulties in estimating American turnout, most "official" turnout figures *underestimate* it. The percentages in Figure 8.1 follow the method of Walter Dean Burnham, which carefully corrects for this underestimation, so they are a little higher than the widely reported turnout figures. Their denominator is an effort to estimate the *eligible* population: the voting-age population minus the number of noncitizens living in the United States. The numerator of the turnout fraction is the number of voters who cast a vote for president or for the office with the highest vote in midterm elections. Estimated turnout would be slightly higher if we had a reliable way to include blank or spoiled ballots, write-in votes for the office with the highest vote total, and voters who did not vote for that office and to exclude from the denominator citizens who are not eligible to vote in various states because they are inmates of prisons or mental hospitals. See Walter Dean Burnham, "The Turnout Problem," in A. James Reichley, ed., *Elections American Style* (Washington, DC: Brookings Institution, 1987), pp. 97–133.

2. Walter Dean Burnham, "The Changing Shape of the American Political Universe," *American Political Science Review* 59 (1965): 7–28.

3. Stephen J. Wayne, *The Road to the White House 2004* (Belmont, CA: Wadsworth, 2004), p. 71.

4. "Suffrage" means the right to vote. See Chilton Williamson, *American Suffrage* (Princeton, NJ: Princeton University Press, 1960).

5. The Supreme Court case overturning the poll tax was *Harper v. Virginia State Board of Elections,* 383 U.S. 633 (1966).

6. *Oregon v. Mitchell,* 400 U.S. 112 (1970).

7. Raymond E. Wolfinger and Jonathan Hoffman, "Registering and Voting with Motor Voter," *PS: Political Science and Politics* 34 (2001): 85–92; and Michael D. Martinez and David Hill, "Did Motor Voter Work?" *American Politics Quarterly* 27 (1999): 296–315.

8. Paul Kleppner, *Continuity and Change in Electoral Politics, 1893–1928* (Westport, CT: Greenwood, 1987), pp. 165–166.

9. U.S. Census Bureau, Table A., Annual Moving Rates By Type of Move: 1990–2000, found at http://www.census.gov/prod/2001pubs/p20–538.pdf (accessed July 30, 2001).

10. Peverill Squire, Raymond E. Wolfinger, and David P. Glass, "Residential Mobility and Voter Turnout," *American Political Science Review* 81 (1987): 45–65.

11. Walter Dean Burnham, "Theory and Voting Research: Some Reflections on Converse's 'Change in the American Electorate,'" *American Political Science Review* 68 (1974): 1002–1023; and Frances Fox Piven and Richard A. Cloward, *Why Americans Still Don't Vote* (Boston: Beacon Press, 2000).

12. See Robert L. Dudley and Alan R. Gitelson, *American Elections: The Rules Matter* (New York: Longman, 2002), pp. 7–15.

13. Ruy A. Teixiera, *The Disappearing American Voter* (Washington, DC: Brookings Institution, 1992), Chapter 4; and Glenn E. Mitchell and Christopher Wlezien, "The Impact of Legal Constraints on Voter Registration, Turnout, and the Composition of the American Electorate," *Political Behavior* 17 (1995): 179–202.

14. See V. O. Key, Jr., *Southern Politics in State and Nation* (New York: Knopf, 1949).

15. The white primary was finally overturned by the Supreme Court in *Smith v. Allwright,* 321 U.S. 649 (1944).

16. Chandler Davidson and Bernard Grofman, eds., *Quiet Revolution in the South* (Princeton, NJ: Princeton University Press, 1994).

17. Thomas B. Edsall, "Parties Play Voting Rights Role Reversal," *Washington Post,* Feb. 25, 2001, p. A1. See also Kevin A. Hill, "Does the Creation of Majority Black Districts Aid Republicans?" *Journal of Politics* 57 (1995): 384–401; and David Lublin and D. Stephen Voss, "Racial Redistricting and Realignment in Southern State Legislatures," *American Journal of Political Science* 44 (2000): 792–810.

18. The cases are *Miller v. Johnson* 515 U.S. 900 (1995) and *Easley v. Cromartie* 532 U.S. 234 (2001), respectively. On majority-minority districts, see David T. Canon, *Race, Redistricting, and Representation* (Chicago: University of Chicago Press, 1999); and Katherine Tate, "Black Opinion on the Legitimacy of Racial Redistricting and Minority-Majority Districts," *American Political Science Review* 97 (2003): 45–56.

19. Robert E. Pierre and Peter Slevin, "Fla. Vote Rife With Disparities, Study Says," *Washington Post,* June 5, 2001, p. A1. See also Michael Tomz and Robert P. Van Houweling, "How Does Voting Equipment Affect the Racial Gap in Voided Ballots?" *American Journal of Political Science* 47 (2003): 46–60.

20. Associated Press, "Crimes Keep Many Blacks from Voting," http://www.nytimes.com/aponline/politics/AP-Felons-Voting.html (accessed Sept. 21, 2000).

21. Robert A. Jackson, "The Mobilization of U.S. State Electorates in the 1988 and 1990 Elections," *Journal of Politics* 59 (1997): 520–537.

22. Steven J. Rosenstone and John Mark Hansen, *Mobilization, Participation, and Democracy in America* (New York: Longman, 2003), pp. 178–188.

23. Burnham, "The Changing Shape of the American Political Universe."

24. Jerrold G. Rusk, "The American Electoral Universe: Speculation and Evidence," *American Political Science Review* 68 (1974): 1028–1049.

25. See Rosenstone and Hansen, *Mobilization, Participation, and Democracy in America.*

26. Data from the National Election Studies, on the Internet at http://www.umich.edu/~nes/nesguide/toptable/tab6c_1a.htm and 1b, 1c, and 2.htm (accessed August 13, 2003).

27. On the mobilization of black voters, see Lawrence Bobo and Franklin D. Gilliam, Jr., "Race, Sociopolitical Participation, and Black Empowerment," *American Political Science Review* 84 (1990): pp. 377–394; and Richard Timpone, "Mass Mobilization or Governmental Intervention," *Journal of Politics* 57 (1995): 425–442.

28. Juliet Eilperin, "Battle for the House: Labor on the Front Lines," *Washington Post,* Aug. 29, 2000, p. A1.

29. Alan S. Gerber, Donald P. Green, and Ron Chachar, "Voting May Be Habit-Forming," *American Journal of Political Science* 47 (2003): 540–550; and Eric Plutzer, "Becoming a Habitual Voter," *American Political Science Review* 96 (2002): 41–56.

30. See John H. Aldrich, "Rational Choice and Turnout," *American Journal of Political Science* 37 (1993): 246–278.

31. Paul R. Abramson, John H. Aldrich, and David W. Rohde, *Change and Continuity in the 2000 and 2002 Elections* (Washington, DC: CQ Press, 2003), pp. 82–85. See also Robert A. Jackson, "Clarifying the Relationship between Education and Turnout," *American Politics Quarterly* 23 (1995): 279–299.

32. Raymond E. Wolfinger and Steven J. Rosenstone, *Who Votes?* (New Haven, CT: Yale University Press, 1980), pp. 35–36.

33. Sidney Verba, Norman H. Nie, and Jae-On Kim, *Participation and Political Equality* (Cambridge: Cambridge University Press, 1978).

34. Amy Goldstein and Richard Morin, "Young Voters' Disengagement Skews Politics," *Washington Post,* October 20, 2002, p. A8.

35. Bobo and Gilliam, "Race, Sociopolitical Participation, and Black Empowerment."

36. Laura Stoker and M. Kent Jennings, "Life-Cycle Transitions and Political Participation: The Case of Marriage," *American Political Science Review* 89 (1995): 421–436; and Nancy Burns, Kay Lehman Schlozman, and Sidney Verba, "The Public Consequences of Private Inequality," *American Political Science Review* 91 (1997): 373–389.

37. Diana C. Mutz, "The Consequences of Cross-Cutting Networks for Political Participation," *American Journal of Political Science* 46 (2002): 838–855.

38. See Rosenstone and Hansen, *Mobilization, Participation, and Democracy in America*, pp. 141–156.

39. See Mark N. Franklin and Wolfgang P. Hirczy de Mino, "Separated Powers, Divided Government, and Turnout in U.S. Presidential Elections," *American Journal of Political Science* 42 (1998): 316–326.

40. Harold D. Clarke, David Sanders, Marianne C. Stewart, and Paul F. Whiteley, "Britain (Not) at the Polls, 2001," *PS: Political Science and Politics* (2003): 59–64.

41. See Richard A. Brody, "The Puzzle of Participation in America," in Anthony King, ed., *The New American Political System* (Washington, DC: American Enterprise Institute, 1978), pp. 287–324.

42. Abramson, Aldrich, and Rohde, *Change and Continuity,* pp. 86–91.

43. Edward G. Carmines and James A. Stimson, *Issue Evolution* (Princeton, NJ: Princeton University Press, 1989); and Claudine Gay, "The Effect of Black Congressional Representation on Political Participation," *American Political Science Review* 95 (2001): 589–602.

44. Paul S. Martin, "Voting's Rewards," *American Journal of Political Science* 47 (2003): 110–127.

45. Wolfinger and Rosenstone, *Who Votes?* Chapter 6.

46. James DeNardo, "Turnout and the Vote: The Joke's on the Democrats," *American Political Science Review* 74 (1980): 406–420. See also Jack Citrin, Eric Schickler, and John Sides, "What if Everyone Voted?" *American Journal of Political Science* 47 (2003): 75–90.

47. Rhodes Cook, "GOP Shows Dramatic Growth, Especially in the South," *CQ Weekly,* Jan. 13, 1996, pp. 97–100.

PART FOUR

1. See Murray Edelman, *Constructing the Political Spectacle* (Chicago: University of Chicago Press, 1988).

CHAPTER 9

1. See Alan Ware, *The American Direct Primary* (Cambridge: Cambridge University Press, 2002). On the spread of the primary to other democracies, see R. K. Carty and Donald E. Blake, "The Adoption of Membership Votes for Choosing Party Leaders: The Experience of Canadian Parties," *Party Politics* 5 (1999): 211–224; and Russell J. Dalton, Ian McAllister, and Martin P. Wattenberg, "Political Parties and Their Publics," in Richard Luther and Ferdinand Mueller-Rommel, eds., *Party Change in Europe* (Oxford: Oxford University Press, 2002), pp. 19–42.
2. Stephen J. Wayne, *The Road to the White House 2004* (Belmont, CA: Wadsworth, 2004), pp. 6–13.
3. See Charles E. Merriam and Louise Overacker, *Primary Elections* (Chicago: University of Chicago Press, 1928).
4. Robert M. La Follette, *La Follette's Autobiography* (Madison, WI: R. M. La Follette, 1913), pp. 197–198.
5. Some states allow third parties to nominate their candidates through conventions.
6. *The Book of the States 2003 Ed.* (Lexington, KY: The Council of State Governments, 2003), pp. 295–296. See also Malcolm E. Jewell and Sarah M. Morehouse, *Political Parties and Elections in American States*, 4th ed. (Washington, DC: CQ Press, 2001), Chapter 4.
7. See Craig L. Carr and Gary L. Scott, "The Logic of State Primary Classification Schemes," *American Politics Quarterly* 12 (1984): 465–476; and Steven E. Finkel and Howard A. Scarrow, "Party Identification and Party Enrollment: The Difference and the Consequence," *Journal of Politics* 47 (1985): 620–652.
8. The numbers of states in each category are drawn from John F. Bibby and Thomas M. Holbrook, "Parties and Elections," in Virginia Gray and Russell L. Hanson, eds., *Politics in the American States*, 8th ed. (Washington, DC: CQ Press, 2003), Chapter 3. Note that experts disagree on these definitions and on the dividing line between an "open" and a "closed" primary.
9. A 1986 Supreme Court decision (*Tashjian v. Republican Party of Connecticut*, 106 S. Ct. 783 and 1257) upheld the Connecticut party's efforts to establish an open primary by overriding the state's closed primary law. This decision affirmed the authority of the party, rather than the state, to control its own nomination process. However, most state parties would prefer a closed primary to an open one.
10. The case was *California Democratic Party v. Jones*, 530 U.S. 567(2000). On blanket primaries, see Bruce E. Cain and Elisabeth R. Gerber, eds., *Voting at the Political Fault Line: California's Experiment with the Blanket Primary* (Berkeley: University of California Press, 2002).
11. Lynn Vavreck, "The Reasoning Voter Meets the Strategic Candidate," *American Politics Research* 29 (2001): 507–529. See also Philip Paolino and Daron R. Shaw, "Lifting the Hood on the Straight-Talk Express," *American Politics Research* 29 (2001): 483–506.
12. Gary D. Wekkin, "Why Crossover Voters Are Not 'Mischievous' Voters," *American Politics Quarterly* 19 (1991): 229–247.
13. The monthly newsletter *Ballot Access News* reports current efforts to change the rules governing ballot access, especially for third parties and independents. It can be found on the Internet (http://www.ballot-access.org).
14. See Harold Stanley, "The Runoff: The Case for Retention," *PS: Political Science and Politics* 18 (1985): 231–236; and Charles S. Bullock, III, and Loch K. Johnson, *Runoff Elections in the United States* (Knoxville: University of Tennessee Press, 1991).
15. See V. O. Key, Jr., *American State Politics: An Introduction* (New York: Knopf, 1956), p. 195.
16. About a third of all state legislative races have been uncontested in recent years. See L. Sandy Maisel, Linda L. Fowler, Ruth S. Jones, and Walter J. Stone, "Nomination Politics: The Roles of Institutional, Contextual, and Personal Variables," in L. Sandy Maisel, ed., *The Parties Respond* (Boulder, CO: Westview, 1994), pp. 148–152.
17. See John G. Geer and Mark E. Shere, "Party Competition and the Prisoner's Dilemma: An Argument for the Direct Primary," *Journal of Politics* 54 (1992): 741–761.
18. See Jewell and Morehouse, *Political Parties and Elections in American States,* pp. 119–120.
19. See, for example, Jewell and Morehouse, *Political Parties and Elections in American States*, p. 123.

20. Theodore H. White, *The Making of the President 1960* (New York: Atheneum, 1961), p. 78.

21. See Walter J. Stone, "The Carryover Effect in Presidential Elections," *American Political Science Review* 80 (1986): 271–280, and Martin P. Wattenberg, "The Republican Presidential Advantage in the Age of Party Disunity," in Gary W. Cox and Samuel Kernell, eds., *The Politics of Divided Government* (Boulder, CO: Westview, 1991), Chapter 3.

22. Studies differ in their conclusions about the impact of divisive primaries, in part depending on the way they define "divisive." See, for example, Patrick J. Kenney and Tom W. Rice, "Presidential Prenomination Preferences and Candidate Evaluations," *American Political Science Review* 82 (1988): 1309–1319; James I. Lengle, Diana Owen, and Molly W. Sonner, "Divisive Nominating Mechanisms and Democratic Party Electoral Prospects," *Journal of Politics* 57 (1995): 370–383; Lonna Rae Atkeson, "Divisive Primaries and General Election Outcomes," *American Journal of Political Science* 42 (1998): 256–271; and Robert E. Hogan, "The Effects of Primary Divisiveness on General Election Outcomes in State Legislative Elections," *American Politics Research* 31 (2003): 27–47.

23. See Paige L. Schneider, "Factionalism in the Southern Republican Party," *American Review of Politics* 19 (1998): 129–148.

24. Matt Bai, "Fight Club," *New York Times Magazine,* August 10, 2003, pp. 24–27.

25. Quoted in David S. Broder and Juliet Eilperin, "Of Primary Importance," *Washington Post,* April 20, 2002, p. A1.

26. Gary F. Moncrief, Peverill Squire, and Malcolm E. Jewell, *Who Runs for the Legislature?* (Upper Saddle River, NJ: Prentice Hall, 2001), p. 39.

27. Sarah McCally Morehouse, *The Governor as Party Leader* (Ann Arbor: University of Michigan Press, 1998), pp. 22–23.

28. Jewell and Morehouse, *Political Parties and Elections in American States*, pp. 109–110.

29. See Maisel, Fowler, Jones, and Stone, "Nomination Politics," pp. 155–156.

30. See Jewell and Morehouse, *Political Parties and Elections in American States*, pp. 118–120.

31. Malcolm E. Jewell, "Northern State Gubernatorial Primary Elections: Explaining Voting Turnout," *American Politics Quarterly* 12 (1984): 101–116.

32. Patrick J. Kenney, "Explaining Primary Turnout: The Senatorial Case," *Legislative Studies Quarterly* 11 (1986): 65–74; and John G. Geer, "Assessing the Representativeness of Electorates in Presidential Primaries," *American Journal of Political Science* 32 (1988): 929–945.

33. Jewell and Morehouse, *Political Parties and Elections in American States*, pp. 124–125.

CHAPTER 10

1. See John S. Jackson III and William J. Crotty, *The Politics of Presidential Selection,* 2nd ed. (New York: Longman, 2001), Chapters 3 and 4.

2. See James W. Ceaser, *Presidential Selection* (Princeton, NJ: Princeton University Press, 1979); and Larry M. Bartels, *Presidential Primaries and the Dynamics of Public Choice* (Princeton, NJ: Princeton University Press, 1988, pp. 17–21.

3. Michael G. Hagen and William G. Mayer, "The Modern Politics of Presidential Selection," in William G. Mayer, ed., *In Pursuit of the White House 2000* (New York: Chatham House, 2000), pp. 1–55.

4. Byron E. Shafer, *Bifurcated Politics* (Cambridge, MA: Harvard University Press, 1988), pp. 181–184.

5. See Gary D. Wekkin, *Democrats versus Democrats* (Columbia: University of Missouri Press, 1983).

6. See Peverill Squire, ed., *The Iowa Caucuses and the Presidential Nominating Process* (Boulder, CO: Westview, 1989).

7. Matthew Robert Kerbel, "The Media: Old Frames in a Time of Transition," in Michael Nelson, ed., *The Elections of 2000* (Washington, DC: CQ Press, 2001), p. 119.

8. Howard Kurtz, "Funny, the Calendar Doesn't Say 2004," *Washington Post,* February 10, 2003, p. C1.

9. See John H. Aldrich, *Before the Convention* (Chicago: University of Chicago Press, 1980); and Paul-Henri Gurian and Audrey A. Haynes, "Campaign Strategy in Presidential Primaries," *American Journal of Political Science* 37 (1993): 335–341.

10. William G. Mayer, "The Presidential Nominations," in Gerald M. Pomper, ed., *The Election of 2000* (New York: Chatham House, 2001), pp. 13–16. See also Andrew E. Busch and William G. Mayer, "The Front-

Loading Problem," in William G. Mayer, ed., *The Making of the Presidential Candidates 2004* (Lanham, MD: Rowman & Littlefield, 2004), pp. 1–43.

11. Richard Herrera, "Are 'Superdelegates' Super?" *Political Behavior* 16 (1994): 79–92.

12. See Patrick J. Kenney and Tom W. Rice, "Voter Turnout in Presidential Primaries: A Cross-Sectional Examination," *Political Behavior* 7 (1985): 101–112; and Barbara Norrander and Gregg W. Smith, "Type of Contest, Candidate Strategy, and Turnout in Presidential Primaries," *American Politics Quarterly* 13 (1985): 28–50.

13. Bartels, *Presidential Primaries and the Dynamics of Public Choice*, pp. 140–148.

14. See Scott Keeter and Cliff Zukin, *Uninformed Choice* (New York: Praeger, 1983); and John G. Geer, *Nominating Presidents* (New York: Greenwood Press, 1989).

15. Samuel L. Popkin, *The Reasoning Voter* (Chicago: University of Chicago Press, 1991), Chapters 6–8.

16. Bartels, *Presidential Primaries and the Dynamics of Public Choice*, Chapter 4.

17. Paul R. Abramson, John H. Aldrich, Phil Paolino, and David W. Rohde, "'Sophisticated' Voting in the 1988 Presidential Primaries," *American Political Science Review* 86 (1992): 55–69.

18. See Walter J. Stone, Ronald B. Rapoport, and Alan I. Abramowitz, "Candidate Support in Presidential Nomination Campaigns: The Case of Iowa in 1984," *Journal of Politics* 54 (1992): 1074–1097.

19. Hagen and Mayer, "The Modern Politics of Presidential Selection," pp. 17–21.

20. L. Sandy Maisel, "The Platform-Writing Process: Candidate-Centered Platforms in 1992," *Political Science Quarterly* 108 (1993–1994): 671–699.

21. Gerald M. Pomper, "Party Responsibility and the Future of American Democracy," in Jeffrey E. Cohen, Richard Fleisher, and Paul Kantor, eds., *American Political Parties: Decline or Resurgence?* (Washington, DC: CQ Press, 2001), pp. 170–172.

22. See Lee Sigelman and Paul J. Wahlbeck, "The 'Veepstakes': Strategic Choice in Presidential Running Mate Selection," *American Political Science Review* 91 (1997): 855–864.

23. "Convention Delegates: Who They Are," *New York Times,* August 14, 2000, p. A19. See also Howard L. Reiter, *Selecting the President* (Philadelphia: University of Pennsylvania Press, 1985), Chapter 4.

24. These figures were provided by Kathleen Frankovic and Jinghua Zou from CBS News/*New York Times* delegate polls taken in June–August 2000.

25. Herbert McClosky, Paul Hoffman, and Rosemary O'Hara, "Issue Conflict and Consensus among Party Leaders and Followers," *American Political Science Review* 54 (1960): 406–427.

26. See Jeane Kirkpatrick, *The New Presidential Elite* (New York: Russell Sage Foundation, 1976).

27. See John S. Jackson III, Barbara L. Brown, and David Bositis, "Herbert McClosky and Friends Revisited," *American Politics Quarterly* 10 (1982): 158–180; and Warren E. Miller and M. Kent Jennings, *Parties in Transition* (New York: Russell Sage Foundation, 1986), Chapters 7–9.

28. See John W. Soule and Wilma E. McGrath, "A Comparative Study of Presidential Nomination Conventions: The Democrats 1968 and 1972," *American Journal of Political Science* 19 (1975): 501–517.

29. Denise L. Baer and David A. Bositis, *Elite Cadres and Party Coalitions* (New York: Greenwood Press, 1988), Chapter 7.

30. Shafer, *Bifurcated Politics*, Chapter 8.

31. Harold W. Stanley, "The Nominations: The Return of the Party Leaders," in Michael Nelson, ed., *The Elections of 2000* (Washington, DC: CQ Press, 2001), p. 35.

32. See Emmett H. Buell, Jr., "The Changing Face of the New Hampshire Primary," in William G. Mayer, ed., *In Pursuit of the White House 2000* (New York: Chatham House, 2000), pp. 87–144.

33. Nelson W. Polsby, *The Consequences of Party Reform* (Oxford: Oxford University Press, 1983).

CHAPTER 11

1. Jerrold G. Rusk, "The Effect of the Australian Ballot Reform on Split Ticket Voting: 1876–1908," *American Political Science Review* 64 (1970): 1220–1238.

2. See Angus Campbell, Philip E. Converse, Warren E. Miller, and Donald E. Stokes, *The American Voter* (New York: John Wiley & Sons, 1960), Chapter 11; and Harold F. Bass, Jr., "Partisan Rules, 1946–1996," in Byron E. Shafer, ed., *Partisan Approaches to Postwar American Politics* (New York: Chatham House, 1998), pp. 230–237.

3. Joanne M. Miller and Jon A. Krosnick, "The Impact of Candidate Name Order on Election Outcomes," *Public Opinion Quarterly* 62 (1998): 291–330.

4. Walter Dean Burnham, "The Changing Shape of the American Political Universe," *American Political Science Review* 59 (1965): 7–28. See also Stephen M. Nichols and Gregory A. Strizek, "Electronic Voting Machines and Ballot Roll-off," *American Politics Quarterly* 23 (1995): 300–318.

5. Guy Gugliotta, "Study Finds Millions of Votes Lost," *Washington Post,* July 17, 2001, p. A1; and Richard G. Niemi and Paul S. Herrnson, "Beyond the Butterfly: The Complexity of U.S. Ballots," *Perspectives on Politics* 1 (2003): 317–326.

6. Robin Toner, "For Those Behind the Scenes, It's Old News That Elections Are Not an Exact Science," *New York Times,* Nov. 17, 2000, p. A23.

7. The classic study is Warren E. Miller, "Presidential Coattails," *Public Opinion Quarterly* 19 (1955–56): 353–368. See also Jeffery J. Mondak, "Determinants of Coattail Voting," *Political Behavior* 12 (1990): 265–288.

8. Walter Dean Burnham, *Critical Elections and the Mainsprings of American Politics* (New York: Norton, 1970), p. 94.

9. The landmark Supreme Court cases are *Baker v. Carr,* 369 U.S. 186 (1962); *Reynolds v. Sims,* 377 U.S. 533 (1964); and *Wesberry v. Sanders,* 376 U.S. 1 (1964).

10. Gregory L. Giroux, "Democrats Regenerating for Long Haul to a Majority," *CQ Weekly,* June 7, 2003, pp. 1364–1367.

11. See Gary W. Cox and Jonathan N. Katz, "The Reapportionment Revolution and Bias in U.S. Congressional Elections," *American Journal of Political Science* 43 (1999): 812–841; Richard G. Niemi and Alan I. Abramowitz, "Partisan Redistricting and the 1992 Congressional Elections," *Journal of Politics* 56 (1994): 811–817; and Andrew Gelman and Gary King, "Enhancing Democracy through Legislative Redistricting," *American Political Science Review* 88 (1994): 541–559. On California, see Bruce E. Cain, "Assessing the Partisan Effects of Redistricting," *American Political Science Review* 79 (1985): 320–334; on Indiana, see John D. Cranor, Gary L. Crawley, and Raymond H. Scheele, "The Anatomy of a Gerrymander," *American Journal of Political Science* 33 (1989): 222–239.

12. See Paul S. Herrnson, *Congressional Elections,* 4th ed. (Washington, DC: CQ Press, 2004); Marjorie Randon Hershey, *Running for Office* (Chatham, NJ: Chatham House, 1984); and on presidential campaigns, Stephen J. Wayne, *The Road to the White House 2004* (Belmont, CA: Wadsworth, 2004).

13. Herrnson, *Congressional Elections*; and Gary C. Jacobson, *The Politics of Congressional Elections,* 5th ed. (New York: Longman, 2001).

14. Robin Toner, "A Political Pulse-Taker Is Back, Without Missing a Beat," *New York Times,* Aug. 28, 2000, p. A10.

15. James A. Thurber and Candice J. Nelson, eds., *Campaign Warriors* (Washington, DC: Brookings Institution, 2000).

16. Kathleen Hall Jamieson, *Packaging the Presidency* (New York: Oxford University Press, 1996); and Darrell M. West, *Air Wars: Television Advertising in Election Campaigns, 1952–2000,* 3rd ed. (Washington, DC: CQ Press, 2001).

17. On content differences in 2000 campaign coverage between mainstream magazines and magazines predominantly read by blacks, see Amy N. Okereke, "Participation, Representation, and Identification," paper delivered to the Summer Research Opportunities Program, Indiana University, July 2002.

18. See Doris A. Graber, *Mass Media and American Politics,* 6th ed. (Washington, DC: CQ Press, 2002), Chapter 4.

19. Dave Barry, "Scandal Sheep," *The Boston Globe Magazine,* Mar. 15, 1998, pp. 12–13.

20. Michael Cornfield, "A User's Guide to 'the Digital Divide,'" *Campaigns & Elections* (2000): 47.

21. John Bart and James Meader, "South Dakota Senate Race 2002," in David B. Magleby and J. Quin Monson, eds., *The Last Hurrah?* (Provo, UT: Center for the Study of Elections and Democracy, Brigham Young University, 2003).

22. See National Election Studies data at http://www.umich.edu/~nes/nesguide/toptable/tab6c_1a.htm (accessed Sept. 5, 2003).

23. See Magleby and Monson, *The Last Hurrah?,* Chapters 1 and 12.

24. See Richard R. Lau and Gerald M. Pomper, "Effectiveness of Negative Campaigning in U.S. Senate Elections," *American Journal of Political Science* 46 (2002): 47–66; Stephen Ansolabehere and Shanto Iyengar, *Going Negative* (New York: Free Press, 1995); and, for a different view, Steven E. Finkel and John G. Geer, "A Spot Check: Casting Doubt on the Demobilizing Effect of Attack Advertising," *American Journal of Political Science* 42 (1998): 573–595.

25. Dan Balz, "Exuberant RNC Seeks More Voters," *Washington Post,* February 1, 2003, p. A5.

26. Paul R. Abramson, John H. Aldrich, and David W. Rohde, *Change and Continuity in the 2000 and 2002 Elections* (Washington, DC: CQ Press, 2003), pp. 261–262.
27. Andrew Gelman and Gary King, "Why Are American Presidential Election Polls So Variable When Votes Are So Predictable," *British Journal of Political Science* 23 (1993): 409–451;, and Thomas M. Holbrook, "Campaigns, National Conditions, and U.S. Presidential Elections," *American Journal of Political Science* 38 (1994): 973–998.
28. See Robert Huckfeldt and John Sprague, "Political Parties and Electoral Mobilization," *American Political Science Review* 86 (1992): 70–86; Peter W. Wielhouwer, "The Mobilization of Campaign Activists by the Party Canvass," *American Politics Quarterly* 27 (1999): 177–200; and Steven J. Rosenstone and John Mark Hansen, *Mobilization, Participation, and Democracy in America* (New York: Longman, 2003), Chapter 6.
29. John C. Blydenburg, "A Controlled Experiment to Measure the Effects of Personal Contact Campaigning," *Midwest Journal of Political Science* 15 (1971): 365–381.
30. Lynn Vavreck, Constantine J. Spiliotes and Linda L. Fowler, "The Effects of Retail Politics in the New Hampshire Primary," *American Journal of Political Science* 46 (2002): 595–610.
31. John P. Frendreis, James L. Gibson, and Laura L. Vertz, "The Electoral Relevance of Local Party Organizations," *American Political Science Review* 84 (1990): 225–235.
32. Harold W. Stanley and Richard G. Niemi, *Vital Statistics on American Politics 1999–2000* (Washington, DC: CQ Press, 2000), Table 4.5, p. 173.
33. Kathleen Hall Jamieson and Paul Waldman, *The Press Effect* (New York: Oxford University Press, 2003), p. 67.
34. See National Election Studies data at http://www.umich.edu/~nes/nesguide/toptable/tab6d_1.htm (accessed Sept. 7, 2003).
35. Daron R. Shaw, "The Effect of TV Ads and Candidate Appearances on Statewide Presidential Votes, 1988–96," *American Political Science Review* 93 (1999): 345–361; and Carroll J. Glynn, Susan Herbst, Garrett J. O'Keefe, and Robert Y. Shapiro, *Public Opinion* (Boulder, CO: Westview, 1999), pp. 436–441.
36. Thomas M. Holbrook, *Do Campaigns Matter?* (Thousand Oaks, CA: Sage, 1996); Daron R. Shaw, "A Study of Presidential Campaign Event Effects from 1952–1992," *Journal of Politics* 61 (1999): 387–422; and Adam Simon, *The Winning Message* (Cambridge: Cambridge University Press, 2002).
37. Thomas E. Patterson, *The Vanishing Voter* (New York: Alfred A. Knopf, 2002), pp. 142–144.
38. D. Sunshine Hillygus and Simon Jackman, "Voter Decision Making in Election 2000," *American Journal of Political Science* 47 (2003): 583–596.
39. Russell J. Dalton, Paul A. Beck, and Robert Huckfeldt, "Partisan Cues and the Media: Information Flows in the 1992 Presidential Election," *American Political Science Review* 92 (1998): 111–126.
40. See Robert Huckfeldt and John Sprague, "Networks in Context: The Social Flow of Political Information," *American Political Science Review* 81 (1987): 1197–1216; and Paul Allen Beck, "Voters' Intermediation Environments in the 1988 Presidential Contest," *Public Opinion Quarterly* 55 (1991): 371–394.
41. The classics are Paul Lazarsfeld, Bernard Berelson, and Hazel Gaudet, *The People's Choice* (New York: Columbia University Press, 1948); and Bernard Berelson, Paul Lazarsfeld, and William McPhee, *Voting* (Chicago: University of Chicago Press, 1954).
42. Donald Shaw and Maxwell E. McCombs, *The Emergence of American Political Issues* (St. Paul, MN: West, 1977). On priming, see Joanne M. Miller and Jon A. Krosnick, "News Media Impact on the Ingredients of Presidential Evaluations," *American Journal of Political Science* 44 (2000): 295–309; and Shanto Iyengar and Donald Kinder, *News That Matters* (Chicago: University of Chicago Press, 1987).
43. Iyengar and Kinder, *News That Matters*; see also Jamieson and Waldman, *The Press Effect*.
44. See Marjorie Randon Hershey, "The Campaign and the Media," in Gerald M. Pomper, ed., *The Election of 2000* (New York: Chatham House, 2001), pp. 46–72.
45. Shanto Iyengar and John R. Petrocik, "'Basic Rule' Voting: Impact of Campaigns on Party- and Approval-Based Voting," in James A. Thurber, Candice J. Nelson, and David A. Dulio, eds., *Crowded Airwaves* (Washington, DC: Brookings Institution, 2000), p. 142.
46. John J. Coleman, "Party Images and Candidate-Centered Campaigns in 1996," in John C. Green and Daniel M. Shea, eds., *The State of the Parties,* 3rd ed. (Lanham, MD: Rowman & Littlefield, 1999), pp. 337–354.
47. See John Kenneth White and Daniel M. Shea, *New Party Politics,* 2nd ed. (Belmont, CA: Wadsworth, 2004), p. 98.

48. See, for example, David B. Magleby, ed., *The Other Campaign* (Lanham, MD: Rowman & Littlefield, 2003).
49. Craig Wilson, "The Montana 2000 Senate and House Races," in Magleby, ed., *The Other Campaign*, pp. 129–148.
50. See Justin Buchler and Raymond J. LaRaja, "Do Party Organizations Matter?" and Brian J. Brox, "Party Mobilization in the 2000 Election," papers presented at the 2002 Annual Meeting of the Midwest Political Science Association.
51. Quoted in David B. Magleby and Eric A. Smith, "Party Soft Money in the 2000 Congressional Elections," in Magleby, ed., *The Other Campaign*, p. 44.
52. See Paul S. Herrnson and Diana Dwyre, "Party Issue Advocacy in Congressional Election Campaigns," in Green and Shea, *The State of the Parties*, pp. 86–104.

CHAPTER 12

1. George Thayer, *Who Shakes the Money Tree?* (New York: Simon & Schuster, 1973), p. 25.
2. Candice J. Nelson, "Spending in the 2000 Elections," in David B. Magleby, ed., *Financing the 2000 Election* (Washington, DC: Brookings Institution, 2002), Chapter 2.
3. See John J. Coleman and Paul F. Manna, "Congressional Campaign Spending and the Quality of Democracy," *Journal of Politics* 62 (2000): 757–789.
4. See Anthony Corrado, "Financing the 2000 Elections," in Gerald M. Pomper, et al., eds., *The Election of 2000* (New York: Chatham House, 2001), pp. 92–124. Unless otherwise noted, specific figures cited in this chapter come from FEC reports.
5. Center for Responsive Politics, http://www.opensecrets.org/overview/stats.asp?cycle=2002 (accessed Sept. 15, 2003). The average figures include major party candidates only.
6. See Paul S. Herrnson, *Congressional Elections,* 4th ed. (Washington, DC: CQ Press, 2004), Chapter 5.
7. Michael Cooper, "At $92.60 a Vote, Bloomberg Shatters An Election Record," *New York Times,* Dec. 4, 2001, p. A1.
8. Malcolm Jewell and Sarah M. Morehouse, *Political Parties and Elections in American States* (Washington, DC: CQ Press, 2001), p. 211.
9. Neil A. Lewis, "Gifts in State Judicial Races Are Up Sharply," *New York Times,* Feb. 14, 2002, p. A27.
10. Gary C. Jacobson, *The Politics of Congressional Elections,* 5th ed. (New York: Longman, 2001), pp. 44–46.
11. See these articles in the *American Journal of Political Science:* Donald Philip Green and Jonathan S. Krasno, "Salvation for the Spendthrift Incumbent," 32 (1988): 884–907; Gary C. Jacobson, "The Effects of Campaign Spending in House Elections," 34 (1990): 334–362; and Donald Philip Green and Jonathan S. Krasno, "Rebuttal to Jacobson's 'New Evidence for Old Arguments,'" 34 (1990): 363–372.
12. On federal races, see FEC press release, June 18, 2003. On state elections, see Michael J. Malbin and Thomas L. Gais, *The Day After Reform* (Albany, NY: Rockefeller Institute, 1998).
13. Benjamin A. Webster, et al., "Competing for Cash," in Paul S. Herrnson, ed., *Playing Hardball* (Upper Saddle River, NJ: Prentice Hall, 2001), pp. 41–69.
14. Larry J. Sabato and Bruce A. Larson, *The Party's Just Begun,* 2nd ed. (New York: Longman, 2002), pp. 84–88.
15. FEC press release, June 3, 2002.
16. Frank J. Sorauf, *Inside Campaign Finance* (New Haven, CT: Yale University Press, 1992), Chapter 4.
17. Gregory Wawro, "A Panel Probit Analysis of Campaign Contributions and Roll-Call Votes," *American Journal of Political Science* 45 (2001): 563–579.
18. See Richard L. Hall and Frank W. Wayman, "Buying Time," *American Political Science Review* 84 (1990): 797–820.
19. John R. Wright, "PACs, Contributions, and Roll Calls," *American Political Science Review* 79 (1985): 400–414.
20. FEC news release, Mar. 20, 2003.
21. See Malbin and Gais, *The Day After Reform,* Chapter 4.
22. 424 U.S. 1 (1976). See Thomas E. Mann, "Linking Knowledge and Action: Political Science and Campaign Finance Reform," *Perspectives on Politics* 1 (2003): 69–83.
23. Anthony Corrado and Heitor Gouvea, "Financing Presidential Nominations under the BCRA," in William G. Mayer, *The Making of the Presidential Candidates 2004* (Lanham, MD: Rowman & Littlefield, 2004), p. 47.
24. Derek Willis, "Private Parties' Last-Minute Spending Spree," *CQ Weekly,* Nov. 11, 2000, p. 2624.

25. From the record in *McConnell v. Federal Election Commission*, quoted in Adam Cohen, "Buying a High-Priced Upgrade on the Political Back-Scratching Circuit," *New York Times,* Sept. 15, 2003, p. A22.

26. See Anthony Corrado, Sarah Barclay, and Heitor Gouvea, "The Parties Take the Lead," in John C. Green and Rick Farmer, eds., *The State of the Parties,* 4th ed. (Lanham, MD: Rowman & Littlefield, 2003), pp. 97–114; and Diana Dwyre and Victoria A. Farrar-Myers, *Legislative Labyrinth* (Washington, DC: CQ Press, 2001).

27. John Kenneth White and Daniel M. Shea, *New Party Politics* (Belmont, CA: Wadsworth, 2004), p. 258.

28. Malbin and Gais, *The Day After Reform*, pp. 11–12.

29. Quoted in Diana Dwyre, "Campaigning Outside the Law," in Allan J. Cigler and Burdett A. Loomis, eds., *Interest Group Politics,* 6th ed. (Washington, DC: CQ Press, 2002). p. 146.

30. Daniel A. Smith, "Strings Attached: Outside Money in Colorado's Seventh Congressional District," in David B. Magleby and J. Quin Monson, eds., *The Last Hurrah?* (Provo, UT: Center for the Study of Elections and Democracy, Brigham Young University, 2003).

31. Paul S. Herrnson, "The Congressional Elections," in Gerald M. Pomper, ed., *The Election of 2000* (New York: Chatham House, 2001), p. 170.

32. Campaign Finance Institute press release, July 14, 2003.

33. John Solomon, "AP: Groups Spend to Sway Elections," AP Online, Nov. 4, 2000 (accessed Nov. 5, 2000).

34. Karen Foerstel and Peter Wallsten, "Campaign Overhaul Mired in Money and Loopholes," *CQ Weekly,* May 13, 2000, p. 1084.

35. Foerstal and Wallsten, "Campaign Overhaul."

36. Mike Allen, "GOP Takes in $33 Million at Fundraiser," *Washington Post,* May 15, 2002, p. A1.

37. Mike Allen, "Interest Groups a Force in Congressional Elections," *Washington Post,* Feb. 6, 2001, p. A5.

38. Raymond J. La Raja, "State Parties and Soft Money," in John C. Green and Rick Farmer, *The State of the Parties,* 4th ed. (Lanham, MD: Rowman & Littlefield, 2003), pp. 132–150.

39. Jonathan Krasno and Kenneth Goldstein, "The Facts About Television Advertising and the McCain-Feingold Bill," *PS Political Science & Politics* 35 (2002): 210.

40. Malbin and Gais, *The Day After Reform,* pp. 13–23.

41. See Harold W. Stanley and Richard G. Niemi, *Vital Statistics on American Politics, 1999–2000* (Washington, DC: CQ Press, 2000), Tables 2.2 and 2.3, pp. 84–87.

42. Richard Morin and Claudia Deane, "Exit Polls in Doubt for Nov. Elections," *Washington Post on the Web,* http://www.washingtonpost.com/wp-dyn/articles/A26071-2002Aug16.html (accessed Aug. 16, 2002).

43. "Campaign Finance Law Provisions," *CQ Weekly,* May 18, 2002, pp. 1347–1352. See also Michael J. Malbin, ed., *Life After Reform* (Lanham, MD: Rowman & Littlefield, 2003).

PART FIVE

1. David Firestone and Richard W. Stevenson, "G.O.P. Leader Brushes Off Pressure by Bush on Taxes," *New York Times,* June 11, 2003, p. 1.

2. See the report of the Committee on Responsible Parties of the American Political Science Association, *Toward a More Responsible Two-Party System* (New York: Rinehart, 1950).

3. Ian Budge and Richard I. Hofferbert, "Mandates and Policy Outputs: U.S. Party Platforms and Federal Expenditures," *American Political Science Review* 84 (1990): 111–131. See also the discussion by Budge, Hofferbert, and others in "Party Platforms, Mandates, and Government Spending," *American Political Science Review* 87 (1993): 744–750.

4. Associated Press, "AP: GOP Changed Spending of Billions," *New York Times on the Web,* August 5, 2002.

CHAPTER 13

1. Jim VandeHei and Juliet Eilperin, "GOP Leaders Tighten Hold In the House," *Washington Post,* Jan. 13, 2003, p. A1.

2. Keith Krehbiel, "Where's the Party?" *British Journal of Political Science* 23 (1993): 225–266.

3. Gary W. Cox and Keith T. Poole, "On Measuring Partisanship in Roll-Call Voting," *American Journal of Political Science* 46 (2002): 477–489; Gerald C. Wright and Brian F. Schaffner, "The Influence of Party," *American Political Science Review* 96 (2002): 367–379. See also Jeffery A. Jenkins, "Examining the Bonding Effects of Party," *American Journal of Political Science* 43 (1999): 1144–1165.

4. The Nebraska legislature is chosen in nonpartisan elections, although the partisan affiliations of its members are usually no secret. Of the 7,611 state legislators and the 535 members of Congress, only 23 were neither Democrats nor Republicans in 2002; see *The Book of the States, 2003 Edition* (Lexington, KY: Council of State Governments, 2003), p. 82.

5. D. Roderick Kiewiet and Mathew D. McCubbins, *The Logic of Delegation* (Chicago: University of Chicago Press, 1991).

6. Even Cannon faced limits, however; see Eric D. Lawrence, Forrest Maltzman, and Paul J. Wahlbeck, "The Politics of Speaker Cannon's Committee Assignments," *American Journal of Political Science* 45 (2001): 551–562.

7. Joseph Cooper and David W. Brady, "Institutional Context and Leadership Style: The House from Cannon to Rayburn," *American Political Science Review* 75 (1981): 411–425.

8. Gary W. Cox and Mathew W. McCubbins, *Legislative Leviathan* (Berkeley and Los Angeles: University of California Press, 1993), pp. 279–282.

9. Barbara Sinclair, "Evolution or Revolution? Policy-oriented Congressional Parties in the 1990s," in L. Sandy Maisel, ed., *The Parties Respond,* 3rd ed. (Boulder, CO: Westview, 1998).

10. David W. Rohde, *Parties and Leaders in the Postreform House* (Chicago: University of Chicago Press, 1991). See also Barbara Sinclair, *Legislators, Leaders, and Lawmaking* (Baltimore: Johns Hopkins University Press, 1995).

11. See, for example, Vincent G. Moscardelli, Moshe Haspel, and Richard S. Wike, "Party Building through Campaign Finance Reform," *Journal of Politics* 60 (1998): 691–704.

12. Barbara Sinclair, *Unorthodox Lawmaking,* 2nd ed. (Washington, DC: CQ Press, 2000), pp. 103–106.

13. See Lawrence C. Evans and Walter J. Oleszek, *Congress Under Fire* (Boston: Houghton Mifflin, 1997); and Lawrence C. Dodd and Bruce I. Oppenheimer, "A House Divided: The Struggle for Partisan Control, 1994–2000," in Dodd and Oppenheimer, eds., *Congress Reconsidered,* 7th ed. (Washington, DC: CQ Press, 2001), Chapter 2.

14. VandeHei and Eilperin, "GOP Leaders Tighten Hold In the House."

15. Sinclair, "The New World of U.S. Senators," in Dodd and Oppenheimer, eds., *Congress Reconsidered.*

16. Steven S. Smith and Gerald Gamm, "The Dynamics of Party Government in Congress," in Dodd and Oppenheimer, eds., *Congress Reconsidered.*

17. The exceptions are some southern states and Nebraska, which is nominally nonpartisan. See Malcolm E. Jewell and Sarah M. Morehouse, *Political Parties and Elections in American States,* 4th ed. (Washington, DC: CQ Press, 2001), Chapter 8.

18. Jewell and Morehouse, *Political Parties and Elections*, pp. 234–235.

19. Jewell and Morehouse, *Political Parties and Elections*, pp. 236–238.

20. See Keith E. Hamm and Robert Harmel, "Legislative Party Development and the Speaker System: The Case of the Texas House," *Journal of Politics* 55 (1993): 1140–1151; and Malcolm E. Jewell and Marcia Lynn Whicker, *Legislative Leadership in the American States* (Ann Arbor, MI: University of Michigan Press, 1994).

21. Thomas Stratmann, "Congressional Voting over Legislative Careers," *American Political Science Review* 94 (2000): 665–676.

22. Juliet Eilperin, "House GOP Practices Art of One-Vote Victories," *Washington Post,* Oct. 14, 2003, p. A1.

23. See Barbara Sinclair, "Majority Party Leadership Strategies for Coping with the New U.S. House," *Legislative Studies Quarterly* 6 (1981): 391–414; and Steven Smith, *Call to Order* (Washington, DC: Brookings Institution, 1989).

24. See Paul S. Herrnson, *Congressional Elections: Campaigning at Home and in Washington,* 4th ed. (Washington, DC: CQ Press, 2004), and Kathryn Pearson, "Congressional Party Discipline: Carrots on the Campaign Trail?" paper delivered at the 2002 Annual Meeting of the Midwest Political Science Association.

25. Julius Turner, *Party and Constituency: Pressures on Congress,* rev. ed., Edward V. Schneier, ed. (Baltimore: The Johns Hopkins University Press, 1970), pp. 16–17.

26. Gregory L. Giroux, "GOP's Effectiveness Shows in Party Unity Votes," *CQ Weekly,* April 19, 2003, p. 923.

27. Jason M. Roberts and Steven S. Smith, "Procedural Contexts, Party Strategy, and Conditional Party Voting in the U.S. House of Representatives, 1971–2000," *American Journal of Political Science* 47 (2003): 305–317.

28. Barbara Sinclair, "The New World of U.S. Senators," p. 3.

29. See Nelson W. Polsby, "The Institutionalization of the United States House of Representatives," *American Political Science Review* 62 (1968): 144–168, and Walter Dean Burnham, *Critical Elections and the Mainsprings of American Politics* (New York: Norton, 1970), pp. 91–134.

30. See Dodd and Oppenheimer, "A House Divided," pp. 38–39.

31. Jewell and Morehouse, *Political Parties and Elections*, p. 251.

32. Stanley P. Berard, *Southern Democrats in the U.S. House of Representatives* (Norman: University of Oklahoma Press, 2001).

33. Gary C. Jacobson, "Congress: Elections and Stalemate," in Michael Nelson, ed., *The Elections of 2000* (Washington, DC: CQ Press, 2001), pp. 204–205.

34. Rohde, *Parties and Leaders in the Postreform House,* Chapter 3. See also M. V. Hood III, Quentin Kidd, and Irwin L. Morris, "Of Byrd[s] and Bumpers: Using Democratic Senators to Analyze Political Change in the South, 1960–1995," *American Journal of Political Science* 43 (1999): 465–487.

35. See Mark A. Peterson, *Legislating Together* (Cambridge, MA: Harvard University Press, 1990); and Cary R. Covington, J. Mark Wrighton, and Rhonda Kinney, "A 'Presidency-Augmented' Model of Presidential Success on House Roll Call Votes," *American Journal of Political Science* 39 (November 1995): 1001–1024.

36. Gary C. Jacobson, *The Politics of Congressional Elections* 5th ed. (New York: Longman, 2001), pp. 254–255.

37. Cox and Poole, "On Measuring Partisanship."

38. See James M. Snyder, Jr., and Tim Groseclose, "Estimating Party Influence in Congressional Roll-Call Voting," *American Journal of Political Science* 44 (2000): 187–205.

39. See Barbara Sinclair, "Party Realignment and the Transformation of the Political Agenda: The House of Representatives, 1925–1938," *American Political Science Review* 71 (1977): 940–953.

40. David W. Brady, *Critical Elections and Congressional Policy Making* (Stanford, CA: Stanford University Press, 1988).

41. Gerald C. Wright and Tracy Osborn, "Party and Roll Call Voting in the American Legislature," paper presented at the 2002 Annual Meeting of the Midwest Political Science Association.

42. Warren E. Miller and Donald E. Stokes, "Constituency Influence in Congress," *American Political Science Review* 57 (1963): 45–57.

43. David Nather and Adriel Bettelheim, "Moderates and Mavericks Hold Key to 107th Congress," *CQ Weekly,* Jan. 6, 2001, p. 49.

44. Jewell and Morehouse, *Political Parties and Elections,* p. 244.

45. David Denemark, "Partisan Pork Barrel in Parliamentary Systems: Australian Constituency-Level Grants," *Journal of Politics* 62 (2000): 896–915.

46. See Jewell and Morehouse, *Political Parties and Elections*, pp. 212–215; Anthony Gierzynski, *Legislative Party Campaign Committees in the American States* (Lexington: University of Kentucky Press, 1992); and Daniel M. Shea, *Transforming Democracy: Legislative Campaign Committees and Political Parties* (Albany: State University of New York Press, 1995).

47. Cox and McCubbins, *Legislative Leviathan*; see also Kiewiet and McCubbins, *The Logic of Delegation.*

48. See Austin Ranney, "Candidate Selection and Party Cohesion in Britain and the U.S.," in William J. Crotty, ed., *Approaches to the Study of Party Organization* (Boston: Allyn and Bacon, 1968), pp. 139–168; Gary Cox, *The Efficient Secret* (New York: Cambridge University Press, 1987); and Leon D. Epstein, "A Comparative Study of Canadian Parties," *American Political Science Review* 58 (1964): 46–59.

49. See Richard Fleisher and Jon R. Bond, "Polarized Politics: Does It Matter?" in Bond and Fleisher, eds., *Polarized Politics* (Washington, DC: CQ Press, 2000), pp. 195–200.

CHAPTER 14

1. See David Von Drehle, Peter Slevin, Dan Balz, and James V. Grimaldi, "Anxious Moments in the Final Stretch," *Washington Post*, Feb. 3, 2001, p. A1.

2. See Clive Bean and Anthony Mughan, "Leadership Effects in Parliamentary Elections in Australia and Britain," *American Political Science Review* 83 (1989): 1165–1180.

3. Quoted in Adam Clymer, "Not So Fast: Suddenly Bush's Smooth Ride Turns Bumpy," *New York Times*, Sec. 4, Apr. 1, 2001, p. 1.

4. Dana Milbank, "Bush Turns More Partisan With Coming of Elections," *Washington Post*, May 19, 2002, p. A1.

5. Quoted in Dana Milbank, "An Election Season Done, Another Just Begun," *Washington Post*, Jan. 7, 2003, p. A15. See also Larry J. Sabato, ed., *Midterm Madness* (Lanham, MD: Rowman & Littlefield, 2003).

6. Quoted in Edwin Chen and Janet Hook, "Bush Team Plays Role Fit for a Kingmaker," *Los Angeles Times*, Apr. 25, 2001, p. A13.

7. Quoted in Jim VandeHei and Dan Balz, "In GOP Win, a Lesson in Money, Muscle, Planning," *Washington Post,* Nov. 10, 2002, p. A1.

8. See John A. Ferejohn and Randall L. Calvert, "Presidential Coattails in Historical Perspective," *American Journal of Political Science* 28 (1984): 127–146; Richard Born, "Reassessing the Decline of Presidential Coattails," *Journal of Politics* 46 (1984): 60–79; and James E. Campbell, "Predicting Seat Gains from Presidential Coattails," *American Journal of Political Science* 30 (1986): 164–183.

9. See Bruce Cain, John Ferejohn, and Morris Fiorina, *The Personal Vote* (Cambridge, MA: Harvard University Press, 1987).

10. Paul R. Abramson, John H. Aldrich, and David W. Rohde, *Change and Continuity in the 2000 and 2002 Elections* (Washington, DC: CQ Press, 2003), pp. 249–250.

11. See James E. Campbell, "Presidential Coattails and Midterm Losses in State Legislative Elections," *American Political Science Review* 80 (1986): 45–63.

12. Robin F. Marra and Charles W. Ostrom, Jr., "Explaining Seat Change in the U.S. House of Representatives, 1950–86," *American Journal of Political Science* 33 (1989): 541–569.

13. The classic statement is Angus Campbell, "Surge and Decline: A Study of Electoral Change," in Campbell, Philip E. Converse, Warren E. Miller, and Donald E. Stokes, eds., *Elections and the Political Order* (New York: John Wiley & Sons, 1966), pp. 40–62.

14. Samuel Kernell, "Presidential Popularity and Negative Voting," *American Political Science Review* 71 (1977): 44–66. See also Richard Born, "Surge and Decline, Negative Voting, and the Midterm Loss Phenomenon," *American Journal of Political Science* 34 (1990): 615–645.

15. Walter R. Mebane and Jasjeet S. Sekhon, "Coordination and Policy Moderation at Midterm," *American Political Science Review* 96 (2002): 141–157.

16. Abramson, Aldrich, and Rohde, *Change and Continuity,* pp. 249–250.

17. See Gary C. Jacobson, *The Politics of Congressional Elections,* 5th ed. (New York: Longman, 2001), pp. 146–153.

18. This translation of votes into seats, called the "swing ratio," was calculated by Edward R. Tufte in "The Relationship between Seats and Votes in Two-Party Systems," *American Political Science Review* 67 (1973): 540–554.

19. See Alan Rosenthal, *Governors and Legislatures* (Washington, DC: CQ Press, 1990).

20. Victoria Allred, "Versatility with the Veto," *CQ Weekly*, Jan. 20, 2001, pp. 175–177.

21. See Hugh Heclo, "Issue Networks and the Executive Establishment," in Anthony King, ed., *The New American Political System* (Washington, DC: American Enterprise Institute, 1979), pp. 87–124.

22. Hugh Heclo, *A Government of Strangers* (Washington, DC: Brookings Institution, 1977).

23. See, for example, B. Dan Wood, "Principals, Bureaucrats, and Responsiveness in Clean Air Enforcements," *American Political Science Review* 82 (1988): 213–234.

24. See Terry M. Moe, "The Politicized Presidency," in John E. Chubb and Paul E. Peterson, eds., *The New Direction in American Politics* (Washington, DC: Brookings Institution, 1985), pp. 235–271.

25. Joel Aberbach and Bert A. Rockman, "Clashing Beliefs within the Executive Branch," *American Political Science Review* 70 (1976): 456–468.

26. Joel D. Aberbach and Bert A. Rockman, "The Political Views of U.S. Senior Federal Executives, 1970–1992," *Journal of Politics* 57 (1995): 838–852.

27. Robert A. Carp and Ronald Stidham, *Judicial Process in America* (Washington, DC: CQ Press, 2001), p. 292.

28. Stuart S. Nagel, "Political Party Affiliations and Judges' Decisions," *American Political Science Review* 55 (1961): 843–850. See also Jeffrey A. Segal and Harold J. Spaeth, *The Supreme Court and the Attitudinal Model* (Cambridge: Cambridge University Press, 1993).

29. See Randall D. Lloyd, "Separating Partisanship from Party in Judicial Research," *American Political Science Review* 89 (1995): 413–420.

30. Sheldon Goldman, "The Bush Imprint on the Judiciary," *Judicature* 74 (1991), 294–306.

31. Sheldon Goldman, Elliot Slotnick, Gerard Gryski, and Gary Zuk, "Clinton's Judges: Summing Up the Legacy," *Judicature* 84 (2001): 244, 249.

32. Editorial, "Avoiding the Senate," *Washington Post*, Dec. 31, 2000 p. B6.
33. Daniel J. Parks, "Senate Judicial Nominations Spat Again Frustrates Appropriators," *CQ Weekly*, Oct. 20, 2001, pp. 2470–2471. See also Sarah A. Binder and Forrest Maltzman, "Senatorial Delay in Confirming Federal Judges, 1947–1998," *American Journal of Political Science* 46 (2002): 190–199.
34. Jennifer A. Dlouhy, "Parties Use Judicial Standoff to Play to Core Constituents," *CQ Weekly*, Oct. 19, 2002, p. 2722.
35. Jennifer A. Dlouhy, "Religion Takes Center Stage in Fight Over Judicial Nominees," *CQ Weekly*, Aug. 2, 2003, p. 1964.
36. *Book of the States, 2003* (Lexington, KY: Council of State Governments, 2003), p. 235.
37. See Henry R. Glick and Craig F. Emmert, "Selection Systems and Judicial Characteristics," *Judicature* 70 (1987), 228–235; and Melinda Gann Hall, "State Supreme Courts in American Democracy," *American Political Science Review* 95 (2001): 315–330.
38. Data from a study conducted by Texans for Public Justice, reported in "Campaign Contributions Corrupt Judicial Races," *USA Today*, Sept. 1, 2000, p. 16A.

CHAPTER 15

1. Susan E. Scarrow, "Party Decline in the Parties State?" in Paul Webb, David M. Farrell, and Ian Holliday, *Political Parties in Advanced Industrial Democracies* (Oxford: Oxford University Press, 2002), p. 77.
2. Paul Webb, "Political Parties in Britain," in Webb, Farrell, and Holliday, *Political Parties in Advanced Industrial Democracies*, pp. 32–33.
3. Ian McAllister, "Political Parties in Australia," in Webb, Farrell, and Holliday, *Political Parties in Advanced Industrial Democracies*, p. 379.
4. E. E. Schattschneider, *Party Government* (New York: Rinehart, 1942), pp. 131–132.
5. Committee on Political Parties of the American Political Science Association, *Toward a More Responsible Two-Party System* (New York: Rinehart, 1950).
6. See Austin Ranney, *The Doctrine of Responsible Party Government* (Urbana: University of Illinois Press, 1964), Chapters 1 and 2.
7. Committee on Political Parties, *Toward a More Responsible Two-Party System*, p. 15.
8. Schattschneider, *Party Government*, p. 208.
9. E. E. Schattschneider, *The Semi-Sovereign People* (New York: Holt, Rinehart, and Winston, 1960).
10. See Evron Kirkpatrick, "Toward a More Responsible Two-Party System," *American Political Science Review* 65 (1971): 965–990; and John Kenneth White and Jerome M. Mileur, eds., *Challenges to Party Government* (Carbondale: Southern Illinois University Press, 1992).
11. See Malcolm E. Jewell and Sarah M. Morehouse, *Political Parties and Elections in American States*, 4th ed. (Washington, DC: CQ Press, 2001), p. 222, and Morris Fiorina, *Divided Government* (New York: Macmillan, 1992), Chapter 3.
12. See Gary Cox and Samuel Kernell, eds., *The Politics of Divided Government* (Boulder, CO: Westview, 1991) and Gary Jacobson, *The Electoral Origins of Divided Government* (Boulder, CO: Westview, 1990).
13. See John J. Coleman, "Unified Government, Divided Government, and Party Responsiveness," *American Political Science Review* 93 (1999): 821–835; George C. Edwards III, Andrew Barrett, and Jeffrey Peake, "The Legislative Impact of Divided Government," *American Journal of Political Science* 41 (1997): 545–563; and David R. Mayhew, *Divided We Govern* (New Haven, CT: Yale University Press, 1991).
14. See Richard Born, "Split-Ticket Voters, Divided Government, and Fiorina's Policy-Balancing Model," *Legislative Studies Quarterly* 19 (1994): 95–115.
15. See A. James Reichley, *The Life of the Parties* (Lanham, MD: Rowman & Littlefield, 2000), Chapter 6.
16. See Ian Budge and Richard I. Hofferbert, "Mandates and Policy Outputs," *American Political Science Review* 84 (1990): 111–132, and the comments on their work in the same journal, 87 (1993): 744–750.
17. Edward G. Carmines and James A. Stimson, *Issue Evolution* (Princeton, NJ: Princeton University Press, 1989); see also Geoffrey C. Layman and Thomas M. Carsey, "Party Polarization and 'Conflict Extension' in the American Electorate," *American Journal of Political Science* 46 (2002): 786–802.
18. Charles Barrilleaux, Thomas Holbrook, and Laura Langer, "Electoral Competition, Legislative Balance, and American State Welfare Policy," *American Journal of Political Science* 46 (2002): 415–427.

19. Jason M. Roberts and Steven S. Smith, "Procedural Contexts, Party Strategy, and Conditional Party Voting in the U.S. House of Representatives, 1971–2000," *American Journal of Political Science* 47 (2003): 305–317.

20. See Geoffrey Layman, *The Great Divide* (New York: Columbia University Press, 2001).

21. See Robin Kolodny, "Moderate Party Factions in the U.S. House of Representatives," in John C. Green and Daniel M. Shea, *The State of the Parties*, 3rd ed. (Lanham, MD: Rowman & Littlefield, 1999), pp. 271–285.

22. See David S. Broder, "Party's Fault Lines Likely to Surface," *Washington Post*, Jan. 21, 2001, p. A22.

23. Nicol C. Rae, "Party Factionalism, 1946–1996," in Byron E. Shafer, *Partisan Approaches to Postwar American Politics* (New York: Chatham House, 1998), pp. 41–74. See also John S. Jackson, Nathan S. Bigelow, and John C. Green, "The State of Party Elites: National Convention Delegates, 1992–2000," in Green and Rick Farmer, eds., *The State of the Parties,* 4th ed. (Lanham, MD: Rowman & Littlefield, 2003), pp. 54–78.

24. Stephanie L. Witt, "Idaho," in Andrew M. Appleton and Daniel S. Ward, *State Party Profiles* (Washington, DC: CQ Press, 1997), pp. 82–88.

25. The seminal study is Philip E. Converse, "The Nature of Belief Systems in Mass Publics," in David Apter, ed., *Ideology and Discontent* (New York: Free Press, 1964), pp. 206–261. Also see Russell J. Dalton, *Citizen Politics,* 3rd ed. (New York: Chatham House, 2002), Chapter 2.

26. Kathleen A. Frankovic and Monika L. McDermott, "Public Opinion in the 2000 Election: The Ambivalent Electorate," in Gerald M. Pomper, ed., *The Election of 2000* (New York: Chatham House, 2001), pp. 76–78 and 88–89.

27. John Zaller and Stanley Feldman, "A Simple Theory of the Survey Response," *American Journal of Political Science* 36 (1992): 579–616.

28. CBS News, "Millennium Poll," December, 1999.

29. Paul R. Abramson, John H. Aldrich, and David W. Rohde, *Change and Continuity in the 1984 Elections* (Washington, DC: CQ Press, 1986), Chapter 6.

30. See Frankovic and McDermott, pp. 73–91.

31. Marc J. Hetherington, "Resurgent Mass Partisanship: The Role of Elite Polarization," *American Political Science Review* 95 (2001): 619–631.

32. Gerald M. Pomper and Marc D. Weiner, "Toward a More Responsible Two-Party Voter," in John C. Green and Paul S. Herrnson, eds., *Responsible Partisanship?* (Lawrence: University Press of Kansas, 2002), pp. 181–200.

33. Philip E. Converse and Roy Pierce, *Political Representation in France* (Cambridge, MA: Harvard University Press, 1986), Chapter 4.

34. See William Crotty, John S. Jackson III, and Melissa Kary Miller, "Political Activists Over Time," in Birol A. Yesilada, ed., *Comparative Political Parties and Party Elites* (Ann Arbor: University of Michigan Press, 1999), pp. 259–286.

35. See Brandice Canes-Wrone, David W. Brady, and John F. Cogan, "Out of Step, Out of Office," *American Political Science Review* 96 (2002): 127–140.

36. John R. Hibbing and Elizabeth Theiss-Morse, "Process Preferences and American Politics," *American Political Science Review* 95 (2001): 145–153.

37. David C. King, "The Polarization of American Political Parties and Mistrust of Government," in Joseph S. Nye, Philip Zelikow, and David C. King, eds., *Why People Don't Trust Government* (Cambridge, MA: Harvard University Press, 1997), pp. 155–178.

38. Leon D. Epstein, "What Happened to the British Party Model?" *American Political Science Review* 74 (1980): 9–22.

39. Jerome M. Clubb, William H. Flanigan, and Nancy H. Zingale, *Partisan Realignment* (Beverly Hills, CA: Sage, 1980), pp. 155–188.

CHAPTER 16

1. See Robert Harmel and Kenneth Janda, *Parties and Their Environments* (New York: Longman, 1982).

2. See Ruy A. Teixeira, *The Disappearing American Voter* (Washington, DC: Brookings Institution, 1992), Chapter 3.

3. These figures are taken from Harold W. Stanley and Richard G. Niemi, *Vital Statistics on American Politics 1999–2000* (Washington, DC: CQ Press, 2000), pp. 44 and 133.

4. Bruce E. Cain, John Ferejohn, and Morris P. Fiorina, *The Personal Vote* (Cambridge, MA: Harvard University Press, 1987).

5. Jeffrey E. Cohen and Paul Kantor, "Decline and Resurgence in the American Party System," in Jeffrey E. Cohen, Richard Fleisher, and Paul Kantor, eds., *American Political Parties: Decline or Resurgence?* (Washington, DC: CQ Press, 2001), pp. 255–257.

6. See Robert Huckfeldt and Paul Allen Beck, "Contexts, Intermediaries, and Political Activity," in Lawrence C. Dodd and Calvin Jillson, eds., *The Dynamics of American Politics* (Boulder, CO: Westview Press, 1994), Chapter 11. On the other hand, organized interests have become more polarized by party since the Reagan years; see Jack L. Walker, Jr., *Mobilizing Interest Groups in America* (Ann Arbor: University of Michigan Press, 1991), Chapter 8, and media coverage frequently refers to party; see Marjorie Randon Hershey, "If 'The Party's in Decline,' Then What's That Filling the News Columns?" in Nelson W. Polsby and Raymond E. Wolfinger, eds., *On Parties* (Berkeley: Institute of Governmental Studies, 1999), pp. 257–278.

7. Larry M. Bartels, "Partisanship and Voting Behavior, 1952–1996," *American Journal of Political Science* 44 (2000): 35–50.

8. Larry J. Sabato and Bruce Larson, *The Party's Just Begun* (New York: Longman, 2002), pp. 2–4.

9. See Ronald Inglehart, *Culture Shift* (Princeton, NJ: Princeton University Press, 1990), Chapters 10 and 11.

10. John H. Aldrich, *Why Parties?* (Chicago: University of Chicago Press, 1995), p. 3.

11. Walter Dean Burnham, *Critical Elections and the Mainsprings of American Politics* (New York: Norton, 1970), p. 133.

12. See Brian F. Schaffner, Matthew J. Streb, and Gerald C. Wright, "Teams without Uniforms: The Nonpartisan Ballot in State and Local Elections," *Political Research Quarterly* 54 (2001): 7–30; and Gerald C. Wright and Brian F. Schaffner, "The Influence of Party: Evidence from the State Legislatures," *American Political Science Review* 96 (2002): 367–379.

13. See Steven J. Rosenstone and John Mark Hansen, *Mobilization, Participation, and Democracy in America* (New York: Macmillan, 1993), Chapter 8.

14. Sabato and Larson, *The Party's Just Begun,* pp. 156–157.

15. Sabato and Larson, *The Party's Just Begun,* pp. 159–160.

Index

343